THE PSYCHOLOGICAL
CROSS-CURRENTS AND
MORAL COMPLEXITIES IN
HAMLET...

the complex political machinations in
RICHARD II...

the theme of racial prejudice and
sexual jealousy in
OTHELLO...

the soaring poetry of
ROMEO and JULIET...

the delightfully barbed wit of
AS YOU LIKE IT...

the dissection of ambition, power and
corruption in
MACBETH...!

These are but a few of the many aspects of
Shakespeare that must be illumined before full
appreciation of his enduring genius is possible.

TEACHING SHAKESPEARE is designed to help provide this essential insight. The product of impeccable scholarship and actual teaching experience at many levels of secondary school, college and university education, it is a volume to be warmly welcomed as a major contribution toward bringing the richness of our cultural heritage to the student of today.

THE COMPLETE WORKS OF
SHAKESPEARE

Superlatively edited paper bound volumes of all of Shakespeare's plays are published in the Signet Classic series. Under the general editorship of Sylvan Barnet of the English Department of Tufts University, each volume features a general Introduction by Dr. Barnet; special Introduction and Notes by an eminent Shakespearean scholar; critical commentary from past and contemporary authorities; and when possible, the actual source, in its entirety or in excerpt, from which Shakespeare derived his play. Among the volumes available at 50 cents each are:

- ☐ MACBETH. EDITED WITH INTRODUCTION AND NOTES BY SYLVAN BARNET, TUFTS UNIVERSITY. (#CD161)
- ☐ JULIUS CAESAR. EDITED WITH INTRODUCTION AND NOTES BY WILLIAM AND BARBARA ROSEN, UNIVERSITY OF CONNECTICUT. (#CD170)
- ☐ THE MERCHANT OF VENICE. EDITED WITH INTRODUCTION BY KENNETH O. MYRICK. (#CD277)
- ☐ HAMLET. EDITED WITH INTRODUCTION AND NOTES BY EDWARD HUBLER, PRINCETON UNIVERSITY. (#CD169)
- ☐ ROMEO AND JULIET. EDITED WITH INTRODUCTION AND NOTES BY JOSEPH BRYANT. (#CD270)
- ☐ A MIDSUMMER NIGHT'S DREAM. EDITED WITH INTRODUCTION AND NOTES BY WOLFGANG CLEMEN, UNIVERSITY OF MUNICH. (#CD171)
- ☐ OTHELLO. EDITED WITH INTRODUCTION AND NOTES BY ALVIN KERNAN, YALE UNIVERSITY. (#CD162)
- ☐ AS YOU LIKE IT. EDITED WITH INTRODUCTION AND NOTES BY ALBERT GILMAN, BOSTON UNIVERSITY. (#CD168)
- ☐ TWELFTH NIGHT. EDITED WITH INTRODUCTION AND NOTES BY HERSCHEL CLAY BAKER. (#CD293)
- ☐ RICHARD II. EDITED WITH INTRODUCTION AND NOTES BY KENNETH MUIR. (#CD163)
- ☐ HENRY IV, PART I. EDITED WITH INTRODUCTION BY MAYNARD MACK. (#CD283)
- ☐ THE TEMPEST. EDITED WITH INTRODUCTION AND NOTES BY ROBERT LANGBAUM. (#CD174)

THE NEW AMERICAN LIBRARY, INC., P.O. Box 2310, Grand Central Station, New York, New York 10017

Please send me the SIGNET BOOKS I have checked above. I am enclosing $_____(check or money order—no currency or C.O.D.'s). Please include the list price plus 10¢ a copy to cover mailing costs. (New York City residents add 5% Sales Tax. Other New York State residents add 2% plus any local sales or use taxes.)

Name_____

Address_____

City_____State_____Zip Code_____

Allow at least 3 weeks for delivery

TEACHING SHAKESPEARE

A GUIDE TO THE TEACHING OF

MACBETH
JULIUS CAESAR
THE MERCHANT OF VENICE
HAMLET
ROMEO AND JULIET
A MIDSUMMER NIGHT'S DREAM

OTHELLO
AS YOU LIKE IT
TWELFTH NIGHT
RICHARD II
HENRY IV, PART ONE
THE TEMPEST

EDITED BY
ARTHUR MIZENER

A MENTOR BOOK

PUBLISHED BY THE NEW AMERICAN LIBRARY, INC.,
NEW YORK AND TORONTO
THE NEW ENGLISH LIBRARY LIMITED, LONDON

Copyright © 1969 by Arthur Mizener

All rights reserved

Library of Congress Catalog Card Number: 71-79101

MENTOR TRADEMARK REG. U.S. PAT. OFF. AND FOREIGN COUNTRIES
REGISTERED TRADEMARK—MARCA REGISTRADA
HECHO EN CHICAGO, U.S.A.

MENTOR BOOKS are published *in the United States* by
The New American Library, Inc.,
1301 Avenue of the Americas, New York, New York 10019,
in Canada by The New American Library of Canada Limited,
295 King Street East, Toronto 2, Ontario,
in the United Kingdom by The New English Library Limited,
Barnard's Inn, Holborn, London, E.C. 1, England

First Printing, May, 1969

PRINTED IN THE UNITED STATES OF AMERICA

THIS GUIDE HAS BEEN COMPOSED BY

BARRY ADAMS, *Cornell University*

SYLVAN BARNET, *Tufts University*

ANTHONY CAPUTI, *Cornell University*

ALAN DOWNER, *Princeton University*

SCOTT ELLEDGE, *Cornell University*

MARIAN ELLIOT, *Ithaca High School*

EPHIM FOGEL, *Cornell University*

SISTER RITA CATHERINE HOMMRICH, *St. Andrews Convent, Roanoke, Va.*

ARTHUR MIZENER, *Cornell University*

MARTIN PARRY, *John Burroughs School*

WILLIAM M. SALE, *Cornell University*

CONTENTS

Foreword	ix
References	xi
Questions and Tests	xi
Macbeth	13
Julius Caesar	49
The Merchant of Venice	77
Hamlet	103
Romeo and Juliet	129
A Midsummer Night's Dream	159
Othello	183
As You Like It	215
Twelfth Night	243
Richard II	269
Henry IV, Part One	297
The Tempest	327

FOREWORD

This book has been written with the hope that it may be useful to those who are teaching Shakespeare's plays. It seemed to us that if a group of experienced teachers were to pool their classroom experience with these plays, they could offer readers something that would be useful to them in their own teaching. This has been our purpose.

We began by making a list of the plays that are most popular with secondary school teachers, as indicated by the survey published by the Cooperative Testing Division of Educational Testing Service in 1964. This survey left us in no doubt at all about the first seven plays to be included. They are: *Macbeth, Julius Caesar, The Merchant of Venice, Hamlet, Romeo and Juliet, A Midsummer Night's Dream,* and *As You Like It.* After that the choices are so scattered that they offer no useful guide, and we have had to depend on our own judgment. We chose *Othello* and *Twelfth Night,* and then, since our list included no history play and none of the so-called Last Plays, we added *Richard II, Henry IV, Part One,* and *The Tempest.*

We then worked out a uniform plan for the treatment of these twelve plays. For each of them we have written an opening statement about the general character of the play, its main themes, and the dramatic design that expresses these themes. This general statement is followed by a detailed discussion of the play's dramatic action, a discussion that represents as closely as possible the actual teaching of the play. Finally, we have added for each play several sets of questions that can be used for various kinds of discussions, essay assignments, and tests, together with samples of how these questions may be selected and arranged to make examinations.

The writers of this book include high school, private school, parochial school, college, and university teachers. One of the most interesting results of our working together on this book was the discovery of how similar are the ideas of all of us about the way these plays should be taught.

ARTHUR MIZENER

REFERENCES

References throughout this book are to the Signet Classic Shakespeare series. Ordinarily a reference will be to the page and line number of the relevant volume; thus, 38.112 means page 38, line 112 of that volume. In the discussion of the action of each play, which is broken down by act and scene, only the line numbers of the scene under discussion are given. In the lists of questions that follow the discussion of each play, the references are to the passages in the text of the play where the answers to the questions will be found. References to plays other than the one under discussion are to the page and line numbers of the Signet Classic editions of those plays. References to the Introductions and Commentaries in each of the Signet Classic volumes are given by page number alone; thus, p. 125 means page 125 of the Signet Classic edition of the play referred to.

QUESTIONS AND TESTS

Sets of fifty short-answer questions and of ten essay questions have been provided after the discussion of each play. The short-answer questions will, we hope, be useful for brief written quizzes or to stimulate classroom discussion of specific passages. The essay questions, directed to the larger meanings of the plays, should make useful subjects for themes or for generalized classroom discussions. Tests can easily be constructed by combining questions from these lists. A sample test constructed in this way is provided for each play.

THE TRAGEDY OF MACBETH

INTRODUCTION

Standing chronologically at the peak of Shakespeare's career, *Macbeth* achieves greatness in a number of ways. If we concentrate on the characters as individuals, we see a play of temptation, sin, and retribution, a nonregenerative drama like the Faust legend; if we think of the historical roles of these characters, we see a play about the fall of a country before a dictator whose tyranny brings widespread suffering until liberating forces establish law and order. In both these ways, the play would have much significance for a Jacobean audience, accustomed to seeing in drama a reflection of what court and public alike thought man ought to be, politically and morally, and to believing that harmony and order derived from the ruler at the top of the hierarchy of their society. To a modern audience, the play has equal significance as a representation of man's ruthless drive for success and of the continuing fight for human freedom against tyranny and oppression.

In the study of *Macbeth*, it is helpful to regard the first two scenes as designed to prepare the audience for the tragic events to follow. Scene i may be looked upon as a prelude to the whole drama, setting the tone and atmosphere; scene ii, as defining the relationship among the principal characters and establishing a base for the subsequent tragic action. (For a more detailed discussion of this subject, see I.i and I.ii under The Action.)

Elements in the dramatic structure of the plot might be considered next. The play is singular in its lack of exposition, of an account of what has already happened before the play opens; everything points to the future while the scenes actually report events that have already occurred. Because the play is not firmly rooted in the past, it is natural to imagine a past for it, to see Macbeth and Lady Macbeth as having al-

13

ready entertained ideas of becoming king and queen. Much in the play—such as the witches' prophecies and the subtleties of verbal irony—does require the audience to imagine past events as the play goes along. Our minds are forced to move back and forth in time. For example, accusing her husband of cowardice, Lady Macbeth snatches at the first argument to hand: "What beast was't then/That made you break this enterprise to me?" (56.47-48). Can the letter be said to broach "this enterprise," or have they discussed the matter before? Before writing the letter, Macbeth had decided that "If chance will have me King, why, chance may crown me,/Without my stir" (46.143-44). This attitude is made to seem practical by the witches, who appear to be reading Macbeth's mind stirred afresh by "things forgotten" (47.150) as he returns from battle, vulnerable like most generals on "the day of success" (49.1-2).

It is also possible to see Banquo as serving an expository function while the play is in progress. He and Macbeth are successful generals in the same wars. Although a foil to Macbeth at the outset, Banquo, it may be argued, undergoes a change while offstage, as many of Shakespeare's characters do. In his last appearance before he is murdered, he seems to be following the same "primrose way to th' everlasting bonfire" (65.19-20) as Macbeth, except that he is a few steps behind: "May they not be my oracles as well/And set me up in hope?" (74.9-10). As A.C. Bradley has pointed out, it is the tone of the passage that is revealing, especially in Banquo's comment, as King Macbeth and his attendants approach, "But hush, no more!" (10). Banquo's character remains equivocal, perhaps for political reasons (see Introduction, p. xxii), perhaps in order to suggest the uncertainty of value judgments in a world where "Fair is foul, and foul is fair" (37.10). In such a view, it might be said that Banquo acts out the exposition, enabling the audience to see, in a parallel career, the course followed by Macbeth before the play opens, and, thus, the universality of the central theme.

The effect of the plot of *Macbeth* is essentially cumulative. The action is bounded by two wars, which are distinguished from one another largely by the depth of Macbeth's degradation: from his initial position as the "noble Macbeth" (40.67) who kills the traitor Macdonwald and fixes "his head upon our battlements" (39.23), to his becoming himself the traitor and another Cawdor, whose "cursèd head" (130.55) is held up "to be the show and gaze o' th' time" (129.24). Once Macbeth has committed murder, he realizes in a double sense that "Renown and grace is dead" (68.96), an evaluation applying morally to himself and literally to Duncan. Having irretrievably lost his own nobility, Macbeth can only go on to repeated murders, until death itself becomes commonplace. Not only does he destroy his relations with Lady Macbeth, so that he scarcely responds to her death, "She should have died hereafter" (124.17), but also, since health of king and state are interdependent, he spreads sickness throughout the land by his repetition of murders, real and rumored, until "The dead man's knell/Is there scarce asked for who" (111.170-71).

In this kind of plot it is important to maintain tension. Suspense, pacing, and dramatic irony—all contribute to this end. Suspense is created, not by the sound of the first shoe dropping on the floor overhead but by the delay of the second. Thus the scenes of suspense tend to cluster around situations of which the audience has some foreknowledge: prophecies set the stage for the murder of Duncan; equivocal statements and crude symbols warn the audience of Macbeth's end; and Macbeth announces his intention to murder Banquo and Macduff's household. As this plot develops, the audience comes more and more to feel that Macbeth cannot control his own life at all, that no matter how desperately he struggles to decide for himself and to will his own acts, he is foredoomed to follow the course he is on to the inevitable end that even he begins to suspect. That end thus becomes merely a matter of time, of the passage of a certain number of tomorrows that are horrible in their monotony because meaningless to a degree almost beyond human conception.

Inseparable from suspense is pacing. Although several different kinds of time are evident in the play, dramatic time, the pace which the audience feels, is the most important. Time races ahead in Act I. Two battles in quick succession; the witches' prophecies, one already fulfilled before it is announced; three men speeding one after the other toward Inverness; and Lady Macbeth reading her husband's letter even while Duncan is coursing him "at the heels" (54.21)—all create a strong sense of inevitability. Macbeth has no time in which to reflect, to be the rational man, except what he steals while entertaining Duncan. With Duncan's entry into the castle at nightfall, the clock stops. With the knocking at the gate, time starts again. When Macduff emerges from Duncan's bedchamber, the tempo, faltering at first, rapidly increases as confusion breaks loose: "Ring the alarum bell. Murder and Treason!/Banquo and Donalbain! Malcolm! Awake!" (67.76-77). The last three acts of the play cover a period of eighteen years in the source materials. This sense of historical time brakes the action before the final onslaught.

When the scene shifts to England, time stalls while Malcolm is testing Macduff's loyalty; then as the forces gather to march on Dunsinane, it gains momentum. In the alternating battle scenes of the last act, there is only a momentary stay when Macbeth, hearing of his wife's death, feels an insurmountable weariness: "Tomorrow, and tomorrow, and tomorrow/Creeps in this petty pace from day to day" (124.19-20). The end comes abruptly as Macduff, bearing the tyrant's head on a pole, declares, "The time is free" (130.55).

Because the play moves rapidly and is full of contrasts, Shakespeare can use dramatic irony to heighten the tension by juxtaposing past and present, good and evil. Duncan reflects that "There's no art/To find the mind's construction in the face" (48.11-12) as Macbeth enters; he sees him as being "full so valiant" (49.54) even as Macbeth is thinking about the Prince of Cumberland; he takes Macbeth's speed in reaching Inverness as a sign of "his great love, sharp as his spur" (54.23); he sees the castle as a place that "sweetly recommends itself/Unto our gentle senses" (53.2-3), while within Macbeth is plotting a murder so vile as to justify the porter's description of this castle as hell; and Macbeth thinks "I have no spur/To prick the sides of my intent" (55.25-26) at the very moment when Lady Macbeth, the sharpest of all spurs, confronts him. These are immediate contrasts not easily missed by the audience. Others are more subtle because they depend for their effects on past events. Banquo's ghost appears to fulfill Macbeth's command, "Fail not our feast" (75.27); Lady Macbeth, about to return the daggers, wonders "If he do bleed" (63.54) and then is astonished to find that Duncan has "so much blood in him" (116.43); or she supposes that "A little water clears us of this deed" (64.66) and learns that "All the perfumes of Arabia will not sweeten this little hand" (117.53-55). Ironies of this kind heighten the dramatic tension.

At this point in the discussion of the play it might be profitable to turn to the source materials in Holinshed's *Chronicles* (see "The Source of *Macbeth*," pp. 136ff.) to examine the contrast between narrative and dramatic techniques in handling the same story, and note significant differences in Shakespeare's use of his source materials. (See Elmer Edgar Stoll, "Source and Motive in *Macbeth* and *Othello*," pp. 183ff.)

Consider, for example, the way the dramatic writer uses dialogue and soliloquy, the action and language of each speaker to reveal his character. It must be remembered that the Elizabethan theater is illusionistic, not realistic: the conventional heaven and hell of the stage invite the audience to see the stage itself as a microcosm in which man occupies a central position. Good and evil are forces existing outside man, but man is the site of their conflict. Thus the characters, though individuals, are given a wider, symbolic significance.

The forces of grace operate chiefly through King Duncan and his rightful heir, Malcolm. At the outset Duncan's character is revealed by both what he says and what he does. At the first royal gathering, where honor and order prevail in contrast to the fear and disorder at Macbeth's royal banquet, Duncan is generous in his praise of and rewards to Macbeth and Banquo, equal subjects under his rule; he is also quick to punish treason. Duncan's goodness is even more strongly suggested by the attitude of other characters toward him, particularly that of Macbeth. The common epithet in everyone's mouth is "The gracious Duncan" (92.3)—even after killing the King, Macbeth uses the term (76.66). Weighing him in the scales, Macbeth can find no fault with his kingship: he "hath been/So clear in his great office" (55.17-18). The murder itself is a symbolic act: an act against order in the state and in the natural world, against authority and every grace that Duncan stands for. On the discovery of the murder, Macduff and the other nobles present act in concert to express their horror. Later, Macduff describes Duncan as "a most sainted king" (109.109). Essentially Duncan presents an ideal of kingship, of God's temporal representative on earth, whose succession will be worthily maintained by his son Malcolm.

The forces of evil operate in part through Lady Macbeth, who invokes their aid. She is marked from the beginning by her inflexibility of will. Knowing that her husband is not devoid of compassion, she steels her heart as she assumes direction of this "great business" (52.69). Later their roles will be reversed. When Macbeth reconsiders "this business" (56.31), she taunts him with cowardice, even questions his love. By force of will she impels him toward the murder of Duncan, until his decision is taken in a moment of amazement: "Bring forth men-children only;/For thy undaunted mettle should compose/Nothing but males" (57.72-74). Although seemingly without pity or conscience, she reveals her other self in her determination to choke all natural feeling; in changing her mind about murdering Duncan himself, "Had he not resembled/My father as he slept, I had done 't" (61.12-13); in having to bolster her courage with wine to face the ordeal ahead. Her calculating mind and will power give strength for immediate action; but lacking Macbeth's poetic imagination, she is incapable of conceiving beforehand the cruelty of murder. The reality is thus all the more shocking for her; her reaction to it is almost the opposite to that of Macbeth. The horror comes suddenly upon her as her husband describes the body, "Here lay Duncan,/His silver skin laced with his golden blood" (69.113-14); but the depth of her horror is not fully revealed until the sleepwalking scene when, recalling the daggers "Unmannerly breeched with gore" (69.118), she exclaims, "Yet who would have thought the old man to have had so much blood in him?" (116.42-43). After Duncan's murder, the positions of Lady Macbeth and Macbeth are reversed, although at this point they share the same state of mind: "Nought's had, all's spent,/Where our desire is got without content" (80.4-5). No longer engaged with the practical planning of the murder, she sinks into the background. Only in the sudden emergency at the banquet does she regain her strength and with it her ascendancy; but once the banquet breaks up in disorder, she relapses into apathy as Macbeth's attention turns next to Macduff. Even though they have drifted apart since the murder of Duncan, there is much pathos in her tenderness. "You lack the season of all natures, sleep" (90.142), she says, sharing his torture of mind. When Lady Macbeth finally reappears in the sleepwalking scene, she is the antithesis of her former self, no longer a calculating murderess, only a very tired woman whose suppressed humanity leads to a disorder of sleep and, perhaps, eventually of mind. It is her retribution that, having denied her heart in murdering Duncan, she can no longer "Stop up th' access and passage to remorse" (51.45). As her gentlewoman says, "I would not have such a heart in my bosom for the dignity of the whole body" (117.58-59).

The character of Macbeth is dealt with at some length in the Signet edition of the text. (See Introduction, pp. xxiiff.; the selection by A.C. Bradley, "From *Shakespearean Tragedy*," pp. 166ff.; and Mary McCarthy, "General Macbeth," pp. 229ff.) It may be noted in passing that Macbeth not only speaks with an individual voice but plays a symbolic role. As an individual his acts have social and political consequences, but we are always conscious that the motives for these acts, being commonplace and familiar, make him Everyman.

There is not space here to analyze the language of individual characters. This can best be done through a close study of one or two representative passages (for example, 51.39-55; 53.1-10; 54.1-28). From this point, the functioning of the poetry in the whole drama may be considered and recognition be given to the fact that without the concrete grasp it affords, Macbeth might be mistaken simply for an evildoer justly punished. A further step will lead into questions about patterns of image, metaphor, or symbol that convey the thought and heighten the intensity of the work—such as the Light-Dark Pattern, the Blood Pattern, the Clothes Pattern, the Sleep Pattern, the Animal Pattern, to name a few. (For an interpretation of some of the image patterns, see Cleanth Brooks, "The Naked Babe and the Cloak of Manliness," pp. 196ff., and Oscar James Campbell, From "Shakespeare and the 'New' Critics," pp.222-28.) From an overall view these patterns group themselves into negative and positive fields which, supported by a certain unity of time and place, relate to the forces of good and evil. Surrounding Macbeth, Lady Macbeth, and their "cruel ministers" (131.68) are negative images such as those of darkness, fear, blood, and cruelty. (See Samuel Johnson, *"Macbeth"* (II.i.49), pp.160-61.) The witches, symbolic of temptation, inhabit the murky weather of their own creation. The play's action concentrates the evil events at Inverness Castle, at night. As evil emanates from the castle, it spreads in a widening circle like a sickness: Banquo is murdered at dusk within the castle grounds; Macduff's household is massacred at Fife. In contrast, Duncan, Malcolm, and "thy kingdom's pearl" (130.56) are surrounded by positive images of light, love, healing, and fertility. Nowhere is this more clearly seen than in Duncan's arrival at Inverness Castle, described as having "a pleasant seat" (53.1), a place where "The temple-haunting martlet" (53.4) builds its nest and procreates its young. The play's good deeds all occur in the daylight and beyond the castle walls. As Macbeth's tyranny spreads through Scotland, help must ultimately come from abroad.

These are, briefly stated, the major characteristics of the play that a teacher ought to keep constantly before his students as the final purposes to which all the minute particulars of the play contribute in their various ways. One of the most difficult problems a teacher faces with Shakespeare's plays— with all their particularity, much of it needing historical explanation before it can be understood at all—is to make the details of the play understandable to the student and, if possible, humanly moving or humorous, and at the same time keep him clearly aware of the larger purposes of the play that all these particulars serve. The discussion of *Macbeth* that follows is intended to suggest ways in which the teacher may deal with the play's details scene by scene and at the same time keep these larger purposes constantly before the students' attention.

THE ACTION

I.i

The opening scene sets the tone for the whole play. The atmosphere is one of "fog and filthy air" (11), of thunder and lightning. By the presence of the witches in an unspecified location, the audience is made aware of forces of evil at work in the world. Man is the focus of their attention, and the man specified here is Macbeth. He is to be the object of a conflict between good and evil. The witches both ask and raise questions: the battle is to be "lost and won" (4). Which battle? For Scotland? For the Crown? Or for Macbeth's soul? All three prove to be related. The prophecy is to be fulfilled in one sense "ere the set of sun" (5), itself premonitory of darkness, even of death. But "The night is long that never finds the day" (114.240), and the end will bring a new dawn. In the meantime, the witches utter a further warning: "Fair is foul, and foul is fair" (10). This is to be a world of topsy-turvy values and appearances, a world of confusion and uncertainty. These tropes, remarkable in the witches' incantation, are to echo through the play: sometimes verbally, to suggest a linking of minds; sometimes actively, to test character. Thus the witches establish the physical and moral climate of the play, a climate marked by unnatural turbulence in the physical world and by a reversal of values in the moral. (For comments on witchcraft, see Samuel Johnson, *"Macbeth,"* pp. 156-59.)

I.ii

The audience is introduced first to the King himself, symbol of order and justice in the realm, ruler by divine right; and, through report, to the tragic hero. Too old to lead the battle himself, Duncan is nonetheless anxious to learn of its progress from firsthand reports. His opening question, "What bloody man is that?" (1), initiates a key image, even a reflection of his own future image, as the symbol fluctuates between the blood of sacrifice and that of slaughter. Here, the Captain has saved the life of the King's own son; Macbeth has "carved out his passage" (19) to the rebel Macdonwald and "unseamed him from the nave to th' chops" (22). As the wounded Captain faints, the outcome of the second battle is held in suspense until Ross brings news of success. The rhetorical flights of both the Captain and Ross—"valor's minion" (19), the analogue of the primates, the eagle and the lion, "Bellona's bridegroom" (54)—contrast with the more reserved style of the King, who refers to Macbeth as "valiant" and "noble" (67). In granting Cawdor's title to Macbeth, Duncan is quick to reward deservers, "What he hath lost, noble Macbeth hath won" (67). Ironically, the theme of treason, central to the play, is introduced in the equivocal terms of the witches, of "lost and won" (37.4), and Macbeth, like Judas Iscariot, is awarded the traitor's title. This scene builds Macbeth up to a figure larger than life, a man of heroic proportions, not without some element of brutality, as he is seen through the eyes of the Captain and Ross; as seen through the eyes of the King, he is a loyal subject, equal in status with Banquo, but highly deserving for his great loyalty and service to his country.

I.iii

The reappearance of the witches at the appointed time and place, now localized, and their subsequent prophecies intensify the sense of evil and of a cosmic tragedy.

Further information about witchcraft is provided in this scene, and the witches themselves are more clearly defined. Unlike their formal counterparts in the Holinshed picture, they appear to Banquo as skinny, bearded old women dressed in rags—Shakespeare has updated them for his audience. Their malice is shown by the first witch, who, shooed away by the sailor's wife eating chestnuts, plans revenge on her husband by sailing in a sieve to his ship, the *Tiger,* and boarding it as a tailless rat, deformed like all of the devil's creatures. The second witch, equally vindictive, has been slaughtering swine while Macbeth has been killing rebels. Then, just as the first witch holds up the thumb of a drowned pilot (any part of a corpse could serve for the witches' magic ritual), a drum dramatically announces the subject of their immediate attention.

Macbeth's first words, "So foul and fair a day I have not seen" (38), while innocent in themselves since he has just wrested victory from defeat in the foulest weather, suggest how close his thoughts are to evil, perhaps to thinking of the kingship. (For comments on the contrast between Macbeth's reported reputation and his present behavior see the Introduction, pp. xxixff.) These witches are not the "goddesses of destiny" seen in Holinshed's *Chronicles;* rather they function as signposts pointing the way, an embodiment of temptation. Ross's confirmation about the prophecy of Cawdor makes the temptation all the stronger and brings Macbeth's thoughts into the open, "The greatest is behind" (117).

By contrast, Banquo reacts quite normally to the witches, questioning their reality and asking for his own fortune to be told. Having no evil in his mind, Banquo is not startled; but their prophecy may have planted the seed of evil. Quick to read Macbeth's behavior, Banquo utters the warning, "oftentimes, to win us to our harm,/The instruments of darkness tell us truths" (123-24).

Although Macbeth has a strong desire to be King, the solicitations of the witches go so "Against the use of nature" (137), that he reaches his first important decision: "If chance will have me King, why, chance may crown me, Without my stir" (143-44). Even so, the decision itself supposes other possibilities.

I.iv

The scene opens as one of light and order, as opposed to the earlier scenes of storm, murkiness, and confusion, insofar as Duncan's grace and integrity prevail; only in the parallel of the two Cawdors and Macbeth's aside is the dark underside revealed, which gives to almost everything the King says a retrospectively ironic undertone.

Somewhat impatient to know that his orders have been carried out promptly, Duncan does not accept his son's mitigation of Cawdor's treason: "He was a gentleman on whom I built/An absolute trust" (13-14). In Duncan's scale of values, integrity is part of a man's worth, more so than courage in facing death. The entry of Macbeth juxtaposes the two Cawdors, past and present. The national danger has been so great and Macbeth's skill and courage so crucial in averting it that Duncan, in conferring the title upon Macbeth, must have felt that he saw in Macbeth all that he had a right to expect in the former Thane, even more. Macbeth has so proved himself in battle that Duncan is moved to tears, allowing his personal feelings to express his gratitude. Macbeth's reply is formal in tone, simply acknowledging his duty to the throne as a loyal subject.

Now that the rebellion has been put down, Duncan takes this formal occasion to proclaim to the assembled court the succession to the throne, instead of leaving the issue to be debated after his death—a Jacobean audience would have seen the wisdom of such foresight. At the same time, the relationship of the King to his nobles is one of graciousness and generosity, not of fear and compunction: "signs of nobleness, like stars, shall shine/On all deservers" (41-42). To show that he is not speaking idle words, Duncan announces his plan to pay a royal visit to Macbeth's castle the same day.

With Malcolm named successor to the throne, Macbeth knows that he can no longer expect chance to crown him King. The King's visit makes the temptation to violence unbearably strong, providing as it does a unique opportunity. The imagery is now reversed: "Stars, hide your fires;/Let not light see my black and deep desires" (50-51); but the image does not imply that Macbeth has reached any final decision, simply that he is sorely tempted. The comment serves to sharpen the irony in Duncan's concluding remarks: "And in his commendations I am fed;/It is a banquet to me" (55-56)—but the food is poisoned.

I.v

It seems apparent from Lady Macbeth's reaction to the letter from her husband that she is no stranger to the idea of his becoming King or even of his catching "the nearest way" (19) to do so. She wastes no words marveling at the witches' prophecy; instead, she decides without hesitation: thou "shalt be/What thou art promised" (16-17). Her analysis of his natural qualities sees in him a gentleness not revealed before, except in the tone of his letter. He is not a wicked man; rather, he lacks any positive moral values. As she weighs his qualities in the scales, she strikes a balance which she herself must tip unless action is to be paralyzed.

When the messenger brings news of the royal visit, for the first time she expresses amazement. It is now that she takes charge. Calling upon evil spirits to change the very nature of her womanhood, she becomes their agent. Her evil plotting at night within the walls of Glamis Castle creates a hellish atmosphere. Images of evil and darkness fill her mind and speech: "The raven himself is hoarse" (39), "Make thick my blood" (44), "thick night" (51), "the dunnest smoke of hell"

(52). She appears to be ready to kill Duncan herself "with my keen knife" (53), or at least sees herself as operating through her husband as agent (see Cleanth Brooks, "The Naked Babe," p. 209, and Oscar James Campbell, From "Shakespeare and the 'New' Critics," p. 224). But with her horror of bloodshed, she rejects even the visual imagining of it. Just when she exclaims "Hold, hold!" (55), Macbeth enters to take, as it were, the words out of her mouth.

Macbeth assumes an innocence, echoing the innocence of the messenger's words: "Duncan comes here tonight" (60). His evasive reply to her question "And when goes hence?/Tomorrow, as he purposes" (60-61) ties in with his wish to "speak further" (72) about the matter, the same desire he had expressed to Banquo in scene iii. He desperately needs time in which to think things over, but time is crowding him.

I.vi

This scene is noteworthy for the ironic contrast which it provides when taken in conjunction with the preceding and succeeding scenes. The castle is located in mountainous country, where the air is nimble and delicate, not filled with "the dunnest smoke of hell" (51.52). Here we have the "temple-haunting martlet" (4) building his "procreant cradle" (8) in niches of the buttressed walls, instead of the raven croaking "the fatal entrance of Duncan" (51.39-40). The imagery suggests innocence as opposed to evil, sacred and life-giving forces as opposed to death and destruction. The point of view is essentially an extension of Duncan's consciousness and way of looking at life, not Lady Macbeth's.

Because Duncan is without guile, he is prone to see others in the same way. Despite his disclaimer "There's no art/To find the mind's construction in the face" (48.11-12), he is an ill judge of persons. In his graciousness to Lady Macbeth, he fails to observe the serpent beneath the "innocent flower" (52.66).

Again stress is placed on the time element, on the speed with which the King's visit has come about; Duncan has not only pursued Macbeth to the castle but had hoped to overtake him. The audience is meant to see that Macbeth has had no time to reflect or to exercise reason; in fact, his absence when the King arrives shows how much he feels the need to reflect.

I.vii

Macbeth has stolen from the banquet to think further about the murder. The issue is clearly a moral one. In looking through Macbeth's eyes, the audience sees temptation as it knows it to be, and grants Macbeth some measure of respect in facing it without pretense or excuse. First, Duncan is a kinsman, first cousin to Macbeth. Then Duncan is the King. Murder in becoming treason takes on another dimension: to kill a king is to let evil into the kingdom, to invite disorder and chaos. More important still, Duncan is a symbol of what kingship meant in Renaissance times when a king was regarded as sacred, as God's representative on earth. Besides all this, Macbeth can find no fault with his rule. It is interesting that Shakespeare presents Macbeth's decision in terms of character, whereas in the source materials Macbeth feels that he has been defrauded of his claim to the throne and knows that his relatives have been hanged for a public spectacle by the King. (See the *Chronicles,* pp. 137 and 144).

Seeing the situation rationally and objectively, Macbeth is ready to abandon the plot; but he has reckoned without his wife. There is no rational answer to her impassioned emotional outburst, her accusation of cowardice, and her appeal to the darker side of his nature: "What beast was 't then/That made you break this enterprise to me?" (47-48). (See Samuel Johnson, *Macbeth* [I.vii.28], pp. 159-60.) By the end of this scene, Macbeth has made his irrevocable decision. In his concluding words he paraphrases his wife's former instructions (52.64-65) saying, "mock the time with fairest show./False face must hide what false heart doth know" (81-82); the coalescence of two minds committed to evil is complete.

II.i

As Act II opens, a new phase of the drama is about to develop, primarily concerned with retribution following hard upon transgression.

The first scene opens at night; the moon has gone down, and the stars are hidden. It is past midnight, the time when evil spirits are abroad, spirits who can put evil thoughts into the minds of sleeping men. Even now, Banquo is disturbed by "the cursèd thoughts that nature/Gives way to in repose!" (8-9). At the sound of Macbeth's footsteps, he calls for his sword as if fearful of treachery; and the next moment his thoughts revert to the witches, who have been troubling his sleep. In reply, Macbeth reveals a mind so settled that he already sees the future as an accomplished fact and solicits Banquo's support: "If you shall cleave to my consent, when 'tis,/It shall make honor for you" (25-26).

In the soliloquy which follows, the offstage murder of Duncan in the next scene is made palpable by being acted out beforehand. As if in league with evil, Macbeth projects the scene visually: the dagger that "marshal'st me the way that I was going" (42) to the completed act, "the gouts of blood" (46). The sense of horror and evil is made corporate in the imagery: "Nature seems dead" (50), "wicked dreams" (50), "witchcraft celebrates" (51), "withered murder" (52), "Tarquin's ravishing strides" (55). The mixture of illusion and reality strengthens the sense of evil external to, but operating within, man; so that the striking of the bell is ironically a summons to both men.

II.ii

The atmosphere of this scene becomes increasingly tense. It is still night. The setting, the interior of the castle, is isolated in time and place, yet transcends both. As Lady Macbeth and Macbeth listen intently but fearfully, the different noises build to a crescendo: the snoring of the drunken grooms, the screech of the night owl, the laughter and cries of nightmare, the voice of Macbeth's conscience, the knocking at the gate. The combination of actual and imagined sounds again unites earthly and unearthly powers, pushing the walls of the castle beyond temporal limits; it also sharply differentiates the reaction of Lady Macbeth from that of Macbeth.

As Lady Macbeth waits at the foot of the stairs for her husband, she suggests a different side to her character in her reason for not killing Duncan herself; yet she is still in charge, her whole mind concentrated on carrying through the murder to a successful conclusion. As Macbeth descends the stairs as if into hell, she greets him, for the first time in the play, with loving intimacy as "husband" (13), wholly unconscious of the incongruity of greeting the bloody-handed Macbeth in these terms. But she retains a firm grip on herself. Her utterances are brief and coldly practical. Even after returning the daggers to Duncan's bedchamber, she remains in charge and directs Macbeth's actions as they hear the knocking at the gate, aware that by her own example she must counteract his lack of firmness. Her literal and practical voice is in strong contrast to his poetic and metaphysical one.

Macbeth is deeply conscious of his guilt. Listening to the

grooms, he can no longer pray. Like the prisoners on either side of the Cross, the grooms react oppositely; yet each, being free of the offense, is capable of salvation. Looking down at his "hangman's hands" (27), symbolic like the red gloves of Herod in the Miracle Plays, Macbeth stands alien, sensible that his hands will turn the whole ocean into a welter of blood, unable to feel, as Lady Macbeth does, that "A little water clears us of this deed" (66). The sleep imagery, increasingly common after the murder, is particularly marked in this scene. The voice Macbeth hears echoes the voice of the witches which hailed him as Glamis, Cawdor, King; now it is Glamis, Cawdor, Macbeth that shall " 'Sleep no more!' " (40), as if in mockery. Sleep, symbolic of innocence, is something that Macbeth has murdered. Later on, when afflicted by terrible dreams himself, he is to feel that "After life's fitful fever" Duncan "sleeps well" (81.23); now he wishes that the knocking could awaken Duncan, that he could undo what cannot be undone.

II.iii

Disregarding the feeling first expressed by Aristotle, that comedy and tragedy do not mix, Shakespeare introduces the porter scene; and, his usual custom, he writes this low-comedy sketch in prose, not merely to make a social distinction between peasant and noble, but to achieve a different effect, a lowering of tension. By having the drunken porter pretend to be the gatekeeper of hell, he sharpens the ironic reference to what has happened within the castle by his physical reference to the "primrose way" (19) outside. After the intense scene of the murder, the knocking at the gate is a reminder of the immediate demands of everyday life, as Thomas De Quincey has pointed out in his essay "On the Knocking at the Gate in *Macbeth*." The microcosmic experience of the individual within the castle must be seen in the broader perspective of the macrocosmic political world. Macduff starts the clock again by saying, "He did command me to call timely on him:/I have almost slipped the hour" (48-49). It is now dawn: the hour of revelation. Lennox alerts the audience by echoing Lady Macbeth's evil inquiry of her husband on his return home, "And when goes hence?" (52-60). Lennox innocently asks, "Goes the king hence today?" (54). Macbeth makes a similar reply to both questions. Ironically, there is to be a difference in the nature of his going, depending on the questioner. Also building to the climax of the discovery is the "unruly" night, the "strange screams of death," the omen of death in the owl's night-long hooting, the rumors of an earthquake (57-63), pointing to repercussions in the universal ordering of the natural world.

When Macduff describes the scene of the murder, he does so in religious terms: "Most sacrilegious murder hath broke ope/The Lord's anointed temple, and stole thence/The life o' th' building" (69-71); for Duncan has ruled "by the grace of Grace" (131.72). His death is "The great doom's image!" (80). Even Macbeth is not unaware of the enormity of his act, as we see when he says that "his gashed stabs looked like a breach in nature/For ruin's wasteful entrance" (115-16); ruin can enter the kingdom when its temporal head has been struck down.

At this stage, Macbeth is sharply conscious of what he has sacrificed at a single blow:

> Had I but died an hour before this chance,
> I had lived a blessèd time; for from this instant
> There's nothing serious in mortality:
> All is but toys. (93–96)

Not only is Duncan dead, but everything that gave meaning to his own life is dead. He is no longer "noble Macbeth" (40.67), but a common murderer. And there can be no return to his former state. As if to prove "Renown and grace is dead" (96), he seals the lips of the grooms. By this further act, he arouses the immediate suspicions of both Macduff and Lennox, as the tone of their remarks reveals.

While the nobles appear to act in concert in agreeing to meet together to discuss the situation further, it is clear that Macduff is already disaffected. Malcolm and Donalbain, the King's sons, know not whom to trust. "Let's not consort with them," says Malcolm (137). Conscious of the danger, they decide to separate and seek safety abroad: Malcolm in England, Donalbain in Ireland.

II.iv

The scene creates a time break and shows what is happening in the world outside the castle. The Old Man, acting like a Greek chorus, suggests the public reaction to current events: to the disturbances in the natural universe (an eclipse would be seen as a portent of disaster, usually political) and to things unnatural (an owl killing the primate of birds, the eagle) "like the deed that's done" (11). The eclipse of the sun is also a symbol of the darkness and evil overtaking the kingdom now that the King is dead.

Although "fair is foul" (37.10), Ross joins those who would try to "make good of bad" (41), now that Macbeth has been duly elected King by the nobles. Macduff, however, disassociates himself entirely by refusing to see Macbeth crowned at Scone, and instead returns home to Fife.

III.i

Act III opens with Macbeth crowned King; thus his acts assume public importance.

Banquo's position at this time is equivocal. As a successful general, his career has paralleled Macbeth's and he is entitled to equal honors. He has seen the witches' prophecies about Macbeth fulfilled. He suspects Macbeth of having played "most foully for 't" (3); yet he has made no attempt to expose him or even to dissociate himself as Macduff has. Macbeth even suspects him of jealousy in saying that "He chid the sisters,/ When they first put the name of King upon me,/ And bade them speak to him" (57-59). Now Banquo looks ahead, "May they not be my oracles as well/ And set me up in hope?" (9-10).

Macbeth himself senses danger. Twice he has expressed eagerness to speak with Banquo and has made overtures for his support. They are, as Banquo himself puts it, knit by "a most indissoluble tie" (17)—the witches' prophecies. It seems expedient to act. Even as Macbeth is eliciting from Banquo information requisite for the murder, ironically he is inviting him to be "our chief guest" (11) at the banquet. He shows no compunction about having Banquo and Fleance put to death, only political caution in convincing the two hired assassins of its necessity. However, his soliloquy gives a deeper insight into his state of mind: his awareness of the ideal of kingship in "the gracious Duncan" (66) whom he has murdered, and his bitterness in having given "mine eternal jewel" (68) to "the common enemy of man" (69) only to make the offspring of his rival kings. His trouble seems to lie less in Banquo than in his sense of loss of what was noble in life, and in his realization that what he hoped for cannot be attained.

III.ii

In sending for her husband, Lady Macbeth is as sensitive to his personal and lonely brooding as she is to his need to create a kingly image at the banquet. Likewise, Macbeth is unwilling to burden her mind further by disclosing his plans for the murder of Banquo and Fleance. Both have been racked by nightmares. Their suicidal feelings at this point intersect: she reflects, " 'Tis safer to be that which we destroy" (6); and a moment later he echoes, "better be with the dead,/Whom we, to gain our peace, have sent to peace" (19-20). There is great tenderness between them at this meeting; yet the meeting is only an intersection. As he comes increasingly to the fore and begins to act without her knowledge, she retires to the background; they are more and more apart. As she is beginning to experience remorse, he is becoming inured to evil, ready to "let the frame of things disjoint" (16) if necessary. While still conscious of moral values, he has now joined in league with "night's black agents" (53) in wishing to have "seeling night,/Scarf up the tender eye of pitiful day" (46-47), convinced that "Things bad begun make strong themselves by ill" (55).

III.iii

Careful beforehand to test the loyalty of the hired murderers, Macbeth now has added to their number to prevent any botches. It is nightfall; rain threatens. The image of the apprehensive traveler spurring his horse to reach "the timely inn" (7) grows audible with the approach on horseback of Banquo and Fleance. As the two men dismount and take the short cut to the castle, they are set upon. The escape of Fleance marks the end of Macbeth's successes. Up to this point fortune has favored him: the witches' prophecies, Duncan's visit, the flight of Malcolm and Donalbain. From here on fortune turns against him.

III.iv

There is much spectacle in this scene to appeal to a Jacobean audience, starting with the royal banquet itself, conducted with the pomp and ceremony due to a king. After the guests have been seated, Macbeth follows his wife's advice by acting the "jovial" host (81.28). Taking her cue from him, she also steps down from the chair of state to join him in mingling with the guests; the duality of Macbeth's role in this scene is stressed by his turning from greeting the guests to greeting the murderers. As he does so, the texture of his language changes too, and the tactile-muscular images increase as he feels himself to be "cabined, cribbed, confined" (25).

Conscious of their public image, Lady Macbeth has to remind the King that "the sauce to meat is ceremony" (37). As Macbeth returns to his duties, he reproves Banquo for failing to attend the feast. Ironically, each time he does so, the ghost appears. Whether or not the director makes the ghost visible to the audience is unimportant. Lady Macbeth sees only an empty stool; innocent of the "twenty trenchèd gashes" (28) in Banquo's head, she is not subject to this spirit of retribution. To Lady Macbeth, "This is the air-drawn dagger which, you said,/Led you to Duncan" (63-64). Both visions can be seen as palpable extensions of Macbeth's conscience, although the distance between the two is great. Largely because Macbeth has a conscience, and because its effect on him is made so plainly visible, he can still win sympathy.

Lady Macbeth rises once more, and for the last time, to her full height as she seeks to cover up for her husband. But the banquet, which began with much ceremony, breaks up in total disorder. "Stand not upon the order of your going," she tells her guests (120); yet order is the foundation of the Elizabethan view of the universe, in which everything has its place. Let something get out of order, and the disruption has serious consequences. The disorder at the banquet is symbolic of the much more widespread disorder in the kingdom, which Macbeth invited by usurping the throne; so that by now there is not a nobleman "but in his house/I keep a servant fee'd." (132-33).

Both action and imagery reinforce one another in this scene. Failing to find peace of mind after having Banquo killed, Macbeth immediately turns his attention to Macduff and seeks out the witches "to know/By the worst means the worst" (135-36). The blood imagery follows the same pattern. It starts with Macbeth's initial remark to the murderer, "There's blood upon thy face" (84.13); then there is the ghostly specter of Banquo, whose "blood is cold" (88.95); that is followed by Macbeth's prophetic "blood will have blood" (89.123); and we reach the climax with his recognition that

> I am in blood
> Stepped in so far that, should I wade no more,
> Returning were as tedious as go o'er. (137-39)

The strong image of wading in blood, reminiscent of bathing "in reeking wounds" (39.39), interacts with the tone of tediousness to measure the distance he has traveled. Even so,

"We are yet but young in deed" (145), he concludes, foreshadowing worse to follow.

III.v

Differences in the verse pattern and in the texture of the language itself suggest an interpolation of this scene, as of the Hecate passage in Act IV (95.39-43). Hecate serves no function in the play. Musical directions for the songs are taken from Middleton's play *The Witch*. (See Textual Note, p. 132.)

III.vi

The ideals of kingship and the machinations of the usurper are juxtaposed throughout this scene. Lennox, again the objective observer, expresses what is in the mind of all. The scornful tone of his accusations against Macbeth contrasts with his continuing use of the epithet "gracious" in speaking of Duncan: the usurper by cold-blooded murder and the king by divine right. The ideal of kingship is further sustained in the Scottish lord's tribute to the "most pious Edward" (27), who shares, in his reception of Malcolm, Duncan's graciousness and, in Lennox's desire to have "Some holy angel/Fly to the court of England" (45-46), Duncan's kingliness. Shakespeare is not merely complimenting the throne but projecting his ideal of kingship. By contrast, Macbeth's tyranny grows daily. Anticipating Edward's permission to secure the assistance of English nobles across the border, Macduff hopes to "Give to our tables meat, sleep to our nights,/Free from our feasts and banquets bloody knives" (34-35). Thus the shape of things to come for Macbeth is foreshadowed even before he seeks out the witches. Disaster will overtake Macduff's household even sooner, as the messenger suggests when Macduff refuses Macbeth's invitation to the banquet. " 'You'll rue the time/That clogs me with this answer' " (42-43).

IV.i

The opening of this scene, in which the weird sisters appear through a trap door in the stage, provides much information about witchcraft. (See Samuel Johnson, *Macbeth*, pp. 162-65.) On this occasion the witches, sought out by Macbeth, greet him no longer by name but as "Something wicked" (45), a measure of his moral deterioration. In trading with the forces of evil, these "secret, black, and midnight hags!"

(48), he is prepared to destroy life itself if necessary to further his own cause. His own images of destruction match in viciousness the ingredients of the witches' brew and stand in strong contrast to the healing and creative images associated with true kingship in the previous scene. Macbeth is never greeted with the royal title except on this one occasion when the first witch refers to him as "this great king" (131).

The popular spectacle of the apparitions offers a sequel to the first appearance of the witches; before, they foretold Macbeth's rise to power; now, his decline and nemesis. Each apparition may, perhaps, suggest a crude symbol of its fulfillment: the Armed Head, Macbeth's decapitation; the Bloody Child, a cesarean section; the Child Crowned, with a tree in his hand, the coming of Birnam Wood to Dunsinane and the restoration of the rightful heir to the throne. Ironically Macbeth has forgotten his own prophetic utterance by now: "blood will have blood./Stones have been known to move and trees to speak" (89.123-24). Able to read Macbeth's thoughts (69) and to forecast future events, the apparitions bring future time into the present and arouse the curiosity of the audience by their equivocal statements.

Macbeth's announcement in this scene of his immediate intentions, to surprise Macduff's castle "before this purpose cool" (154), increases the tension of the next.

IV.ii

More clearly than ever the audience sees the savage brutality of Macbeth in the spiteful revenge he takes on the innocent and defenseless household of Macduff, and feels an additional pathos when it remembers Macbeth's statement of purpose in the preceding scene. Learning from Ross that her husband has departed for England, Lady Macduff assumes that he has deserted to save his own life. In this disordered land, where "All is the fear and nothing is the love" (12), the mother feels that she must turn to the natural kingdom, to "the poor wren,/The most diminutive of birds" (9-10), to find what should be the father's instinct to protect his young. But we know that Macduff has consistently refused to compromise his position once he sensed Macbeth's guilt in killing Duncan: instead of attending the coronation he returned home to Fife (72.35-36) and aroused Macbeth's anger by flouting his invitation to attend the royal banquet (93.39-40). In the meantime, he has left on his mission to seek help from the King of England (93.29-31), without involving his wife in any part of his military plans to save Scotland. As Ross, himself about to join Macduff secretly, replies, "cruel are the times, when we are traitors/And do not know ourselves" (18-19), a reminder of the witches' paradox that "Fair is foul, and foul is fair" (37.10). No longer can man be judged aright in this disordered kingdom.

In seeing Lady Macduff and her son alone together, the audience is made aware of their utter defenselessness. The son, quick to parry his mother's suppositions about the death of his father, can also sense the topsy-turviness of the times, in which "there are liars and swearers enow to beat the honest men and hang up them" (54-56). There is something quixotic in the mother which makes her peculiarly defenseless. Warned by the messenger to fly, she can only proclaim her innocence and then recall that "I am in this earthly world, where to do harm/Is often laudable" (73-74). Both die courageously, and perhaps the most moving thing of all is that Lady Macduff dies without knowing that her husband has escaped only to bring succor to a land in which the people "float upon a wild and violent sea" (21).

As Shakespeare directs attention and sympathy toward Lady Macduff, he creates a transition to prepare for the coming of the forces of freedom to reestablish law and order. No longer looking through Macbeth's eyes, the audience sees Macbeth reach his lowest ebb in having the household of Macduff slaughtered because Macduff himself has escaped.

IV.iii

As the scene shifts to England, the forces of retribution gather to a head. For the eventual restoration of Scotland, the characters who take part in it must be uncontaminated by the prevailing evil. During this testing period, time lengthens, both chronologically and dramatically, before events rush to their foreseeable conclusion.

In the first part of this scene Malcolm is play-acting, probing Macduff. At the outset he assumes a passive and despairing role, although he has already secured from the King of England an army of ten thousand men under the command of Old Siward (134-35). Macduff wants action. Unaware of what has happened to his own family, he testifies to the widespread massacre which Macbeth has used to quell resistance: "Each new morn/New widows howl, new orphans cry" (4-5). Ironically Macduff does not realize that he will be the one to cry for the death of his own family. Malcolm, however, in distrust, holds back the action Macduff so greatly desires. Such distrust is understandable. Malcolm, like his father, had once trusted Macbeth, had thought him "noble," had fought in the same battle to save his country from rebellion. Yet he had lived to see this same man murder his father. At the moment, Macduff might well be a man of such a pattern. He is openly suspicious for two other reasons: first, that Macduff had loved Macbeth well (13); second, that Macduff had left his family unprotected in Scotland (26-28), a fact never explained. Malcolm echoes the witches' paradox "fair is foul" when he says, "Though all things foul would wear the brows of grace" (23).

When Malcolm acts out the part of "fair is foul," he not only tests the worth of Macduff's loyalty but establishes the basis of true kingship, the conditions necessary for a healthy society. In denigrating himself, he enumerates those graces a king should possess: "As justice, verity, temp'rance, stableness,/Bounty, perseverance, mercy, lowliness,/Devotion, patience, courage, fortitude" (92-94). These virtues are the foundation upon which an ordered society can be reconstructed. He gets from Macduff the kind of reaction that restores his faith and a tribute to the ideal of kingship which Duncan symbolized:

> Thy royal father
> Was a most sainted king: the queen that bore thee,
> Oft'ner upon her knees than on her feet,
> Died every day she lived. (108-11)

Having shed his cloak of assumed evil, Malcolm tells of the alliance formed among the Scottish nobles, and between them and the English forces placed at his disposal by the King of England. The doctor's testimony to the power of the English king, whose faith-healing has defied medical science, further allies the kingship with its source of divine authority, "sundry blessings hang about his throne/That speak him full of grace" (158-59).

When Ross enters he bears additional witness to the spreading tyranny of Macbeth's rule and disorder in Scotland, "Where sighs and groans, and shrieks that rent the air,/Are made, not marked" (168-69). His tone arouses in Macduff suspicion about the well-being of his family, but Macduff has to drag from him the unwilling news of "these murdered deer" (206). Macduff's loyalty to Scotland has cost him his family; the price exacted for "the universal peace" is the loss of "the sweet milk of concord" (98-99)—all that Macbeth was prepared to "Pour . . . into hell." Macduff's silent anguish and frustration rise to rage as he determines to execute personal vengeance on Macbeth. The forces of "light" are now united; Malcolm is ready to overthrow those of "darkness" and bring about a new dawn: "The night is long that never finds the day" (240). And with this, time speeds up again.

V.i

Lady Macbeth, last seen at the banquet when she was still capable of strong and vivid action, has undergone so deep a change that she is cut off from all human contact by her hallucinations. Ironically her thoughts about the murder are now those she tried to suppress in Macbeth. Now she reenacts what before she could not envision. "A little water clears us of this deed," (64.66) she had once thought; now "All the perfumes of Arabia will not sweeten this little hand" (53-55). The audience is made grossly aware of the effect upon her of having to replace the dagger in Duncan's bedchamber and smear the faces of the grooms with blood as she exclaims, "who would have thought the old man to have had so much blood in him?" (42-43). She has also heard about Lady Macduff—"The Thane of Fife had a wife. Where is she now?" (45-46). These broken utterances reveal the weight of past events. While actively engaged in directing the murder of Duncan, she could "Stop up th' access and passage to remorse" (51.45); but now, with nothing further to do and left to her own thoughts, her heart becomes "sorely charged" (56-57). The disorder of her mind parallels the disorder in her relationship to Macbeth and the disorder in the realm. As the doctor points out, "Unnatural deeds/Do breed unnatural troubles" (75-76). His advice to "Remove from her the means of all annoyance" (80) may suggest what is later rumored.

V.ii

In the succession of short scenes that follow, time speeds up as the forces of freedom join to liberate Scotland.

While Macbeth waits for his castle to be besieged, the English soldiers from across the border, led by Malcolm, Macduff, and Siward, are heading toward Birnam Wood. Many young men, including some of the Scottish nobles, have joined this liberating force.

Reports pour in of widespread disaffection among Macbeth's own followers, as once they "Came post with post" (44.98) praising him. Macbeth's present situation is defined in an image recurrent throughout the play, the image of ill-fitting clothes. Macbeth himself introduced it when, in answer to the witches' addressing him as Thane of Cawdor, he asked in all honesty, "why do you dress me/In borrowed robes?" (45.108). His new titles become "strange garments" (46.144) to which he is unaccustomed, or "Which would be worn now in their newest gloss" (56.34). After he has gained the crown, his title of King is symbolized by garments which do not belong to him. In this scene, he is described as a grotesque whose title hangs "loose about him, like a giant's robe/Upon a dwarfish thief" (21-22). (For some detailed discussion of the imagery of clothing, see Cleanth Brooks, "The Naked Babe and the Cloak of Manliness," pp. 205-12.) Further, the parallel between the health of a king and the health of his kingdom is made explicit as Macbeth, whose power is rapidly disintegrating, is likened to a man whose body is so swollen with dropsy that he can no longer "buckle his distempered cause/Within the belt of rule" (15-16). The medical metaphor is continued as the liberating army is seen as the cathartic which shall purge the sickly commonwealth (27-29) and restore health to Scotland.

V.iii

As the armies surround the castle, Macbeth becomes increasingly distraught. Volatile in temper, he suffers fits of elation and depression, scorning with false confidence the approaching enemy, cursing his servant, arming and unarming, turning now to Seyton and now to the doctor. There is a moment of melancholy calm when he reflects on his life: "My way of life/Is fall'n into the sear, the yellow leaf" (22-23). At the beginning of the play, he was a vigorous man in the prime of life. Although in chronological time the play is brief, Shakespeare creates the sense here that after what Macbeth has been through he has lived a lifetime, that there is nothing further for him in life. Macbeth sees himself as clearly as when he assessed the murder of Duncan. By cutting himself off from mankind, he has lost "honor, love, obedience, troops of friends" (25) and gained instead "Curses," "mouth-honor" (27)—a king and no-king. This ability to look at himself unflinchingly is one of his rare qualities and draws sympathy, as does his concern for Lady Macbeth. From now on he must fight his battle alone; and the audience is made to feel that the end is very near.

V.iv

As the liberating armies approach Birnam Wood, we see how one of the witches' prophecies is to be fulfilled when Malcolm instructs his soldiers to advance behind a camouflage of branches to conceal the strength of their numbers—ten thousand English foot soldiers supplemented by Scottish nobles who have joined the cause. Macbeth, whose generalship has favored attack rather than defense, is compelled to await the siege in his castle, fearful that too many will desert if he takes the offensive.

V.v

As Macbeth awaits the approaching enemy, there is a sense of immediacy and desperation in his order to "Hang out our banners on the outward walls./The cry is still 'They come!'" (1-2). But "the cry of women" (8) diverts his attention to what is happening inside the castle, an echo that recalls the night of Duncan's murder; only his reaction now, as he recognizes, is one of satiety: "I have supped full with horrors" (13). There is pathos in Seyton's announcement, "The Queen, my lord, is dead" (16); it is the first time that Lady Macbeth has ever been accorded her royal title, and in the same breath we find that her inability to "stop up th' access and passage to remorse" (51.45) has brought about her death. As Macbeth reflects on the death of his wife and on mortality in general, his tone is one of great weariness, of a man who, reviewing his life, sees no further meaning to it. The tone is all the more emphatic because of the ironic contrast between dramatic time and chronological time. Inside the castle at this point, Macbeth sees the broad perspective of his life as a slow and reiterated monotony, "Tomorrow, and tomorrow, and tomorrow/Creeps in this petty pace from day to day/To the last syllable of recorded time" (19-21); outside, events are hurrying forward to bring about his nemesis. It takes the messenger's news that Birnam Wood is moving to stir him again to anger, to the immediate situation, to action. If the witches' prophecy is to be fulfilled, he will face without flinching his own fate and their stormy blasts: "Blow wind, come wrack!/At least we'll die with harness on our back" (51-52). This flash of his old heroic courage wins a degree of admiration.

V.vi

After Malcolm has mapped out the plan of attack, the trumpets sound for the liberating forces to advance. The clarion echoes from another battle for freedom, a battle which Macbeth won and the Thane of Cawdor lost. Since then Macbeth has imagined Duncan's virtues as angels pleading "trumpet-tongued against/The deep damnation of his taking-off" (55.19-20). Now the warlike trumpets signal the advance against another Thane of Cawdor, and it is the avenger Macduff who gives the order: "Make all our trumpets speak; give them all breath,/Those clamorous harbingers of blood and death" (9-10). As a director, Shakespeare is well aware of this stage effect.

V.vii

The odds are so overwhelming that Macbeth feels like a bear tied to the stake; however, with desperate faith in the last of the witches' prophecies, he fights on and gains a momentary feeling of security in killing the Young Siward. Once again, with renewed vigor, he seems to be the cannon "overcharged with double cracks" (39.37) as Macduff, seeking personal vengeance, locates him by "the noise" (14), "this great clatter, one of greatest note" (21). But by now the castle has surrendered, and Macbeth's troops are joining the liberating army.

V.viii

The scene opens (See Textual Note, p. 132) with a typical contrast. Cornered, deserted by his troops, Macbeth will fight "Whiles I see lives" (2) rather than commit suicide; seeking revenge and with victory in sight, Macduff spares the lives of professional soldiers "hired to bear their staves" (127.18). When they meet face to face, Macbeth can still feel a sense of guilt, of betrayal of what is meant by nobility, at having had Macduff's family slaughtered. When Macduff reveals the final equivocation of the witches, for a moment Macbeth is overcome; even the forces of evil seem to have betrayed him. But he reacts to Macduff's taunt of cowardice as he did to Lady Macbeth's. Now he is fighting not just against a mortal, but against fate and his own deep damnation. Just as Malcolm could not help admiring the way in which the former Thane of Cawdor met death, Macbeth's final challenge invites admiration: "Lay on, Macduff;/ And damned be him that first cries 'Hold, enough!' " (34).

The play closes with a convention common to Jacobean drama: an expository summation of the fate of the characters unaccounted for. This scene, which may seem commonplace and dull to a modern audience, had, however, great significance for the Jacobeans. Here the world is restored to order. The vanquishing of the tyrant, the creator of disorder, is made vivid by the bringing onstage of the head of Macbeth. Once more the crown is in rightful hands, and Malcolm acts immediately as the steward of kingship. He creates a new rank for those who have been on the side of moral and political right, "thy kingdom's pearl" (56), and pledges himself to rule "by the grace of Grace" (72). Shakespeare's audience could leave the theater with order, the primary requisite of their lives, properly restored.

MARTIN PARRY

SHORT-ANSWER QUESTIONS

1. What specific facts about witches can be gathered from the first scene? (37.1-11)

2. What two battles are "lost and won" early in the play and by whom? (38.9-23; 40.51-58)

3. What does Duncan refer to in saying, "What he hath lost, noble Macbeth hath won"? (40.63-67)

4. When the witches have vanished from the heath, what decision does Macbeth reach about becoming King? (46.143-44)

5. What is the irony in Duncan's remark, "There's no art/To find the mind's construction in the face"? (48.11-12)

6. What is the reason for Macbeth's saying, "The Prince of Cumberland! That is a step/ On which I must fall down, or else o'erleap"? (49.48-49)

7. After reading his letter, what does Lady Macbeth reveal about her husband's nature? (50.17-26)

8. What reasons does Macbeth give for not wishing to kill Duncan? (55.12-28)

9. What kind of pressure does Lady Macbeth exert in persuading her husband to kill Duncan? (56.39-43; 47-48)

10. What part do "time and place" play in relation to Duncan's murder? (51.35-38; 54.20-24; 54.1-2; 55.29-30; 56.51-54)

11. On the night of the murder, how does Macbeth try to win Banquo's support? (59.25-26)

12. How does Macbeth act out the murder before doing it? (59.33-59)

13. What reason does Lady Macbeth give for not killing Duncan herself? (61.12-13)

14. What marked difference is there between the speaking voices of Macbeth and Lady Macbeth immediately after the murder? (61.14-73)

15. What functions does the Porter Scene serve? (64.1-21)

16. What does Macduff imply about Duncan in saying "Most sacrilegious murder hath broke ope/The Lord's anointed temple"? (67.69-70)

17. In the discovery scene, what does Macbeth mean in saying, "There's nothing serious in mortality"? (68.95)

18. What does the following remark mean and to whom does it apply: "the near in blood,/The nearer bloody"? (70.142-43)

19. In the scene following the discovery of Duncan's murder, what does Ross mean when he says: "By th' clock 'tis day,/And yet dark night strangles the traveling lamp"? (71.6-7) Is there any special significance to this remark?

THE TRAGEDY OF MACBETH 43

20. Which one of the nobles did not attend the coronation of Macbeth and why? (72.35-36; 69.108-9)

21. Once Macbeth has been crowned King, what attitude does Banquo express toward his own future? (74.8-10)

22. In what way are Banquo and Macbeth "with a most indissoluble tie/For ever knit"? (75.17-18; 45.117-28)

23. What are Lady Macbeth's feelings once she becomes Queen? (80.4-7)

24. What argument does Macbeth use to persuade the two murderers to kill Banquo? (77.75-91)

25. What change takes place in the relationship between Macbeth and Lady Macbeth following the murder of Duncan? (80.8-9; 82.45-46)

26. How does Macbeth's royal banquet in Act III compare with Duncan's in Act I? (48.15-42; 84.1-122)

27. Lady Macbeth compares her husband's vision of the ghost to what other situation in the play? (86.63-64) In what ways are they alike?

28. How does Lady Macbeth excuse Macbeth's behavior at the sight of Banquo's ghost? (86.54-58)

29. What facets of Lady Macbeth's character are revealed in the banquet scene?

30. What does the tone of Lennox' speech indicate when he says: "The gracious Duncan/Was pitied of Macbeth: marry, he was dead"? (92.3-4)

31. What is "the usual form in which familiar spirits are reported to converse with witches"? (94.1; p. 162)

32. What does each of the apparitions prophesy to Macbeth? (97.71-94)

33. What is the meaning of the line of eight kings, some "That twofold balls and treble sceptres carry"? (99.121-24)

34. In what way does Lady Macduff's feeling about her husband's absence relate to the paradox of the witches, "Fair is foul, and foul is fair"? (101.3-4)

35. What effect does the murder of Lady Macduff and her children have upon the outcome of the play? (113.228-29)

36. Why is the scene of Lady Macduff and her child introduced so late in the play?

37. What reasons does Malcolm give for distrusting Macduff? (105.12-17)

38. In talking to Malcolm, how does Macduff describe Duncan and the former queen? (109.108-11)

39. Why does Malcolm give himself a bad character? (109.114-17)

40. What is the meaning of the last line in Act IV: "The night is long that never finds the day"? (114.240)

41. In her delirium in the sleepwalking scene, what specific events does Lady Macbeth recall? (116.38-43; 65-71)

42. In what way does the doctor attending Lady Macbeth provide a contrast to the King of England? (117.62; 110.147-49)

43. How does the sleepwalking scene change or modify our views about Lady Macbeth? (117.53-59)

44. What do we learn from Malcolm about Macbeth's military strategy? And why does he change it? (123.8-14; 125.46-48)

45. How does Macbeth's reaction to the news of his wife's death contrast with the reaction of Macduff on hearing about the death of his wife and children? (124.17-18; 113.207-27)

46. How does Young Siward's part in the battle help to bring true one of the witches' prophecies? (127.11-13)

THE TRAGEDY OF MACBETH 45

47. How is each of the witches' prophecies fulfilled? (45.105-06; 129.15-16)

48. When faced by Macduff, how does Macbeth react when he learns that the last of the prophecies has come true? (129.17-34)

49. When Macduff enters at the end of the play, in what way has Macbeth's career come full circle? (130.54-55)

50. Why is it fitting for Malcolm to make the closing speech in the play? (130.59)

QUESTIONS FOR DISCUSSION

1. How does the impression given of Macbeth before he comes onstage (38.7-58) differ from that when he first makes his appearance (42.38-154)? How do you account for this difference?

2. In what ways are the situations of Macbeth and Banquo alike? In what ways are the reactions of these two generals to such situations either alike or different? (39.33-42; 42.39-155; 48.27-43)

3. To what extent is Lady Macbeth a mirror revealing her husband's character? What particular qualities does she reveal in him?

4. It has been said that Macbeth's natural element is darkness, whereas Duncan is associated with light. Illustrate this statement and discuss the significance of these symbols in terms of the kingship and the moral scheme of the play.

5. Discuss Macbeth's motives for killing Banquo. (76.48-72; 80.8-22)

6. Some critics see the escape of Fleance as the climax of the play; others see Macbeth's loss of control at the sight

of Banquo's ghost as the climax. To what extent can it be argued that each of these is correct?

7. How do the prophecies of the apparitions affect Macbeth? (96.50-154) Is Macbeth's destiny controlled by fate or is he free to act for himself?

8. How far is it true to say that mistrust reaches its culmination in the scene in which Macduff meets Malcolm in England? (Pp. 104-14)

9. To what extent are Lady Macbeth's reactions in the sleepwalking scene similar to those which she tried to suppress in Macbeth at the time of Duncan's murder? (116.29-72; 62.20-68)

10. How far has Macbeth been stripped of social and humane qualities before the play is over?

SAMPLE TEST

I. (25 minutes)

Answer each of the following questions in one or two sentences.

1. Once Macbeth has been crowned king, what attitude does Banquo express toward his own future?

2. In what way are Banquo and Macbeth "with a most indissoluble tie/For ever knit"?

3. What are Lady Macbeth's feelings once she becomes queen?

4. What argument does Macbeth use to persuade the two murderers to kill Banquo?

5. What change takes place in the relationship between Macbeth and Lady Macbeth following the murder of Duncan?

6. How does Macbeth's royal banquet in Act III compare with Duncan's in Act I?

7. Lady Macbeth compares her husband's vision of the ghost to what other situation in the play? In what ways are they alike?

8. How does Lady Macbeth excuse Macbeth's behavior at the sight of Banquo's ghost?

9. What facets of Lady Macbeth's character are revealed in the banquet scene?

10. What does the tone of Lennox' speech indicate when he says: "The gracious Duncan/Was pitied of Macbeth: marry, he was dead"?

II. (20 minutes)

Write a short essay in which you discuss the following topic:

Some critics see the escape of Fleance as the climax of the play; others see Macbeth's loss of control at the sight of Banquo's ghost as the climax. To what extent can it be argued that each of these is correct?

Be specific. Remember that how well you write is more important than how much you write.

THE TRAGEDY OF JULIUS CAESAR

INTRODUCTION

The First Folio (1623) groups Shakespeare's plays under the headings of Comedies, Histories, and Tragedies. *Julius Caesar* is, of course, in the last group, though were the histories not limited to plays on relatively recent English history, it might well have been called a history play. When he turned to *Julius Caesar*, Shakespeare probably had recently completed his eighth play on English history, and in *Julius Caesar* he seems to be extending his territory, looking now at ancient history. Some of the English histories—notably *Richard II* and *Richard III*—are more or less tragic, but unlike such later tragedies as *Hamlet* and *King Lear* they seem as much concerned with political problems as with the fall of an individual, as much concerned with England as with her particular kings. And in *Julius Caesar*, which deals with the assassination of a world ruler and with the subsequent destruction of the assassins, we get some sense of the political concern that we find in the history plays. Shakespeare seems, in large measure, to be writing about Rome in a way that he later does not write about, say, Hamlet's Denmark or Lear's pre-Christian Britain or Macbeth's Scotland. Furthermore, although he did not write of the ensuing Roman events until six or seven years later (in *Antony and Cleopatra*), even when he wrote of the fall of Caesar and of his assassins he must have seen the matter as only a portion or chapter of Roman history (just as each English history play was a portion of a larger story), rather than as something like *Hamlet* or *King Lear* or *Macbeth*, complete in itself.

But if *Julius Caesar* bears some resemblance to the English histories, it also anticipates the great tragedies: we find noble men doing violent deeds and coming to see the irony of their actions. For a moment, however, let us postpone a discussion of the tragic aspects and look briefly at the style of the play. At first glance—if any of us can pretend to see the play for the first time—we notice an apparent simplicity of style. Where Shakespeare's first tragedy, *Titus Andronicus*, had its elaborate, highly evident rhetoric and its fifty or so allusions to mythology to make it "Roman," *Julius Caesar* shows us that Shakespeare has learned that the Roman world need not be created by a display of book learning. Here he apparently tried to create a spare, dry, "simple" or austere Roman world. There is no bawdry, no song, little lyricism, little cryptic expression, and little comedy. (The comedy is almost entirely confined to the opening scene, and perhaps extended a little into Casca's description of Caesar in the second scene; it rather looks as though by the end of the second scene Shakespeare abandoned the idea of making the sour Casca a comic figure and, indeed, abandoned comedy for the rest of the play). There seems, then, to be a remarkable uniformity of tone, and one is not surprised to learn that statistical examinations have shown that the vocabulary in *Julius Caesar* is (for Shakespeare) unusually small and unusually simple. Yet the play is never dull, partly because a fair amount happens, and partly because the language is not slack. "Forget not in your speed, Antonius,/To touch Calphurnia; for our elders say/The barren, touchèd in this holy chase,/Shake off their sterile curse" (36.6-9). (In this random sample are revealed Caesar's easy sense of command, his equally easy shifting of the superstitious belief to "our elders," and his deep concern to free Calphurnia not from mere sterility but from a "sterile curse.") And so on; one must look hard to find a line that does not live, that does not sound like memorable speech. One can open the text at random without fear of disappointment. Consider this brief exchange: Antony is beginning his funeral oration:

For Brutus' sake, I am beholding to you.

Fourth Plebeian. What does he say of Brutus?
Third Plebeian. He says, for Brutus' sake
        He finds himself beholding to us all.

Fourth Plebeian. 'Twere best he speak no harm of Brutus here!

(90.67-70)

How right that is. The plebeians scarcely wish to hear Antony, but his reference to Brutus catches them; Antony knows that the best way to engage the attention of the crowd is to begin by referring to its hero. The Third Plebeian patiently explains to the Fourth what Antony has said, and then comes the wonderful touch, the Fourth Plebeian's complacent threat: " 'Twere best he speak no harm of Brutus here!" But it is not merely that Shakespeare had an ear for reproducing popular speech; there is a good deal of figurative language that he never heard, and he is cunning at using unobtrusively all of the devices of rhetoric. Only very rarely, as at 84.204-06, where we have a pun and a mythological reference, do we feel we are getting "poetry" or prettiness rather than dramatic speech. Among the most highly wrought speeches, of course, are the funeral orations. Notice, for example, Brutus' use of isocolon (successive phrases or clauses of approximately equal length) in these three successive sentences, each of about the same length, and each with three clauses:

> hear me for my cause,
> > and be silent,
> > > that you may hear.

> Believe me for mine honor,
> > and have respect to mine honor,
> > > that you may believe.

> Censure me in your wisdom,
> > and awake your senses,
> > > that you may the better judge.
> > > > (88.13-18)

Notice, too, the embroidery: "hear . . . hear," "mine honor . . . mine honor," "Censure . . . senses." Later in this speech we get "*b*ase . . . *b*e . . . *b*ondman," and "*r*ude . . . *R*oman" (89.29-32), etc. But the devices are unobtrusive, and the speech is fully in accord with our conception of Brutus. It is in prose, perhaps to suggest that it is not impassioned and is not meant to arouse passions. Then, after the plebeians' lines quoted a moment ago, Antony speaks. We notice that his speech is in verse. He must use every device possible if he is to sway the mob from its loyalty to Brutus, who has a reputation for honesty. We get antitheses, parallels, and, especially, we get playing with words. The conspirators are praised as honorable, Caesar dispraised as ambitious, but these words are so harped on, and so interlarded with statements that undercut them, that they come to have meanings quite the reverse of their usual ones. Chiefly, of course, Antony relies on what Roman rhetoricians called paralipsis, the figure of pretending to pass over a matter while really stressing it: "It is not meet you know how Caesar loved you" (93.143), " 'Tis good you know not that you are his heirs" (93.147). Gestures and props (e.g., Caesar's bloodstained and slashed mantle—the one he wore "That day he overcame the Nervii," 94.175) reinforce the language. In short, the language of these two speeches, as of the rest of the play, is lucid and compelling, apparently effortless but certainly not artless.

A teacher should try to get students to see the shapeliness of the utterances, and should try to communicate the pleasure that one can take in memorable speech—for example, in the simple-minded, brutal loyalty of the Fourth Plebeian's " 'Twere best he speak no harm of Brutus here!' " The flyting, or exchange of insults at Philippi (120.30-44), is yet another example of impassioned language that is not noble but that exhilarates us by its revelation of strong feeling.

Almost every line will afford us the pleasure we get from shapely utterance, but of course it would be precious or idle to suggest that we value Shakespeare only—or chiefly—because we get neat utterances. The utterances reveal people; they embody attitudes and they contain a plot. The plot is clear enough: Cassius cajoles Brutus into joining the conspiracy against Caesar, Caesar is killed just before the middle of the play, the conspirators enjoy a brief moment of triumph, and then at the middle Antony (preceded by his servant, who speaks for him on p. 81) enters, and we get the turning point or catastrophe; from here on the conspirators are on the down-turn, though they do not know it until the next scene (III.ii). To some extent this is the usual Shakespearean tragic pattern, with a turning point in the middle. For example, the first half of *Romeo and Juliet* shows Romeo winning Juliet, but in III.i he kills her cousin Tybalt, and he thus sets in motion (it is often said) the losing of Juliet. In *Macbeth* the protagonist reaches his height in III.i—"Thou hast it now: King" (74.1)—but he then quickly finds that the crown brings no delight. *Julius Caesar*, however, has a particular problem: who is the tragic hero, Caesar or Brutus? There are critics who write Caesar up (and write Brutus down), insisting that it is Caesar's play, and that although he does not appear in the second half, Antony is his surrogate. And of course evidence can be adduced, notably Cassius' tribute to Caesar (126.45-46) and Brutus' tribute (128.94-96). One can add that the play is named for Caesar and (more important) that Caesar follows a usual tragic formula: a great man is brought low through overconfidence. He is traduced in the first scene, but in the second he is clearly a great man, however unlovely he may be. In the first four lines of I.ii, his imperiousness and his associates' servility are disturbing, but his analysis of Cassius (43.192-210) reveals his powers of perception, the more so because Brutus is unable to read Cassius with equal accuracy. And yet Shakespeare reminds us even at this point that Caesar is only a man: "Come on my right hand, for this ear is deaf" (43.214), and he precedes this line with a braggartly or thrasonical line (so-called from the braggart Thraso in Terence's comedy *The Eunuch*) which is hard to take straight: "I rather tell thee what is to be feared/Than what I fear; for always I am Caesar" (43.211-12). There are other thrasonical bits (e.g., 69-70.44-48, and the notorious "Wilt thou lift up Olympus?" 79.74), and there is no use trying to overlook them, though it should be added that it is not certain that we are to see Caesar as ridiculous in these passages. Tragic heroes commonly use hyperbole, and they commonly speak of their greatness (*cf.* Othello, who says he suffers "the plague of great ones"); possibly Shakespeare failed to handle these passages adequately, though it certainly looks as though he were trying to make his Caesar both a hero and a braggart. There is yet another relevant point: when Caesar compares himself to the Northern Star and to Mount Olympus, he is, in a way, right. He is constant to his purpose that Publius remain banished, and, furthermore, we can hardly scorn Caesar for his language and his posture when we know that he is about to be murdered by hypocrites. Our scorn is for Caesar's adversaries; our sympathy is for the man who we know will be killed in a moment. Still, there is no doubt that Caesar suffers from the tragic vice the Greeks called hybris, the proud illusion that one is free of mortal limitation. Calphurnia tells him his "wisdom is consumed in confidence" (70.49) and Artemidorus tries to warn him (73.7) that "security" or overconfidence makes him vulnerable. We may wish to say he has a tragic flaw, but we should recognize his greatness and we should note that in his last line (*"Et tu, Brutè?* Then fall Caesar," 79.77) he reveals his admiration for Brutus and he seems to die as much from a broken heart as from the daggers. If he has a flaw, and if it is overconfidence, it manifests itself in his too generous view of Brutus, rather than in tyranny. Cassius' accusation of tyranny gets very little substantiation; Brutus says quite explicitly that Caesar has not acted pitilessly or unreasonably (55-56.10-27). Even late in the play Brutus will speak of

Caesar as "the foremost man of all this world" (105.22). Caesar indeed is this, and Cassius' detractions do not make him less, though Caesar is also arrogant, deaf, blind, and (in III.i) dead. Antony sees both aspects: Caesar the hero and Caesar the man who must endure the end common to all flesh (82.148-50). Similar words can be spoken of Hamlet, Lear, Othello, and Macbeth.

But of course there is much to the view that Brutus is the tragic hero. He has about him at the start that divided spirit, those "passions of some difference" (38.40) that make him something of an anticipation of Hamlet, and, like Hamlet, at the end of the play he gets a soldier's funeral. Throughout, though involved in public affairs, he is a private man who is in some degree a symbol of the human condition. In such scenes as that with Portia or with the sleeping Lucius, or when he soliloquizes on the interim "Between the acting of a dreadful thing/And the first motion" (57.63-64), he has the humanity we expect of a tragic hero. And just as one can speak of Caesar's hybris, so one can speak of Brutus': Brutus is proud of his integrity and confident of his statesmanship and of his military ability, yet he is putty in Cassius' hands, and as a general he plays into Octavius' hands. But the nobility of his mind is scarcely called into question. In the second scene Cassius can manipulate Brutus precisely because Brutus *is* noble (47.308-12); compare with Hamlet, who, Claudius knows, is too high-minded to examine the foils to see if they are other than they are said to be. Even Marc Antony at the end insists that Brutus alone of the conspirators was pure of motive.

We cannot here study closely all of Brutus' actions, but we might glance at two episodes, the decision to kill Caesar and the ensuing meeting with the conspirators, both in II.i. In lines 10-34 we find Brutus meditating *"in his orchard"* (55.1s.d.). The pensiveness he revealed in I.ii we can reasonably believe was due to unspoken doubts about Caesar, and now that Cassius has whetted Brutus against Caesar we hear Brutus give voice to his thoughts. The first line of his speech about Caesar reveals that he has already come to his conclusion: "It must be by his death" (55.10). Brutus admits he knows "no personal cause" (55.11), and he admits Caesar has not been unjust, but he fears that if Caesar is crowned he may change his nature, and so he decides that Caesar must be killed. Because Caesar "may" change (56.27) and become unjust, Brutus decides to take the law into his own hands and to do Caesar the injustice of murdering him. The motives are high, but the tragic error is plain. (It is perhaps better to speak of a tragic hero as making an "error" than as having a "flaw." The former is probably closer to Aristotle's hamartia —literally a "missing of the mark"—and closer to our vision of the heroes.) Later in this scene, conferring with the conspirators, we see Brutus deluding himself that he is a "sacrificer" and not a "butcher" (61.166). Despite the wry joke about Antony dying of melancholy for Caesar (62.186-87), a jibe not to Brutus' credit, we must feel that Brutus is highminded but is deceived by Cassius and by his own language. It is Brutus, not Caesar, who disjoins remorse from power (56.18-19). After the murder—which Brutus prefers to call a sacrifice—we can only be horrified to see him invite the Romans to bathe their hands in Caesar's blood. (Unable to imagine Brutus speaking such words, Pope gave the speech to the sour Casca, but Shakespeare's scene is right; remorse has been disjoined from power, and the tragic Brutus is momentarily exhilarated by his misdeed.)

The scene-by-scene summary that follows offers some detailed comments but one point must be mentioned before we give up this sketch of Brutus. Cassius seems to mature, to come to some sort of self-awareness or "recognition" such as we expect in a tragic hero (122-23.71-88), but the closest Brutus comes to such self-awareness—and it is not very close —is in 128.94-96: "O Julius Caesar, thou art mighty yet!/Thy spirit walks abroad, and turns our swords/In our own proper entrails." Indeed, when he says he joys "that yet in all my life/I found no man but he was true to me" (132.34-35), we wonder what he makes of Cassius, who worked upon him, and of Antony, who turned the mob against him. (On this passage see the comment in the discussion of The Action.)

Little has been said of Cassius, nothing of Casca, Calphurnia, Portia, the Soothsayer, and others who will require discussion in class. But probably the ambiguities in Caesar's and in Brutus' characters will be the center of most of the discussion, and it would be unjust to the play and to ourselves to flatten out either: Caesar is not simply a braggart, nor is he simply a great man murdered; Brutus is not simply a dupe, nor is he simply a noble man who is undone. As in his other major plays, Shakespeare here gives us a sense of the complexity of life, along with the pleasure of art.

THE ACTION

I.i

The very first stage direction invites comment. The Prefatory Remarks in the Signet Classic edition (pp. xiv-xv) describe the stage, but the teacher should make certain that the students understand the convention of an unlocalized place. And the students should also be made aware of the drama in this opening: two men compelling a group across a broad stage. First we see, then we hear, what is happening. The play begins by showing the power of forces opposed to Caesar, but we later learn (46.285-86) that Flavius and Marullus, though effective here, are overpowered by Caesar. The first scene is not primarily one of exposition. It does, of course, give us some information: Caesar has conquered Pompey's sons, it is the feast of Lupercal, etc., but if it were judged merely by the facts it conveys it would get a low mark. More important, of course, it eases the audience into the play, beginning with some more or less "realistic" dialogue about humdrum affairs—though what real cobbler is so apt at punning? Jokes are seldom funny after they have been explained, but it is worthwhile eliciting a few jokes involving puns. The initial small talk probably gets the audience in rapport with the imaginary world on the stage. Shakespeare's Romans, by the way, probably wore costumes resembling togas, but these were symbolic rather than historically accurate. We are, for example, several times told in the play that the characters wear cloaks and hats (e.g., 58.73), which, like clocks that strike (62.191), were unknown in Rome. Indeed, the togas may have been worn over doublets, the usual Elizabethan close-fitting jackets. (See 42.179 and 45.265.) After the small talk comes Marullus' "Roman" speech, with its rather obvious rhetoric: "Wherefore . . . What . . . What . . . You . . . you . . . O you . . . you" (34-39). Note too

THE TRAGEDY OF JULIUS CAESAR 57

the repetition of "Rome" (41, 45, 54) in long "Roman" sentences. The speaker evokes a glimpse of the Roman mob's adulation of Pompey (Caesar is not even named), and introduces the idea of the fickleness of the mob. His own skill is enough to vanquish these citizens (65); later the skill of Antony (III.ii) will again reverse the mob's direction. The reference to Lupercal (70) is not much more than local color, though it anticipates the explicit reference to Caesar's childlessness in the next scene (36.6-9). Flavius' statement that he

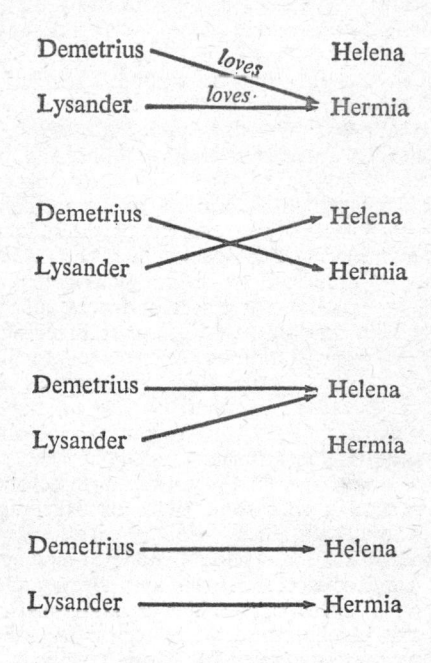

```
Demetrius           loves      Helena
Lysander            loves  →   Hermia
```

```
Demetrius                      Helena
Lysander                       Hermia
```
(crossed arrows)

```
Demetrius           ──────→    Helena
Lysander            ──────→    Hermia
```
(both to Helena)

```
Demetrius           ──────→    Helena
Lysander            ──────→    Hermia
```

and Marullus will pluck feathers from Caesar's wing so that he "Will . . . fly an ordinary pitch" (76) anticipates the efforts of the conspirators to pull Caesar down lest he grow too lofty, and in the later report of Flavius' and Marullus' failure we get an anticipation of the self-destruction of the conspirators. Finally, note that the metaphor of the soaring hawk imperceptibly melts into an image of Caesar as a god, "above the view of men," keeping men in "servile fearfulness" (77-78).

I.ii

In the opening lines we hear and see something of the "servile fearfulness" just mentioned. Caesar is imperious, first commanding Calphurnia merely by calling her name (his "Calphurnia" is short for "Calphurnia, come here and listen to me"), and then using the imperative form, "Stand you" (3), "Forget not" (6). Calphurnia's deference is equaled by Antony's. There is indeed something servile in Antony's "When Caesar says 'Do this,' it is performed" (10). Students should be made to understand the initial impression that Caesar makes. However supercilious the Tribunes of the first scene are, their words do appear to find confirmation in the beginning of the second scene. But suddenly, with the Soothsayer's exclamation of "Caesar!" (12), the situation changes, and momentarily Caesar is the one commanded. His question, "Who calls?" (13), indicates, however briefly, that he is not master of the situation, but the next line, delivered by Casca, further illustrates the servility of Caesar's followers. The triple repetition of "Beware the ides of March" is ominous, but Caesar's imperative "Set him before me," (20) is in his usual manner, and his last sentence here is, characteristically, a single word: "Pass" (24). Later, of course, Caesar will similarly disregard Calphurnia's dream, and still later he will brush aside Artemidorus' warning. One can argue that Caesar suffers from the overweening pride usually described in the Greek word *hybris* or *hubris,* but, on the other hand, one hardly expects a statesman to enter into earnest discussion with an unknown man who calls from the crowd. Caesar would be less than heroic if he worriedly asked for further details.

Brutus' first substantial speech (28-31) shows his affinities with Romeo, an earlier tragic hero, and with Hamlet, a later one. He is not "gamesome" (28); to go further, he has a touch of that melancholy or uncertainty that marks him as a sensitive man who is troubled by things that others take for granted, as (for example) Hamlet is troubled by his father's death and his mother's marriage although his mother seems to see nothing in her action to worry anyone. Brutus says he is "with himself at war" (46), and shortly, when he says he fears that the people will crown Caesar (79-80), we get a further glimpse of his anxieties. Cassius' first speech to Brutus (but his second in the play, because he has already acted as one of Caesar's menials in line 21) reveals that note of selfishness, or at least of concern with the self ("I have not from your eyes that gentleness/And show of love as I was wont to have"—33-34) that becomes more apparent later in the scene. In line 61 he says the age groans under Caesar's yoke, and he presumably believes this unsupported assertion. After the assassination the conspirators proclaim "Liberty" (79.78), but Antony, Octavius, and Lepidus put to death a hundred senators (112.172-74). Cassius' offer to be a mirror to Brutus so that Brutus can understand himself (68-70) quickly becomes a revelation of Cassius rather than of Brutus. Cassius says his subject is honor (92), but the remainder of the speech is less about honor than about Cassius' gnawing sense of inferiority. Caesar's alleged inferiority as a swimmer, and his sickness, have nothing to do with his political ability. The last lines especially, with their mimicking of Caesar's words, their indignation, and (most important) their resentment that Caesar bears the palm "alone" (131) reveal that Cassius is motivated less by political concerns than by pride. Brutus remains cautious; perhaps we can hear, mixed with his caution or reasonableness, some notes of priggishness in lines 167-70, but caution rather than priggishness dominates the speech. Line 175, with its statement that hard times are "like" to come, sets Brutus apart from Cassius, who has said that Rome groans "underneath this age's yoke" (61), and yet it indicates that Brutus leans toward Cassius' view. Caesar, at his reentry, reveals in his remarks about Cassius that he is a keen analyst, but mingled with the shrewd analysis are touches of arrogance (211-12) and revelation of physical weakness (213). Shakespeare puts into Casca's mouth the description of the offer of the crown. Cassius had cued us that Casca will speak "after his sour fashion" (180), and indeed we get a sour rather than an impartial description of the offer. (Note, by the way, that Casca here uses prose and is something of a comic figure. Later his lines are indistinguishable from those of the other conspirators.) Furthermore, the offer takes place offstage. That is, Shakespeare does not let us see Caesar himself acting thus discreditably; we get only a prejudiced report. The scene concludes with Cassius' only soliloquy. We catch a tone of condescension at the start, and we are not surprised to hear in the next lines that Cassius proposes, quite cynically, to work on Brutus. In short, Brutus' nobility or generosity of mind makes him a singularly easy, unsuspecting victim of the manipulator Cassius. We have seen almost nothing of an oppressed Rome that requires Brutus' aid.

I.iii

The Elizabethans created thunder by rolling a cannonball or some such object in a trough, and they created lightning by blowing resin through a candle flame. The storm suggested by the thunder and lightning at the beginning of this scene is presumably a sign of the disorder that we have seen Cassius hatching, rather than a sign of any disorder in Caesar; compare it to the storm and the unnatural happenings in *Macbeth* II.iv, following the murder of Duncan. The storm in *Julius Caesar*, like the Soothsayer's warning and like Calphurnia's dream, enhances Caesar's stature by suggesting that invisible forces are concerned with his well-being. In the early part of this scene Shakespeare apparently means to contrast Cicero's equanimity with Casca's base terror. Note especially Cicero's statement that "men may construe things after their fashion,/ Clean from the purpose of the things themselves" (34-35), which might almost be said to summarize the action of this tragedy—and most tragedies. Cassius (46-52) tells Casca he has been exposing himself to the storm. Students should discuss what this tells us about Cassius' nature; they ought to be able to sense something of his desperation, and to see the justice of Casca's reply to Cassius (53-56). Cassius' reply that the prodigies are a kind of analogue to Caesar—ominous, but in fact weak—is not quite satisfying to us; we sense Cassius' usual envy, and we perhaps recall Cicero's words about men's ability to misconstrue. Cassius sees Romans as "sheep" and "hinds" (105-06), as "rubbish" and as "offal" (109)—scarcely a view appropriate to a champion of liberty, though perhaps he is here adjusting his diction to appeal to the currish Casca, and he quickly wins Casca over, in contrast to the more thoughtful Brutus. But the scene concludes with reference to the forged letters that will help to win Brutus, and with Cassius' confident assertion that Brutus is three-fourths won. Note too that Cassius, like Casca, values Brutus as window-dressing.

II.i

The last speech in the previous scene mentioned that "it is after midnight" (54.163), helping to prepare the setting for this scene (enacted in broad daylight on the open Elizabethan stage), but Shakespeare takes no chances; in his first speech Brutus indicates that the time is between midnight and dawn. How Brutus' "orchard" (1 s.d.) or garden was indicated is not

THE TRAGEDY OF JULIUS CAESAR   61

certainly known, but *As You Like It* is of about the same period as *Julius Caesar,* and it seems reasonable to think that property trees were used. (See Prefatory Remarks, p. xvi.) The orchard affords a contrast to the tumultuous street scenes that precede, and it suggests that the meditative Brutus is in a retreat. Notice that there are still meteors (44-45), but Brutus is undisturbed by them. Students should be helped to see the richness of the scene: Brutus, disturbed, seeks refuge in his garden, but his first five lines reveal uncertainty, impatience, and sleeplessness (usually in Shakespeare a sign of a troubled conscience). Brutus' second speech begins *in medias res.* He apparently has been debating the matter, and he reveals to us, in the first line of his second speech, that he has already decided that Caesar must die. This speech is of great importance in understanding Brutus; students should study it closely so that they see Brutus acts not (like Cassius) out of any sense of injured merit, but only "for the general" (12). Shakespeare has deliberately suppressed historical scraps (e.g., Caesar had crossed the Rubicon and entered Rome as a conqueror) that could have strengthened Brutus' point; he forces Brutus to rely merely on the possibility that a crown "might" (13) change Caesar's nature, and on an analogy between Caesar and an adder still in the egg. Brutus aptly defines the abuse of greatness as a separation of mercy or pity from power (18-19), but his fair-mindedness compels him to admit that Caesar has not acted in fits of power. By line 27, Brutus is arguing that because Caesar "may" prove unjust, he should be killed. In short, Brutus is capable of seeing that Caesar has not acted mercilessly, and yet he is also capable of acting unjustly toward Caesar. Lucius' second entry, at line 34 (he will enter yet twice more), serves to get Brutus some sympathy by allowing him to speak paternal words to the young servant. Brutus' sleeplessness is emphasized (61-62), anticipating the wonderful episode in IV.iii when he sees the ghost. (Lucius' sleep is anticipated in the present scene in 229-33.) The business of the oath is Shakespeare's invention. Plutarch had praised the conspirators for working loyally without an oath, but Shakespeare introduces Cassius' proposal to swear, so that Brutus may object and overrule Cassius as he will later overrule him in more critical matters. Brutus' dismissal of Cicero, another minor matter, nicely reveals Brutus' smugness. Students may well be asked to examine the degree in which Brutus fits his own description of Cicero in 150-52. (Plutarch had given the conspirators a good reason for omitting Cicero. He was a coward and might betray them. Shakespeare omits this and gives Brutus a less good reason, thus emphasizing Brutus' self-centeredness.) Both of these decisions by Brutus, of course, serve to prepare for the much more important decision to spare Antony. Students should examine this speech (162-83) very closely, first so that they clearly see Brutus' distinction between "sacrificers" and "butchers," second so that they see—given the context—the impossibility of the distinction. Brutus never seems to understand that the assassins are indeed butchers. In one of his most unlovely moments he smugly jests about Antony's loyalty to Caesar: "If he love Caesar, all that he can do/Is to himself—take thought and die for Caesar" (186-87). Again Shakespeare alters Plutarch to lessen Brutus' case: Plutarch says that Brutus argued that it was unjust to kill Antony, and, secondly, that because Antony was noble-minded he would understand the assassins' honorable motives and would join them in recovering liberty. This degradation—though perhaps that is too strong a word—of Brutus is continued when Brutus counsels that they put on the smiling faces (224-25) that he had scorned earlier (79-85). But his tenderness for the sleeping boy and for his wife Portia does much to restore the balance, to remind us that Brutus is preeminently a virtuous man. The scene concludes with Caius Ligarius' tribute to Brutus, another substantiation of Brutus' high repute.

II.ii

We have seen Cassius and others amid the thunder, then Brutus and his associates (where the setting of the orchard somewhat reduced the celestial disturbance), and now we see Caesar. Caesar rejects his wife's plea that he stay at home, and his speeches are increasingly arrogant. In lines 28-29 it is perhaps chiefly his habit of speaking of himself in the third person that grates upon our ear; but in the lines about danger (44-45) he is surely insufferable. Meanwhile, between these two speeches is one that may seem hybristic but that rises out of the context to present a universal thought—that is, in the speech in which Caesar says that "The valiant never taste of death but once" (33), we hear not only the voice of a single definable character speaking in a particular circumstance but also the voice of mankind addressing mankind. And it should be mentioned that the Caesar we see does indeed die bravely. (We probably do not recall—or if we recall it we do not believe—Cassius' statement that Caesar feared drowning.) In any case, Shakespeare omits Plutarch's statements that Caesar feared the omens, and goes so far in the other direction that Caesar at times seems arrogant in his disregard. For a mo-

THE TRAGEDY OF JULIUS CAESAR   63

ment he thinks of lying to explain his absence from the Senate (55), but to his credit he rejects this thought (63-64). He finally yields to Decius' flattery, but if we think less of Caesar for yielding, we are also horrified by Decius' hypocritical profession of "dear dear love" (102). And from here to the end of the scene Caesar is portrayed as noble and sympathetic. He greets his visitors with unfeigned enthusiasm, and he invites them to taste wine with him (126). Probably there is an echo of the Last Supper (where, however, there was but one traitor). Note the Sophoclean irony (i.e., utterance that has one meaning for the speaker and quite another for the audience) in Caesar's "Be near me" (123), underscored by Trebonius' wry aside. The scene concludes with a pair of lines spoken by Brutus, the only one of the conspirators who is distressed by their hypocrisy.

II.iii

This short scene continues the favorable depiction of Caesar, to which the latter part of the previous scene was devoted. Here we get a letter (in prose, as usual, setting it off from the verse that is the normal utterance of speakers) which speaks of Caesar's "security" (7) or overconfidence, but which has been written by a man who sees "virtue" in Caesar and "emulation" or envy in Caesar's enemies (12-13).

II.iv

Portia's concern for Brutus is a sort of parallel to Artemidorus' concern (in the previous scene) and to the Soothsayer's concern (later in this scene) for Caesar, but chiefly it serves to gain sympathy for Brutus by showing his wife's uneasiness. Line 9 indicates that Brutus has told her of his plan. (We ought not to ask when he had the opportunity to do so.)

III.i

The anxiety and private quality of the previous scene now give way to an elaborate public entry of dignitaries. Caesar, who was rehabilitated in the latter part of II.ii, opens the scene somewhat smugly, but the Soothsayer replies ominously. The loyal Artemidorus and the deceitful Decius compete for Caesar's attention, and Caesar grandly—but self-destructively—brushes aside Artemidorus' petition with "What touches us ourself shall be last served" (8). Note Caesar's ar-

rogance in the early part of this scene, in such details as the
royal "us ourself" and in his reference to "Caesar and *his*
Senate" (32). And of course lines 58-73 are full of self-
praise. But attention should be called to the effect on the
stage: Caesar is speaking grandly of himself while he is surrounded by fawning would-be murderers. Their "couchings
and . . . lowly courtesies" (36) are more offensive to the
spectator than Caesar's self-praise, and, indeed, in lines 35-48
Caesar is only praising himself for a quality he is exhibiting:
he remains constant to the decree that banished Cimber's
brother. Even Brutus, who presumably cares little about Cimber's brother and is using him merely as a pretext to get near
to Caesar, behaves basely when he says "I kiss thy hand, but
not in flattery, Caesar" (52). (Later, 120.30-32, Antony will
remind Brutus of his hypocrisy.) Caesar's speech in lines 58-
73 continues his high view of himself, but, again, he displays
the constancy he boasts of, and our disapproval is concentrated on the hypocrites who surround him. True, he (or
Shakespeare) strains our patience with "Wilt thou lift up
Olympus?" (74), but his dying words convey dignity. If Caesar committed a tragic error, it was, apparently, to trust Brutus, rather than any violation of Roman liberty. The conspirators' high words (78-83) that follow the murder are less
impressive than the blood that flows. The conspirators themselves go on to emphasize the bloodiness of the spectacle, inviting the Romans to bathe their hands "in Caesar's
blood/Up to the elbows" (106-07). This business of the
blood bath is probably not metaphoric; we see the men, who
had claimed to be "sacrificers, but not butchers" (61.166),
now momentarily infatuated with blood, fulfilling Calphurnia's dream (71.78-79). Then follow two speeches (111-13,
116-18), both by Cassius, full of Sophoclean irony: the deed
will be enacted in future ages, as in this very play, but it will
not show the conspirators as "The men that gave their country liberty." And now, in the middle of the play, when the
assassins are almost intoxicated with their success, a Servant
from Antony enters; with the entry of this humble figure
comes the turning point, or catastrophe. If the students have
read another of Shakespeare's tragedies they can perhaps
compare the turning points. Almost at once Antony appears,
daringly ignoring Brutus' greeting and apostrophizing Caesar
(148). Cassius had seen only Caesar's infirmities; Antony
sees the mortality and yet retains a vision of Caesar's grandeur. Note the nice distinction between Brutus' offer of an
explanation (164-76, 179-84) and Cassius' offer of power
(177-78). Antony feigns friendship, but emphasizes the

blood (185, 191, 198, 200, 206) and envisions Caesar as a noble stag pulled down (204-10), not (it should be noted) as a hero who brought his own destruction upon himself through some fault. And, indeed, if we recall the assassination we see the aptness: Caesar, constant to his purpose, was met with "base spaniel fawning" (43). If Antony's picture in the present speech is false, it is so not in its picture of Caesar as a hart but in its implication that the destroyers were brave hunters. Antony's allusion to the murderers as "many princes" (209) apparently continues his politic flattery of Brutus and the others. Students will have no difficulty in finding Brutus overbearing in his dispute with Cassius concerning the funeral orations (231-43), but even though they may see the smugness of Brutus' insistence that his plan "shall advantage more than do us wrong" (242), they may not notice that here the noble Brutus is trying to be the cunning politician. His fatuousness continues in his next speech (244-51); clearly this is not a man who can help to fill the vacuum created by Caesar's death, and Antony, when left alone, scornfully dismisses these "butchers" (255)—the very word that Brutus had said must not describe the assassins (61.166)—and praises Caesar as "the ruins of the noblest man/That ever lived in the tide of times (256-57). Then comes a vision of the chaos that will overcome a divided Rome as Caesar's ghost ranges for revenge. Here the play approaches the genre of revenge tragedy, and a good deal of what follows can be conceived of as Caesar's revenge (*cf.* Cassius' words, 126.45-46, and Brutus', 128.94-96), but we ought not to insist that the whole play is Caesar's if this means that we deny that in the second half Brutus is seen as a tragic hero. The scene concludes with Antony revealing (in his statement that Rome is not safe for Octavius, line 289) a shrewdness that Brutus has not displayed.

III.ii

Brutus' use of prose here presumably is meant to suggest his unwillingness to appeal to the emotions, although he does ask some rhetorical questions, and he concludes theatrically when he offers to use his dagger upon himself (47-48). The failure of Brutus' deed, which was motivated by a desire to keep Rome free, and of his speech, is seen immediately when the Third Plebeian cries out, "Let him be Caesar" (52). That is, even the crowd's favorable response to Brutus indicates Brutus' failure. Antony succeeds. He is cunning but also truthful. He calls attention to Caesar's fidelity, military skill, and compassion. Mingled with these facts are the ironic harpings on Brutus' allegation that Caesar was ambitious, and on Brutus' honorable nature. Never was a virtue made to sound more odious. And never was better use made of *paralipsis*, the rhetorical figure in which the speaker effectively tells what he pretends to pass over. Antony assures his hearers that he will not tell them of the contents of Caesar's will, but in the process he tells all he needs to (130-59). In line 159 he at last seems about to read it entire, but, in fact, he contrives to delay, first arousing pity and anger by showing Caesar's toga. Note, too, in line 215 his cunning insinuation that the assassins have been motivated by "private" feelings, not by public spirit, and note in line 219 the disclaimer that he is an orator. He does his work well, and we can sympathize, though in lines 263-64 and 269-70, as he watches the enraged plebeians leave, he seems to reveal a disquieting delight in violence.

III.iii

This short scene makes visible the chaos that has followed Caesar's death. Antony, of course, has stirred the plebeians, but Cassius is ultimately responsible for the lawlessness terrorizing Rome.

IV.i

The destructiveness revealed in the previous scene has its parallel here, as we watch Antony, Octavius, and Lepidus calmly marking men for death. Such is the liberty that the assassins have introduced to Rome. Note, too, Antony's Machiavellianism, which perhaps was first overt in 86.254-55 and in 97.263-64, 269-70. Now we see him quite willing to tamper with Caesar's will (8-9) and to betray Lepidus. Note, too, the tiff with Octavius, another instance of dissension in Rome.

IV.ii

Brutus is astute enough here, when he detects a change in Cassius' attitude toward him (18-21). (Note the parallel to the dissension between allies in the previous scene; with Caesar gone, Rome is divided into factions, and even the factions are divided.) In Cassius' greeting (37) we detect that very "enforcèd ceremony" (21) that Brutus has spoken of, but in

THE TRAGEDY OF JULIUS CAESAR 67

Brutus' reply (38-39) we are probably right in detecting some of the self-satisfaction that marks his earlier speeches.

IV.iii

The quarrel continues in the tent. Probably Brutus is right in his first speech, but more important is the fact that the allies are quarreling. Brutus' second speech (9-12) is reasonable enough, but in a few minutes we will find that Brutus is apparently quite willing to have the money that he rebukes Cassius for having acquired. During the quarrel neither man is attractive: Cassius is egotistic (note the abundance of first person pronouns in 28-36), and Brutus is sanctimonious (37, 42-50). Brutus' composure in line 58 is almost priggish, and his use of first-person pronouns in 67-69 does not lessen the effect. Cassius at length makes peace, craving Brutus' friendship (94-95); Brutus replies, condescendingly at first (107-08). When we learn later in this scene that Portia has died, possibly we take a more charitable view of Brutus' words to Cassius, but the earlier impression cannot really be eradicated. (Of the various theories about the double report of Portia's death, that given in the footnote to lines 180-94 is the most reasonable.) And though Brutus gains sympathy with the news, he loses some of it a little later with his complacent "Good reasons must of force give place to better" (202), and in "Under your pardon" (212), where the polite self-deprecation does little to mask a sentiment that is more or less "Excuse me, but let me now correct you." But in his famous speech with the figure of "a tide in the affairs of men" (217), we detect, under the optimistic theory, a note of pessimism as we hear of the "miseries" (220) that may follow, and indeed, in his next speech he informs us that "night" (literal, of course, but also symbolic) "is crept upon our talk" (225). Brutus puts on a dressing gown (230, 234 s.d.), and this action, along with the departure of his allies (237), marks a change in Brutus from public to private man. Now he is the kindly master of loyal servants, especially when he ministers (270-71) to the sleeping boy. The motif of sleeplessness is introduced (see comments on II.i), and if the ghost is Caesar's it is also, in a way, Brutus' bad conscience.

V.i

Octavius' first line indicates things are going well for his side: the conspirators are unwittingly complying with his hopes. There is some bickering between Octavius and Antony

(16-20), but it quickly gives way (note that in line 25 Antony calls Octavius "Caesar") to more formal contention, a flyting, or exchange of taunts between the opposing commanders (28-44). This flyting shows Brutus unfavorably in various ways: it allows Antony to call attention to Brutus' hypocritical dealings with Caesar (30-44); it allows even Brutus' ally Cassius to turn upon Brutus and remind him that he erred in letting Antony outlive Caesar (45-47); and in Brutus' frosty reply to Octavius we detect again the self-righteousness that regularly mars Brutus' words (56-57). Note, by the way, how much Shakespeare can convey in Antony's three words, "Old Cassius still!" (63). Caesar had early called attention to Cassius' envy, and in the line that Cassius utters to provoke Antony's brief speech we see that he continues as Caesar had described him. When Caesar was alive, Antony rejected Caesar's estimate of Cassius (43.196-97), but Antony has come to see the aptness of Caesar's estimate. Shakespeare now attempts the impossible and succeeds: he begins to make Cassius a sympathetic figure. We had earlier felt some sympathy for him in the quarrel in Brutus' tent, but only because Brutus was so maddeningly complacent. But now Cassius acquires sympathy not only because he is the underdog (though that is important); he acquires it also because at last his words are not marked by corrosive envy. He admits that he is changing his opinions, and now believes in a cosmic order, whereas earlier he seemed the thorough materialist in, for example, his insistence that he was no less than Caesar because he was a better swimmer. In this important speech (70-88), note especially his sense of loss of freedom (presumably because he is compelled by Brutus), his identification of himself with Pompey (Caesar's earlier conquest), and his belief in omens, which leads him to sense that his cause is lost. Note, too, that it is his birthday (71); we get a sense of completion, of a wheel come full circle, of a life that has reached its end. Brutus' speech rejecting suicide (100-07) requires a bit of explaining, the more so because he soon commits suicide. The point, of course, is that the Stoic sees suicide as cowardly and vile because it wrongly implies that changes of fortune are of consequence and can affect the soul. In his next speech (110-12), however, he speaks as a Roman soldier determined not to face capture and humiliation. Though perhaps we find Brutus' device of speaking of himself in the third person (111) a little stuffy, as we found it in Caesar, Brutus here (like Cassius) is becoming increasingly sympathetic. His last two lines in the scene suggest

THE TRAGEDY OF JULIUS CAESAR 69

something of Cassius' acceptance of a plan beyond the workings of men.

V.ii

This very short scene gives an effect of the bustle of preparation for war, in contrast to the melancholy of the previous speech. Note especially line 5; it is Brutus alone who must bear the responsibility for the premature attack.

V.iii

The ennobling of Cassius continues, partly by his words and deeds, partly by the authentication afforded by Titinius. Cassius refers again to his birthday (see comment on V.1), and the sense of completion is underscored by the fact that he dies on the very sword with which he stabbed Caesar (41-46). And almost immediately we hear Titinius' unconsciously ironic words, "These tidings will well comfort Cassius" (54). Cassius has needlessly killed himself, for Pindarus' report was inaccurate. Although there is no doubt that Brutus has botched things (e.g., in failing to kill Antony), it must be said that Cassius dies not only by his own hand but (aided by Pindarus) by his own error. Titinius puts it simply: "Alas, thou hast misconstrued everything!" (84). But of course it is too simple to credit the defeat merely to Cassius; Brutus sees in it the power of Caesar, too (94-96), and though Brutus determines to continue the fight, his tribute to Caesar suggests that he cannot have much hope.

V.iv

As we see from the stage directions, Brutus' old companions are gone; the currish Casca, the fawning Decius, the envious Cassius are no more seen, and Brutus achieves some new dignity by being freed from them and by being seen in the company of the loyal Cato and Lucilius.

V.v

Brutus' opening line reveals that he is a broken man; victory is impossible, and the best he can do is to retain friendship. His friends refuse to kill him; their love for him adds to his stature, but insofar as he is an unsuccessful petitioner he loses stature too. About all he can do is suggest that he and his allies run to their death rather than be driven to it (23-

25). There is dignity in his farewells, but one wonders what to make out of his assertion that "I found no man but he was true to me" (32-35). Cassius had manipulated him, and Antony had hoodwinked him; is Brutus blind, or are we supposed to forget the earlier happenings? Or did Shakespeare err by imperfectly reproducing Plutarch, who has Brutus say, "It rejoiceth my heart, that not one of my friends hath failed me at my need," which is quite different from the more inclusive statement of Shakespeare's Brutus. In any case, death comes to Brutus as a release, bringing him an earnestly desired rest. And as he kills himself, there is again the sense of fulfillment (42, 50-51), partly because he is freed from the burden of living, partly because he dies by his own hand. Immediately we note that the efficient Octavius takes over (60), allowing Antony to be once more the orator. Antony pays tribute to Brutus, clearly distinguishing him from the other conspirators, and then Octavius has the last word, the new leader of Rome.

Sylvan Barnet

SHORT-ANSWER QUESTIONS

1. What is unusual about the dress of the commoners? (33.4-5,8)

2. What are the commoners celebrating? (34.34 and 35.55)

3. Why do the Tribunes strip the images of Caesar's trophies? (35.71-78)

4. Why does Caesar ask Antony to touch Calphurnia during the race? (36.6-9)

5. Who warns Caesar to beware of the ides of March? (37.18)

6. How did Cassius once save Caesar's life? (40.100-15)

7. Explain "Yond Cassius has a lean and hungry look"? (43.194-210)

THE TRAGEDY OF JULIUS CAESAR   71

8. According to Casca, what was the crowd's response when Caesar rejected the crown? (44.220-30)

9. According to Casca, what was Caesar's attitude when he rejected the crown? (44.239, 240-41)

10. Why does Cassius plan to forge letters? (47.321-22)

11. Who is the man Cassius has in mind when he speaks to Casca of "a man/Most like this dreadful night,/That thunders, lightens, open graves, and roars/ As doth the lion in the Capitol"? (57.79)

12. According to Brutus, what would be the effect on Caesar if Caesar were crowned? (55.13-16)

13. Why has Brutus been sleepless? (57.61-62; but note too that he was ill at ease earlier, in 38.39-41)

14. What is Brutus' reason for sparing Mark Antony? (61.162-65)

15. According to Decius, what trait in Caesar makes him vulnerable to Decius? (63.206-08)

16. According to Calphurnia, what are some of the strange sights that the watchmen have reported? (69.17-24)

17. Describe Calphurnia's dream. (71.76-79)

18. What two things does Decius say that persuade Caesar to go to the Capitol? (71.93-99)

19. How does Decius interpret Calphurnia's dream? (71.83-90)

20. How does Artemidorus hope to warn Caesar of the conspiracy? (73.10-11)

21. How does the Soothsayer hope to warn Caesar? (75.37-38)

22. How does Caesar prevent Artemidorus' warning from being successful? (76.8)

72   TEACHING SHAKESPEARE

23. What makes Cassius think that the conspiracy is known to men other than the conspirators? (77.13-17)

24. What pretext do the conspirators use to crowd around Caesar? (78.44, 51, 57)

25. What trait does Caesar claim to share with the Northern Star? (78.60-70)

26. Why does Brutus think it is advisable for Antony to give an oration? (85.238-42)

27. What points does Brutus insist that Mark Antony make in his oration? (85.245-47)

28. What is the effect on the populace of Brutus' speech? (89.48-54)

29. At the outset of his speech, what does Antony say his purpose is? (91.76)

30. Which of Caesar's virtues does Antony call attention to in his funeral oration? (91.87-93)

31. What are the contents of Caesar's will? (93.147; 96.243-44; 97.249-53)

32. What effect does Antony's speech have on the populace? (97.255-61)

33. What happens to Cinna the Poet? Why? (99.28-36)

34. What is Antony's attitude toward Lepidus? (101.12-15, 35-40)

35. What is the cause of the quarrel between Brutus and Cassius? (105.1-6; 108.69-77)

36. What does Brutus mean when he tells Cassius that Cassius has an "itching palm"? (105.10-12)

37. Why did Portia commit suicide? (111.151-55)

38. Why does Cassius think it best to let Antony and Octav-

ius "seek us," while Brutus thinks it best to advance to Philippi to seek Antony and Octavius? (113.198-211)

39. What prophecy does Caesar's ghost make? (117.282)

40. In the verbal battle that precedes the military battle, what does Antony accuse Brutus of? (120.30-32; 121.39-44)

41. How does Cassius interpret the omens? (123.80-88)

42. Though Brutus at first says he does not approve of suicide, he changes his mind. What does Cassius say to him that makes Brutus find suicide acceptable? (124.107-09)

43. What is the purpose of the errand Cassius sends Titinius on? (125.14-18)

44. Why must Cassius rely on Pindarus to tell him what is happening to Titinius? (126.21)

45. What does Cassius think happens to Titinius? (126.32)

46. How does Cassius die? (126.41-46)

47. Why do some soldiers mistakenly think they have captured Brutus? (130.14-27)

48. What request does Brutus make that his servants refuse to grant? (131.11-12)

49. How does Brutus die? (133.47-51; 134.65)

50. According to Mark Antony, how did Brutus differ from the other conspirators? (134.69-72)

QUESTIONS FOR DISCUSSION

1. Cassius says that Brutus' "honorable mettle may be wrought/From that it is disposed" (47.309-10). Exactly

how does he work upon Brutus, and what in Brutus' nature allows Cassius to be as successful as he is?

2. There are a number of passages concerning sleep, ranging from the brief implication that Cassius does not "sleep a-nights" (43.193) to the scene (IV.iii) in which Lucius sleeps while Brutus sees the ghost. Examine the references to sleep and relate them to the characters.

3. Trace the development of the relationship between Antony and Octavius.

4. Cassius says that Rome is "groaning" under Caesar's "yoke" (38.61). How much support for this view does the play provide?

5. Titinius says of Cassius, "Alas, thou hast misconstrued everything!" (128.84). Discuss Cassius' misconstructions.

6. Brutus early says "Antony is but a limb of Caesar" (61.165), and when he is facing defeat at Philippi he says, "O Julius Caesar, thou art mighty yet!" (128.94). But do we feel, as we see or read the play, that in the latter part it is Julius Caesar who conquers, using Mark Antony as his agent?

7. Discuss the role of the supernatural in *Julius Caesar*.

8. Examine Shakespeare's use of prose, and discuss the possible reasons why some passages are in prose rather than in blank verse.

9. Describe the relationships between Brutus and Portia and between Caesar and Calphurnia, and discuss the degree to which these relationships contribute to our understanding of the two men.

10. What are the qualities in Mark Antony's oration (III.ii) that make it more effective than Brutus' oration?

SAMPLE TEST

I. (½ hour)

Write a well-organized essay on ONE of the following subjects.

1. Cassius says that Rome is "groaning" under Caesar's "yoke" (38.61). How much support for this view does the play provide?

2. What are the qualities in Mark Antony's oration (III.ii) that make it more effective than Brutus' oration?

II. (½ hour)

Write briefly on FIVE of the following.

1. How did Cassius once save Caesar's life?

2. According to Brutus, what would be the effect on Caesar if Caesar were crowned?

3. According to Decius, what trait in Caesar makes him vulnerable to Decius?

4. Why does Brutus think it is advisable for Antony to give an oration?

5. What is Antony's attitude toward Lepidus?

6. How does Cassius die?

7. According to Mark Antony, how did Brutus differ from the other conspirators?

THE MERCHANT OF VENICE

INTRODUCTION

The Merchant of Venice has always been a popular play. It was twice issued as a separate text (Quarto) before it appeared among the comedies in the first collected edition (Folio), 1623. It has been constantly on the stage since the Restoration period: the characters of Shylock and Portia are continuously appealing to tragic actors and romantic actresses; its interweaving of melodramatic excitement, witty love play, and fairy tale adventure is continuously appealing to audiences. The play should be readily accessible to today's students.

To insure the students' understanding, however, it is best to prepare them to see Shylock in the perspective of Shakespeare's work. When *The Merchant* was first revived during the Restoration, and for nearly a century thereafter, Shylock was presented as a comic character. But, as the English theater approached the Romantic period, humanitarianism recast the role: Shylock became a tragic figure, Shakespeare became anti-Semitic, and the play's clear and simple theme was corrupted by emotionalism. A Jew is presented in an ugly light, therefore the play is anti-Semitic; by the same reasoning, *Macbeth* is anti-Caledonian and *Richard III* anti-monarchist.

That is to say, the issue is irrelevant, but more, it leads to a misunderstanding of the dramatic function of Shylock. Shylock happens to be a Jew, but his dramatic function lies in his profession as a usurer and his belief in the legalistic principle of an eye for an eye. His hatred of Antonio derives less from the indignities the Christian has visited upon him than from interference with the profits of his usury. Shylock's famous self-justification (87.55-69) is not a defense of his race but of the principle of revenge. The Elizabethan audience (and their most representative playwright) knew that usury was illegal and that revenge was immoral. Shylock's insistence on adherence to the strict performance of his cruel bond is analogous to strict adherence to the letter of the law, the "old" law of the Old Testament. The "new law," promulgated by the commentators on the New Testament, gave primacy to the spirit behind the letter, for "in the course of *justice,* none of us/Should see salvation" (116.198-99). In simplest terms, Shylock represents the dramatic force of the old law in conflict with the new, represented by Portia, and it is a pleasing comic irony that the new law triumphs finally by threatening Shylock with the legal consequences of the strict performance of his own bond.

The action of *The Merchant,* then, is constructed on an allegorical basis, a conflict of values of utmost familiarity to the audience. But it should be quickly added that the play itself is not an allegory; the action is not, in Dryden's terms, "the example built upon the moral, which confirms the truth of it to our experience." As generally in Shakespeare, habitual principles ("the moral") make possible the creation of conflicts which provide the audience with the satisfaction of experiencing characters in action.

As the principal characters of the action are more directly motivated by morality than psychology, so the location of the action is more symbolic than geographic. The Venetian world as developed through the action and dialogue is not the shimmering panorama of canals, great houses, piazzas, and iconographic lions made familiar by Canaletto and tourism. Shakespeare's Venice is the Rialto, the area of commercial exchange, and the courtroom where even the presiding Duke is powerless to go beyond the letter of the law. Its sole concern is with material things: argosies, ducats, substances that "chance or nature's changing course" (Sonnet 18) can transmute into shadows. The most extreme manifestation of the Venetian world is, of course, Shylock's bargain: a pound of flesh (a man's life) for his three thousand ducats.

In this world, virtue lies in the selfless friendship of Antonio for Bassanio. Saddened though he is by the inevitable severing of their companionship, Antonio is willing to chance his life that Bassanio may have funds to pursue his wooing of Portia. Male friendship was, for the Elizabethans, the purest and most disinterested of relationships, but as Shakespeare's early sonnets reiterate, it was the responsibility of the good and the beautiful to defeat time and death through marriage and reproduction. Antonio's noblest act is to enable Bassanio to get an heiress and an heir; his generosity to Bassanio mitigates the folly of his trust in worldly things.

THE MERCHANT OF VENICE

Remote from Venice geographically, Belmont is a world of very different values. Actions in this world are governed by Portia's determination to obey the stipulations of her father's will: to marry the suitor who can discover the spirit behind the letter. It is a world of love and charity and, in the last act, harmony. It is a world where Jessica and Lorenzo find shelter from the harshness of Venice. It is a world where the fortune-seeker, Bassanio, is easily converted by his love for the genius of the place to "choose not by the view" (94.131). Yet Portia and Belmont are not easily won; there is a harsh stipulation in her father's will that those who dare to choose and choose wrongly must leave without protest and remain celibate forever. Indeed, Bassanio, having demonstrated his wisdom in winning Portia, must endure a second trial before possessing her. Portia, then, embodies the values of Belmont as Shylock those of Venice.

The action of the play reaches its climax in IV.i, with the confrontation of Portia and Shylock both as persons of the plot and as the forces they embody. The following scheme is one way of representing this confrontation:

Shylock	*Portia*
	embodies
the world of Venice	the world of Belmont
	based on
the letter of the law	the spirit of the law
	as exemplified in
the trial of Antonio's bond	the trial of the caskets
	made possible by
the old law	the new law
	motivated by
revenge	charity ("mercy")
	ending in
capitulation	harmony

Such a scheme is, of course, only a scheme; it is not the play, but only some of the operative forces that make the play possible. The spectator at a performance is not expected to see the action with such objectivity that he is directly aware of its moral pattern; perhaps Shakespeare, at this time writing three or four plays a year, was himself only dimly aware of the structure that underlay his action. Yet the structure not only underlies but unifies and gives point to the joining of two romantic fictions; a tale of lovers' wooing and a tale of male friendship.

The scheme, too, fails to account for some of the most attractive secondary elements of the drama: Jessica and Lorenzo; Gratiano and Nerissa; and the Gobbos. None of these characters is to be found in any of the possible "sources" of *The Merchant,* yet each complements the central action, and in a peculiarly Shakespearean way.

The proper concern of romantic comedy was the honest wooing and winning by a man of a maid, for

> Then is there is mirth in heaven
> When earthly things made even
>   Atone together. (*As You Like It,* 134.108-09)

It was Shakespeare's particular delight to reinforce this theme by doubling and tripling the love chase. Earlier there had been Valentine and Sylvia, Proteus and Julia in *Two Gentlemen of Verona;* later there would be Orlando and Rosalind, Silvius and Phebe, Touchstone and Audrey in *As You Like It,* Benedict and Beatrice, Claudius and Hero in *Much Ado About Nothing.* It is Shakespeare's way, however, that the secondary and tertiary couples be not simple echoes of the hero and heroine.

In *The Merchant,* the force of love rescues Jessica from the tyranny of her father's house, close-shuttered, barren of art or music. She is borne away to Belmont by a group of masquers in gay disguises, accompanied by music, and is last glimpsed with her husband in a garden under a starry sky enveloped in a "concord of sweet sounds" (130.84). The Jessica-Lorenzo action makes a succinct statement of the conventional romantic theme, which has been complicated in the main action by the interwoven and perhaps weightier story of the bond. There is, moreover, a foreshadowing of the outcome of the bond action in Jessica's elopement. As she leaves her father's house she takes with her a casket of his gold and jewels to bestow upon her Christian lover. So, at the conclusion of the trial, Shylock is to be stripped of his possessions for the benefit of Antonio and the state of Venice.

Gratiano and Nerissa provide a variation on the theme. Nerissa is only sketched: the shadow of her mistress, witty enough and wise enough to respond to a cue with the appropriate answer, and to play skillfully the game whose rules are established by Portia. Gratiano, however, is an early draft of a character Shakespeare was to develop into a unique figure: Touchstone, Feste, Lear's Fool, the "chorus character" whose foolish or glib wit is a trenchant commentary on the action. "Let me play the fool!" Gratiano cries on his first entrance (44.79) and declares that the material world should not be taken too seriously. In a later speech (74.8-19) he makes a memorable development of the familiar theme of the vanity of worldly pleasures. He must not, however, be mistaken for a solemn moralist; he is not altogether sage. With a couple of mildly risqué puns, he retains his membership in the young-men-about-San Marco (or the Mermaid Tavern) and sustains the high-hearted tone of the play.

The Gobbos, in transferring their service from Shylock to Bassanio, ring another change upon the theme. It is easy to dismiss Launcelot (called simply "The Clown" at his first entrance) as the necessary role for the company's low comedian, provided with obscure foolery and irrelevant business to amuse the groundlings. His speeches are often difficult—and, with his blind father, brutal—yet they, too, grow out of the relation of surface appearance to inner reality, the letter as opposed to the spirit, which is the unifying idea of the total action. "It is a wise father that knows his own child" (63.76-77) is a most familiar proverb, and II.ii is a comic metaphor reminding the spectator that any man may be "sand-blind" (74), be he Shylock on the Rialto or the Prince of Morocco in Belmont; the very structure of the play, with the Prince departing to make his choice as the Gobbos perform their turn of deception-perception, confirms their relevance.

The structure of the play, in modern versions, seems to correspond to the classical five-act formula. Act divisions, however, were introduced by the editors of the First Folio; they do not appear in the First Quarto, which may have been printed from a scribe's copy of the author's manuscript. In an Elizabethan play five-act divisions are seldom organic, and in Shakespeare's theater there were few breaks in the performance. One set of characters had hardly made its exit through the stage door before another set bustled on to maintain the action's relentless progress; this is one of the ways in which an Elizabethan performance resembled more a feature film than the conventional fare of the present-day legitimate theater. It is only through such an unbroken succession of scenes that the structural principle of significant juxtaposition can make its effect.

It is possible, however, to identify major units within the total structure; in *The Merchant,* as in most of Shakespeare's plays, they are three in number. In *The Merchant,* also, these three major units correspond to the old dramaturgical principle of Rising Action, Climax, and Falling Action, though this is more coincidence than typical Shakespearian practice. The first major unit in which the conditions of Antonio's bond and of Bassanio's election are established culminates with Act II, scene ix. The second, encompassing the two major trials, concludes with Act IV, scene ii (a scene which prepares for a further trial). The final unit is Act V, reunion in Belmont, with the harmony of the spheres portending and echoing the harmony of earthly things.

The following scene-by-scene commentary is intended to interrelate the surface and the moral action of the play, but it must be read with a firm commitment to the theatrical experience: the *play* is the thing, the moral is only one of the means by which the dramatist achieves his end, a happy generalization about the quality of human relationships, wherein wit, charity (and a reasonable income) can outpoint malice, despair, and the other Sisters of Sin.

THE ACTION

I.i

Before attempting an analysis of the play, the student should have securely in his mind the nature of the Elizabethan playhouse (see Prefatory Remarks, pp. xiv-xv). While scholars disagree tediously about details, they have generally accepted as its basic elements: 1) a large undecorated platform, the main acting area, around three sides of which stood a considerable portion of the audience; 2) two doors in the rear wall at opposite ends of the platform; 3) a small curtained area set into or against the rear wall between the doors; 4) an upper stage, or balcony, above the curtained space. This playhouse is one of Shakespeare's major tools and he makes dramaturgical capital out of both its limitations and its freedoms. The following account of the action of *The Merchant* will call attention to the variety of uses of the theater as they occur.

For example, the opening scene. By all the rules of playwriting this should be expository, telling the spectator what he needs to know to follow the subsequent action: the time, the place, the principal characters, their relationships, the inciting incident. Each of these requirements the scene fulfills. The time is during the business day (183-84), the place is Venice (115), the principal characters are to be Antonio, Bassanio, Portia, and the inciting incident is carefully laid out (see the following). Yet the scene is more than half over before any of these elements (except the characters of Antonio and Bassanio) is introduced. Are the first 112 lines mere chatter to get the attention of the groundlings?

A playwright is necessarily the most economical of narrative artists, and Shakespeare employs his opening moments with skill and purpose. The first 56 lines are a kind of prelude evoked by Antonio's unaccustomed depression. Salerio

83

and Solanio are little more than pieces of scenery, yet their attempts to explain Antonio to himself sketch in the basic pattern of the moral world called, for the purposes of the action, Venice. Typical "Venetians," they account for his depression as concern about his argosies (9). The hourglass symbol of the transitory nature of life, reminds Salerio of cargoes lost on sandbars (25-29); in church his mind would turn to vessels torn apart by rocks (29-34). Antonio's denial that his sadness stems from financial concerns involves a clear admission (41-45) that his various ships are at sea and that he has confidence in their return.

Lines 57-68 introduce a new group of young Venetians who will be parties to the romantic action of the play. Salerio and Solanio, having contributed to establishing the tone and character of the locale, make a formal, poised departure.

Gratiano now takes the audience's attention in lines 73-112. His long speech declaring his intention to "play the fool" quickly changes the mood of the play from sad to comic-satiric as he mocks those who assume a melancholic pose to gain an undeserved reputation for wisdom. In his speech, and in the cue which Antonio gives him (77-79), however, is introduced one of the main lines of imagery in the play, that the world is a theater. It is one of the most constant metaphors in Shakespeare's works: all men and women are merely actors, playing to the best of their ability the parts they have been cast in or have chosen for themselves. Sometimes the basic tension of an entire play arises from this metaphor: his father's ghost "casts" Hamlet as the revenger, Hamlet himself would "play the antic." In *The Merchant* the climactic scene depends upon the success of Portia's deliberate role-playing; other scenes create suspense or amusement as the audience experiences the effect of the roles Portia's suitors have chosen to play.

The final lines (113-185) of scene i find Antonio and Bassanio alone on the stage, and the subject of Bassanio's quest is introduced. Antonio knows something of Bassanio's "secret pilgrimage" (which may be the reason for his serious mood, although Shakespearean comedy does not require such attention to motivation), and Bassanio's account at first suggests that he is a fortune hunter. The audience is meant, however, to accept him as a proper young gentleman, hitherto careless of material things, suddenly overcome with a sense of the responsibilities he has acquired, and fully persuaded that he has found the solution to his problems in Portia. To understand Bassanio it is important to notice the order in which he lists Portia's characteristics (161-63): first, that she is an heiress;

second, that she is a beauty; third—and most important—
that she has remarkable "powers and gifts" of mind, imagination, and understanding. Although her reputation has brought
her suitors from the four corners of the earth, Bassanio's own
mind (imagination, understanding) persuades him that if he
can afford a trip to Belmont, he can possess the golden fleece.
Although Antonio's fortunes are at sea, he is willing to back
the expedition; he and Bassanio go to inquire "Where money
is" (184).

I.ii

As the two men leave the stage through one door, Portia,
the object of their quest, and her handmaid, Nerissa, enter
through the other to establish the nature of the world of Belmont.

The first lines (1-11) echo the opening scene: Portia is
moody and Nerissa reads her a lesson a la Gratiano. Yet the
reason for Portia's discontent is very clear—the restriction
that her father's will has put upon her choice of a husband.
Nerissa urges the reasonableness of her father's action: first,
that holy men are often inspired by the approach of death;
and second, that Portia's own choice would doubtless coincide with her father's. To test the latter point the ladies play
a game of character analysis, Nerissa naming and Portia assessing each of her suitors (35-110). The dialogue here resumes the theatrical image initiated in the first scene, for Portia's speeches indicate that each suitor is acting a role, each is
motivated by some passion or humor, is something less than a
whole man. The listing ends with the mention of Bassanio, "a
Venetian, a scholar and a soldier" (112), a promising combination of manly qualities—a man of the world, a man of
mind, and a man of courage. But before Portia can be led to
further indiscreet revelations, a servant announces the arrival
of the Prince of Morocco to try his fortunes.

I.iii

As Portia and Nerissa leave the stage, Bassanio enters to
try his fortune with Shylock. The scene once more is Venice,
"Where money is" (47.184). True to his character as usurer,
Shylock temporizes with Bassanio (1-35), half-yielding, half-withholding, obviously enjoying the power which the situation
has put into his hands. At the entrance of Antonio, Shylock's
aside (38-49) makes unmistakably clear the motive of his future actions. He refers to the historical enmity of Christian

and Jew, "But more" (140): Antonio lends money without interest and publicly condemns usury, thus threatening the profits of the usurer. The motive for Shylock's actions, then, is revenge, to "feed fat the ancient grudge" (144) he bears him.

As was conventional, the other actors in the scene assume that the speaker of the aside is wrapped in his own thoughts, and Bassanio recalls Shylock to business. Shylock continues to toy with his quarry, twitting Antonio about his stand against money-lending, twisting an Old Testament story into a parable defending usury (Antonio, commenting to Bassanio, is really underlining for the audience the role Shylock is playing: "O what a goodly outside falsehood hath!", line 99). Shylock cites Antonio's contemptuous treatment, and Antonio is driven to such righteous rage that the usurer changes his approach and advances the terms of his bond as an offhand jest. Bassanio, sensing danger, protests, but Antonio has confidence in the fortune of his ships; he will sign to the bond.

II.i

As the Venetian friends exit to complete "this merry bond" (58.170) at the notary's office, the Prince of Morocco, all in white, enters with his followers and with Portia and Nerissa. Since there is no break in the action, the audience cannot fail to see the relationship of this scene with its predecessor. The Prince, whose dark complexion is emphasized by his contrasting costume, immediately begs that he be not judged by his outward appearance. Unlike Antonio, he is conscious of the tricks that Fortune can play (36-38). And Portia makes no effort to deceive him with a jesting manner about the seriousness of the bargain he is about to enter into (38-42). Thus the two stories are knit together by related ideas as well as common characters; the relationship is made plain when Portia and Morocco exit to prepare for the decisive act, as did Antonio and Bassanio in the preceding scene.

II.ii

The stage is immediately taken by "the Clown," that is, the lowest in social rank of the characters of the play. He identifies himself at once as Shylock's servant and performs a familiar comic routine, debating with his good and evil angels about leaving Shylock's employ. As the textual glosses indicate, his soliloquy is full of blunders and malapropisms, but it is not unrelated to one of the principal themes of the play.

THE MERCHANT OF VENICE 87

Lines 33-113 extrapolate in action this farcical version of the problem: Old Gobbo can be deceived because he is physically blind, as other characters are spiritually blind through self-delusion or false values. There is even a foretaste of the courtroom scene as Launcelot, having convinced his father that his son is dead, has some difficulty in escaping from his own trap (88).

The comic problem resolved, Bassanio enters with several young men. It is evident that Antonio has signed Shylock's bond, since Bassanio is preparing for his trip to Belmont. In lines 114-65 the Gobbos accost him and beg that Launcelot may become his servant. Bassanio accepts him, and this marks the first (and the least important) of Shylock's losses in the play.

The entrance of Gratiano returns to the major business of the action—Bassanio's quest—for Gratiano, too, has business in Belmont. Bassanio adds him to the party, but not without some cautionary remarks which continue his, and the play's concern with false appearance and inner reality (178-86). Gratiano promises to suit his behavior to the demands of the situation, and the friends part, planning to meet again at the bon voyage dinner.

II.iii

The brief scene between Jessica and Gobbo, who has come to bid her farewell, introduces still another subplot which will be rapidly developed in the next three scenes. Jessica trusts Gobbo with a message for Lorenzo and, in an aside, informs the audience that Shylock is about to suffer a second loss.

II.iv

The subplot is continued in the next scene as the young men of Venice make preparations for a masque, with costume and merry music. Gobbo delivers Jessica's letter, and the audience learns that she has determined to disguise herself as a page and elope with Lorenzo, taking certain jewels and gold of Shylock's with her.

II.v

As the young men depart, Gobbo enters and encounters Shylock, who has come home to leave instructions for Jessica. He will dine with Bassanio "in hate" (14), and he has agreed to Bassanio's engagement of Gobbo since that will "help to waste/His borrowed purse" (49-50). Informed that a masque is in preparation, he orders Jessica to lock the shutters and stop her ears against the sounds of music, for he is one that "hath no music in himself" (130.83), a characteristic that we must recall in the opening moments of the final act.

II.vi

In this scene, the Jessica-Lorenzo subplot (which is, in a nutshell, a conventional plot for an entire romantic comedy) is brought to a climax as the very masquers Shylock so despised appear under his "penthouse" (1) (that is, before the upper stage of the theater). Lorenzo describes Jessica's virtues much as Bassanio had Portia's ("wise, fair, and true," 56) and then calls out for her. Jessica appears on the upper stage disguised as a page boy. She throws down a casket "worth the pains" (line 33; note that this is Shylock's second loss). In the next scene Portia will offer her lover a casket, too; it will contain a different kind of treasure, "Fair Portia's counterfeit" (93.115). Jessica is embarrassed by her costume and by her assignment to bear the torch, "an office of discovery" (43). The function of the candle held to her shame is to reveal the true state of things, which she would keep dark. Lorenzo, however, laughs away her hesitation and the masquers set off for the entertainment, with Jessica—Shylock's third loss. But a sudden shifting of the wind cuts short their plans; the expedition to Belmont will set forth at once.

II.vii

As Bassanio and his companions embark, the action resumes the story of the caskets. Portia and Morocco enter and stand before the curtained space where the caskets are placed. The curtains are drawn and we watch Morocco's downfall. He reads the inscription on one casket after the other and interprets each, much as Shylock had interpreted the Old Testament story, to accord with his own mistaken values. Thus Morocco, the first threat to Bassanio's success, by not knowing himself, eliminates himself.

II.viii

Salerio and Solanio enter for an interlude of exposition, informing the audience of the safe departure of Bassanio's ship, Shylock's discovery of his daughter's elopement, and Antonio's noble farewell instructions. Since these are matters which could have furnished effective dramatic scenes, it must be asked why the playwright chose to confide them to such undistinguished and indistinguishable utility figures. The answer lies in an important aspect of Shakespearean dramaturgy: shifting focus. After the resolution of the elopement subplot, the audience is to focus its attention on the resolution of the casket story. Yet the suspense of Bassanio's trial will be weakened if the three scenes of choosing are played without interruption; likewise will they be weakened if too many incidents are allowed to intervene. Thus the spectacular scene of Morocco's choice, with its high rhetoric and rich imagery, is followed by a narrative of events, in a lower key, which keeps alive the story of the bond (25-32) without seriously detracting from the suspense of the story of the caskets.

II.ix

The suspense action is resumed as Nerissa enters to arrange the caskets for the "election" (3) of the Prince of Aragon. Once again, though more briefly, the audience hears the terms of the will and the inscriptions on the caskets. As Morocco had chosen from ambition, so Aragon chooses according to his own prized value, "clear honor" (41), but it is the honor of Hotspur in *1 Henry IV,* the honor which is really pride of place. Thus Aragon, the second threat to Bassanio's success, by not knowing himself, eliminates himself. Aragon departs, but before the tension can fall, a messenger enters to announce the arrival of Bassanio. The climax is at hand.

III.i

Again an interlude postpones the event the audience is awaiting, and although the first speakers are those of II. viii, the information they convey is more serious. There is very circumstantial "news on the Rialto" (1) that Antonio has lost one of his ships. Next Shylock appears, for the playwright is preparing the way for the bond story to take the focus of attention from the caskets. Salerio and Solanio tease Shylock about Jessica's elopement, and he replies with an increasing fury that once again leads him to betray his true motives: Antonio's flesh will feed his *revenge*. It is easy to misread line 50-69; anti-Semitism is very much on the conscience of today's world. However, Shylock deliberately misinterprets Antonio's past behavior (51-55), refusing to see that Antonio despised usury and usurers; and four times in the twenty lines he proclaims the justice of revenge (as Salerio says, "That's certain, if the devil may be [the] judge," 31).

But the reaction the audience is expected to give to Shylock's passionate defense is perhaps most clearly indicated in the subsequent dialogue with Tubal (73-123). Shylock's rapid shifts from bitterness about Jessica's elopement to glee about Antonio's misfortunes, repeated several times, can only be intended for comic effect. Indeed, his sense of loss is more commercial than paternal, and is hardly calculated to arouse sympathy. And the scene ends on a firm note of menace; Antonio is to be prevented from leaving Venice if his ventures fail: Shylock "will have the heart of him" (120).

III.ii

The increasing importance of the bond adds a new tension to the third casket scene, which might otherwise be somewhat anticlimactic. Portia makes it very clear that Bassanio is the only venturer to her taste, and their witty exchange (24-38) informs the audience that they are, in the way of romantic lovers, properly suited.

Portia, however, does what she can within the limitations of her father's will. She provides a musical background for the choice and an extended comparison between Bassanio and Hercules, as if the myth could prefigure victory. The musical accompaniment is one of Shakespeare's most famous songs, and the recurrence in it of words rhyming with "lead" has persuaded some commentators that Portia was exceeding the terms of the will in giving Bassanio a clue. This seems oversubtle for dramatic effectiveness, however; and the song is more cautionary than revealing, its theme the distinction between true love and mere fancy. Bassanio is more than ready to develop the theme and relate it to one of the principal themes of the play: the difference between appearance and reality, "The seeming truth which cunning times put on/To entrap the wisest" (100-01). Knowing himself, he chooses the leaden casket and wins Portia.

Portia eagerly accepts her fate in Venetian terms ("account," "full sum," "converted," 155, 157, 167) and symbolizes their union with a ring which will enable the comedy to end (to use Gobbo's term) in happy "confusions" (62.37).

Gratiano and Nerissa now announce their betrothal, and Lorenzo and Jessica arrive to complete the assembly of lovers. Salerio is there, also, with a message from Antonio. While Fortune has smiled on Bassanio, she has frowned on

THE MERCHANT OF VENICE 91

his friend; his bond, and therefore his life, are forfeit to Shylock. Although Antonio asks nothing of Bassanio, Portia determines that the money shall be paid twice over and the bond redeemed. The wedding ceremony performed, Bassanio and Gratiano are to depart at once for Venice.

III.iii

The instant juxtaposition of significantly related events which is the essence of Shakespearean dramatic structure calls for the representation of Antonio's unhappy fortune, as Shylock swears he will have his bond, immediately after the previous scene's display of Bassanio's happy fortune in winning Portia. After Shylock, unmoved by either pleas for mercy (a Christian idea) or offers of payment (an idea that ought, in theory, to seem more relevant to Shylock), Shylock departs, and Solanio assures Antonio that the Duke of Venice will not permit such barbarity, but Antonio knows that the Duke is bound to uphold the law, lest Venice lose its "trade and profit" (30).

III.iv

The action returns to Belmont where a carefully inverted scene prepares the audience for Portia's entry into the story of the bond. She first invests Lorenzo with responsibility for the management of her estate, pretending to retire to a monastery until her husband's return. She next sends her servant to Padua to fetch "notes and garments" (51) from Dr. Bellario, a lawyer and her relative. Finally she reveals to Nerissa some of her true purpose. Disguised as men, they will follow their husbands to Venice, for sport.

III.v

This scene serves as a buffer between the happy end of Bassanio's quest and the high events preparing in Venice. Involving Gobbo, Jessica, and Lorenzo, characters whose fate can have caused little anxiety to the audience, it has only the minimum of dramatic tension. It has been suggested that time was needed to allow Portia and Nerissa to shift costumes, though it would be only a matter of moments to slip into a lawyer's gown. It has been further suggested that a scene was needed to cover the passage of time, while the Belmont ladies journey to Venice; it should be remembered, however, that Shakespeare is never bound by the clock, and that he allows his audience to be aware of passing time only when it is dramatically significant (as in *The Winter's Tale*). The relevance of the buffer scene is in the idea which is at its heart.

Gobbo, as has been pointed out, is a malaprop, yet in his attempts at wit and his misuse of words he associates himself with the play's concern with appearance and reality, mask and face, outward show and inward fact, letter and spirit. "How every fool can play upon the word!" exclaims Lorenzo (43) and fall to "quarreling with occasion!" (55), refusing to "understand a plain man in his plain meaning" (57-58). After Gobbo's exit, Lorenzo explicitly joins the semantic issue with the imagery (and action) of disguise that has run through the play. In lines 64-69 he says, in effect, that if Gobbo's diction disguises what he would really say, many men of greater power and status deliberately choose to hide the truth behind false verbiage. And thus is the way prepared for the legal quibbling of the fourth act.

IV.i

The confrontation of the world of Belmont and the world of the Rialto is at hand. But before it occurs, the playwright must establish: 1) the idea of the place of the confrontation; and 2) Shylock as in firm possession of the upper hand.

Since there is no scenery to indicate locale, Shakespeare must rely on his actors, not just to name the place of the action but to give some sense of its nature; with the means at his disposal he creates a solemn spectacle. Enter the Duke of Venice with his Magnificoes, the Venetian Senate, an impressive sight since the Elizabethan actors more than made up in costume for what they lacked in scenery. The Duke summons Antonio, who enters as prisoner accompanied by his friends. The Duke regrets the inflexible nature of the accuser, Antonio declares his resignation, and Shylock is called. In lines 16-34, in stately formal language, the Duke expresses his hope that Shylock will eventually forgive Antonio, and Shylock, in an equally formal reply (35-62), justifies himself; Shylock's speech is a good example of that false rhetoric, that "play upon the word" (106.43), that Lorenzo had condemned in the preceding scene. At the end, of course, Shylock reveals his true motive, "a lodged hate and a certain loathing" (60) which he will twist the law of Venice to serve. This is not merely a courtroom, but the place where the Law will be observed with ruthless inhumanity.

Shylock must seem to have the upper hand because the playwright intends the audience to experience one of the most satisfying of dramatic situations: the villain defeated by his own devices, the biter bit, or, as the title of a popular play of Shakespeare's time puts it, *Wily Beguiled*. Point by point, Shylock turns aside Bassanio's moral aphorisms (63-69), rejects his offer of double compensation (85-87), and points out that the Duke is powerless to countermand the laws of the state (101-03), as Antonio had earlier recognized (101.26-31). Antonio's resignation seems justified by the place (the idea of Venetian justice) and the confidence of his prosecutor, who sums up the situation in a threatening sentence, "I stand here for law" (142).

Wrapped in professional robes, Portia and Nerissa enter also to "stand for law." Portia begins, discouragingly for the audience, by admitting the legality of Shylock's claim. Yet her famous speech on the nature of mercy is intended to remind us that beneath the costume representing the letter of Venetian law is the spirit of Belmont. Shylock, however, sees only the costume, the letter, as does Bassanio when he begs her to "Wrest once the law to your authority" (214). But Portia is true to her assumed role; there must be no tampering with the legal order of things lest chaos result. Is the audience to be uneasy at her position, or to recognize a conventional situation, that Shylock will somehow fall victim to the very law he stubbornly upholds? The whole tone of the play up to this point suggests the latter; still everything seems to weigh on Shylock's side. Portia examines the bond, declares it forfeit, and once again offers Shylock the opportunity to be merciful. He replies that he stays "here on my bond" (241). Portia orders Antonio to bare his bosom to the knife. "So says the bond," cries Shylock (252). She once again advances the idea of charity, but "'tis not in the bond" (261). To remind the audience that there is another plot to be resolved there is some byplay with the new-made husbands, but Shylock cuts it short with a demand that the sentence be decreed (297). Portia adds the final weight to Shylock's triumph with the formula, once repeated, "The court awards it, and the law doth give it" (299). Antonio kneels, and Shylock raises his knife pointed at the merchant's heart.

But Portia stops him with her quiet (and expected?) "Tarry a little" (304). Once more she appeals, as Shylock has over and over again, to the bond, and insists, as he had, on strict execution of the letter: a pound of flesh, but no drop of blood. "Is that the law?" asks Shylock (313), and collapses immediately; he will take the proffered money. Portia, however, will not allow him this escape from the trap he has constructed for himself: "The Jew shall have all justice"

(320), that is, the letter of the bond, and nothing else. Shylock is content to regain his principal: "He shall have merely [strictly] justice and his bond" (338). Shylock now tries to abandon his suit, but the law of Venice is still relentless; it provides the severest of penalties for attempted murder.

At this point it is the duty of the court to practice the mercy so frequently advocated. The Duke and Antonio exercise their options under the law, allowing Shylock the use of some of his money and conferring on him the grace of Christian baptism. They thus, from the point of view of the play and its times, effectively answer Shylock's charge (87.65) that a Christian will avenge any wrong done him by a Jew. With Shylock's submission the matter of the bond is happily resolved.

It has been the frequent practice of star actors to end the play with Shylock's exit. But it must be remembered that Portia's trip to Venice was not merely to rescue Antonio but to try "confusions" with Bassanio. Small as it is, the business of the rings is analogous to the caskets and the bond in working the theme of the play to its conclusion. The rings had been given by Portia and Nerissa to their husbands-to-be as tokens of the bond they were about to enter into. After her victory, Portia tries to claim Bassanio's ring as a remembrance, but he is true to his bond. She leaves with doubting words but a light heart. Bassanio, however, must yield to Antonio's plea; Antonio has risked not only money and skill but his very life to be of service to his friend. Gratiano, whose sharp tongue has often cut shrewdly into the scene, is dispatched with the ring, and the two friends make ready to return to Belmont.

IV.ii

The delivery of the ring is central to the events of the final act; it is, therefore, allowed a brief scene to itself. Portia and Nerissa are on the way to Shylock's house when Gratiano overtakes them and hands Portia Bassanio's ring. There is an echo here of Shylock handing her the bond which will be his own undoing. Nerissa requests him to escort her, for this will be her chance to reclaim *her* ring, and thus continue the parallel between her romance and Portia's.

V

The final scene resolves the action instituted by Portia's gift of her ring to Bassanio, sums up and restates the unifying ideas of the play, and restores the tone of gaiety and romance that may have been threatened by the menacing presence of Shylock. The dialogue between Jessica and Lorenzo establishes the time of the action as night; this must, of course, be done with words since the performance took place in broad daylight on a scenery-less stage. Their dialogue, though jesting, reminds the audience of the Elizabethan convention that night was a time for confusion, if not chaos and downright evil. Sounds of music from the house provide the text for Lorenzo's thematic speech about the harmony which maintains the proper order of things in the heavens, in nature, in society, and within the individual. (For Shakespeare's most detailed treatment of this basic Elizabethan concept, see the speech of Ulysses in *Troilus and Cressida,* 66-67.75-137.) It has its most domestic and familiar manifestation, of course, in the harmonious relationship of man and wife, the business of this act. Shylock, "The man that hath no music [i.e., harmony] in himself" (83), has been defeated; only the rings remain to be accounted for.

They are accounted for rather quickly. Neither Portia nor Nerissa is inclined to do more than tease, though the teasing touches lightly on the major ideas of the earlier action: the inviolability of a bond, the difference between appearance and reality, letter and spirit (for example, 192-208). That the confusions are not more spun out, and that Portia refuses to tell Antonio how she has come by her happy news for him (278-79) are evidence of the playwright's purpose in adding this coda to his play. He would reestablish the world of Belmont as the final dramatic experience for his audience. Even Gratiano's concluding, characteristic, and rather adolescent pun is no more than the final tootle of a pennywhistle to signify the play's end. The mood is unbroken.

ALAN DOWNER

SHORT-ANSWER QUESTIONS

1. What is Antonio's mood on his first entrance? (41.1-7)

2. What three comparisons does Salerio make to account for Antonio's mood? (42.22-34)

96   TEACHING SHAKESPEARE

 3. What two reasons does Solanio advance for Antonio's mood? (42.46-48)

 4. Lorenzo is planning to dine with Bassanio (43.70). How many times is this meeting referred to as a point toward which the action is moving? (45.104-05; 53.30; 65.115; 67.169; 68.203; 69.1; 70.17; 71.11; 75.48)

 5. Why will Gratiano "play the fool"? (44.79-102)

 6. For what three reasons will Bassanio woo Portia? (47.161-63)

 7. What is the cause of Portia's "weariness"? (48.22)

 8. How does Nerissa defend Portia's father's will? (49.27)

 9. According to Nerissa, what qualities in Bassanio make him "best deserving"? (51.111)

10. By what biblical story does Shylock defend his profession? (55.68-87)

11. According to Shylock, how has he been treated by Antonio? (56.103-16)

12. How, then, does Antonio justify his application for a loan? (57.127-34)

13. Shylock declares that he will not eat with a Christian (53.34); what is his reason for dining with Bassanio? (71.14-15)

14. What is Shylock's attitude toward music and masquing? (72.28-36)

15. Gratiano says that anticipation is sweeter than satisfaction. Of the three examples he cites, which is most pertinent to Venice? (74.8-19)

16. What does Jessica take with her in eloping? (74.33; 75.49-50; 89.111)

17. Why is the masquing cut short? (76.64)

THE MERCHANT OF VENICE 97

18. What three conditions are laid down in Portia's father's will to govern those who sue for her hand? (81.9-15)

19. In your own words, what are the inscriptions on the three caskets? (76.4-9)

20. By what reasoning does Morocco select the gold casket? (77.39-47, 54-59)

21. What does the gold casket contain? (78.63)

22. By what reasoning does Aragon select the silver casket? (82.36-48)

23. What does the silver casket contain? (83.53)

24. Why does Portia compare Bassanio to Hercules? (91.60-61)

25. By implication, what is the difference between "fancy" and true love? (91.63-70)

26. By what reasoning does Bassanio select the leaden casket? (92.74-107)

27. What does the leaden casket contain? (93.115)

28. What is Shylock's reaction to Jessica's elopement? (79.4, 12-22)

29. What reasons does Shylock advance before the trial for insisting on his bond? (87.50-69)

30. Shylock speaks of "loss upon loss"; to what does he refer? (88.87-89)

31. What is Portia's initial plan to rescue Antonio? (100.306-07)

32. How do we know what Shylock's reaction to this offer will be? (99.284-88)

33. Why, according to Antonio, does Shylock seek his life? (101.22-24)

98   TEACHING SHAKESPEARE

34. Why cannot the Duke "deny the course of law"? (101.27-31)

35. How does Portia know that Antonio is a "true gentleman"? (102.11-18)

36. Who is Dr. Bellario? (103.50; 112.105-06)

37. Why, according to Gobbo, is Lorenzo to be blamed for converting Jessica? (106.22-25)

38. Lorenzo says that "many fools . . . in better place . . . for a tricksy word/Defy the matter" (107.67-69). How many characters in the play exemplify this precept?

39. What is Antonio's attitude as his trial begins? (109.10-13)

40. Interpret the Duke's opening plea to Shylock. (110.17-34)

41. With what three reasons does Shylock reply? (110.45-46, 53, 60)

42. What distinction does Portia make between justice and mercy? (116.183-202)

43. Why does Portia refuse to "Wrest . . . the law to [her] authority"? (117.217-221)

44. How is Shylock frustrated by his own bond? (120.305-11)

45. Why does Shylock offer his life to the Duke? (122.374-76)

46. Portia invites Antonio to show mercy to Shylock. How does Antonio respond? (122.379-89)

47. Bassanio at first refuses to part with his ring; why does he eventually submit? (125.448-50)

48. What is Portia's purpose in accepting the ring? (126.13-15)

49. What is the common theme of the love stories which Jessica and Lorenzo exchange? (127.4-22)

50. How is Portia "convinced" of Bassanio's faithfulness? (137.266-73)

QUESTIONS FOR DISCUSSION

1. The play begins with Antonio's sadness and ends with the harmony of Belmont. Scene by scene, and sometimes within scenes, Shakespeare contrasts moods of gravity and gaiety, tension and relaxation. Trace these variations through the play and consider their effect on an audience.

2. The elopement of Jessica and Lorenzo is initiated and completed in an unbroken sequence of scenes (II.iii-vi). Contrast this with the initiation, development, and completion of the story of the bond; of the caskets. To what extent does it govern the tone of the major actions?

3. Shylock is as insistent as the other Venetians on the natural antipathy of Christians and Jews. To what extent is this a mask for the true motivation of his actions? How is this related to the explanations that Morocco and Aragon advance for their "elections"?

4. In Act I, scene ii, Portia criticizes each of her suitors as governed by a single excessive passion. To what characters in the play may this principle be applied?

5. Relate the three "trials" in the play (the caskets, the bond, the rings) in terms of the characters involved, the conditions laid down, related ideas, and their outcomes.

6. Antonio observes that "the devil can cite Scripture" (56.95) after Shylock's account of Jacob and Laban. What other characters in the play see Shylock as a devil? What effect has this recurrent comparison on our reaction to the bond?

7. Gobbo's malapropisms disguise his true meanings. How is this related to the major actions of the play?

8. Antonio, in his first speech, concludes that he has "much ado to know myself" (41.7). What other characters in the play lack self-knowledge, and how are they enlightened?

9. As a city engaged in maritime commerce, Venice is much concerned about "ventures" (41.8ff.) and "merchandise" (42.40). To what extent do the images of the play and their occasional manifestation in dramatic symbols (Shylock's "balances") cluster around this "Venetian idea"?

10. Lorenzo warns Jessica not to trust "The man that hath no music in himself" (130.83). Shylock despises music (72.29-36), but the implications of Lorenzo's speech go deeper. In what kinds of situations is music actually employed in the play? In how many situations is the idea of music (i.e., harmony) important?

SAMPLE TEST

I. (30 minutes)

Write a well-organized essay on ONE of the following subjects.

1. In Act I, scene ii, Portia criticizes each of her suitors as governed by a single excessive passion. To what characters in the play may this principle be applied?

2. Lorenzo warns Jessica not to trust "The man that hath no music in himself" (130.83). Shylock despises music (72.29-36), but the implications of Lorenzo's speech go deeper. In what kinds of situations is music actually employed in the play? In how many situations is the idea of music (i.e., harmony) important?

THE MERCHANT OF VENICE

II. (30 minutes)

Write briefly on FIVE of the following.

1. What is Antonio's mood on his first entrance?

2. By what biblical story does Shylock defend his profession?

3. By what reasoning does Bassanio select the leaden casket?

4. Why cannot the Duke "deny the course of law"?

5. What is Antonio's attitude as his trial begins?

6. What distinction does Portia make between justice and mercy?

7. How is Shylock frustrated by his own bond?

THE TRAGEDY OF HAMLET, PRINCE OF DENMARK

INTRODUCTION

Hamlet is the most fascinating of Shakespeare's plays; as Hazlitt says, "It is the one of Shakespear's plays that we think of the oftenest . . ." (p. 197). The first of the great tragedies, it has some of the gracefulness of the romantic comedies that immediately precede it and some of the harshness of the tragedies that follow it. We cannot date Shakespeare's plays exactly, but *Hamlet* appears to have been written about 1600–01, shortly after the melancholy romantic comedies—*As You Like It* and *Twelfth Night*—and *Julius Caesar*. It was followed by the so-called "dark comedies," *Troilus and Cressida* and *Measure for Measure,* and by the other major tragedies. (For the approximate chronological order of Shakespeare's plays, see Prefatory Remarks, Signet Classic Shakespeare edition of *Hamlet*, p. xii.)

Hamlet has a good deal of the romantic comedies' lyric grace. Its treatment of the dramatically necessary indication of time (40.166-67), of the political significance of restless ghosts (38.112-25), of the allusion to Christmas (39.158-61) in the first scene is typical; these lines have a verbal grace that Shakespeare will stop using when he comes to the harsher attitudes of the later tragedies. These lyric effects are reinforced by a marvelously natural use of rhetorical artifices, the easiest of which to show students is hendiadys, the substitution of a pair of coordinated nouns for the ordinary combination of an adjective and a noun—for example, "the gross and scope of my opinion" (36.68) for "the gross scope of my opinion." Hendiadys is capable of a good deal of subtlety. For example, "the dead waste and middle of the night" (47.198), which means "the middle hours of the night that are a wasteland, spiritually dead" (when "hell itself breathes out/Contagion to this world," 112.397-98). Here the relation between the nouns is slightly causal: because it is the middle of the night it is a dead waste. It becomes specifically causal in "the sensible and true avouch/Of mine own eyes" (36.57-58); this means "true because it is proved by one of the senses, my eyes." This remark of Horatio's is, incidentally, wonderfully revealing of his character. Horatio is quiet and cautious, a man of steady common sense who never leaps to conclusions, especially about such things as ghosts. The ghost is to him a thing that appears "*Together with* that fair and warlike form" of the senior Hamlet (35.47); though it is dangerous to speak to a ghost at all, Horatio nonetheless sticks to his doubts and addresses it as "illusion" (38.127). It is characteristic of Shakespeare's dramatic skill that this quality of Horatio's character—so crucial to the play as a whole because it makes him a sustained contrast to Hamlet—is, in this scene, used to persuade the audience of the ghost's reality. Horatio firmly expresses the audience's doubt; "Tush, tush," he says, " 'twill not appear" (35.30); he is then confronted by the ghost and has to accept "the sensible and true avouch" of his own eyes.

But if *Hamlet* has a good deal of the verbal grace of the romantic comedies that precede it, it also has a good deal of the bitter disgust at the human condition that is evident in the plays like *Measure for Measure* and *Lear* that follow it. At one point Hamlet suggests that his "imaginations" may be "as foul/As Vulcan's stithy" (100.85-86); but they are not, for what he imagines is true, and it is the world that is—measured by his high standards—thus foul. For that world Hamlet can feel only a nauseated disgust, and whenever he thinks of it his mind is filled with images of disease, corruption of the flesh, decay, rot, and vile smells. This disgust is given marvelous dramatic focus in the sexual disgust created in Hamlet by the "dexterity" with which his mother posts "to incestuous sheets" (45.157; to the Elizabethans, marriage with a brother-in-law was incest). It is a perfect dramatic image. The young man cannot conceive of "old folk" like Gertrude feeling passionate love ("Rebellious hell,/If thou canst mutine in a matron's bones,/To flaming youth let virtue be as wax/And melt in her own fire," 119.83-86); the son cannot bear to think of his mother making love ("In the rank sweat of an enseamèd bed,/Stewed in corruption," 119.93-94).

Hamlet is thus deeply concerned with its hero's personal experience of life. But it is also, like most of Shakespeare's plays, concerned with the public life of society. Hamlet himself is not simply a brilliant and deeply troubled individual;

he is also a prince, a man who, throughout the play, rightly thinks of himself as "the Dane" (158.260), that is, the true king of Denmark. The play as a whole is as deeply concerned with the public, political fate of the kingdom as it is with the private, personal fate of its hero. This double perspective on experience, this concern for both the individual and society, for private feeling and public responsibility, is anticipated in a simpler but very similar way in *Julius Caesar*. Caesar is Brutus's dearest friend, and Brutus decides that, for the good of society, he must kill Caesar. So closely bound up are the private and public responsibilities for Brutus that he thinks of his private consciousness as a state when he is making up his mind to kill Caesar; at such a moment, he thinks, "the state of a man,/Like to a little kingdom, suffers then/The nature of an insurrection" (*Julius Caesar*, 57.67-69).

In *Hamlet*, the interaction of the public problem—the "rottenness" in the state of Denmark—and the private one—the radical disorder of Hamlet's soul—is continuous, so deeply embedded in the play's action that it cannot be fully described except in a line-by-line analysis; but its importance is clear as soon as we recognize that Claudius and Hamlet are genuinely the "mighty opposites" that Hamlet calls them (162.62), that each represents one of the great human choices, neither of which can be denied its importance in life.

Claudius is a brilliant statesman: with what skill and restraint he handles the delicate international problem created for him by Fortinbras, which comes at the most dangerous moment of his career, when he is scarcely on the throne he has won by evidently questionable means. With what tact and charm he deals with his rebellious nephew, Hamlet. With what intelligence and courage he manages Laertes. It is men like Claudius who keep society orderly and peaceful; without them it would quickly fall back into chaos and anarchy. The Elizabethans knew enough of social chaos to understand—as perhaps we no longer do—how precious a gift an orderly world is; they would have sympathized with Claudius' genuine desire to keep Denmark a peaceful and happy country and would have admired his skill as a ruler. But in order to acquire and keep the power to rule, Claudius has been driven to the most horrible crimes. He has murdered his own brother ("It hath the primal eldest curse [of Cain] upon't," 114.37); he has in effect seduced his brother's wife; he has tricked his nephew out of the throne. When the time comes, he will not hesitate to persuade Laertes to the shameful murder of Hamlet, to arrange to poison Hamlet twice over, and to refuse to reveal the truth when the innocent queen, whom he loves as much as he loves anything in this world, drinks the poison he has meant for Hamlet. None of this happens because Claudius is a coldly wicked villain; he is not. He is deeply shocked by his own crimes: "O, my offense is rank, it smells to heaven" (114.36). But what he does follows, with a logic he cannot escape, from what he is.

Hamlet too is a great man. We have only to watch him with Horatio, whom he loves and admires, to see how intelligent and generous he is; how clearly he recognizes, for example, Horatio's possession of the steadiness of character he himself lacks, calling Horatio "one, in suff'ring all, that suffers nothing,/A man that Fortune's buffets and rewards/Hast ta'en with equal thanks"(100.68-70). Hamlet has a range of insight and understanding, a fineness of mind and feeling, that is a constant delight, and his wit is dazzling. He is everything a prince ought, ideally, to be; and as a prince—politically speaking—he is hopeless. He understands his princely obligations, none better, and he suffers greatly at the thought of how humiliatingly ineffectual he appears beside "a delicate and tender prince" like Fortinbras who, "with divine ambition puffed"—so filled with enthusiasm by his ambition's dreams of honor that he seems almost divinely inspired—"Makes mouths at the invisible event" (131.48-50). Hamlet's trouble is not, of course, a lack of courage, an inability to look with scorn at the impenetrable risks of heroic action. His trouble goes deeper than that; it is an overwhelming conviction that every kind of action is utterly pointless, that life itself—"*all* the uses of the world"—are "weary, stale, flat, and unprofitable" (44.133-34). The only felicity he can imagine is not being at all.

There is no more question of Hamlet's ability and his courage than of Claudius'; he shows both clearly when he is forced by circumstances to act without time for brooding, as when he murders Polonius, thinking he is stabbing the King (117.25), or when he springs forward at Ophelia's funeral to claim his right to grieve for her (157.256). But the minute these acts are completed, the old, sardonic sense that all action—compromised as it is by the insuperable limitations of life itself—is futile returns to mock him, to make him mock himself: "Nay, an thou'lt mouth,/I'll rant as well as thou" (159.285-86). Hamlet is disqualified for effective action in the world by his radical disbelief in the value of the world; and that disbelief is a product of the very excellence, the delicacy of insight and the refinement of feeling, that make him so admirable.

Thus both these mighty opposites are the victims of their

own natures and their conceptions of life. Neither deceives himself (for Claudius' self-awareness, see 114.51-55; for Hamlet's, see 90.610-15). Claudius cannot truly repent his crime, bad as he knows it is, because he cannot bring himself to surrender its rewards, above all perhaps that queen on whom his voice lingers so lovingly when he lists those rewards—"My crown, mine own ambition, and my queen" (114.55). Hamlet cannot make himself be "Rightly . . . great" (132.53) much as he longs to. Even as he tells himself that he ought to emulate Fortinbras and his twenty thousand men "That for a fantasy and trick of fame/Go to their graves like beds" (132.61-62), he cannot repress his ironic sense of the absurdity of their conduct, cannot resist calling it meaningless, "a fantasy and trick of fame," cannot keep himself from elaborating this judgment with his corrosive wit— "fight for a plot/Whereon the numbers cannot try the cause,/Which is not tomb enough and continent/To hide the slain" (132.62-65).

Around these two central figures, who are as opposed in their characters and their conceptions of life as they are in the immediate circumstances of the play's plot, all the other characters are grouped by parallels and contrasts of every kind. The most significant of these is, perhaps, the play's series of father (or uncle) and son (or nephew) relations: the Ghost and Hamlet, Claudius and Hamlet ("But now, my cousin Hamlet, and my son," 42.64), Polonius and Laertes, Norway and Fortinbras, the rich father and Osric. The circumstances of the play—fathers dying in questionable circumstances, challenges to military heroism—"all occasions" in their lives bring them constantly into contrast with one another and, as Hamlet puts it, "inform against" him (131.32).

In this way a plot filled with varied characters is focused on the central theme that is so beautifully dramatized by the conflict between the main characters. That theme is further reinforced by a series of dramatic images, events that occur perfectly naturally but have symbolic overtones. A good example is the company of strolling players and their play. Traveling actors of this kind were common in Shakespeare's time, and Shakespeare even seems to be making an allusion to his own company at the Globe Theatre when he introduces the players (see 82.370 and the note). It is almost enough to make one think Shakespeare dragged these players in so that he could indulge in a little talk about his own trade.

But in fact one of the major problems for Hamlet is the problem of outward action and inward feeling. It is a crucial aspect of his dilemma that he can never act in a way that truly represents what he feels. The only time he seems able to speak freely what he feels is when he has put on his "antic disposition" (64.172) and is "acting" mad. It confounds him that "this player here,"

> But in a fiction, in a dream of passion,
> Could force his soul so to his own conceit
> That from her working all his visage wanned,
> Tears in his eyes, distraction in his aspect,
> A broken voice, and his whole function suiting
> With forms to his conceit? And all for nothing! (88.561-67)

Yet he, with a beloved father and king murdered, a mother "whored" (162.64), a kingdom stolen, can say and do nothing. This problem of appearance and reality, of outer conduct and inner feeling, is almost the first thing Hamlet speaks of in the play. When his well-meaning, conventional mother says to him, "Why seems it so *particular* [unique] with thee?" he answers as if she too were deeply preoccupied with the gap between seeming and being.

> Seems, madam? Nay, it is. I know not "seems."
> 'Tis not alone my inky cloak, good mother, ...
> Nor windy suspiration of forced breath,
> No, nor the fruitful river in the eye, ...
> That can denote me truly. These indeed seem,
> For they are *actions that a man might play,*
> But I have *that within which passes show.* (43.75-85)

Something like this, then, is what we must try to convey to our students: first, the profound issues raised by the dramatic conflict between Hamlet and Claudius; then the complication and enrichment of these issues by the varied secondary characters that the plot brings into parallel with the central characters; and then the refinement of these issues by the dramatic and verbal images that surround both.

THE ACTION

I.i

This is a scene of exposition, in which necessary information is conveyed to the audience. Such material is undramatic, but in this scene the appearances of the Ghost are very cleverly used to keep the audience alert. From the start we are made edgy: notice that Barnardo, the relief, nervously challenges Francisco, the man on duty and therefore the natural challenger. Barnardo is nervous; so is Francisco (see 8-9). The time of the scene is midnight (7), the "dead hour" of the night (65), "When churchyards yawn, and hell itself breathes out/Contagion to this world" (112.397-98). We soon learn—"What, has this thing appeared again tonight?" (21)—the specific reason for the watch's nervousness. Students ought to ask themselves why these men are nervous. Only Horatio, the man of skeptical common sense, is calm. Horatio's character is clearly suggested by what he says (for example, 29, 33-34, 46-47, 66-68, 165). As Barnardo begins what sounds as if it were going to be a long and circumstantial description of the Ghost's previous appearances (34), we relax; no sooner do we do so than we are made to jump with surprise by the Ghost. Horatio decides the Ghost is astir because there is about to be trouble in the country (69). He then explains the political situation of Denmark (79-125). This is the real exposition; it is important to our understanding of the play that we should see clearly the relations between Denmark and Norway and what the nephew of the King of Norway, young Fortinbras, has been up to. Horatio brings us back to the problem of ghosts with his beautifully phrased recollection of the ghosts of Rome "a little ere the mightiest Julius fell" (114)—and the Ghost reappears. Horatio challenges it and—as Elizabethan learning about ghosts recommended—asks about the three things that usually cause ghosts to walk, the first two of which—has the Ghost unfinished personal business? is there trouble coming for the country?—are linked to the play's double concern with private and public life (see the preceding Introduction). The Ghost appears ready to answer but is forced by the coming of dawn to leave, and it is decided that "young Hamlet" (170), the Ghost's son, must hear of this.

I.ii

As the first scene takes place during the dark "witching time of night" (112.396), when the supernatural seems very real, the second scene takes place the following morning in a blaze of worldly splendor, when men are most confident that they can govern their own fates by intelligence and effort. This is the sphere of Claudius, the skillful worldly statesman, as the dubious dark of scene i is the sphere of Hamlet, acutely aware that "There are more things in heaven and earth, Horatio,/Than are dreamt of in your philosophy" (64.166-67; the "your" is generic; Hamlet does not mean Horatio's personal philosophy but philosophy in general; "philosophy" is short for natural philosophy, what we call science). The scene is a formal one, the King and Queen splendid in their royal robes, the courtiers in brilliant colors—all except Hamlet, whose "inky cloak" (77)—the scene's only sign of mourning for the dead king—makes him stand out even though he does not speak until line 65. The visual aspect of this scene is full of meaning, and to experience it fully, we need to remind ourselves of the physical character of the Elizabethan stage (see Prefatory Remarks, pp. xiii-xvi), particularly the largeness of the stage compared to ours, and the scope it offers for such visually impressive spectacles as we have in this scene.

Claudius' opening speech in scene ii is brilliant. This is his first formal meeting with the full court since the death of Hamlet's father and Claudius' marriage, both questionable affairs that Claudius "must with all our majesty and skill/Both countenance and excuse" (125.31-32). He begins with a skillfully phrased, deliberately formal reference to the death of Hamlet's father (1-7) and an official justification of his marriage (8-16). His tone then changes strikingly, becoming brisk and businesslike, almost as if in relief at having got over the dangerous ground (17-39). The dramatic effect of this shift in tone is very evident when Claudius' speech is read aloud. Claudius' plan for dealing with Fortinbras is skill-

THE TRAGEDY OF HAMLET   111

fully conceived, as is evident when his ambassadors return at 72.60-80 with their report of triumphant success.

From the business of the state, Claudius turns to personal matters, first to young Laertes, the conventionally proper young man, and his father. That settled, he then takes up the more delicate matter of Hamlet. For reasons of state (Hamlet is politically popular, as we know from 142.18-21), and for personal reasons (he loves Hamlet's mother), Claudius wants Hamlet's friendship. Claudius' use of the word "son" (64) emphasizes the parallel between Laertes and Hamlet here. It is almost pathetic that in seeking to be gracious to Hamlet—"But now, my cousin Hamlet, and my son" (note that Claudius uses the personal "my" rather than the more formal royal "we")—Claudius hits on just the way of speaking that will most annoy Hamlet, as Hamlet's bitter, punning aside (65) shows us. There follows Hamlet's first expression of the problem of feeling and action (see the preceding Introduction). Hamlet is very rude to Claudius, seizing the chance his mother unintentionally gives him to turn his back on Claudius and say to her, "I shall in all my best obey *you*, madam" (120). Claudius makes the best he can of it, and Hamlet is left alone for his first, overwhelmingly revealing soliloquy.

The soliloquy opens with a passionate assertion of Hamlet's longing "not to be" (93.56). This phrase must be taken literally; it expresses a desire for complete nonexistence. This desire dominates Hamlet's feelings; it is the logical attitude for a man to whom "all the uses of this world," which men cannot escape so long as they are conscious at all, "Seem . . . weary, stale, flat, and unprofitable" (133-34). Hamlet is not thinking of a continued existence in a better world; on the contrary, he is as discouraged about life in that "undiscovered country, from whose bourn/No traveler returns" (94.79-80) as he is about life in this world. What he longs for is "not to be," a total cessation of consciousness, a dreamless sleep. This longing is the true subject of this first soliloquy, as it is also of the more famous one at 93.56-88. Hamlet explains his reasons for not wanting to be in the rest of his soliloquy, his feeling that "all the uses of this world" (134), all the possible ways of living—not some of them, but all of them—are meaningless, that the world is a once beautiful garden now completely ("merely," 137) choked with ugly and disgusting weeds. Notice how his mind then jumps, by psychological association rather than logical progression, to the thought of his mother's marriage to Claudius. That marriage offends him deeply, because he loved his father and scorns Claudius, because the marriage was indecently hasty and Hamlet cannot but suspect there is a large element of physical passion in it, because it is, at least technically, incestuous. Such is Hamlet's fastidious nature.

Hamlet's soliloquy is interrupted by the men who have seen the Ghost, and Hamlet decides he "will watch tonight" (242).

I.iii

The events of this scene follow very shortly after those of I.ii, in which the King gives Laertes permission to return to France (42.62-63). In it we see three related conversations, between Laertes and Ophelia, Laertes and Polonius, and Polonius and Ophelia. Its primary function is to show us a conventional father-son relationship that stands in marked contrast with the one between Hamlet and his "uncle-father" (82.384) shown in the previous scene and the one between Hamlet and his ghostly father in the succeeding scene. Polonius is a conventional worldly-wise man just beginning to decline into dotage. He should not be treated as a comic fool; his advice to Laertes is excellent as far as it goes, but it goes only as far as the practical wisdom of this world will take men. It might have been given by Claudius, except that Claudius has none of Polonius' slightly pompous complacency. Laertes is a younger Polonius. Perfectly sincere in his conventional righteousness, he is nonetheless, as we shall see, capable under pressure of the meanest kind of unscrupulousness. Ophelia's obedience to her father is not to be taken as a sign of weakness; in Elizabethan times children were expected to obey parents implicitly.

I.iv

Here we are back, one night later, at the same place and the same time of night as in the play's first scene. Again we are put in a relaxed mood, here by Hamlet's thoughtful analysis of the way a single flaw may ruin an otherwise admirable nation or man (it is difficult to avoid the conviction that Hamlet is thinking of himself) and are again taken by surprise when the Ghost appears. Hamlet insists on speaking to the Ghost; "By heaven," he says with grim humor, "I'll make a ghost of him that lets me!" (85). Marcellus, remembering the conventional lore about ghosts, is now sure that "Something is rotten in the state of Denmark" (90).

I.v

The Ghost at last reveals to Hamlet and to us the true story of the death of Hamlet's father, and Hamlet's instinctive dislike of his uncle is now justified. He swears to carry out the revenge the Ghost asks for, and the Ghost reinforces his impulse—natural in a man of his temperament—to live by the very highest standards of conduct, standards that allow no compromise with the weaknesses of human nature or the imperfections of the world. The uncompromising morality of the Ghost and of Hamlet is as extreme in its way as is the worldliness of Claudius and Polonius in its acceptance of the need to compromise with men's frailties.

When Hamlet's friends catch up with him, his sensitive nature has been deeply disturbed by the shocking revelations he has just heard; he is on the edge of hysterics, as we know from the hectic quality of such speeches as 121-24 and 126-32. When Hamlet calms down a little, he explains to Horatio that hereafter he may "put an antic disposition on" (172). This is important. It tells us that Hamlet's "wild and whirling words" (133) in later scenes are a deliberate pretense, the acting out of the role of the melancholy madman familiar to Elizabethans (compare Burton's *Anatomy of Melancholy*). But though Hamlet is always acting this role and is never truly mad, it nonetheless allows him to express real feelings he could otherwise not express, as he has already pointed out (45-159). Hamlet is radically out of accord with the ways of the world and often nearly beside himself with distress at what he sees. "Let me not think on't" (45.146) is a cry from the heart; life pains him almost beyond endurance. But he is, as he himself puts it, "but mad north-northwest: when the wind is southerly I know a hawk from a handsaw" (83.387-88). Hamlet pretends to be melancholy mad and is never truly so, but, though his bitterness never destroys his essential sanity, he is so painfully outraged by the world that he often feels as bitter as the melancholy madman says he is.

II.i

Six or eight weeks elapse between Acts I and II, but the play deliberately fails to emphasize that fact because it wants the parallel between I.v and II.i to be as striking as possible. Hamlet's discovery of the profound evil implicit in Claudius' subtle worldliness and Hamlet's consequent determination to follow at any cost the advice of his true father, the Ghost

(59.22-25), and to resist to the death the attitude toward life of his false uncle-father, Claudius (43.92-108), is thus followed immediately by a scene in which a second and even more obvious example of worldliness is displayed by Polonius, the cunning, though in his way loving, father of Laertes, in his scheme for managing the education of his son. The contrast between this scene and preceding one is maximized by the continuity of the action on the curtainless Elizabethan stage.

Polonius' scheming is interrupted by Ophelia with her report of Hamlet's strange behavior during an offstage scene in which Hamlet has taken mute, sad leave of the girl he loves and does not wish to involve in the dangerous course his promise to the Ghost has committed him to. With his usual self-confidence, Polonius pronounces Hamlet mad from frustrated love. He is as wrong in this conventional diagnosis as he is confident of his rightness ("Hath there been such a time . . ./That I have positively said ' 'Tis so,'/When it proved otherwise?", 75.153-55). Hamlet quickly discovers that this is Polonius' theory and, in order to conceal the truth, takes advantage of every opportunity to encourage Polonius to believe it.

II.ii

Just as Polonius has a clever plan for managing Laertes' life, so, we now discover, Claudius has one for managing Hamlet's; he has brought a pair of Hamlet's casual acquaintances from the university, two conventional young men, to pump Hamlet. We then see the ambassadors reporting the success of their embassy to Norway and hear Polonius' amusingly long-winded exposition of his theory of Hamlet's madness. The King and Polonius agree to test this theory, and suddenly Hamlet is upon them. Polonius, in his ill-advised self-confidence, undertakes to "board" (170) Hamlet, and under the guise of his antic disposition, Hamlet thoroughly insults him and, at the same time, encourages him to believe Hamlet is mad for love of Ophelia ("How say you by that? Still harping on my daughter," Polonius says with satisfaction, 188-89).

Hamlet also manages to suggest, with his mad eloquence, his extreme horror of the world in general and of sex in particular. "For if the sun breed maggots in a dead dog, being a good kissing carrion——Have you a daughter?" (181-83). The notion that the sun bred maggots in carrion is good Elizabethan science (compare *Antony and Cleopatra*, 94.30-33).

THE TRAGEDY OF HAMLET 115

Hamlet does not need to finish this sentence; its obvious conclusion is that the son and heir to the crown of Denmark is equally likely to breed something as disgusting as maggots—that is, children—in the momentarily attractive but mortal flesh of Ophelia ("let her [my lady] paint an inch thick, to this favor she must come" he later says, looking at a skull, 155.195-96). Conception of children will be no blessing for Ophelia, whatever the adage says about the value of mental conception—nor, in Hamlet's estimation, for any woman, since to him men are so vile that the race ought to be brought to an end, a result that might be achieved if all women got them to nunneries and ceased being breeders of sinners (95.121-22).

With this tedious old fool, as Hamlet calls Polonius, thus disposed of, Hamlet turns to the tedious young fools Rosencrantz and Guildenstern. He quickly sees through their game and realizes that they have another conventional theory of his madness—ambition; he sets to work to encourage them in this mistaken belief as he had encouraged Polonius in his. Plain examples of this encouragement are 101.95-97 and 110.351-52; Rosencrantz suggests Hamlet's trouble is ambition at 256-57.

This passage is followed by the arrival of the players (see the preceding Introduction) and the Player's recitation of the slightly old-fashioned but beautiful tragic speech about Hecuba that sets off Hamlet's second soliloquy. Its description of the death of a king and the grief of his queen has an obvious relevance to the story of Hamlet. In the soliloquy that follows, Hamlet contrasts the almost miraculously complete physical expression of the Player's merely imagined grief with his own inability to act—to say nothing of acting on—his own real grief. He calls himself (560) a "rogue" (that is, a vagrant) and "peasant slave" (that is, a man without the nobility to respond to the demands of honor); he even begins to think he must be a coward. Then, hearing his own conventional "rant" (as he will later call it, 159.286), he turns on himself with characteristic scorn for the inadequacy to his real feelings of these conventional complaints (594-99). Finally, more calmly, he works out an ingenious plan for trapping the King into exposing himself (600-17). This plan is necessary because, as Hamlet points out (610-15), the Devil frequently disguises himself as the spirit of a much-loved person and persuades a man to damn himself (compare 56.69-74).

III.i

This scene occurs the day after the events of the previous scene (see 88.546-47). But again we are not reminded of this gap in time, and see Claudius about to put into effect his ingenious scheme for trapping Hamlet immediately after we have heard Hamlet planning his scheme for trapping Claudius. Just as Hamlet appears, Polonius accidentally forces the King to speak an aside that, for the first time, reveals to us what he feels (49-54). It shows us not only that the King is indeed guilty but that he is suffering for his guilt. Our interest in this dramatic revelation is abruptly suspended when Hamlet begins his most powerful soliloquy. Its tone is weary, as if Hamlet had been going over these arguments endlessly. Indeed, we know he has; they are essentially the arguments of his first soliloquy (44.129-59), that the world is drearily evil, that no man with any sense would continue to exist were it not that the next world might be worse. With acute but unamused irony Hamlet concludes by noting that even the act necessary to end the need for all other acts has been frustrated by his own insight into his situation.

Hamlet emerges from this profoundly depressing meditation to find Ophelia before him. She goes through her pathetic little act as her father has ordered her to, and Hamlet, pained to think that if the world is hopelessly evil, Ophelia, whom he loves, must be too, bursts out in rage against the world and particularly women. In modern productions it is common to have Polonius reveal himself during this scene and thus to motivate Hamlet's outburst to Ophelia as really an attack on Polonius. To do so is both crude and unnecessary. Hamlet has a better reason than the knowledge that Polonius and the King are listening for speaking as he does, namely, his horror of human experience itself. It has, as he truly says, "made [him] mad" (149), in the sense of driving him to a despair such that he truly believes life were better brought to an end.

Claudius, the only man in the play intellectually capable of dealing on equal terms with Hamlet, sees at once that both Polonius' theory of frustrated love and Rosencrantz' of ambition are inadequate (165-67). He at once suspects Hamlet knows something that endangers the King's life, and with a promptness in decision as striking (and, in the end, as ineffectual) as Hamlet's delays, he determines to send Hamlet to England and, as we soon learn (129.58-65), to his death.

III.ii

This scene takes place the evening of the same day. It begins by reminding us of the play Hamlet has planned. Hamlet then arranges to have Horatio help him watch the King's reaction to the performance, and the guests arrive. Hamlet puts on his antic disposition, and his first "idle" (92) remark is calculated to encourage the theory that he suffers from frustrated ambition. It puns on air/heir (96), and says in effect, "I am fed with promises of being your heir; but promises are mere words, so much air; only chameleons can live on air (this was a common Elizabethan idea); if you tried to fatten capons for slaughter with air, you would fail, as you will fail in trying to fatten me for slaughter with your promises of making me your heir." Claudius did in fact specifically promise to make Hamlet his heir at 44.108-12. Hamlet's words here sound wild and whirling to everyone but the King. Next, Hamlet is attentive to Ophelia in a way that confirms Polonius in his theory that Hamlet is mad from frustrated love ("O ho! Do you mark that?" 114).

The play is then performed, the King finds it unendurable and leaves abruptly, and Hamlet becomes almost hysterically excited at this confirmation of his suspicions. In this mood he is—beneath the disguise of his antic disposition ("my wit's diseased," 328-29)—brutal to poor Rosencrantz and Guildenstern when they bring him Gertrude's message, and also to Polonius when he repeats this message.

III.iii

This scene follows without pause. The King is in his private apartments. Polonius passes through on his way to the Queen's apartment, and when he leaves, the curiosity roused by the King's brief aside at 93.49-54 is finally satisfied by a soliloquy that fully reveals the King's guilty suffering. As the King prays, Hamlet passes through on his way to his mother's apartment. He is tempted to kill the King but desists for just the kind of subtle reason that would appeal to him, it is impossible to doubt the sincerity of his conduct here.

III.iv

When Hamlet joins his mother, she begins with her usual lack of understanding by tactlessly saying, "Hamlet, thou hast thy father [that is, Claudius] much offended" (10). Deeply offended himself at hearing Gertrude call Claudius his father, Hamlet replies rudely, "Mother, you have *my* father much offended" (11), and almost immediately adds, even more rudely, that she is "the Queen, your husband's brother's wife,/ And, would it were not so, you are my mother" (16-17). Gertrude mistakes Hamlet's bluntness for madness, and when he roughly thrusts her into a chair (19), she panics and cries out for help. Polonius, who can never keep quiet, cries out too, only to find that "to be too busy is some danger" (34), for Hamlet, assuming he is the King, whips out his sword and strikes through the arras. "A bloody deed—almost as bad, good Mother,/ As kill a king, and marry with his brother" (29-30). Hamlet is deliberately testing the Queen to find out if she knows about the murder. Her shocked astonishment at the question makes her innocence clear. Hamlet then goes on to try to make Gertrude share his horror of her sexual relations with Claudius. She is quickly persuaded, but Hamlet, once launched on this subject, cannot stop himself (92-102), and the Ghost intervenes. Since the Queen cannot see the Ghost, Hamlet's conversation with him convinces her once more that he is mad and he has to persuade her all over again of his sanity. She then agrees to side with him, as she does throughout the rest of the action.

The scene ends with Hamlet dragging Polonius' corpse offstage with a series of those almost magically brilliant remarks that express his feelings about life. Who but Hamlet, with his sensitive, fascinated horror of mortality, could have called what he was doing "lug[ging] the guts into the neighbor room" (213) or sardonically addressed Polonius' corpse with, "Come, sir, to draw toward an end with you" (217).

IV.i

The next four brief scenes occur without any break in time. In this one Gertrude reports to Claudius what Hamlet has done without revealing to Claudius Hamlet's secret.

IV.ii

Here we see Hamlet playing his antic role for Rosencrantz and Guildenstern.

IV.iii

Here Hamlet is brought before the King; he is still playing the antic, which allows him to express once more his horror

THE TRAGEDY OF HAMLET 119

of mortality ("But if indeed you find him not within this month, you shall nose him as you go up the stairs into the lobby," 35-37), and, incidentally, to talk in a way Claudius alone understands about how kings must, like all men, die (23-25).

IV.iv

Hamlet is now on his way to the ship to sail for England. He meets a captain of Fortinbras' army crossing Denmark to attack Poland, and the thought of this gallant, gratuitous attack once more drives him to anguished contemplation of his own failure to act as an heroic prince should.

IV.v

Enough time passes between scenes iv and v for the news of Polonius' death to reach Laertes in France and for Laertes to return to Denmark. During that time Ophelia, having endured the strain of her unhappy love for Hamlet, has broken under the further strain of learning that he has killed her father and that her father has been buried in haste, as if his death were somehow shameful. Claudius explains this carefully (75-86) and then tells Gertrude, and us, of Laertes' dangerous response to the news of Polonius' death, and Laertes arrives, intent on his revenge. "To hell allegiance, vows to the blackest devil,/Conscience and grace to the profoundest pit!/I dare damnation," he says (131-33). The egotistical lack of insight of this attitude and its immorality are in striking contrast to Hamlet's earlier response to similar news. Claudius meets Laertes with great courage; he knows well enough that the "divinity doth hedge a king" (123) will not protect a man who has murdered his own king; he has to depend entirely on his own courage. When he has almost calmed Laertes, Ophelia appears again and upsets Laertes once more.

IV.vi

This brief scene interrupts Claudius and Laertes just long enough to let the audience know that Hamlet is returning.

IV.vii

Here the King completes with his customary skill the work

of persuading Laertes to murder Hamlet. He flatters Laertes crudely ("Can you devise me?" he asks when Hamlet's letter arrives, 53); it works: a moment later, when he asks "Will you be ruled by me?" (59), Laertes is happy to be. They then make their plan for murdering Hamlet, and the scene ends with Gertrude's report of Ophelia's death.

V.i

Enough time passes between IV.vii and V.i for Hamlet to get back to Denmark. Since his ship had been two days at sea when the pirates attacked (141.15-16), we can assume Hamlet has been out of Denmark about four days. The scene opens with the wonderful and relevant comedy of the gravediggers, with their paradoxical complaint against the privileges of the great, the "count'nance [they have] in this world to drown or hang themselves more than their even-Christen" (28-30). With characteristic extravagance, Hamlet canvasses the effects of death on human ambitions. His thoughts are governed by his disgust with death, his vivid sense of rottenness and stench ("And smelt so? Pah!" 202). He is interrupted by Ophelia's funeral. He is deeply shaken by Ophelia's death, and as he listens to Laertes' extravagant but conventional expressions of his grief, he cannot control himself. He steps forward to try to express his feelings, only to be brought up in ironic self-scorn as he hears himself ranting like Laertes (285-86).

V.ii

This scene follows almost immediately on the previous one. Hamlet is seizing the first opportunity to relate the events of his abortive sea journey to Horatio and us. The experience has shown him that his worst suspicions of Claudius are the only safe guides in dealing with him. Even the usually calm Horatio is badly shaken to learn what Claudius has tried to do (25, 28). Hamlet's narrative is followed by Osric's report of the King's proposal of a fencing match. (Do not attempt to work out the betting odds described by Osric; they are incomprehensible; all we need to know is that the odds are on Hamlet as supposedly the less skillful fencer.) Osric gives the play yet another example of young manhood, the most absurd one we see. He illustrates what the fool makes of the refinement of manners that Hamlet, with his intelligence and sensitivity, makes so attractive (see 96.156).

Hamlet is changed since his voyage. His mood is neither

that expressed in the hopeless brooding of the play's early soliloquies (44.129-59; 93.56-88) nor the almost hysterical excitement that is his alternate mood there. He has now achieved the stoic calm of Horatio and can "defy augury" (220) in the conviction that "the readiness is all" (225), that true moral courage consists in accepting, without either despair or optimism, what life brings.

When people arrive for the fencing match, Hamlet apologizes handsomely to Laertes (who receives the apology rather coldly), and the fencing begins. Properly performed, this is an intensely exciting scene: no one moves except the two skilled fencers; nothing is heard except the shuffle of their feet and the clash of their rapiers, until Hamlet—suddenly and surprisingly—scores a touch and claims it by saying, "One" (281). The King tries to get him to drink from the poisoned cup but he refuses. He and Laertes then fence a second bout, and again Hamlet scores. His mother is so pleased that she innocently drinks his health from the poisoned cup. The carefully laid plot of Claudius and Laertes has now gone seriously wrong: Laertes appears unable to touch Hamlet with the unbated and poisoned rapier, and only minutes remain before they will be exposed by the Queen's collapse. In the pause after the third bout, then, Laertes dishonorably stabs a defenseless Hamlet. Grasping the situation in a flash and moving swiftly, Hamlet snatches Laertes' rapier which he now knows is unbated (though he does not yet know it is poisoned), tosses Laertes his rapier so that Laertes, unlike him, can defend himself, and then scores yet another touch. As Laertes is wounded as fatally as Hamlet already has been, the Queen collapses, realizing as she does so that she has been poisoned. Again Hamlet moves like lightning, now against the King; as the dying Laertes confesses the whole of the plot, Hamlet forces the King to drink from the poisoned cup after wounding him too with the poisoned rapier. When the King and Laertes are dead, Hamlet turns to Horatio and asks him to tell the true story of his life to the world. It is a princely request, for reputation meant nearly everything to a renaissance prince (compare *Love's Labor's Lost*, 37.1-7). Nor does he forget his public responsibilities; almost with his dying words he speaks for Fortinbras as his successor on the throne he has held with such effectiveness for the few minutes since Claudius' death. Fortinbras arrives as Hamlet dies, claims the throne, and is supported by Horatio; and Hamlet, who "was likely . . . /To have proved most royal" had he lived (174.398-99), is carried off to the slow booming of a

122　TEACHING SHAKESPEARE

peal of ordinance, the solemn "soldier's music" (400) he has at last earned.

ARTHUR MIZENER

SHORT-ANSWER QUESTIONS

1. The first speaker in the play is Barnardo; what is he doing when the play begins? (33.6-8)

2. At what time of day does the Ghost make its first appearance? (33.7)

3. Why does the Ghost not answer Horatio when he questions it? (39.147-56)

4. What is unusual about the circumstances of Danish life at the opening of the play? (36.71-79)

5. Explain why Claudius sends Cornelius and Voltemand as ambassadors to Norway. (41.27-35)

6. Explain Hamlet's reply to the King, "Not so, my lord. I am too much in the sun." (42.67)

7. How soon after they have seen the Ghost do the watchers report to Hamlet? (40.169-75; 46.189)

8. What is Laertes' advice to Ophelia about Hamlet? (49.5-9)

9. What comparison is Hamlet using when he describes the Ghost's wandering by saying, "the sepulcher/Wherein we saw thee quietly interred/Hath oped his ponderous and marble jaws/To cast thee up again"? (56.48-51)

10. Summarize the Ghost's description of the murder. (60.59-73)

11. What does Hamlet write in his notebook after his conversation with the Ghost? (61.107-09)

THE TRAGEDY OF HAMLET 123

12. What was unusual about Hamlet's appearance when he visited Ophelia in her "closet" on the occasion she describes to her father? (68.75-100)

13. What is Polonius' diagnosis of the illness that caused Hamlet to behave so strangely when he came to see Ophelia? (69.102-06)

14. When Rosencrantz and Guildenstern arrive, the King says to them, "What it should be,/ More than his father's death, that thus hath put him [Hamlet]/ So much from th' understanding of himself,/ I cannot dream of" (70.7-10); is this true?

15. What report do Voltemand and Cornelius bring back from Norway? (72.60-80)

16. The letter from Hamlet to Ophelia that Polonius reads to the King and Queen ends, "Thine evermore, most dear lady, whilst this machine is to him" (74.123-24). What does "whilst this machine is to him" mean?

17. What is Hamlet's purpose in talking to Polonius about the sun's breeding maggots in a dead dog? (76.181)

18. When Rosencrantz says it must be ambition that makes Hamlet think Denmark a prison, what does Hamlet say? (78.256-60)

19. Hamlet says to Rosencrantz and Guildenstern about their coming to see him, "I will tell you why; so shall my anticipation prevent your discovery" (80.301-02). What does this last phrase mean?

20. Why is the company of players traveling about instead of staying in the city? (81.338-52)

21. What incident is described in the speech Hamlet persuades the Player to recite? (85.457-60)

22. Hamlet tells Polonius that he ought not to treat the players according to their deserts but "much better"; that is, according to what? (88.542)

23. The King and Polonius have secretly arranged the first

meeting between Hamlet and Ophelia that we see (92.28-37); why?

24. In the soliloquy that begins "To be, or not to be," Hamlet is convinced that to kill himself is too risky. Why? (93.66-69)

25. Why does Hamlet urge Ophelia to "Get thee to a nunnery"? (95.122-23)

26. When Hamlet is attacking marriage, he says, "Those that are married already—all but one—shall live. The rest shall keep as they are" (96.150-52). But the logical point is not who shall live but who shall be married. Why does Hamlet say "live"?

27. Who is the one who shall not live in the previous question's quotation?

28. What is, according to Hamlet, the purpose of drama? (98.21-25)

29. What does Hamlet most admire about Horatio's character? (100.67-70)

30. When the company arrives to watch the play, Hamlet manages to hint that the cause of his madness is both ambition (Rosecrantz and Guildenstern's theory) and love (Polonius' theory). How does he do so? (101.95-97; 101.111-13)

31. How long has Hamlet's father been dead when Hamlet and Ophelia discuss the matter just before the play begins? (102.129-32)

32. What does Queen Gertrude think about the play? (106.235-36)

33. What is the name of the play? (106.243) *Nick name*

34. Why is the play named as it is? (106.243)

35. Hamlet insists that Rosencrantz and Guildenstern play the recorders, even when they protest they do not know how; why? (111.371-80)

THE TRAGEDY OF HAMLET 125

36. Claudius says his offense "hath the primal eldest curse upon't" (114.37). What curse is that?

37. Why does Hamlet not kill the King when he finds him praying? (115.73-95)

38. Why did Hamlet strike instantly at the figure behind the arras in his mother's room? (117.32-33)

39. What reasons does the Ghost give Hamlet for his second appearance? (120.111-14)

40. When Hamlet is on the way to the ship that is to take him to England, he meets a captain from Fortinbras' army; where is that army going? (130.12; 130.18-20)

41. What does Hamlet think of the purpose of Fortinbras and his army? (132.60-65)

42. How is it that Hamlet is the only man captured by the pirates when they attack the ship that is carrying him to England? (141.17-21)

43. Why does the King decide he must persuade Laertes to murder Hamlet? (144.57-59)

44. What plans have the King and Laertes for killing Hamlet? (146.136-62)

45. Who was Yorick, whose skull the gravedigger shows Hamlet? (155.181-82)

46. Why is Ophelia's funeral so brief and unceremonious? (156.229-32)

47. What finally happens to Rosencrantz and Guildenstern? (161.44-47)

48. How many hits does Hamlet score against Laertes in their fencing match? (170.281; 170.286)

49. How does Hamlet kill the King? (171.323-28)

50. What does Horatio plan to do when he knows Hamlet is dying? (172.341-43)

QUESTIONS FOR DISCUSSION

1. In what ways are the situations of Hamlet and Laertes alike? How do these two young men differ in their reactions to the similar situations in which they find themselves?

2. Hamlet calls himself and the King "mighty opposites" (162.62); discuss the ways in which they are "opposites."

3. In the King's soliloquy (114.36-72), when we can safely assume he is telling the truth, he gives three reasons why he has acted as he has; these are his desires for "my crown, mine own ambition, and my queen." Discuss the ways these desires fit the King's character.

4. Hamlet is bitterly disillusioned about women: "Frailty, thy name is woman," he says (45.146). Discuss the extent to which his mother's "o'er hasty marriage" to Claudius is responsible for this feeling.

5. Hamlet is dominated throughout the play by a desire "not to be"; he expresses that desire in both the famous soliloquy in which the phrase occurs (93.56-88) and in his first soliloquy (44.129-59). Discuss the reasons he gives for feeling this way.

6. Polonius advises Laertes, Ophelia (51.58-135), Reynaldo (65.7-68), and the King and Queen (73.92-151). Select one or two of these occasions and discuss what they show about Polonius' opinions of life.

7. Polonius is very self-confident (see 75.153-55); yet he is almost invariably wrong about Hamlet. Discuss the reasons he is.

8. Hamlet greatly admires Horatio and tells him why

THE TRAGEDY OF HAMLET 127

(99.56-76). Discuss the aspects of Hamlet's own character that make him admire Horatio for being as he is.

9. Whenever Hamlet thinks about life in general, his mind turns to thoughts of rank gardens, sickening diseases, decaying corpses (for example, 44.129-59 and 151.76-218). Select one or two examples of this habit of mind and discuss them in such a way as to show why Hamlet feels as he does about life.

10. When the Player reminds Hamlet of his inability to express his grief, he finds his trouble so inexplicable that he even suggests he may be a coward (88.560-91). That is not the trouble with him; discuss what is.

SAMPLE TEST

I. (30 minutes)

Write a well-organized essay on ONE of the following subjects.

1. Hamlet is dominated throughout the play by a desire "not to be"; he expresses that desire in both the famous soliloquy in which the phrase occurs (93.56-88) and in his first soliloquy (44.129-59). Discuss the reasons he gives for feeling this way.

2. Hamlet greatly admires Horatio and tells him why (99.56-76). Discuss the aspects of Hamlet's own character that make him admire Horatio for being as he is.

II. (30 minutes)

Write briefly on FIVE of the following.

1. Explain why Claudius sends Cornelius and Voltemand as ambassadors to Norway.

2. Explain Hamlet's reply to the King, "Not so, my lord. I am too much in the sun."

3. What is Hamlet's purpose in talking to Polonius about the sun's breeding maggots in a dead dog?

4. Why is the company of players traveling about instead of staying in the city?

5. In the soliloquy that begins "To be, or not to be," Hamlet is convinced that to kill himself is too risky. Why?

6. What plans have the King and Laertes for killing Hamlet?

7. How does Hamlet kill the King?

THE TRAGEDY OF ROMEO AND JULIET

INTRODUCTION

Shakespeare's lyric tragedy *Romeo and Juliet* was his first great popular success and, although it clearly does not rank with the tragedies of his later career, it remains the world's most famous love story and its protagonists have become the very archetypes of young lovers. Separated by chance, by quarreling families, even by their own rashness, they have, as lovers, been transmuted by Shakespeare into something more enduring than the pure gold of the statues their grieving fathers vowed to erect in their honor.

The play has often been called a tragedy of fate. Its hero and heroine are "A pair of star-crossed lovers" (41.6). Before entering Juliet's home for the first time, Romeo experiences a sudden premonition of disaster, "Some consequence yet hanging in the stars" (64.107), and later, when his joy has so quickly been overtaken by disaster, he cries out, "O, I am fortune's fool!" (103.138). Juliet, too, senses some kind of impending evil, even in the happiness of the balcony scene, and says of their love, "It is too rash, too unadvised, too sudden" (78.118). However, in spite of the many references to fortune and the stars, the play is not truly a tragedy of fate. The fate which operates in it is more chance or plain bad luck than the ordained workings of a controlling destiny. It is by chance that Romeo learns of the Capulet feast; it is by chance that neither he nor Juliet discovers the other's identity until after they have met and fallen in love; it is by chance that Romeo's well-intentioned interference with Mercutio and Tybalt brings about the death of his friend; it is by chance that Friar Lawrence's letter does not reach Romeo, that the Friar does not precede Romeo to the Capulet tomb. There is no denying that chance is important in this play, more crucial than in any of the later and greater tragedies.

But if chance were the only controlling force, we might well have a melodrama, not a tragedy. Shakespeare may have intended to write a tragedy of fate, but he very nearly wrote a tragedy of character. Romeo's impulsiveness, his rashness, is the quality which makes him able to love Juliet at once, deeply, completely, at their first meeting. It is the same quality which makes him accept Balthasar's report of her "death" at once, completely, without hesitation. "Is it e'en so? Then I defy you, stars!" (145.24). And so he returns to Verona, not to seek out Friar Lawrence with questions, but to go to the Capulet tomb to lie with Juliet. The rashness of the lovers does not seem out of place in Verona, a hot and sultry city where young men may gaily crash a party or suddenly and grimly die in the streets. Their love springs from the same soil that nurtured the family feud.

It is easy, however, to exaggerate the importance of the feud. True, the Prologue warns us of the "ancient grudge" (41.3), and Escalus, at the end, seems to place the ultimate responsibility for the tragedy on the hatred of the parents (158.292). But there is much evidence that the quarrel was being kept alive by such people as the servants and the vindictive Tybalt. After the opening street brawl, both Montague and Capulet accept the Prince's warning without grumbling; Capulet has no objection to Romeo's presence at his feast; Romeo's good friend Mercutio was a guest of the Capulets; before meeting Juliet, Romeo fancied himself in love with Rosaline, a niece of Capulet; and when he speaks of the street quarrel, he seems bored, as though it is an old and dull story: "What fray was here?/Yet tell me not, for I have heard it all" (49.176-77). It is ironic that a feud, apparently so nearly ripe for settling, had to be settled at so terrible a cost.

The conflict between the families is, nevertheless, of major importance in the environment in which Romeo and Juliet live. The conflict between the generations is also part of this environment and is shown most dramatically in the Capulet household. Juliet, who at first seems like an attractive, obedient youngster, is transformed by the intensity of her love into a young woman who takes the responsibility for her own actions. She is forced into this responsibility since she cannot turn to her parents for help and even the Nurse ultimately fails her. When Capulet berates her for refusing to marry Paris, his fury appalls his wife and the Nurse, but it is clear that they will or can do nothing to protect Juliet. Lady Capulet's "I would the fool were married to her grave!" (123.141) is as heartless as his threat: "And you be not, hang, beg, starve, die in the streets,/For, by my soul, I'll ne'er acknowledge thee,/Nor what is mine shall never do thee good" (125.194-96). And the Nurse's advice to Juliet that she forget Romeo and marry Paris is perhaps even more cruel, since she is the only one of the three who knows of Juliet's marriage. She knows of the marriage, but she understands nothing of the quality of Juliet's love. We have no scenes showing Romeo with his parents, but their inability to understand him is suggested in their conversation with Benvolio in the first act. The one adult both Romeo and Juliet turn to is Friar Lawrence, and he does help them, though not because he fully sympathizes with their love, but because he hopes to end the family feud. His wise, calm reason is not always welcome, as when Romeo tells him, "Thou can'st not speak of that thou dost not feel" (113.64). He goes on with the eternal protest of youth to age, "Wert thou as young as I . . ." (65). We should notice, though, that it is not only the older generation that fails to understand Romeo and Juliet's love. Romeo's friends, even the quick and responsive Mercutio, do not perceive the reason for the change in Romeo after he has met and fallen in love with Juliet. The isolation of the young lovers grows from their first meeting, when for a few moments they are alone in the midst of a crowd, to the scene when Juliet, utterly alone, takes the potion, and then to the final scene in the tomb, where they are again alone in the midst of the crowd that gathers to hear the explanation of their death.

If their elders and their friends failed Romeo and Juliet, perhaps it was simply that there was not enough time. Time as the enemy of love is a theme found both here and in the Sonnets, probably written about the same time. One of the major changes Shakespeare made in the story he took from Arthur Brooke's *Tragicall Historye of Romeus and Juliet* was to compress the action from months to days. The action begins on Sunday with the street brawl, the Capulet party, and the first meeting of Romeo and Juliet. On Monday, Romeo and Juliet are married, Tybalt and Mercutio killed, and Romeo is banished. On Tuesday, Romeo and Juliet part after their one night together, Juliet's wedding to Paris is planned, and she drinks the potion. On Wednesday morning, she is discovered, presumably dead; and on Thursday night, Romeo returns to Verona to join Juliet in the tomb. The headlong pace is reinforced by the excitement and tension of many of the scenes, the impatience of Juliet as she waits for word from Romeo, the quick wit of Mercutio, the quick tempers of Tybalt and Capulet, the busy movements of the servants, and, as is characteristic of Shakespeare, in the metaphorical language. In the balcony scene, Juliet likens their love to the lightning (78.118-20), and in the tomb Romeo refers to "A lightning before death" (151.90). The Friar uses another image suggesting swiftness and danger when he says, "These violent delights have violent ends/And in their triumph die, like fire and powder,/Which, as they kiss, consume" (96.9-11). The reckless, breathless pace should not be ignored while the students spend more time reading and examining the play than Romeo and Juliet did in living it.

Lightning and gunpowder are only two of the many images of light that run throughout the play, beginning with Romeo's first glimpse of Juliet when her beauty suggests the warmth and brilliance of the torch (67.46). To him, she is the sun rising in the East (74.3), and "The brightness of her cheek would shame those stars/As daylight doth a lamp; her eyes in heaven/Would through the airy region stream so bright/That birds would sing and think it were not night" (74.19-22). To Juliet, Romeo is "day in night;/For thou wilt lie upon the wings of night/Whiter than new snow upon a raven's back" (106.17-19). Caroline Spurgeon has pointed out in her study of Shakespeare's imagery that this controlling image of light suggests that Shakespeare saw the love of Romeo and Juliet as a swift and brilliant light illuminating a dark world for a few moments before it was extinguished.

Close attention to the language of the play can be one of the most stimulating aspects of reading *Romeo and Juliet*, even for students who may have known little of Shakespeare before this. There is both good and bad poetry to compare here; there is rich evidence of the fun Shakespeare took in playing with words, in the puns, the riddles, the sonnet-dialogue of Romeo and Juliet's first meeting; there is the affectation of Romeo's early dialogue, bad poetry, but psychologically right for the self-conscious young poseur; there is the language of the balcony scene, the scene of parting, the death scenes, where the metaphors are not mere decoration but the unconscious, lyric expression of honest emotion. Students can see how the light imagery, for example, is not ornamentation but the means by which Shakespeare creates a mood, reveals his characters, and, consciously or not, also reveals his own attitude toward his subject. By close and imaginative reading of particular passages such as the pivotal scene in which Mercutio and Tybalt die, they can discover something of Shakespeare's ability to create character and action in dramatic dialogue.

Romeo and Juliet is a young man's play about young love.

That young people have always responded to it is indicated by the condition of the First Folio, chained to the shelves of the Bodelian Library in Oxford. Its pages show more wear than those of any other play, and the pages of the balcony scene show the greatest evidence of having been turned and re-turned. The play is as moving an experience today as it was then.

THE ACTION

The Prologue

Romeo and Juliet is one of the few plays in which Shakespeare uses a formal prologue, spoken by an actor designated as Chorus, to announce the subject matter of the drama. In sonnet form, the Prologue introduces the theme of fate in the famous reference to "A pair of star-crossed lovers" (6); the family feud in the references to "ancient grudge" (3), "parents' strife" (8), and "parents' rage" (10); and the tragic end in reference to "their death-marked love" (9). The setting is also announced, "In fair Verona" (2). The several references to parents and children suggest one of the basic conflicts in the play, one which all students will understand even if they have difficulty with the language. Since this is one of the few Shakespearean tragedies in which the protagonist is not a king, a prince, a general, whose rise and fall are directly involved with the welfare and stability of the state, perhaps Shakespeare used the Prologue to suggest a seriousness the story would not automatically have commanded. Romeo and Juliet were not just two attractive young people whose love affair ended badly. They came of families of great dignity, whose affairs did affect the welfare of the entire city. What is more, the fact that the tragic outcome had been written in the stars might have suggested that this was more than just a pathetic story.

I.i

In this introductory scene, we meet some of the principal characters and see, almost at once, how easily the peace can be broken by the Montagues and Capulets. In the opening dialogue between Sampson and Gregory, two servants of the house of Capulet, we learn of the family quarrel even before the two Montague servants enter. Students should notice that the servants, as they usually do in Shakespeare's other plays, speak in prose; the blank verse begins with the arrival of their betters, Benvolio and Tybalt. With a succession of puns, most of them bawdy, a quarrel erupts, first with words, then with gestures, then with weapons. Displaying a certain caution, or perhaps comic cowardice, Sampson does not draw his sword until Benvolio arrives. He may be thinking that his superior will take any legal responsibility for the fray. Benvolio, Romeo's cousin, sensibly tries to quiet the brawling servants, but the fiery Tybalt, Juliet's cousin, arrives, eager to fight; he hates the very word "peace" (72). The elder Capulets and Montagues also appear, both men ready to join the quarrel. Lady Capulet's rather scornful advice that her husband wield a crutch instead of a sword probably suggests a great difference in their ages. This opening quarrel, of course, highlights the family feud, which is of prime importance in the play. It also serves the practical purpose of gaining the attention of what in Shakespeare's day was probably a very noisy audience. Almost everyone will stop in his tracks to watch a fight.

Escalus, Prince of Verona, arrives on the scene and quiets the quarreling foes. He has reached the end of his patience with both families, who have three times caused open breaches of the peace, and announces that if either fights in the streets again, their lives will be forfeit. Students should notice too that the citizens who gather, attracted by the fight, seem disgusted with the feud, crying with complete impartiality, "Down with the Capulets! Down with the Montagues!" (76-77).

The second part of the scene introduces Romeo, a lovesick young man. We hear about him first from Benvolio in a conversation with Lord and Lady Montague. Notice Lady Montague's maternal relief that her son was not involved in the street quarrel. We learn that Romeo has been behaving strangely, keeping to himself, sighing and weeping, avoiding the daylight hours, and his parents ask Benvolio to find out the cause of his unnatural behavior. In the conversation between Romeo and Benvolio, we see a young man not truly in love but in love with the idea of love. His sighs and groans, his extravagant paradoxes—"O brawling love, O loving hate" (179)—are in sharp contrast to his language in scene v when he meets Juliet and knows at once what real love is. Benvolio again shows himself a young man of good will and common sense.

I.ii

We move now from the Montagues to the Capulets. The scene begins in the midst of a conversation between Lord Capulet and the County Paris, a young nobleman, relative of the Prince. They have evidently been talking about the Prince's order to stop fighting and Paris' request to marry Juliet. Capulet sounds as though he is not reluctant to keep the peace and speaks gently of his daughter, "the hopeful lady of my earth" (15). He tells Paris that Juliet is too young for marriage (8-11) and that, in any case, she will marry the man of her own choice; "My will to her consent is but a part" (17). Students should remember his comments and attitude when they come to Act III and see his anger at Juliet's refusal to marry Paris. Capulet is obviously pleased by Paris' suit and invites him to the party he is giving that evening, suggesting that he compare Juliet with the other young women who will be there.

The servant who is sent out with a list of guests to be invited to the feast cannot read and, by chance, meets Romeo and Benvolio to whom he appeals for help. When Romeo sees the name of his fair Rosaline, Capulet's niece, among the guests, he is quite willing to accept Benvolio's suggestion that they too attend the party, although he is sure that his friend is speaking nonsense when he says that he will see some other lady there whose beauty will outshine Rosaline's. Thus the first meeting of Romeo and Juliet will occur quite by chance, the accidental meeting of Romeo and the illiterate servant.

I.iii

This scene introduces Juliet, her mother, and the Nurse. If Romeo impresses us at first as a rather foolish, moon-struck young man, Juliet seems like a docile child. She comes when she is called, speaks scarcely more than half a dozen lines, and when her mother asks her about marriage, she answers, "It is an honor that I dream not of" (66). After Lady Capulet has told her to pay particular attention to Paris at the party that night, Juliet agrees, obediently saying that her interest in him will be limited by her mother's consent. Her lack of excited interest in the subject of love contrasts sharply with that of Romeo, who thinks of little else although he does not know that he has not yet experienced it.

The Nurse, garrulous and earthy, easily takes part in the family conversation; in fact, she very nearly dominates it. She has taken care of Juliet since her birth almost fourteen years before, and she obviously loves to tell and retell all sorts of details she remembers. Lady Capulet at first dismisses her, but then calls her back and allows her to ramble on at length before trying to cut her off. Perhaps the most noticeable characteristic of Lady Capulet's conversation with her daughter is her bluntness: "Well, think of marriage now" (69), she tells her, with emphasis on the *now*. And twice she asks her, "What say you? Can you love the gentleman?" (79); "Speak briefly, can you like of Paris' love?" (96). She recognizes her obligation to help marry her daughter to an eligible young man, but she seems to take no very idealistic view of love; her long speech about the "book of love" (81-94) may reflect resentment at the lack of romance and excitement in her own marriage.

I.iv

Romeo and his friends, with masks and torches, are on their way to the Capulet house, which they will enter uninvited and unannounced. They intend to stay long enough for one dance and then leave. Mercutio, one of the most attractive characters in the play, jokes with Romeo, who cannot compete with his friend's puns and wit because he is concentrating on his role of unhappy lover. Still moody, self-absorbed, sentimental, Romeo says that he will not dance, he will be a mere onlooker: "I have a soul of lead/So stakes me to the ground I cannot move" (15-16). He mentions a dream, and Mercutio is off and running with his famous Queen Mab speech, a set piece which does not advance the plot but which shows us Mercutio as a man of lively imagination, poetic, humorous, earthy. Whenever Mercutio is onstage, his intellectual and physical vigor captures our attention. It is little wonder that some critics like to say that Shakespeare was forced to kill him midway through the play or he would have stolen it from Romeo and Juliet. Romeo interrupts, but Mercutio is not an easy man to turn aside, whether he is talking or fighting. But then Benvolio, always sensible and sometimes ironic, warns them that they may reach the Capulet house "too late" (105). Romeo picks up this phrase in his response, "I fear, too early" (106). He goes on to refer to a strange foreboding he feels "for my mind misgives/Some consequence yet hanging in the stars" (106-07). And so Romeo enters Juliet's home with an uneasy presentiment that "this night's revels" (109) may somehow lead to "some vile forfeit of untimely death" (111). Such an idea is dramatically right for the self-conscious young man who has been expressing all the conventional literary symptoms of love, but we sense that he is not posing here and that psychologically his intuition is right.

I.v

During the first few moments, we see the Capulet servants bustling about before the family and their guests enter. When they do, Capulet, jovial and fully enjoying himself at his own party, orders the music and dancing to begin. He is having a very good time indeed, being the gracious host and recalling his youth. He is not at all outraged when Tybalt tells him that Romeo, a hated Montague, is at the party. He even has a few good things to say about Romeo's reputation and becomes furious when Tybalt, hot-tempered as always, threatens to disrupt the gathering. His quick anger, which is rather like Tybalt's, is directed not against the conventional enemy but against his nephew who is crossing him. Capulet's acceptance of Romeo's presence suggests that the family feud is not so all-important to him as to Tybalt, the troublemaker, who now must nurse his anger since he is not allowed to vent it on Romeo at once.

The most important development in this scene, of course, is the meeting of Romeo and Juliet, and for both of them it is love at first sight. Rosaline never receives another thought from the young man who went to the feast to see her. Neither Romeo nor Juliet knows who the other is. Romeo asks a servingman, "What lady's that which doth enrich the hand/Of yonder knight?" (43-44). By chance he must have asked a servant hired for the occasion, not a regular member of the household, because the man does not know Juliet's identity. Romeo's first words about Juliet, "O, she doth teach the torches to burn bright!" (46), introduce a metaphor that runs throughout the play. Both Romeo and Juliet use many images of light—the torch, the sun, the stars, the lightning—to refer to each other and their love. There are both tension and quiet in their first meeting. They are, in a sense, isolated, although there are many other people all about them. Their first exchange of words is in the form of a sonnet (95-108), one of the most popular lyric forms of Shakespeare's day. There is a playful quality about the rather elaborate literary symbols of pilgrims, palmers, and prayers that does not entirely hide the intensity of feeling each is experiencing. In its way, this first exchange between them is a kind of sacrament.

Only after the Nurse interrupts the meeting, sending Juliet

to her mother, does each discover the other's identity. It is the Nurse who tells Romeo that Juliet is the daughter of the house, and it is the Nurse, later their go-between, who finds out Romeo's name for Juliet after she has pretended interest in some of the other guests. Juliet's immediate response, "My only love, sprung from my only hate!" (140) and her careful hiding of her feelings from the Nurse, are significant. She is no longer the child we saw in her first scene.

By the end of Act I, the young people have met, fallen in love, and discovered that they belong to warring houses. By the end of this act, we have also seen the principal elements that will lead to tragedy: the family quarrel representing a world antagonistic to youth and love; fate, or fortune, which seems to govern at critical junctures; and an impulsiveness or rashness of character, which makes possible both the love of Romeo and Juliet and its tragic outcome.

II. Prologue

Like the first act, this one begins with a prologue in sonnet form. This is the last time the Chorus appears to comment on the play. Students who have read *Henry V* might compare these prologues with the ones in that play, where a prologue introduces each of the five acts. The Chorus here points out that Rosaline is forgotten, refers to "foe" twice to emphasize the family quarrel and the consequent difficulties which will face the young people, but concludes with the thought that their love will enable them to meet extraordinary difficulties. Unlike the earlier prologue, this one seems unnecessary, almost obtrusive, since it tells us nothing that we do not already know.

II.i

This scene follows shortly after the scene at the feast. Romeo is near the Capulet garden, avoiding his friends. Benvolio, sure that he has seen Romeo leap over the wall into the Capulet orchard, asks Mercutio to call him. The exuberant Mercutio, who thinks that Romeo is still pining for Rosaline, pretends to try to conjure him with many lighthearted and bawdy suggestions. Romeo, however, does not answer, although he must hear them, and his friends leave.

II.ii

Romeo's opening line, rhyming with Benvolio's last one of

the preceding scene, shows that he has heard the jests of his friends, but he does not linger on them for Juliet appears (2) and Romeo is conscious only of her. For almost the first fifty lines the two are speaking about but not to each other, because Juliet is unaware of Romeo's presence until he comes forward (49) after hearing her express her love for him. The quality of Romeo's language, beginning with his opening speech, is quite different from the language he used about Rosaline. His imagination soars on the wings of love, not rhetoric. His language should also be contrasted with that of Juliet. Her love is as great, but her imagination does not soar quite so far from earth as his. She is practical, direct, and honest. "How camest thou hither?" she asks (62), and he answers, "With love's light wings did I o'erperch these walls" (66). Each of her practical questions receives such a reply, and, before they part, it is Juliet who has spoken of marriage and arranged for them to communicate with each other. Her tremulous excitement, her fear that he may think her too quickly won, her fear for his safety coupled with her reluctance to have him leave, her complete joy in loving and being loved are youthful but not childish. This hour is their happiest one, and although the voice of the Nurse interrupts them it does not shatter their world. But in the midst of this happiness, Juliet feels a sudden presentiment of evil, even as Romeo did before the feast. "I have no joy of this contract tonight./It is too rash, too unadvised, too sudden;/Too like the lightning, which doth cease to be/Ere one can say it lightens" (117-20). The lightning, another image of light, is an apt one in its brilliance, quickness, and danger.

After Juliet's third "good night," Romeo leaves to seek out Friar Lawrence and ask his help. One technique which Shakespeare consistently used to heighten dramatic intensity was that of sharply contrasting scenes. And so we have the intensity and purity of this most famous of love scenes heightened by Mercutio's exuberant bawdry which precedes it and Friar Lawrence's quiet philosophic comments which follow it.

II.iii

Friar Lawrence, confessor to both Romeo and Juliet, is gathering herbs at dawn, mediating on the paradox that the earth is at once nature's mother and tomb, that the same plant can be both poison and medicine, that departure from the natural order can turn virtue into vice and vice into something worthy. In man too, he finds conflicting powers, "grace and rude will" (28). The Friar's knowledge of herbs prepares us for the potion he gives Juliet in Act IV, and his comments also point to the poison Romeo will buy from the Apothecary in Mantua.

Romeo hears the last part of the Friar's speech but probably does not pay great attention to it. We see again that Romeo likes to speak in riddles, but eventually he tells the Friar that he wants to marry Juliet. Friar Lawrence is quite naturally surprised since he has recently heard Romeo sighing about Rosaline. He sensibly points out that he had reproached Romeo "For doting, not for loving" (82). Although he is skeptical about Romeo's sudden change and the wisdom of such a hasty marriage, he agrees to marry the young people, hoping that it will end the family enmity.

II.iv

This scene is almost entirely a comic one. The only serious note is the reference to a letter, presumably a challenge, Tybalt has sent to Romeo (6-7). It reminds us for a moment of Tybalt's fury when he recognized Romeo's voice at the Capulet party and perhaps saw him watching Juliet. Mercutio clearly despises Tybalt, not because of his quick temper but because he fights "by the book." The fencing terms and puns should not overwhelm the student. Even if he misses some of them, he should see that when Romeo enters he is not only able to match wits with Mercutio but that he thoroughly enjoys doing so. After a series of exchanges, Mercutio, delighted that Romeo is himself again, exclaims, "Why, is not this better now than groaning for love? Now art thou sociable, now art thou Romeo . . ." (92-94). Now that Romeo is truly in love, not simply pretending to be, he is his natural self.

The Nurse and Peter appear, looking for Romeo, and Mercutio has more fun at their expense. Left alone with the Nurse and Peter, Romeo is eventually able to stop her talking and get her to listen to his message to Juliet, to meet him that afternoon at Friar Lawrence's cell to be married. He also tells the Nurse to leave a rope ladder so that he may join Juliet that night.

II.v

Juliet is impatiently waiting for the return of the Nurse, who has been gone three hours. Again she uses a beautiful image of light in her reference to Love's messengers, which should move even faster than the sun's beams "Driving back shadows over lo'ring hills" (4-6). When the Nurse does arrive, she is, as always, garrulous and not particularly coherent. She may be teasing Juliet by not telling her at once what she wants to hear, or it may be completely impossible for her ever to be brief. When she finally does relate Romeo's message, she does so with remarkable directness. In this scene, as in Romeo's conversation with the Friar, we have a contrast between the impetuosity of youth and the slowness of age.

II.vi

The act ends with a brief scene in Friar Lawrence's cell, where he and Romeo welcome Juliet. Romeo is sure that one moment with Juliet can balance all the sorrow that may come to him, that their love can "devour" even death (7), but the Friar is concerned about the haste of the marriage. "These violent delights have violent ends" (9). In spite of the haste, secrecy, and excitement, there is a quiet dignity about the scene, which ends with the three leaving to take part in the marriage ceremony.

III.i

In this climactic scene, Mercutio and Tybalt are killed and Romeo banished, all in a few moments and only twenty-four hours after the street brawl which opened the play. The scene begins with Benvolio, the peacemaker, suggesting to Mercutio that they leave the streets; the day is hot, the kind of day that stirs "mad blood" (4) and brings violence. The high-spirited Mercutio pretends that the mild Benvolio is eager for a fight, describing him as a man who will fight for any and all reasons or no reason at all. Actually, he is describing Tybalt, the "King of Cats" (78), who arrives looking for Romeo. Mercutio taunts him, but Tybalt is saving his sword for Romeo.

However, when Romeo arrives, happy and content because of the marriage ceremony that has just taken place, he refuses to accept Tybalt's challenge when he calls him villain (62) and even expresses friendship for him. The others, of course, know nothing of his feelings for Juliet, Tybalt's cousin, and his behavior must seem like inexplicable cowardice. Benvolio is speechless, but Mercutio, astonished at Romeo's "calm, dishonorable, vile submission" (74), draws on Tybalt. Romeo tries to stop the fight which follows, and in so doing strikes at the rapiers in such a way that Tybalt is able to thrust his weapon under Romeo's arm and stab Mercutio. In this one moment we have the principal forces of the tragedy converging: the sultry heat of the day and the family feud, the impulsiveness of Romeo in trying to stop the fight, the chance of the timing and the position of Romeo's body so that he brings about the death of his friend Mercutio. There is both anger and wit in Mercutio's last lines: anger that he is dying because of a stupid quarrel which means nothing to him—"A plague a both your houses!" (92, 108, 110)—and that he is dying at the hand of "A braggart, a rogue, a villain, that fights by the book of arithmetic!" (102-03); humor, even at this moment, in his pun on a "grave man" (99-100).

Accepting at once the responsibility for Mercutio's death, Romeo fights with Tybalt and kills him. Benvolio's warning, "Stand not amazed. The Prince will doom thee death" (136), suggests that Romeo is almost stunned by the rapid turn of events whereby he has directly or indirectly caused two deaths. He sees himself a victim of fate, "fortune's fool" (138), and leaves to find refuge with Friar Lawrence.

A great crowd gathers, and Benvolio explains the cause of the quarrel to the Prince. Students should see that even honest Benvolio stretches the truth at one point in his eagerness to exonerate Romeo; Tybalt did not seek the quarrel with Mercutio; it was Mercutio who insisted on fighting (76-82; 160-61). The fact that Mercutio was a kinsman of the Prince may influence Benvolio's version of the quarrel. The Prince banishes Romeo instead of ordering his death; he also levies a heavy fine against both families. It is interesting that it is Lady Capulet, not her husband, who vehemently, almost hysterically, demands Romeo's death. Presumably the Prince mitigates the sentence he had previously threatened (46.100) because Romeo had avenged the death of Escalus' kinsman.

III.ii

From the violence of the preceding scene, we move to Juliet, alone in her father's garden, impatiently waiting for the end of the day. "Gallop apace, you fiery-footed steeds," (1) suggests the excitement and passion with which she waits for the night and Romeo. Ironically, she is pleased when the Nurse arrives because she will bring news of Romeo. The Nurse says what she has to say at such length and so incoherently that Juliet at first thinks that it is Romeo who is dead, then both Tybalt and Romeo. When the Nurse finally tells her the ugly news, she does so directly, even brutally: "Tybalt is gone, and Romeo banishèd;/Romeo that killed him, he is banishèd" (69-70). Juliet is genuinely shocked and grieved by the news of her cousin's death, but when the Nurse speaks ill of Romeo, Juliet turns on her sharply (90), for her love for and loyalty to Romeo are stronger than any other emotion. "Some word there was, worser than Tybalt's death" (108), and that is Romeo's banishment. She does not want the Nurse to take her to her parents, grieving over the death of Tybalt, but sends her to Romeo with a ring as a symbol of her love.

III.iii

Having just seen Juliet's reaction to the news of Romeo's banishment, we next see Romeo's reaction. He is not grateful that the Prince has spared his life; banishment from Verona, from Juliet, seems a worse punishment than death. He speaks of suicide, asks for poison, and, when the Nurse describes Juliet's grief, tries to stab himself. The Friar reproaches Romeo for his near hysteria, his extravagant grief, and points out reasons for a calmer, even happier, mood. He is alive; Juliet is alive and loves him; the Friar will keep in touch with him in Mantua until it is appropriate to announce the marriage, and then, he predicts, the Prince will forgive him and allow him to return. He sends Romeo to Juliet, warning him to leave by daybreak. The Nurse turns back after she has started to leave, remembering the ring that Juliet has sent. With the ring, and probably because of the Friar's reasonable remarks, Romeo is much calmer, saying, "How well my comfort is revived by this!" (165).

III.iv

On the surface, this scene is a calm one. Lord and Lady Capulet have been talking with Paris, who is willing to postpone his courtship until Juliet recovers from her grief over the death of Tybalt (8). He has already said good night to Lady Capulet and is apparently leaving when Capulet suggests that the wedding take place in a few days. Wednesday will be too soon after Tybalt's death—it is now Monday—but Thursday will be an appropriate day. Paris, naturally, is happy at the suggestion; Capulet undoubtedly feels that he will be introducing joy into a house of grief.

III.v

It is dawn, and Romeo and Juliet are saying their farewells. The tremulous happiness of their "good nights" in the balcony scene is replaced by a quieter, sadder, but even stronger feeling. At first, it is Romeo who is the practical one, who says that the bird song they hear is that of the lark, not the nightingale. He yields to Juliet's plea that he stay, but at once she changes, knowing that her wishful thinking will not keep the day of banishment from growing more and more light. The poignancy of the scene is increased by their ignorance of the plans Juliet's father has just been making for her happiness. Romeo, who had been so distraught in Friar Lawrence's cell, has control of himself as he tries to comfort Juliet. When she asks, "O, think'st thou we shall ever meet again?" (51), he can answer, "I doubt it not" (52), and even suggests that all their troubles will someday be only the subject for "sweet discourses" (53) and reminiscence. Juliet, however, feels some kind of foreboding, saying, "Methinks I see thee, now thou art so low,/As one dead in the bottom of a tomb" (55-56). He is "so low" because he has climbed down from the balcony and is looking up at her, both of them pale with grief and tension though they do not know that this is the last time they will speak together. As he has done twice before, Shakespeare here uses the unconscious premonition of disaster to reinforce the sense of tragic fate.

Juliet must at once begin playing a role, for her mother enters to tell her of arrangements for the wedding. First, however, she talks of Juliet's reactions to Tybalt's death and is almost painfully blunt: "Some grief shows much of love;/But much of grief shows still some want of wit" (73-74). She also calmly announces her intention of arranging the poisoning of Romeo, a remarkable statement from a respectable matron. Throughout the first part of the scene (75-103) all of Juliet's responses are deliberately ambiguous, meaning one thing to Lady Capulet and something quite different to Juliet. When her mother tells her of the wedding plans (113-16), Juliet is shocked into open defiance. Her father and the Nurse then enter, and Juliet arouses her father's temper. He is furious that she does not appreciate his efforts to find her a worthy husband. Both the Nurse and Lady Capulet try to soften his anger, but his rage seems almost uncontrollable and, in his cruelty, he threatens to turn Juliet out of the house if she does not obey him. At his departure, Juliet appeals to her mother, who clearly does not intend to cross her husband. She is not in a rage, but her words are no less final than her husband's: "Talk not to me, for I'll not speak a word./Do as thou wilt, for I have done with thee" (204-05). Juliet then turns to the Nurse for comfort, the person who has petted and spoiled her all her life, and who knows of her marriage to Romeo. The Nurse's advice is, in brief, to commit bigamy. Romeo is banished, as good as dead; forget him! Her amorality could not be shown more clearly. Juliet's one-word answer, "Amen" (230)—so be it—suggests that she recognizes her situation, that she is alone and can no longer count on father, mother, or nurse for help. There is still Friar Lawrence, however, and she resolves to seek his counsel. Her last line, "If all else fail, myself have power to die" (244), indicates that she is ready to take her life if the Friar too fails her.

IV.i

The scene opens with the Friar and Paris talking about the coming wedding. Paris believes that Capulet is speeding the marriage because he fears that Juliet's excessive grief for Tybalt is dangerous. The Friar's aside, "I would I knew not why it should be slowed" (16), may suggest both honest concern for the troubled people and regret that he is personally involved. After Juliet's entrance, she and Paris converse, with Juliet again showing remarkable ability to control herself and answer ambiguously while apparently being very forthright though subdued. As soon as Paris leaves, she breaks down and begs the Friar for help, saying that she prefers to die if he cannot offer her any hope. When the Friar speaks of a desperate remedy, she says that no remedy would be too terrifying for her, that she would even hide "in a charnel house,/O'ercovered quite with dead men's rattling bones" (81-82), not knowing that she will indeed wake soon in the family tomb. Friar Lawrence gives her a potion which will insure a deathlike trance, telling her to take it on Wednesday night. On her supposed wedding morning, she will seem to be dead and will be carried to the Capulet vault. Forty-two hours after taking the potion, she will awaken "as from a pleasant sleep" (106) and find both the Friar and Romeo beside her, for he will send for Romeo at once. Juliet takes the potion eagerly, "Give me, give me! O, tell me not of fear!" (121).

IV.ii

Back in Capulet's home, he is sending out a servant with a list of guests to invite to the wedding, even as he had done just two days earlier when he planned the feast at which, by chance, Romeo and Juliet met. Juliet returns from confession, seemingly repentant and willing to be ruled by her father. Capulet is so delighted by the change in her attitude that he impulsively changes the wedding date to the next day. The sudden shift, the chance act of an impetuous man, drastically reduces the time in which Friar Lawrence must send word to Romeo and carry out his plans. Lady Capulet is concerned about not being able to have everything ready for the next day, but her husband, excited and pleased, says that he will stay up all night if necessary and "play the housewife" (43) to see that all preparations are made.

IV.iii

After selecting the clothes for the wedding, Juliet asks the Nurse to leave her to her prayers, since her prospective marriage is leading her into a complicated moral state (3-5). She also asks her mother to leave on the grounds that she has many household needs to attend to before tomorrow. Thus, Juliet plays her great scene, as she must, alone, in great fear but with great courage. She starts to call the Nurse back, perhaps the last gesture of the child she was until so recently, but recognizes at once, "My dismal scene I needs must act alone" (19). She shows her determination when she brings forth a dagger which she will use if the potion does not work. Her next fear is that the potion will actually be poison, mixed by Friar Lawrence so that his part in the affair will never be discovered. She discards this idea, remembering, ". . . he hath still been tried a holy man" (29). Then she fears that she may wake before Romeo comes; her vision of the grim sights and smells that will assail her in the tomb further excites her, makes her fear that she will go mad. She knows that she will see Tybalt's body there, perhaps his ghost "Seeking out Romeo" (56). Calling out, "Stay, Tybalt, stay!/ Romeo, Romeo, Romeo, I drink to thee" (57-58) in her last moment of consciousness, she tries to protect Romeo from Tybalt's vengeance.

IV.iv

This is a busy scene, with Lord and Lady Capulet, the Nurse, and various servants hurrying about, preparing for the wedding feast, all in conspicuous contrast to the stillness that we know prevails in Juliet's room. Again we see the familiarity with which the Nurse is treated by the family.

IV.v

The Nurse, coming to awaken Juliet, at first jokes about

her being a sleepyhead until she discovers, she thinks, that the girl is dead. The grief of the parents, the Nurse, and Paris is all genuine, although students may well find their speeches exaggerated (49-64). It has been suggested that in these three speeches Shakespeare was satirizing rhetorical devices used in Senecan tragedies. Even so, the family's sorrow is honest, and Capulet seems to speak from a full heart when he says, "Death lies on her like an untimely frost/Upon the sweetest flower of all the field" (28-29). Friar Lawrence has a difficult role to play here; he knows that Juliet is not dead, but he must offer the consolations of religion to her grieving family and friends.

The most difficult part of the scene for most students is the last section, involving Peter and the musicians in a bit of comedy. Some critics suggest that Shakespeare was creating a piece of stage business for Will Kempe, a popular comic actor of the day; others have justified the episode on the grounds that Shakespeare intended to show that tragedy and comedy are always rubbing shoulders, that to the hired musicians a wedding and a funeral were just two jobs, neither more significant than the other as long as they would be paid and get their dinner. In his later works, Shakespeare became more skillful at using comedy to underscore tragedy, as in the drunken porter scene in *Macbeth* or the gravedigging scene in *Hamlet*.

V.i

This scene takes us to Mantua, where Romeo is waiting for word from Juliet. He is tense, excited, happy, sure that his dreams mean good news. He has dreamed that Juliet found him dead but revived him with a kiss. This indeed seems like a forerunner of the scene in the tomb, but when the dream comes true, Romeo will be dead, with Juliet soon to follow him. When his servant, Balthasar, arrives from Verona, Romeo asks him a rapid series of questions about Juliet, his father, the Friar, and Balthasar can only tell the story of Juliet's reported death. Romeo questions him no more but impulsively accepts the worst: "Is it e'en so? Then I defy you, stars!" (24). From his servant's reference to Romeo's pallor and wild looks, we know how deeply Romeo has been shaken, but his behavior is quite different from that of the hysterical boy in Friar Lawrence's cell learning of his banishment. He is decisive, gives some necessary orders to Balthasar, and plans his death with resolution: "Well, Juliet, I will lie with thee tonight" (34). He describes the Apothecary's shop, knowing that the man's poverty will make him willing to break the law and sell him poison. The Apothecary does not need much urging, and Romeo, more philosophical or more cynical now, tells him, "There is thy gold—worse poison to men's souls,/Doing more murder in this loathsome world,/Than these poor compounds that thou mayst not sell" (79-81).

V.ii

One of the principal elements of chance in the tragedy is related in this scene. Friar John tells Friar Lawrence why he was unable to deliver the letter to Romeo. Delayed by the authorities because he and another friar were in a house where plague was suspected, he was unable to deliver the letter himself or get a messenger because of the fear of infection. Thus because of an accident, which none of the characters could foresee or control, Romeo did not learn of Juliet's presumed death and the Friar's plan for their reunion.

V.iii

The final scene occurs in the churchyard where the Capulet tomb is located. Accompanied by a page, Paris comes bearing flowers and perfumed water, intending to carry out the first of a series of nightly rituals at Juliet's grave. Just why he does not wish to be seen is not entirely clear, but he asks his page to warn him if anyone approaches. The whistling of the boy alerts him, and, recognizing Romeo, he assumes that he has come to do some act of desecration, since he knows nothing of the love of Romeo and Juliet and thinks of Romeo only as a Montague, enemy of the Capulets. He, therefore, challenges Romeo, who has come with Balthasar and, like Paris, has told his servant to wait for him. Romeo has also given Balthasar a letter for his father and has warned him not to interrupt him, no matter what he hears or sees, on pain of death. Romeo has no desire to fight with Paris and does so only out of desperation, not anger. He who a few days ago seemed like a boy speaks to Paris as "Good gentle youth" (59), and truly Romeo, like Juliet, has grown up during the course of the play. He views the body of Paris, and even that of Tybalt, with a kind of compassion; they are his companions in misfortune and death. His final soliloquy is filled with his consciousness of Juliet's beauty and their love. Even in death "her beauty makes/This vault a feasting presence full of light" (85-86). With his poison he drinks a toast to his love, gasps as he recognizes the speed of the drug, and dies with a kiss just before Friar Lawrence enters, too late.

Juliet's first words as she rouses are, ironically, "O comfortable friar!" (148), but he has poor comfort for her. He urges her to come with him, now that Romeo and Paris are dead, and he will place her in a convent. Juliet refuses to leave, but the Friar dare not stay. We may not admire his flight, but we can understand his fears, and, dramatically, it is necessary that he leave so that Juliet can join Romeo in death. She tries to drink any remaining poison in the cup but there is none, and so she dies by Romeo's dagger sheathed in her breast.

The final moments of the play are concerned with the discovery of the deaths and the explanation of them. One after another arrive various watchmen, Balthasar, Friar Lawrence, Prince Escalus, Lord and Lady Capulet, Lord Montague, and their attendants. The explanation, of course, can come only from the Friar. The fact that Shakespeare has him recount the story in detail and at length in a speech, none of which is new to the audience, indicates that he thought it essential that the two families understand their responsibility for the tragedy and that civil order be restored. The Prince justly points out that not only are Capulet and Montague responsible for what has happened, but that he too for "winking at your discords" (294) bears some of the blame. And all have been punished.

The feud is buried as Montague, mourning the death of his wife as well as his son, vows to build a statue of Juliet in pure gold; Capulet, offering his hand to his old enemy, promises to raise a statue of Romeo. Pure gold the statues may be, but they are poor substitutes for the young lovers, who lived, loved, and died so quickly, so intensely—poor sacrifices of their parents' enmity.

MARIAN ELLIOT

SHORT-ANSWER QUESTIONS

1. In the Prologue to Act I, what indicates that the outcome will be tragic? (41.5, 6, 8, 9, 11)

THE TRAGEDY OF ROMEO AND JULIET 151

2. What is Benvolio's first action in the play? (45.66-67) What is Tybalt's? (45.68-69)

3. What penalty does Prince Escalus pronounce on the Montagues and Capulets? Why does he regard the street quarrel as more than a casual disturbance of the peace? (46.84-106)

4. What do Romeo's words about the street fight show about his attitude toward the family quarrel? (49.176-77) How can we tell from this passage that he is entirely preoccupied with what he thinks is his love for Rosaline?

5. What advice does Benvolio give Romeo about Rosaline? (51.230-31; 55.85-90)

6. What advice does Capulet give Paris about Juliet? (53.30-33)

7. What is Juliet's reaction to her mother's news that Paris wants to marry her? (59.97-99)

8. Romeo introduces the subject of dreams (62.49), and Mercutio launches into his Queen Mab speech. How does this speech reveal both his imagination and his sense of humor?

9. What is Romeo's immediate reaction when he first sees Juliet? (67.46-55)

10. How does Juliet discover Romeo's identity? (70.130-39) What is her reaction? (140-45)

11. After the feast, Romeo avoids his friends so that he can stay near the Capulet house. How do we know that he probably overhears Mercutio and Benvolio when they call him? (74.1)

12. Why does Romeo not tell Juliet at once who he is after he speaks to her in the balcony scene? (75.49-58)

13. When Juliet says that she would not want her kinsmen to find Romeo there (76.74), he says, "I have night's

152   TEACHING SHAKESPEARE

cloak to hide me from their eyes." What do these lines suggest about differences in their characters?

14. Why does Juliet tell Romeo not to vow his love for her by the moon? (77.109-11)

15. Where is Romeo going when he leaves Juliet at the close of the balcony scene? (80.188-89)

16. What is Friar Lawrence doing when he first appears? (81.5-8)

17. Why does the Friar agree to marry Romeo and Juliet? (84.90-92)

18. Why has Tybalt apparently sent Romeo a challenge? (84.6-8)

19. What message does Romeo send Juliet by the Nurse? (91.186-89)

20. Juliet is impatient to hear Romeo's message, but the Nurse does not tell her at once what it is. Why not? (pp. 94-95)

21. How much time elapses between Romeo and Juliet's first meeting and their marriage?

22. Why is there a reference to the weather at the beginning of Mercutio's and Benvolio's conversation? (98.2)

23. When Tybalt sees Romeo approaching, he says, "Here comes my man" (100.57). Mercutio responds with "But I'll be hanged, sir, if he wears your livery" (58). What is the difference between their definitions of "man"?

24. After Mercutio's death, why does Romeo say, "O sweet Juliet,/Thy beauty hath made me effeminate/And in my temper soft'ned valor's steel!"? (102.115-17)

25. What does Romeo mean by his exclamation, "O, I am fortune's fool!" after the death of Tybalt? (103.138)

26. What penalty does Prince Escalus pronounce after the death of Tybalt? (105.188-99) Why is it not the penalty he had earlier vowed he would exact?

THE TRAGEDY OF ROMEO AND JULIET   153

27. The Nurse's disconnected garrulity is comic in some scenes, but not when she tells Juliet of Tybalt's death and Romeo's banishment (pp. 107-10). What is the effect here?

28. In what ways does Romeo's behavior in Friar Lawrence's cell seem hysterical? (pp. 11-14)

29. What message does the Nurse bring Romeo from Juliet? (110.142-43; 116.163-64)

30. Why does Juliet at first say it is the nightingale, not the lark, that sings? (118.1-5) Why does she say, a few minutes later, that it is the lark? (119.27) Why does its song seem discordant?

31. When Capulet berates Juliet for refusing to marry Paris, he calls her "tallow-face." (124.158) What does this epithet tell us about her appearance at this point?

32. What is the Nurse's advice to Juliet after her father has told her she is to marry Paris? (126.215-27)

33. When Juliet goes to Friar Lawrence for help, she finds Paris with him. Why is Paris there? (p. 128)

34. What is to be the effect of the potion Friar Lawrence gives to Juliet? (131.95-103) How long is the effect supposed to last? (131.105)

35. When Juliet tells her father that she will marry Paris, what does he say about the wedding date? (133.24) What is the importance of his decision?

36. Why does Juliet tell the Nurse that she wants to be alone? (134.2-5) What excuse does she give her mother? (135.9-12)

37. Why does Juliet have a dagger with her? (135.21-23)

38. Why does she think that the Friar may have given her a real poison? (135.24-27) What other fears does she express about the potion?

154   TEACHING SHAKESPEARE

39. When she calls out "Stay, Tybalt, stay!", what does she mean? (136.57)

40. Who discovers that Juliet is apparently dead? (138.1-16)

41. Why is Romeo in a happy frame of mind before Balthasar arrives? (144.1-11)

42. If Balthasar had not faithfully followed Romeo's instructions to bring him news from Verona, how might the outcome of the play have been different?

43. Why is the poverty of the Apothecary emphasized? (146.50-54)

44. Why was Friar John unable to deliver Friar Lawrence's letter to Romeo? (147.5-12)

45. Why does Paris go to the tomb of Juliet? (149.12-17)

46. When Paris challenges him, Romeo says, "I beseech thee, youth,/Put not another sin upon my head/By urging me to fury" (150.61-63) What other sin or sins is he referring to?

47. When Romeo refers to "Beauty's ensign" in Juliet's lips and cheeks, what is he noticing about her appearance? (151.94-96)

48. What is ironic about Juliet's first words to the Friar? (153.148)

49. What do we learn about Romeo's mother in the final scene? (156.210-11)

50. After hearing Friar Lawrence's story and the explanations of Balthasar and Paris's page, Prince Escalus says, "All are punished" (158.295) Does "All" include the Prince himself? How? Why? (158.294-95)

QUESTIONS FOR DISCUSSION

1. In the opening lines, the Prologue to Act I refers to Romeo and Juliet as "A pair of star-crossed lovers" (41.6), suggesting that their fate is beyond their control. Discuss the ways Shakespeare develops the theme of fate, or fortune, as a controlling force in the play.

2. Romeo's character is developed partly by contrasting characters or foils. Among these are three other young men, for whose deaths Romeo is directly or indirectly responsible—Mercutio, Tybalt, and Paris. Discuss the differences and similarities between them and Romeo.

3. The family feud is a powerful factor in the play, but there are many indications that the quarrel is not of primary importance to anyone but Tybalt and the servants. Discuss these indications and their significance.

4. Romeo's impulsiveness is shown many times throughout the play, from his first sight of Juliet to his immediate acceptance of her death. How does his rashness contribute to the tragic outcome?

5. Friar Lawrence tries earnestly to help Romeo and Juliet, but his good intentions are not enough. In what ways does his well-intentioned help fail? Does it contribute in any way to the final tragedy?

6. Romeo and Juliet consistently speak of each other and their love in terms of light. Even in the tomb Romeo says, "For here lies Juliet, and her beauty makes/This vault a feasting presence full of light" (151.85-86). Choose some of these images to explain, pointing out what they show about Romeo and Juliet's feelings and the ways their minds work.

7. During the course of the play, less than five full days, Juliet changes from a docile child to a brave and passionate woman. Discuss some of the ways these changes

are shown. Is there any aspect of the child suggested in her climactic scene, in which she drinks the potion?

8. Romeo, too, changes during the course of the play, not so steadily perhaps as Juliet, but just as dramatically. Compare his attitudes and actions in the final scene in the tomb with those of earlier scenes.

9. Romeo and Juliet are both young and passionately in love, but they are quite different in temperament and personality. Juliet, for example, often seems more practical than Romeo, her imagination more earthbound. Choose some passages which show differences in their characters and discuss them.

10. Friar Lawrence's soliloquy (81.1-30) quite appropriately uses many images drawn from nature, particularly gardening. What is he saying about the natural order? How can you relate his ideas expressed here to the play as a whole and to the other characters?

SAMPLE TEST

I. (30 minutes)

Write a well-organized essay on ONE of the following subjects.

1. In the opening lines, the Prologue to Act I refers to Romeo and Juliet as "A pair of star-crossed lovers" (41.6), suggesting that their fate is beyond their control. Discuss the ways Shakespeare develops the theme of fate, or fortune, as a controlling force in the play.

2. Romeo and Juliet consistently speak of each other and their love in terms of light. Even in the tomb Romeo says, "For here lies Juliet, and her beauty makes/This vault a feasting presence full of light" (151.85-86). Choose some of these images to explain, pointing out what they show about Romeo and Juliet's feelings and the ways their minds work.

THE TRAGEDY OF ROMEO AND JULIET 157

II. (30 minutes)

Write briefly on FIVE of the following.

1. What penalty does Prince Escalus pronounce on the Montagues and Capulets? Why does he regard the street quarrel as more than a casual disturbance of the peace?

2. How does Juliet discover Romeo's identity? What is her reaction?

3. Why does the Friar agree to marry Romeo and Juliet?

4. Why is there a reference to the weather at the beginning of Mercutio's and Benvolio's conversation?

5. Why does Juliet at first say it is the nightingale, not the lark, that sings? Why does she say, a few minutes later, that it is the lark? Why does its song seem discordant?

6. What is the Nurse's advice to Juliet after her father has told her she is to marry Paris?

7. When Romeo refers to "Beauty's ensign" in Juliet's lips and cheeks, what is he noticing about her appearance?

A MIDSUMMER NIGHT'S DREAM

INTRODUCTION

This play was not called *A Midsummer Night's Dream* because the action occurred on the eve of Midsummer, June 24, the "longest day in the year," the birthday of John the Baptist; in fact the action occurs in May, perhaps early in the month when people "observe[d]/The rite of May" (102.136). Why it was called a dream of any sort (or time) is a question our study of the play should try to answer, for the play implicitly and explicitly deals with similarities between two products of the imagination: dreams and works of art. All plays can be said to be dreams, but some plays, like *A Midsummer Night's Dream*, are more dreamlike than others because they contain incongruities—mixtures of the possible and the impossible, of the reasonable and the irrational—that remind us of some dreams (*cf.* "antique fables" 108.3, and "palpable-gross play," 122.369). This play is a *Midsummer Night* dream, because in Shakespeare's England there were many pleasant, half-believed superstitions about that holiday, one of which was that the man a girl dreamed of on the eve of Midsummer would become her husband.

But a good way to begin the study of the play is to recognize that it is an "occasional" play; Shakespeare seems to have written it to help celebrate an occasion, that is, a noble wedding; the action of the play is set against another occasion, the marriage of Theseus and Hippolyta; and the play is full of the spirit of celebration that characterized the occasions of both May Day and Midsummer. Spring, courtship, fertility, even the breaking of conventions, were themes of festivals of May; and with Midsummer there was an ancient association of "madness," or a brief period of irrational behavior. Some discussion of the nature of holidays, of special occasions, may be a useful introduction to one of the aspects of drama that our play illustrates extremely well. For a holiday may be defined as a period of time during which we do not work, during which we pass the time, or please ourselves by forgetting what daily life demands of us.

Every child knows that holidays can be a bore if they bring only idleness. They must be filled with something to do—with activity, or pseudo-activity. Boredom produces melancholy; idleness produces time to think about our troubles; and if we cannot forget our troubles by working, we must do so by playing games or watching others play games. In the study of *A Midsummer Night's Dream,* we may think of reading or seeing a play as a kind of spectator sport in which we lose our sense of ourselves by becoming imaginatively involved in the contest or story that someone else presents us with. To be sure, not all stories or plays are comedies: tragedies and serious stories also take us out of ourselves. But when we are in a holiday mood, we are not likely to take seriously the sad story of Piramus and Thisby even when it is well written or enacted by professional actors.

Students of our play, therefore, may at the start be made to see that Shakespeare seems to have been sufficiently delighted by the occasion of a noble wedding to write a play about the occasion of a noble wedding, and to fill it with words and characters and actions that would produce the kind of escape from boredom, the kind of positive feelings of fun, that are appropriate to the celebration of a marriage. Then, in the course of their study they should be helped to a growing awareness that this entertainment, this collection of song and dance and slapstick, of poetry and illiteracy, and of the comic and the serious, is in fact more than just a way to kill time or avoid boredom; they should see that it is also an almost miraculous revelation of the ways in which man's imagination may be more useful and more humane than his reason. One way to work toward this discovery is to show them the variety of ways in which they can answer the question, *What is the play about?*

First, we may say the play is about a group of people, or about a place, or about what happens to these people in that place. Characters, setting, and plot ought to be clearly understood before we go on to other less specific matters. Theseus and Hippolyta are on the stage only about one fourth of the time, and they are not sufficiently involved in the plot for us to feel that we know much about their characters. We know Theseus is the Duke of Athens; we watch him act and hear him speak with masculine dignity and authority in the first scene. We get a glimpse of the real man in his lyrical description of his hounds (101.122-29). And in the last act, our impression that he has the typical strengths and limitations of a man of action is confirmed by his somewhat condescending but good-natured tolerance of lovers and poets. He is not without a sense of humor, and we do not much blame him for rejecting the epic of the Centaurs, the ballet or pantomime of the "tipsy Bacchanals," and the satire on the death of learning (110.44-60). Shakespeare has not made him an intellectual or a highly sensitive patron of the arts, but neither has he made him a caricature of the boorish man of action without taste. To have done so would have been not only to insult Shakespeare's patron or the bridegroom of the wedding for which the play was written but also to have coarsened the quality of the contrast between the world of action and the world of poetry. If the poet is not usually a madman, the nonpoet is not usually a dolt. The Theseus-Hippolyta plot is a background for the play involving the innocent mischief of the young lovers, the fairies, and the crude mechanicals; and that background has the elegance or good taste the truly noble should possess. There is no need to talk of Theseus and Hippolyta as flat characters: students who try to imagine the play on the stage and who listen carefully to their speeches can discover that we know as much about them as the world in general ever knows about its dukes and their fiancées.

Only in a very limited way, then, is the play about Theseus and Hippolyta. It is more about Lysander, Demetrius, Helena, Hermia, and Hermia's father, Egeus; it is more about them, perhaps, but again we do not feel we know them very well. Egeus is simply a stern and unrelenting father. Lysander and Demetrius are hard to distinguish from each other, and Helena and Hermia are only slightly more distinct. The truly memorable characters in the play are, of course, the rest of the cast—the artisans and the fairies; and the answer that the play is about Oberon and Bottom comes nearer the truth than that it is about three pairs of lovers. We know this simply because we know that in the most engrossing parts of the play those two characters seem to dominate the action. Bottom's energy, enthusiasm, and imagination, his love of acting and his remarkable human dignity beneath all the indignity of his illiteracy should be pointed out so that students do not think of him as simply a farcical figure or as the product of a satirical attitude toward the lower classes. Bottom is the man without whom the show cannot go on, and a man with the kind of right instincts that make him equal to the social demands of the consortship of Queen Titania.

Oberon and Titania, though sometimes conceived of as no

bigger than your thumb, were also thought of as life-size, and on the stage, therefore, it should not be difficult to think of Oberon as a human being, nor is the ridiculousness of the Titania-Bottom scenes compounded by a great discrepancy in their sizes. Puck should be thought of as somewhat smaller than men, perhaps the size of a little boy—comparable in build and movement to Ariel in *The Tempest*. Mustardseed and his fellows were thought of as very, very small. The other point to be made in the study of Oberon, Titania, and Puck is that of all the characters in the play they seem the most human—in many ways the most real and true to life.

The play is also, of course, about what happens to these characters, and the study of plot should begin with an analysis of the articulation of the parts of the four stories, as will be suggested in the scene-by-scene commentary following. But such an examination of the play's structure should be followed by an attempt to explain what happened. All the efforts of the human beings to influence the course of events, to control their own lives, to establish their own destinies, are in fact either frustrated or assisted by forces beyond their control—all except those of the presiding figures of Theseus and Hippolyta, and even in their case we are made to feel that if their marriage is happy and their children strong and lovely, the blessing of the fairies will have been partly responsible. On the whole what the characters do and what happens to them (the "plot" in one sense of the word) are influenced by something supernatural, super-rational.

Finally, at this level of discussion, students may say the play is about life in Athens (and "A wood near Athens," 55.1) a long time ago, and in exploring this observation, they will discover how the romantic setting of far away and long ago can be understood only in the imagery of English Elizabethan life in town and country.

But these answers, about characters, plot, and setting, are not ends in themselves and should not satisfy a good student who knows that they have reference only to the *fiction* of the play: the characters are not real people (never lived, in history); the plot is not realistic (not like life as we know it); and the place and time both have an obvious air of make-believe. Surely, they will say, the play is better explained as being about love and hate, about illusion and reality, about waking and dreaming, about order and disorder, about poetry and the prosaic, about imagination and reason, about free will and fate, about the natural and the supernatural, about life in the city and life in the "green world" of nature, about the upper classes and the lower classes, about good art and bad art, about good audiences and bad audiences. These antitheses are referred to, more or less, in the scene-by-scene analysis following, but students should be shown how the whole play may be illuminated by an effort to see it as a poetic way of discussing one or more of these topics. The country (the *"wood"*) is where the man-made complications are resolved, where the dreams occur and the visions appear, where the healing force of the imagination redirects the egocentric reason, where May Day is celebrated, where youth and love triumph over age and hate. Dreams are human experiences in which we are sometimes made to wonder whether life is not a dream, or at least whether dreams are not somehow more real than what happens when we are awake. Though such metaphysical criticism can easily become idle or simply ingenious talk, it should not be shut off until the exercise of supporting the generalizations seems to produce little new understanding of the play.

The question of what the play is about is not our only master key; *How does it work?* will also help us move about freely in our exploration, for *How does it work?* is a way of asking how and why we are affected by the play, why we like it, what it is that makes it so much like a wonderful dream. "past the wit of man to say what dream it was" (104.208-09). A large part of the most satisfactory explanation will consist simply of pointing to passages of poetry that enchant us, or charm us like the action of magic juices. For example, those beginning with the lines: "Your eyes are lodestars, and your tongue's sweet air" (47.183); "As wild geese that the creeping fowler eye" (79.20); "Tomorrow night, when Phoebe doth behold" (48.209); "The cowslips tall her pensioners be" (55.10). And there is Titania's description of the effect in nature of her quarrel with Oberon (58.81-117), as well as the story of her love for the mother of the changeling (59.122-37). There is also Oberon's account of the origins of pansies (60.155-69), and his lines beginning "I know a bank where the wild thyme blows" (64.249); and many more. The rhythms of accent and juncture, the quality of the sounds that make up the words as well as the imagery (the things and actions referred to in the passages) are all sources of pleasure and answers to the question, *How does it work?*

Shakespeare put into this play in one way or another a remarkably large number of the sports, pastimes, and amusements that were in fact part of the typical lavish program of entertainment at the elegant house parties given by wealthy lords in Queen Elizabeth's day. As the play opens, Theseus is discussing with the master of the revels the "merriments"

(41.12) that are to constitute the "pomp," "triumph," and "reveling" (42.19). And without denying the strong unity of the play, we may look on it as a collection of entertainments —or at least as a series of little parts: scenes, speeches, and actions that please us. The play "works" by keeping us constantly pleased as we move from one little pleasure to another. Only, perhaps, in some of the long passages involving the thwarted lovers and the comedy of errors may our interest lag. Almost always there is something comic or something lyrical to listen to, something that sounds funny or sounds beautiful.

But finally students will need something more than these two master questions if they are to discover how and why they felt as they did at the end of the play. Why, we must ask, is our pleasure greater than the sum of the pleasures we have picked out and discussed? For Shakespeare's play is more, it turns out, than just something to watch (or read) on a holiday. It seems to be "worth remembering," or "unforgettable," as the movie critics have called so many movies we have forgotten. Students, in short, will want to know what the play means; and though we may first wish to argue that it does not have and does not need a meaning, any more than a lovely piece of music or a pure ballet has or needs a meaning, we must still be sure not to neglect the difference between literary art and other arts: if we allow or encourage discussion of what *Hamlet* or *Macbeth* means, we should be prepared to direct a discussion of the possibility that this entertainment, this dream, has meant something to those students who liked the play because it seemed to reveal some truths they may not have known they knew. Not all good things in life come from acts of our own reason and will. Language is more than a means of communicating ideas. Dreamers, lovers, poets, and other madmen need not be superhuman or subhuman. Not all serious men are somber. Boredom and its common product melancholy are evils, enemies of life, and sometimes they may be warded off by the magical sounds, images, and perspectives of a dream.

So the study of this lighthearted play should be taken seriously, and should be directed toward discoveries not only of all the elements (character, plot, setting, language, and imagery) by means of which it creates the world of the play but also of all the aspects of human life that it seems to represent in a way we recognize as true to life. The study of dreams was therapeutic centuries before Freud.

THE ACTION

I.i

There are probably enough "facts" to get straight in the opening scene without adding irrelevancies about who Theseus and Hippolyta were in Greek mythology. It is enough to say that Shakespeare wanted the story to seem romantic and far away, but that he could scarcely keep a character called the Duke of Athens from seeming to be much like an Elizabethan nobleman, with his Master of the Revels, Philostrate, whose position and function in the noble household should be explained. The characterization of the four young lovers is so faint that students should be given some hint about how to remember which is which. The relationship at the opening of the play can be diagramed thus:

Neither man loves Helena; both love Hermia. Helena is unhappy because she loves Demetrius; Hermia is unhappy because although Lysander returns her love, her father wants her to marry Demetrius. Later, Puck's mischief changes the relationship (67.78).

That is, Lysander switches his affection from Hermia to Helena. Both women are now wooed by the wrong men. After the second application of the magic juice (82.102), the relationship changes again:

Now both men love Helena; neither loves Hermia; but finally (95.452) Puck puts things right:

Of the four "plots" in the play, two are introduced in this first scene (the third, in the second scene, and the fourth in the next—i.e., II.i). Both plots have to do with marriage, and the relationship between the two may be suggested by facing up to modern objections to the cruelty or injustice of Egeus' insistence that his daughter, Hermia, marry the man he prefers instead of the one she loves. Theseus, presumably a good ruler, supports the "cruel" father. Why? The end of the play, or the effect of the play, is partly to establish order; and the ideas of order, rank, and authority and their relation to society (or family structure) should be considered. It may be useful to remind students that in Elizabethan times there *were* marriages for love, sometimes in spite of parental objection. And it would also be appropriate to point out two things about literary convention: first, we do not find the father-daughter conflict unreal or unconvincing, because we know it is a commonplace in *stories,* especially in fairy tales, myths, and romances; second, in plays in general, and especially in Shakespeare, we accept as given the facts that produced the conflict we are about to watch—we ask only that everything growing out of the given situation be convincing. The opening scenes of a Shakespearean play usually contain the exposition of what produced the conflicts that constitute the play. We are not disposed to argue about it; we want to get on with the play. Two questions about the verses in I.i.: what is there about lines 135-49 that reminds us of opera, and why, if this play were an operetta, might 141-49 be one of its most famous arias? The other is, why the rhymed couplets toward the end of the scene? And what is the effect of the rhymes in the stichomythia in 192-201?

I.ii

Though students may understandably think this scene has more to do with what makes things fun on Stunt Night at Camp Hoki Hoki than with what makes a play a success, it should not be difficult to discover how many standard problems of theatrical productions are glanced at in this short scene of low comedy. This company of players is like many others: it has only one real actor, and is lucky to have him. Bottom's genius seems to be related to his passion to "play many parts" (see *As You Like It,* 77.142). If Shakespeare is satirizing his own profession as an actor, he is also satirizing his profession as a playwright—the play and the company deserve one another; and if this is satire, it certainly is good-natured, since we are made to feel the good will of the company and are convinced that the impulse to put on a play is a civilized, human, and humane impulse—that organized, artful make-believe is somehow a good thing.

In discussing this exposition of the third plot, students should be led to recognize that the play being cast is about frustrated young lovers and has some faint and comic resonance with the story of our four young Athenians (just as

Oberon and Titania, in the fourth plot, have some similarity to Theseus and Hippolyta: both pairs are more mature, all are noble figures of state). And in respect to style, one ought not to miss Shakespeare's comic treatment of such serious questions as verisimilitude (Bottom's concern lest the audience be overpersuaded and forget that it's only a play, III.i,) and the contemporary taste for bombastic dramatic poetry (Bottom's "This was lofty!", 40).

II.i

This is a good point at which to remind students that Shakespeare did not himself mark the act and scene divisions in his plays: they were put in later by editors. Where one scene ends and another begins is easy to see: when all the characters have left the stage the scene is over. But no such single formula governs the act divisions. One could, for example, make a good case for including II.i in Act I, since it is the last of the three introductory or expository scenes.

On the other hand, the break between Acts I and II is a break between the real world of Athens and the fairy world of the *"wood near Athens"* (1 s.d.), and the fourfold plot is only one of several ways to see the structure of the play, which is also held together by the opposition between the world of men and the world of fairies. Having noticed this, students might then be asked which of these two worlds, Athens or fairyland, has the most real life in it. The terms "real" and "life" need not worry us at this point. Being in love but not married and being married but not constantly in love are both conditions experienced in real life, but we tend to think of the conditions or facts of married life as being more true to life than those of courtship, perhaps simply because courtship is short and marriage is long. So we are amused to discover that it is not till we get into fairyland that we see and hear so much that is like real life: not lovers, but man and wife; not lyrical, dreamlike eternal love, but love and jealousy mixed; not life in a never-never land of dukes and Athenian counts, but life in an English village, with stallions and young mares, old women exchanging gossip and drinking English ale flavored with (pickled?) crab apples; not life in a romantic wood, but life in a real English countryside afflicted by the meteorological vagaries described in 81ff.; not the little-girl love of Helena for Hermia, but the mature love of one woman for another, as we discover it in one of the best speeches in the play (122-37).

The folklore should be discussed with the help of the notes

and the Introduction, and Puck's character and motivation might be compared with those of some of Shakespeare's fools, on one hand, and with those of Ariel in *The Tempest* on the other. The great poetry in the play is by and large spoken by Oberon, Titania, and Puck; and students should be set thinking about the propriety of putting the best art and poetry and some of the best scenes of real life in the fairy (dream, poetic) world rather than in the real (waking, reasonable, prosaic) world.

II.ii

This scene is a straightforward continuation (in *"Another part of the wood,"* 1 s.d.) of the action in the previous scene, and together these scenes bring three of the play's plots together (Oberon has come to Athens to bless the marriage of Theseus and Hippolyta). Bottom & Co. will become involved in the next scene (III.i). Here students should be reminded that when produced, these scenes are full not only of the poetry which we can all hear, but of color and movement, of costumes and dances; and that such scenes help give the play its tone of a revue, light opera, operetta, or musical comedy —works we may admire only for the individual scenes or routines that make up the whole. But having recognized that, we must not neglect our pleasure in noticing such thematic facts as that even the supernatural agents (Oberon and Puck) with supernatural powers (the juice) seem to be able to make errors, and that even when the gods try to help men, men sometimes help to make the divine plans go awry. And what are we to think about Hermia's dream? Both Helena and Hermia are now part of a bad dream.

III.i

This scene and IV.i enclose, or bracket, the central scene of the plot, III.ii, in which the four young lovers suffer the climax of Puck's mischief as well as the beneficent magic that resolves the confusion and assures us that "Jack shall have Jill" and "Nought shall go ill" (96.461-62). The conventional human trials of love and self-deception are set in a context of high caricature—an outrageously funny incongruity involving a clown who does not know that he is an ass and a fairy queen who does not know that her beloved is a clown. The scenes revealing the dreams of Titania and Bottom are the most comic in the play. They are the most dream-like. They are also an essential part of the play's meaning. This scene, III.i, should be worked out carefully in class so that students hear the dialogue and see the action. As the scene opens, we feel at once the grotesque contrasts produced by the presence of the rude mechanicals in the world of the fairies, for as Quince and his fellows enter, we notice Titania asleep in the background. The rehearsal of "Pyramus and Thisby" is full of comedy that depends on the contrast between the players' assumptions about how the imagination works and a poet's or playwright's assumptions about imagination. The players think the audience will confuse art and reality just as they themselves do. Like many unskilled actors, they trust neither the play nor the audience. But the first one hundred lines are low comedy compared with the exquisite fancy of the meeting of "translated" (120) Bottom and deluded Titania. Incongruity is the most common cause of laughter, and the scene is a dazzling composition of incongruities. It may spoil the fun to point them all out. It may be best simply to read the dialogue as well as possible, emphasizing not only Bottom's supreme self-confidence and native wit, but his natural courtesy as well. In dreams we are ourselves, only more so.

Students will doubtless notice that when Bottom plays the role of the sophisticated satirist and utters his sententious observation that "reason and love keep little company together nowadays" (144-45), he makes a statement that could serve as an epigraph for the play. Shakespeare put it in the mouth of an illiterate weaver and ham actor.

III.ii

This scene, the midpoint in the play, contains the high point of the mischief, or the confusion; after it everything rolls downhill toward happy resolutions. Offstage during this scene Bottom and Titania are in the height of their deceptions, and onstage Oberon and Puck, making their second effort to help smooth the course of true love, succeed only in introducing more perturbation—confusion worse confounded. Part of our pleasure in this episode is what we feel whenever a variation is made on a variation: it is like our pleasure when a juggler, having extended himself to what we assume must be his utmost, produces one more complication into his already breathtaking performance. We may also enjoy the suffering of all four lovers because we are sure they will soon be blest with a happy ending. Like Puck, we laugh to see what fools these mortals be, and are pleased by the errors because we find their "jangling" to be "a sport" (353). Within limits we all like mischief; teasing is often the product of boredom; watching a quarrel may be better than watching a love scene. But on the whole, we find this part of the comedy (a kind of variation on old Roman comedy of disguises that Shakespeare had imitated in several earlier comedies) not really so engrossing as the rest of the play. Shakespeare helps us through this dull stretch by some individualization of the two quarreling women (little Hermia's sensitivity about her shortness reminds us of Cleopatra's similarly feminine anxiety about her own stature); and the romantic picture of their girlish loves contrasts with the love of Titania for the mother of the foundling. Oberon's elaborate practical joke (also an example of a very old comic device) of misleading Lysander and Demetrius when they are trying to fight makes for some broad-humored stage business, a little like the confusion Prospero asked Ariel to produce in *The Tempest*.

The parody of Puck's last speech in this scene may be a good place to consider the form and function of the tetrameter verse, to notice that the song is a chant, and that chants that weave spells are "enchanting."

IV.i

In a way this scene concludes the action—that is, the true lovers are reunited, Oberon wins the child, Titania is released from her spell, and Bottom is freed to return to rehearsal. Though in such a comedy we are not much distracted from the fun by considerations of fairness, or justice, it may be that we are dimly aware that both the lovers and Titania suffer the appropriate bad dreams, for what delights us in the irony of Bottom's pompous observation that "reason and love keep little company together nowadays" (76.144-45) is the fact that lovers think they are reasonable. Indeed we enjoy being reminded that most of the time we assume we are acting more reasonably than in fact we are; and most of the time we think we have more control over our own lives than in fact we have. Titania may seem to us to have had a right to the changeling, but in fact she deceived herself in thinking that she was right to resist the authority of her husband. Bottom comes out of his experience enriched: the dream was not a testing or a punishment to him; it was a release.

The three speeches of Theseus and Hippolyta upon their return to the stage (106-130) have been much admired. Without going seriously into the complexities of a discussion of the development of Shakespeare's verse, or trying to decide why these speeches may remind experienced readers of the mature Shakespeare, we may still profitably ask students to compare these twenty-five lines with other passages in the play and, by analyzing the syntax, diction, imagery, and patterns of accent, to make some explanation of their effect. Perhaps students should be told that educated Elizabethans were generally able to sight-read and sing parts—and that in fact Elizabethan gentlemen *did* try to constitute their packs of hounds so that the various pitches of their cries would produce an harmonious tone, or kind of chord. Students should consider the dramatic function of the speeches and discover how they help to reestablish our sense of Theseus, whom we had almost forgotten.

In the last thirty lines of the scene, the five mortals who have spent the night in the wood under the spell of Oberon and Puck speak of their experience as if it had been a dream and are uncertain about whether they are now awake. Which is dream and which is real life has always been a fascinating question, and it fascinated Shakespeare. It is, of course, no problem for Bottom, who when he promises to have Quince write a ballad about it is doing what an Elizabethan might well do. Ballads were more like newspapers than what we think of as folk songs: they were accounts of newsworthy happenings; some of them, naturally, were sensational!

IV.ii

Broad comedy seldom reads well. It depends for its effect on the speaking and gestures of actors and upon the contagiousness of laughter in an audience. A good deal of what apparently tickled Shakespeare's audiences—especially the malapropisms—does not amuse us. The great comic powers of Shakespeare are illustrated not by Quince's "he is a very paramour for a sweet voice" (11-12), but by Flute's reply: "You must say 'paragon.' A paramour is, God bless us, a thing of nought" (13-14). The genius of the line is not easily explained, but it should nonetheless be pointed at, just as it should be in that fine speech of Bottom a little earlier: "I have a reasonable good ear in music. Let's have the tongs and the bones" (98.31-32).

V.i

The play ends with a song and dance and a benediction; and the whole last scene (all of Act V, that is) is more like an epilogue or grand finale than most fifth acts, simply because all the conflicts have been resolved and order restored by the end of Act IV. Dr. Johnson noticed that Shakespeare often finished up his plays carelessly and hurriedly, as if he had not had the patience to finish them carefully. But in *A Midsummer Night's Dream* Shakespeare prolonged the action of the last act just enough to throw the central action into perspective, to suggest that his own play was only part of a celebration of a great event, just as *Pyramus and Thisby* is just a part of the program of festivities for the marriage of Theseus and Hippolyta ("A fortnight hold we this solemity,/In nightly revels and new jollity," Theseus says, at lines 371-72).

Of the three parts of this scene—the conversation of the audience before the play (1-105), the play itself (106-372), and the return of "fairy time" (373-440)—the second and third should be discussed first. About the great performance of Peter Quince's Company, students should be told that "audience participation" at such amateur theatricals was common in Elizabethan houses, and that our fun in the grotesqueries of the performance is considerably increased by the competition in wit that it stimulates in the noble audience. Having members of the class read the parts as they were spoken by the rude mechanicals will help to suggest how funny the scene can be when all this illiteracy is *heard*. But with some help students can also be made to see how the performance of *Pyramus and Thisby* seems to reinforce some of the meaning of *A Midsummer Night's Dream:* if we go back to the rehearsal scene (71.1–74.103), we can see the irony of Bottom's anxiety about what Coleridge called the audience's willing suspension of disbelief, that is, their desire (and their ability) to forget that they are in a theater and that what they are watching is not real life. Bottom is afraid the play will have more verisimilitude than the audience can stand, whereas of course no one will be able to take the play seriously. On the other hand, the players are afraid that if someone does not play the moon and the wall, the audience will not be able to imagine the setting of the play. The rehearsal and the performance are a kind of in-joke about the theater and aesthetic theories about the workings of the imagination; and so the whole thing plays a variation on the theme of what is real and what is only our imagination, or how do you tell a dream (or a play) from real life.

At midnight Theseus puts an end to the fun and bids all good night; everyone leaves the stage (in fact, marking an end to a scene), and Puck enters with a broom. Once again it is the fairies who bring us closest to real life: the imagery is full of the workaday world, of English life, of basic human concerns about the forces of nature that can bless as well as torture men, about love and children. The rhythms remind us again of chants and charms, and though we know folklore can be called a body of superstitions, we can hardly resist feeling that this is a religious blessing, true in its central human values, and that in the dream and its "shadows" (425) we have seen reality.

But the students' final discussion of the play should center on the famous speech with which Theseus opens Act V. Some students will want to learn the speech, and if they are encouraged to do so, they may also be warned about the dangers of thinking that what they are learning is "what Shakespeare said" about poetry. We cannot know what Shakespeare *believed;* we don't know whether he agreed with what he made Theseus say. Sometimes, in other words, people who learn famous speeches from the plays of Shakespeare forget the context: the circumstances under which the speech was uttered and the character of the person who uttered it (was he a good person? or a wise person?).

Now we do not, in fact, know much about Theseus, but the fact that he is a duke disposes us to believe that he is at least not stupid, and his wisdom and goodness in first supporting Egeus' conception of the family and then in recognizing the higher claims of love have already reinforced our respect for him. Still these virtues—intelligence, justness, kindness—do not make him an authority on poetry, or love, or psychology. He sounds, in fact, more like an able soldier or businessman who "knows what he likes" than like a literary critic. We do not, in short, believe that this warrior (and duke, and lover of hunting) has the same character we imagine the actor and poet Shakespeare to have had. The two men could have admired one another without agreeing about art.

The only way to judge whether what Theseus says is what Shakespeare believed is to see whether what the speech affirms is consistent with what the play as a whole seems to affirm. We can, of course, notice that what Theseus says about the madman, the poet, and the lover had been said many times during the two thousand years since Socrates had pointed out that all three kinds of madness produced versions of truth; but that historical argument—that Theseus' opinion is an old and respectable one—will not help to prove that Shakespeare agreed with it.

Students should be given plenty of time to consider the speech, proposition by proposition, especially from the point of view of its relevance to the play, the work of art, the product of Shakespeare's imagination, which they have just read,

Emphasizing the words "shaping" and "bodies forth" (14) and "shapes" (16) may lead to some discoveries about the function of the imagination and about the way to conceive this play, all plays, all poems, all works of art. "Forms" (15) probably means "ideas," which are of course not "things" (*cf.* "airy nothing" in line 16). Thinking about what language does to ideas when they are given a name may lead to discoveries about what distinguishes literature from other arts as well as about how our sense of the reality of this play on all its levels of improbability is created simply by words.

After they have considered the shaping function of the imagination, its power to *make* a work of art, students may turn to the question of whether what the imagination makes is true; and this question may be approached by asking whether the lover is right in seeing Helen's beauty in the face of a homely (or ugly) girl (Elizabethans thought fair complexions beautiful, dark complexions ugly). Certainly Titania was foolish about Bottom; on the other hand Lysander sounds pretty foolish when he talks about the reason in love: "The will of man is by his reason swayed/And reason says you are the worthier maid" (68.115-16).

Perhaps a study of the speech along these lines will lead to the conclusion that Theseus' argument can be used against him. He seems to argue that we should not believe what the imagination of a lover or a poet makes us see because these things are "More than cool reason ever comprehends" (16). But *A Midsummer Night's Dream,* the work of Shakespeare's "shaping fantasy," makes a strong case for the proposition that we do and *should* (at least sometimes) believe what art and love make us see *because* such visions allow us to see a kind of truth or reality that transcends the limits of "cool reason."

SCOTT ELLEDGE

SHORT-ANSWER QUESTIONS

1. Why does Theseus in the opening speech compare the moon to a "stepdame"? Does the comparison suggest anything more than Theseus' wit?

2. What words in Hippolyta's reply (41.7-11) suggest that her attitude about the delay is different from Theseus'?

3. Does Egeus think Lysander's style of wooing was unfair? What would have been more "fair"? (42.28-38)

4. When Hermia wishes that her father would see Lysander with her eyes, what can she mean? How could he "look" with her "eyes"? (43.56)

5. What does "course" mean in 46.134, and what does the metaphor contribute to the idea of love?

6. Is the effect of Lysander's listing of the hardships of love comic or tragic? (46.135-49) What is the effect of the last line?

7. Consider the things Hermia swears by in 47.168-76. What does "simplicity" (171) mean? Should this speech be read with passion or with laughter? What difference does it make how it is read?

8. In Helena's speech at the end of Act I, scene i, what is the evidence that she is very wise about love, and what is the evidence that this wisdom is useless to her?

9. The speeches of the rude mechanicals are in prose; what is the difference between the verse of the speechs of the four lovers and that of the speeches of Hippolyta and Theseus? And what distinguishes the verse of the fairies' speeches from that of all the others in the play?

10. In Act I, scene ii, how, and how soon, do we get the idea that Bottom is the leading spirit of the company?

11. What does Bottom mean by saying that his speech (51.32-39) was "lofty"? What makes it funny? What might have made it funnier to Shakespeare's audience?

12. Lysander (48.209) promises to meet Hermia in moonlight; Quince calls his first rehearsal (53.102) in moonlight; and Oberon and Titania are "Ill met by moonlight" (57.60) When we consider that the play opens with a reference to the moon, shouldn't we feel that Shakespeare

is emphasizing the moon? If he is, what could be his reason?

13. In the Fairy's first speech (55.2-17), what is the effect of the rhyme and meter?

14. In 56.18-31, Puck gives the Fairy (and us) the story of the quarrel between Oberon and Titania. How does the story help to characterize them?

15. In 56.33-57.57 what is it that makes our impression of Puck so vivid?

16. Titania's speech beginning at 58.81 is one of the finest passages of poetry in the play. Why does it make such an instantaneous appeal? Could this account of disordered nature and its cause be thematically related to the meaning of the play as a whole, or is it simply a handsome addition to a collection of poetic passages? How is it like a long cadenza?

17. What is Titania's reason for refusing to give up the changeling? (59.122-60.137) What makes us sympathize with her? Why is the remembered laughter important? The scene Titania recalls so vividly is both concrete and witty; what is the wit in comparing the votaress with "embarkèd traders"? What were the "trifles" (133), and to what did they correspond in the ships? (127)

18. Oberon's account of the origin of the magic juice (60.148-61.172) is a little set piece; does it also make some contribution to the general meaning of the play?

19. Most of the dialogue of the lovers is in rhymed couplets; how do you account for the blank verse in the Demetrius-Helena scene? (62.188-63.242) (Compare 80.41ff.)

20. Oberon's description of Titania's bower (64.249-57) is not necessary to our understanding of the fairies' character or of the action; why not cut it out?

21. In Oberon's charm (65.27-66.34) what have the animals in common?

22. What makes Lysander's speech (68.115ff.) funny?

23. What did Hermia see in her dream (69.145-56), illusion or reality?

24. In the conversation preceding the rehearsal (71.1-73.77) Bottom considers four problems of illusion and four solutions; of course the discussion is funny, but is it not somehow a comic variation on a theme of the play as a whole?

25. What is the effect of "nowadays" in 76.145?

26. What is the effect of the confrontation of the extremes in the last part of III.i? What makes the contrast between Bottom and the fairies seem so sharp?

27. In Puck's account of the transformation of Bottom (79.6-80.4) what does the simile of the birds add to our delight or understanding? Is it simply decorative?

28. What new meaning does the context give to the famous line "Lord, what fools these mortals be!"? (83.115) What does Puck mean by "And those things do best please me/That befall prepost'rously"? (83.120)

29. Notice the rhyme schemes of Lysander and Helena's speeches. (83.122-33) How do you account for this oddity?

30. Demetrius' praises of Helena's beauty (84.137-44) are in the fashion of hyperbolic comparison; is it only the dramatic situation (the context) that makes them funny, or are they in themselves ridiculous?

31. Are our efforts to distinguish Helena from Hermia assisted by Helena's memory of their early friendship? (86.202-14)

32. Hermia is sensitive about her shortness (89.290-98); how do we react to her anger? What does Puck mean in line 353?

33. The long speech of Oberon beginning at 91.354 is in couplets, just as are the speeches of the lovers; why do Oberon's lines sound more like poetry than do the lines of the lovers?

178   TEACHING SHAKESPEARE

34. How is our impression of Oberon affected by his lines beginning at 92.388?

35. What is the rhyme scheme of 95.431-36 and 442-47? How do you account for the variation from couplets?

36. Though he is onstage only part of the time, Oberon presides over the unraveling in the first scene of Act IV. How does Shakespeare reinforce our understanding of Oberon's powers? Does he make us feel that what happened to Bottom, the lovers, and Titania was completely out of their control? Or did they "assist" Oberon in his magic? That is, was Bottom still Bottom, Titania still Titania, and were the four lovers still themselves?

37. Oberon (99.49-66) seems in a way to have "cured" Titania more than tricked her; how do you explain that?

38. What do you think Oberon means by saying "Dian's bud o'er Cupid's flower/Hath such force and blessed power"? (100.76-77) What are the overtones of "blessèd" and why are they appropriate in this play?

39. With the coming of dawn, the winding of the horn, and the appearance of Theseus, Hippolyta, and Egeus, we move suddenly to another world. What is there in 101.106-102.130 that makes us feel the change?

40. In the end Bottom (see his speech beginning at 140.203) and Oberon seem to be complementary figures rather than contrasting ones. Explain.

41. In Theseus' famous speech at the beginning of Act V: (a) Paraphrase "Are of imagination all compact" (8). (b) What are good synonyms for "seething" and "shaping"? (4-5) (c) What is implied by "cool"? (6) How is the statement about the poet different from the statements about the madman and the lover? (d) What is a "fine frenzy"? (12) (e) Study the definitions of "form" in a good dictionary and discover some of the ideas Shakespeare may have meant to imply in the phrase "bodies forth/The forms of things." (14-15) (f) Theseus seems to say that "things unknown" (15) are "nothing" (16); is a product of the imagination which has been given a

A MIDSUMMER NIGHT'S DREAM 179

local habitation and a name a "thing" or "nothing"? (g) Explain the last five lines of the speech.

42. Does Theseus say anything in this speech (108.2-109.22) that you think Shakespeare would have disagreed with?

43. The audience at a performance of *A Midsummer Night's Dream* should agree with Hippolyta (109.23-27); why?

44. What, apparently, does Philostrate mean by "sports" (110.42)? Describe the four items from which Theseus makes his choice. What art forms do they seem most to resemble?

45. The discussion of the "production" by the "rude mechanicals" (110.61-112.105) can be read as a dialogue on art, with Theseus and Hippolyta representing different attitudes toward art (or bad art). Both positions are commendable, and each is appropriate to the character of the person expressing it. Discuss.

46. What is wrong with the Prologue's first speech? (112.108-17) In his second speech (113.127-114.151), mark all the expressions you think the audience will laugh at.

47. Are the comments by the members of the audience heard by the actors? Are the comments intended to make the players uncomfortable? In lines 211-18 we see again the difference between the taste of Theseus and Hippolyta. Explain. If Theseus were alive today, what would he say about plays and movies?

48. How do the verse form and the diction of the great speeches of Pyramus (119.273-120.308) and Thisby (120.326-121.349) make them hilarious?

49. Do you think it is right to end the play with the fairies on stage. Would it not have been better to end, as we began, in the "real" world of Theseus and Hippolyta and the four other lovers? Why all the horror in Puck's first twelve lines? (122.373-84) How are we made to feel a blessing in the "song and dance"? (123.403)

50. Oberon and Puck have the last speeches. Would it have been better to give Oberon the last speech? What is the

theme of Oberon's speech? What sort of speech is it? That is, is it a song of praise? A declamation? An argument? Or what? And what sort of speech is Puck's? Compare it with the last lines of *The Tempest*.

QUESTIONS FOR DISCUSSION

1. Discuss the role of, or the importance of, the moon in the play.

2. By what means does Shakespeare make Oberon, Titania, and Puck seem so human?

3. Does the play make us seriously consider the problem of evil in the world or the pointlessness of most men's lives? Explain.

4. If the play ends on an optimistic note, what is the source or cause of the optimism?

5. The play seems full of parallels, contrasts, pairs, symmetries, and regular patterns. Discuss.

6. How and why does Bottom emerge as one of the chief characters?

7. Titania promises to "purge" Bottom's "mortal grossness," but how well does she succeed?

8. What is it about this play that makes it seem more like a dream than most other plays of Shakespeare that you know?

9. In this play what has the poet Shakespeare given "a local habitation and a name" to?

10. Is Puck inferior or superior to the mortals he calls "fools?"

A MIDSUMMER NIGHT'S DREAM

SAMPLE TEST

I. (15 minutes)

Why wouldn't the play be just as good if all the action occurred in Athens? Or if the problems of the fairy world (such as the quarrel between Oberon and Titania) were solved in the "real" world?

II. (10 minutes)

Why wouldn't the play be better without the actual production of *Pyramus and Thisby*?

III. (20 minutes)

Answer briefly eight of the following questions:

1. What happened in the natural world as a result of the quarrel between Oberon and Titania?

2. How did Oberon persuade Titania to give back the changeling?

3. How did the juice of love-in-idleness acquire its peculiar power? What kind of love will it induce?

4. Who is Robin Goodfellow and what does he do?

5. Why do the rude mechanicals decide to produce a play?

6. Are there any average middle-class people in the play? Explain.

7. What are some of the verse patterns in the play? Explain the variety.

8. What are some of the reasons why "the course of true love never did run smooth"?

9. What does Bottom think of his dream?

10. What does Oberon say in his benediction?

THE TRAGEDY OF OTHELLO, THE MOOR OF VENICE

INTRODUCTION

Othello is the second of the five great tragedies by Shakespeare composed and produced between about 1601 and 1607, of which *Hamlet* is the first, and *King Lear, Macbeth,* and *Antony and Cleopatra* the third, fourth, and fifth, respectively. (For the approximate chronology of the plays, see Prefatory Remarks, pp. xii-xiii.) None of these five can rightly be ranked above the others, for all are incommensurable in their poetry and dramatic power, but each of them may be singled out for certain special qualities. By common consent, the special distinction of *Othello* lies in its superb construction, its sheer theatrical intensity and effectiveness. As playgoers from Shakespeare's day onward have testified, its unitary, relentlessly progressing plot holds audiences in the grip of mounting fear, suspense, and pity. Toward the end of the century in which the play was written, even the wrongheaded Thomas Rymer was forced to admit, more in anger than in sorrow, that playgoers customarily ranked *"Othello* above all other tragedies on our theaters" (p. 193).

The reasons for such popularity are not far to seek. To adapt the words of Samuel Johnson, the tragedy shows how "the cool malignity of Iago, silent in his resentment, subtle in his designs," working upon "the fiery openness of Othello, magnanimous, artless, and credulous, boundless in his confidence, ardent in his affection, inflexible in his resolution, and obdurate in his revenge," causes the Moor to murder his bride—the delicate, tender, and loving Desdemona, "confident of merit, and conscious of innocence," yet beautifully forgiving and protective of the husband who has "falsely murdered" her (155.116-24). We should add to this that the Moor, seeing the diabolical Iago as an honest and just friend and the saintly Desdemona as a foul and perjured devil, kills her in the conviction that he is performing a sacrifice in heaven's name; shortly afterward, learning the truth, he kills himself at the end of a speech reviewing the genesis of his terrible deed and characterizing it as an ignorant, savage, and unchristian act. Even in this summary, it is clear (to adapt Johnson once again) that we have in *Othello* "such proofs of Shakespeare's skill" in drama "as it is vain to seek in any [other] modern writer." To find comparable power of dramatic construction, harrowing irony, stunning reversal, and heroic self-confrontation, we have to turn to Sophocles' *Oedipus Rex*.

There is far more to *Othello*, of course, than the thrilling progression of its linear and ironic plot. The power and beauty of the play are greatly enhanced by its complex, multilinear progressions of character, motif, and language. By "motif" is meant a frequently repeated situation, idea, sensory object, class of objects, word, or phrase. Heavy use of motifs to enrich and refine the primary meanings generated by plot and character is characteristic of Shakespeare. Among opposing words and concepts frequently repeated and interwoven in *Othello* are hate against love, selfishness against obligation or duty, cynicism against idealism, being against seeming (inner reality against outward appearance, heart against tongue, performance against profession), love against lust, ocular proof against reason and faith, honor against material things, heaven against hell, black or dark against white or fair, justice against injustice, and honesty against dishonesty. (Beside the usual modern meaning of *honest* as truthful, the class should be aware of such Elizabethan meanings as chaste, honorable, decent, frank, trustworthy.) Other important ideas are witchcraft in both a literal and figurative sense and poisoning the mind and heart through the ear. Among the most important sensory objects in the play are the black skin of Othello in contrast with Desdemona's ("that whiter skin of hers than snow,/And smooth as monumental alabaster," 150.4-5), the handkerchief which Othello gave her and which Iago transmutes into the "evidence" that destroys her, images of illicit and animal copulation, and a whole array of references to lustful or loathsome animals (goats, monkeys, wolves, toads, asps).

Especially striking is the reduplication of incidents involving deception, jealousy, and judgment, in various senses of the term. All three of these motifs are introduced in the first scene and run throughout the play. The prime deceiver is Iago, who dupes successively Roderigo, Brabantio, Cassio,

Emilia, Desdemona, various Venetian officials, and, most destructively, Othello. The notion of benign or at least excusable deception is introduced in the clandestine marriage of Desdemona and the Moor and in her minor lie denying the loss of her handkerchief. Roderigo, Iago, Bianca, and Othello exhibit various forms of jealousy. "Judgment" is used again and again in two main senses. In one sense, it is the clear-eyed rational faculty which in everyday life is responsible for sifting reported information and sensory evidence, as the Duke and the Senators do in I.iii. According to a strong tradition older than Plato, the testimony of the eye or the ear was to be regarded skeptically, as very possibly dealing with appearance rather than with reality. Compare Henry V's remarks to Lord Scroop, "Not working with the eye without the ear,/And but in purgèd judgment trusting neither" (*Henry V*, 70.135-36). In his desperate state at the end of III.iii, Othello elevates "ocular proof" above the purged eye of reason and above faith, which is "the substance of things hoped for, the evidence of things not seen" (*Hebrews* 11.1); he thereby plays into the hands of Iago, who does not believe in "an essence that's not seen" (119.16). In another sense, "judgment" (as in the phrase "brought to judgment") refers to a judicial or quasi-judicial process, a trial in which a person is accused and defended, evidence being presented for and against him, and sentence thereupon being passed and in due course executed. Such judicial processes occur in the "trial" of Othello before the Senators (52-58.52-217), of Cassio before Othello and the night watch (83-85.161-250), of Desdemona before the private court of Othello's warped and clouded judgment (105.330 through 153.88), and of Othello once again before the Venetian officers and before the bar of his now purged and rectified judgment (163.334-52). In his great final speech, Othello is simultaneously plaintiff, defendant, prosecutor, defense attorney, jury, judge, and executioner. Never in the history of drama has a motif been pursued to a more remote, complete, and powerful conclusion.

Equally impressive is the dramatist's pursuit of the whole truth about the nature of the hero as he is placed in a field of force between Iago and Desdemona. All three characters are at once more particular and more universal than their counterparts in Cinthio's *Hecatommithi*. Without turning them into sterile allegorical abstractions, Shakespeare has nevertheless touched them with ideality. Desdemona comes much closer than Cinthio's character to a feminine ideal of purity, kindness, patience, obedience, and love. Othello is not merely a grave, middle-aged black African;* he has become, in A.C. Bradley's words, "the most romantic figure among Shakespeare's heroes. . . . There is something mysterious in his . . . wanderings . . . among marvellous peoples; in his tales of magic handkerchiefs and prophetic Sibyls; in the sudden and vague glimpses we get of numberless battles and sieges in which he has played the hero and has borne a charmed life; even in chance references to his baptism, his being sold to slavery, his sojourn in Aleppo." So too, Cinthio's ensign has not merely taken on a name and a particular set of resentments; he has also come to embody the very idea of evil—its emptiness and negation, its complete severance from and hatred of the life-enhancing virtues. Iago is the very antithesis of Othello. Whereas Iago, the hypocrite who hides his true identity under shifting masks, is the negation of authentic being ("I am not what I am," 41.62), Othello, in all he does and says, radiates a sense of defined and assured selfhood ("I fetch my life and being/From men of royal siege," 47.20-21)—a unity of the inner and outer man (contrast 41.58-60). Whereas Iago brags that he never acts out of "love and duty" (41.56), Othello in his first complete speech (47.16-27) emphasizes his services to the Signiory and his love for "the gentle Desdemona" (24).

A good way of getting students to enrich and refine this contrast is to have them compare Iago's and Othello's different modes of speech, their opposing voices (see Maynard Mack, "The Jacobean Shakespeare," pp. 213-23). In Iago we hear the voice of nihilism disguised as the voice of experience, bluff and undeceived; a diction devoid of poetic overtones but blossoming into a fertile lewdness on the subject of sex, giving the "worst of thoughts/The worst of words" (98.132-33). In I.ii and especially in I.iii, we hear the voice of Othello. It is in part the voice of a man who "commands/Like a full soldier" (66.36)—virile, spare, and pointed: " 'Tis better as it is" (46.6), "Let him do his spite" (47.16), "Not I. I must be found" (47.29); in part, the voice

---

* There is no doubt that Shakespeare's Othello is black, a Negro. Roderigo calls him "the thick-lips" (41.63), and the references to his black skin by others, in and out of his presence, and by Othello himself, are abundant (42.85,88 [the devil is of course black], 49.69, 54.98, 59.247, 60.285, 74.225, 101.230, 102.262, 107.384-85, and 155.130). Incidentally, Shakespeare might well have seen Negroes in England. In both 1596 and 1600, Queen Elizabeth announced that there were "already here too many" Negroes ("Negars and Blackamoores"), that "in these hard times of dearth" they were competing for employment and for "relief" with "her own natural" and Christian subjects, and that they should be transported out of England.

of open and generous comradeship: "The goodness of the night upon you, friends" (47.34), "How does my old acquaintance of this isle?" (73.201). But it is above all a voice remarkable for its eloquence and its rare poetry. Othello's language before his fall is noble and spacious, the product of a clear and wholesome spirit. His images are fresh, rich, and often exotic, rising naturally from fullness of experience in strange and distant places. They have magnitude and suggest greatness of mind. We get these qualities in abundance when Othello tells in I.iii how he spoke to Desdemona "of most disastrous chances,/Of moving accidents by flood and field,/ . . . of anters vast and deserts idle,/Rough quarries, rocks, and hills whose heads touch heaven" (55.133-40). (Note how the alliteration in 140 accentuates the rugged grandeur of the scene.) But there are also vivid touches in I,ii, as in the sweep of Othello's assertion that, but for Desdemona, he "would not [his] unhousèd free condition/Put into circumscription and confine/For the seas' worth" (47.25-27), or when he halts an incipient fray with the famous command, "Keep up your bright swords, for the dew will rust them" (48.58).

The grave, dignified, magnificently self-possessed Othello turns out, then, to be quite the opposite of the conventional stage blackamoor—the arrogant, bombastic, stealthy, and lascivious African described by Iago and Roderigo in I.i. Desdemona's first appearance on stage parallels Othello's, in that she too turns out to be quite different from the "still and quiet" tender maiden of her father's description (49.65, 54.95). In her society, to marry a Negro is to "incur a general mock" (49.68). But when she politely replies to her father's challenge (57.178-87), she is, like Othello earlier in the scene, absolutely calm and unwavering. Theirs is a "marriage of true minds" (Sonnet 116) which refuses to admit impediments of race, "Of years, of country, credit [i.e., reputation], everything" (54.97). She "saw Othello's visage in his mind" (59.247), and fell in love without reservation, body and soul, even to the extent of identifying completely with her husband's life-commitment as a soldier. She can no longer be "A moth of peace" (59.251), but is now Othello's "fair warrior" (72.179; cf. 116.151) and must follow him to the wars.

How Iago destroys this heroic union of Venetian and African, youth and middle age, tenderness and strength, beauty and valor, is the tragic burden of the play and will be examined in detail in the commentary following. At this point, it is proper to note that the pollution of Othello's mind by Iago is reflected also in the pollution of his language. His imagination and his speech become tainted with the Iago imagery of copulating and loathsome animals, of foul and monstrous evil.

In teaching the play, then, one must do justice not only to the thrilling plot but also to the wonderfully patterned, entirely convincing transit of the mind and soul of its hero—the noble Moor who moves from love and a beautiful, though somewhat overconfident and only partially tested, magnanimity and dignity to degrading jealousy, hate, darkening of judgment, and corruption of soul, then back again to love and a superb largeness of spirit, achieved this time through an agonizing, unsparing clarity of vision. Othello's recovery and recognition are all the more astonishing because they come so late, after he has fallen so far, and because they coincide with his sudden, overpowering suicide.

"O thou Othello that was once so good/Fall'n in the practice of a cursèd slave,/What shall be said to thee?" (161.287-89). Lodovico's question is the central question of the play. It is the question Elizabethans raised of man himself. When Hamlet saw man as "the beauty of the world" and "the paragon of animals," yet at the same time as the "quintessence of dust" (80.315-17), he was giving voice to a common and crucial paradox. Sir John Davies, in his poem of 1599, "Nosce Teipsum" ("Know Thyself"), put the paradox in this way:

> I know the heavenly nature of my mind,
> But 'tis corrupted both in wit and will;
>
> I know my soul hath power to know all things,
> Yet is she blind and ignorant in all;
> I know I am one of nature's little kings,
> Yet to the least and vilest things am thrall.
>
> I know my life's a pain and but a span,
> I know my sense is mocked with everything;
> And to conclude, I know myself a man,
> Which is a proud and yet a wretched thing.

No tragedy excels *Othello* in portraying both the grandeur and misery of being human. At the end of the final scene, we are aware of "the tragic loading of [Desdemona's] bed," the work of Iago, which "poisons sight" (164.359-60). But we are also aware of the words of the wronged and forgiving

Cassio when Othello, "Killing [himself], to die upon a kiss" (163.355), joins his ill-starred wife in death:

> This did I fear, but thought he had no weapon;
> For he was great of heart. (163.356-57)

THE ACTION

I.i

In the exciting opening scene, Shakespeare puts us in possession of the facts essential to the understanding of the action by allowing us to infer, piecemeal and gradually, as in life, something about the characters and the circumstances in which they are involved. He also presents us with some intriguing uncertainties: What is Othello really like? How did he persuade Desdemona to marry him? How will he meet Brabantio's potent challenge to the marriage, or the insidious—and greater—threat represented by Iago? The scene also sets an appropriately somber mood (both the first three and last three scenes take place at night, and in each case lives are at stake). Furthermore, it strikes the notes of judgment and jealousy at the very beginning of the play (Roderigo is jealous of Othello's success with Desdemona, Iago of both Cassio's and Othello's good fortune). And it does all this in such a way that it becomes a "mirror scene," one that in its design and inner dynamics reflects the action of the play as a whole. (On mirroring devices, see Maynard Mack, "The Jacobean Shakespeare," pp. 227-33, and, especially, p. 243.)

At the beginning of this scene two men enter carrying torches. They are arguing in irritated tones about a third man at first unidentified ("him . . . his . . . him," 6-9) and an event as yet unspecified ("this . . . such a matter," 3-5). Their tantalizing vagueness is entirely natural, for they know perfectly well whom and what they are talking about and need not spell things out to each other. The result of exposition of this sort is that information about Iago and Roderigo comes quickly and clearly, whereas that about Othello and Desdemona (she is not named until the second scene, 47.24, and he is not until the third, 52.48) comes slowly and in uncertain form. As a consequence, we can arrive at rapid and accurate conclusions about the first two speakers on stage, but we must suspend our judgment about the unnamed Moor and his relationship with the lady (not until 45.165 do we learn that they have in fact been *married*) until we can see and hear them for ourselves. We are thus involved, as audience, in a process of judgment which is crucial to the play from beginning to end and which involves, as characters, first Roderigo ("Now, sir, be judge yourself," 35), then Brabantio and the other Senators, and finally, Desdemona and Othello (see the preceding Introduction).

About Roderigo and Iago there is no question. From the opening lines (see Coleridge, "[Comments on *Othello*]," pp. 205-06), Roderigo appears as a dupe, "a gulled gentlemen" (38.5), and Iago as "a villain" (38.4) who is milking him for every penny in his purse (2-3). Notice how clearly Iago's character is defined by the dialogue. He is a person full of hate (note the cluster in 4-6 of "abhor," "hate," and "despise"). He also seems full of pride ("I know my price; I am worth no worse a place," 10), though in his comments on Cassio there is a trace of a nagging sense of inferiority which will later on emerge full blown: "If Cassio do remain,/He hath a daily beauty in his life/That makes me ugly" (144-45.18-20). Iago is certainly a materialistic manipulator and intriguer (in addition to controlling Roderigo's purse, he got "Three great ones of the city" to intercede for the lieutenancy, 7-9), a systematic dissembler whose words and actions belie what is really in his heart ("I am not what I am," 62), and, above all, a man who in his utter egoism ("I follow but myself," 55) rejects completely "love and duty" (56), rejects, that is to say, those instincts and habits of response—a fellow feeling ranging from friendliness to deepest love, a sense of obligation to others—without which any social life becomes impossible.

Can we accept the testimony of such a witness? Is Michael Cassio as inexperienced and unqualified as Iago implies (15-30)? If we focus, in particular, on Iago's (and, to a lesser extent, Roderigo's) view of Othello, Othello at first appears merely a "he" (6, 9, 11) of some authority who is said to be proud, arbitrary, and bombastic (10-15); he is then identified as a Moor (30, 37, 54), which to an Elizabethan would mean a Negro (see footnote to preceding Introduction), soon afterwards as "the thick-lips" (63), a thief (78), and, among other animals, "an old black ram/ . . . tupping [Brabantio's] white ewe" (85-88; 108-09, 113-14, 123). This language of animal copulation is "profane" (112) and false even to the literal fact—the marriage is not consummated until Othello and Desdemona are in Cyprus (78.9-11, 16-17). Such language comes readily to Iago's lips; it initiates an important strain of imagery, with which Iago will eventually "poison" and "plague" Othello's mind (65, 68). By the end of the scene, we know that whatever the Moor will turn out to be like, he will enter under a shadow. He is vulnerable because, despite his high position, he is to some extent an alien with no strong roots in Venetian society, a "stranger/Of here and everywhere" (133-34). Moreover, the Moor is a Negro in a white world; though Brabantio has "loved [him]" and "oft invited [him]" (55.127), the Senator is horrified by the thought of Othello as a son-in-law. Othello is even more vulnerable, of course, because he has for an enemy the cunning, cynical Iago, who conceals his malignancy under the mask of blunt, friendly honesty and loyal service. Henceforward, for the audience, all such professions of humanity by the nihilistic Iago will be bitterly ironical. Among other things, then, this first scene prepares for the piercing dramatic irony that pervades the rest of the play.

I.ii

It is still night (notice, at lines 1 and 28, the stage direction *"with torches"*), and the Moor enters with Iago, now displaying his "flag and sign of love" (45.153) and posing as a man of conscience, a bluff honest soldier who could barely restrain himself from striking Roderigo for his "scurvy and provoking terms" against Othello (1-9). (The foul language was mostly Iago's, of course.) Othello's entrance in colorful costume, with attendants carrying torches, is impressive. But even more impressive is his grave, dignified bearing, his manly sense of his inherent and earned merit, and his magnificent self-possession. To Iago's suggestion that he run and hide (as Iago himself did after he stirred up a commotion in scene i), Othello calmly replies: "Not I. I must be found./My parts, my title, and my perfect soul [i.e., my abilities, my position as general, and my unstained conscience]/Shall manifest me rightly" (29-31). Whereas Iago in I.i stirred up primitive, anarchic emotions, Othello here invokes restraint and reason, and with firm authority keeps the peace between two groups eager to fight: "Keep up your bright swords, for the dew will rust them" (58; cf. 80-83). But Brabantio cannot be persuaded to a peace by the black general (cf. "the sooty bosom/Of such a thing as thou," 69-70). He has already judged Othello a "thief" (Iago's word, 42.78) and an enchanter, and he formally arrests him in order

THE TRAGEDY OF OTHELLO 193

to deliver him up to justice (84-86). Hearing that the Duke and the Senator are in council (we already know that they are discussing the news from Cyprus, 38-46), Brabantio decides that they will judge his case against the Moor.

I.iii

The first and longer portion of this scene develops the judgment motif, as the Duke and his council first discuss Turkish intentions and then listen to Brabantio's charges, Othello's defense, and Desdemona's corroboration. In both instances reason prevails over confusion and hysteria, but at the end of the scene the stage is left to that powerful sower of discord, Iago.

The richly costumed Duke and council, in post-midnight session, are sifting ambiguous and contradictory evidence in order to arrive at a sound "judgment" (9) by "assay of *reason*" (18). Honors in this enterprise go to the canny First Senator. He rightly concludes that the Turk intends to attack Cyprus rather than Rhodes (18-30), convinces the Duke (31), and is immediately proved right by the messenger (33-42). Certain of his grounds, the Duke acts at once. This model of a proper relation between thought and action is duplicated as the "Valiant Othello" enters (48) and Brabantio repeats before the council his charges of theft and witchcraft. The Duke offers Brabantio severe, impartial justice (65-70), but he knows that mere assertion and "poor likelihoods" are "no proof" (106-09), and both he and the First Senator ask Othello for his side of the story (74, 110-14). Othello sends for the material witness, Desdemona (cf. 169, "Let her witness it"), and, meanwhile, in an admirable account of his courtship, proceeds to set matters straight. Othello's skillful oratory (he is, of course, anything but rude in his speech, 81-89) is a sign of his self-command. The benevolent white magic of Othello's words which awakened love in Desdemona (144-67), is in contrast to the malevolent black magic of Iago's words earlier and later in the play. "This only is the witchcraft I have used," Othello concludes as Desdemona enters (169). Once again, the Duke is convinced (170), and this before he even hears Desdemona.

For Desdemona's speeches (179-87, 243-54), see the preceding Introduction. Desdemona has deliberately defied convention by her "downright violence, and storm of fortunes" (244). A father's consent to his child's marriage was of enormous importance in those days, but knowing that Brabantio would never grant it, Desdemona and Othello have married without it (compare Jessica's marriage to Lorenzo and Juliet's to Romeo). This was a necessary deception, and Shakespeare does not want us to regard it as culpable. Nevertheless, it is a deception, and Brabantio has something of a case, for his paternal rights *have* been violated. Hence the Duke's mollifying reference to "this mangled matter" (171) and his "sentence" (197) which ends by advising Brabantio, "The robbed that smiles, steals something from the thief" (205). (It was a convention to put such maxims and aphorisms in rhymed couplets.)

Iago will later use the necessarily clandestine marriage and Brabantio's agitation as weapons in his assault on Othello's mind: "She did deceive her father, marrying you; . . . He thought 'twas witchcraft" (100.206, 211). For those who know the whole play, there is therefore a poignant prospective irony (that is, an unconscious or conditional prophecy, the partial, complete, or curious fulfillment of which is apparent to the audience but not the characters) in Brabantio's warning, "She has deceived her father, and may thee," and in Othello's reply, "My life upon her faith!" (288-89). There is irony, too, in Othello's next words, "Honest Iago/My Desdemona must I leave to thee" (289-90). By the end of the scene, honest Iago is planning "to abuse Othello's ears" and to destroy Desdemona's honor by charges that Cassio "is too familiar with his wife" (386-87). Words, then, are not just words, as Brabantio implied, and Othello's heart is certainly "piercèd through the ear" (216).

Coleridge calls Iago's soliloquy (374-95) "the motive-hunting of motiveless malignity" (p. 206). By this he means that Iago's malice, like the devil's with which Coleridge compares it (cf. Iago's self-association with "Hell and night," 394; cf. 353), is primary, compulsive, and fundamental, and that the reasons given for exercising this malice are secondary and accidental. Notice, too, that Iago's soliloquy is a parody of the process of judgment displayed earlier in the scene. He admits he has no evidence of adultery, only rumor and "mere suspicion," but he will act as if the proof is certain (378-81). Thus in Iago's case, far more than in the erring Gertrude's, "reason panders [i.e., is corruptly subservient to] will" (*Hamlet*, 119.89), inverting what Elizabethans regarded as a divinely ordained hierarchy of reason over will and will over appetite. Throughout Iago's amusing and sinister little sermon to Roderigo (296-373), egoistic will (cf. 316, 321, 331, 343) controls both reason and appetite. One is impressed, also, by the preacher's dedication to what is obviously a primary article in his creed: "Put money in thy purse."

II.i

In the Globe Theatre there was no curtain-plus-intermission to indicate the lapse of time for the voyage to Cyprus (at least a week has passed, 76-77), but the audience would know from the opening dialogue, and probably from sound effects under the stage (p.xv), that a fierce sea storm is in progress (1-19). Watching anxiously for approaching ships, the Cypriots soon learn that the Turkish fleet has been destroyed by the storm (9, 20-21). But fears for Othello's safety (33 ff.) are not dispelled until the ship sighted at line 92 turns out to be indeed the Moor's (176). In *Othello* the storm anticipates, whereas in *King Lear* (cf. 111.12) it simultaneously reflects, the "foul and violent tempest" (34) in the hero's mind (Acts III-V). Ironically, the lovers escape from nature's storm (67-73, 181-91) only to be shipwrecked by man's. Iago's evil presence is prominent in the scene. He enters with Desdemona (81), and the audience knows that the cynicism which he offers her as if in lighthearted banter (108-58) is his actual creed. He fairly drips with malice as he promises to ensnare Cassio in his own courtliness (note the special foulness of "clyster pipes," 175) and to untune the harmony of the lovers (197-99). (On the parallel between Iago's and Othello's observation of Cassio, see the commentary on IV.i.110-45, following.) As in the previous scene, the stage is surrendered to Iago, who first, with his usual ease, manipulates Roderigo, and then steps forward to bare to the audience his twisted and tormented soul. Note that his irrational jealousy, which gnaws his innards "like a poisonous mineral" (297), must follow necessarily from his poisonous creed—if all women are sluts and all men lechers, then Iago had better "fear Cassio," Othello, or any likely man, with his "nightcap" (307)—and that his program, as it has so far defined itself ("Tis here, but yet confused," 311), is to reproduce in Othello an identical "jealousy so strong/That judgment cannot cure" (301-02). In effect, Iago's program is to make the mind of Othello like the mind of Iago.

Such a task would seem almost impossible of accomplishment, were it not that the scene has revealed a new and special vulnerability in Othello. Self-assured, self-sufficient, the Othello of old—the Othello we see in Act I—has seemed a "nature/Whom passion could not shake" (129.265-66; cf. 115.135-37). But Othello's marriage has put him "into circumscription and confine" (17.26) as no previous relationship has done. Despite his later suggestion to the contrary,

Desdemona is not a falcon whom he can simply whistle off and let fly down the wind, for the thongs by which she is attached to her falconer are indeed his own "dear heartstrings" (102.259-63). Shakespeare demonstrates this, in thirty brilliant lines (180-210), when Othello lands at Cyprus. Unafraid of death, the Othello of old would never have been overcome with emotion just because he himself had survived a storm. What accounts for his present spontaneous overflow of feeling is his delighted astonishment at finding in Cyprus the wife who had sailed a week after he had and who, he had thought, was still exposed to the terrible storm. This is the "too much of joy" that makes him forget decorum, mention the destruction of the Turks almost as an afterthought, "prattle out of fashion, and . . . dote/In [his] own comforts" (195-205). So Othello's heart is no longer sovereign but subject to Desdemona, now "our great captain's captain," as Cassio sees (74). Iago sees this too—"Our general's wife is now the general" (87.314-15)—and he senses that Othello's "soul is so enfettered to her love" that she can "play the god/With his weak function [reason]" (88.345-48). What to normal humanity would be, at worst, the forgivable weakness of late and unrestrained love gives the antihuman Iago his unique opportunity to destroy Othello.

II.ii and II.iii

II.ii is not printed as a separate scene in the early texts, nor would it have been felt as such as the action flowed continuously across Shakespeare's open stage. (From II.ii to the end of the play, each scene follows close in time upon the previous one.) The scarcely intermitted echo of "honest Iago's" soliloquy puts a blight on the herald's proclamation of general rejoicing and on Othello's and Desdemona's brief passage to their nuptial bed (1-11). Iago concludes a small try at dragging Cassio's mind to his own level with "Well, happiness to their sheets!" (27) and then mounts a successful major effort. He gets Cassio drunk and embroils him in a quarrel with Montano, one of several Cypriot gentlemen whom Iago has likewise "flustered with flowing cups" (56). Note how Iago's explanatory soliloquy (46-61) clarifies, and thereby makes more ominous, the action to come; how plainly he functions as the prime mover of this action (27-44, 65-97, 133-34, 154-55); how quickly he slanders Cassio's "infirmity" (124) while pretending to be his friend; and how cleverly he plays the part of reluctant witness against the lieutenant (176, 178-86, 219-47). When information about the brawl is withheld from Othello, he almost loses his habitual self-command, "and passion, having [his] best judgment collied,/ Assays to lead the way" (205-06). Once the "facts" are in, however, he pronounces swift and severe sentence against Cassio (247-48). This is very characteristic. Othello is a military commander; in battle, lives have depended on his translating his "best judgment" into instant, vigorous action. He cannot dally with uncertainty. His instinct is to resolve doubts by an immediate appeal to further evidence, and then to act with utmost decisiveness, with an awesome kind of follow-through whose "compulsive course/ Nev'r keeps retiring ebb" (109.451-52).

Iago's rough, soldierly chaffing about the unreality of reputation (265-70) conceals his genuine hatred for good name and other time-honored values. By using Desdemona's kindness to slander her good name, Iago is typically pluming up his "will/ In double knavery" (64.384-85). To destroy someone through a weakness—say, a poor head for drinking—is great fun, "Pleasure and action" which "make the hours seem short" (379). But it is a far greater pleasure to destroy people through their merits—Othello through his love for Desdemona, his free and open nature, his passion for truth and justice, his habit of decisive action; Cassio through his honesty and trust (cf. 353), his good looks and courtliness; and Desdemona through her generosity and virtue. To "turn her virtue into pitch,/ And out of her own goodness make the net/ That shall enmesh them all" (360-62)—that is, after all, the cream of the devilish jest.

III.i

The action is continuous in the three scenes of this act. Morning has already come in the previous scene (89.378, 91.31), and Cassio appears before Othello's house with musicians. Like most bridegrooms, though, the general doesn't appreciate being awakened by the traditional serenade. The exchange with the clown supplies an interval before Iago enters again and offers "to draw the Moor/ Out of the way" (35-36), so that Cassio may speak freely to Emilia and then to Desdemona.

III.ii

Othello passes across the stage with Iago and others in his military retinue.

III.iii

Powerful in the poetry, pity, and terror of Othello's reversal from love to hate, unslacking in its momentum, this crucial "temptation scene," the longest in the play, is a magnificent tour de force. It follows brilliantly from everything that has been implied in the preceding action.

There are two resonant prospective ironies early in the scene. First, Desdemona assures Cassio, "For thy solicitor shall rather die/Than give thy cause away" (27-28). Othello, fondly recognizing Desdemona's affectionate sense of control over him, puts her off temporarily, and gives voice to the second prospective irony: "Excellent wretch! Perdition catch my soul/But I do love thee! And when I love thee not,/Chaos is come again" (90-92). Chaos thereupon moves toward Othello as Iago begins his jealousy-inflaming insinuations about the already tarnished Cassio.* His method is one of indirection: he advances an insinuation, withdraws it, and then reintroduces it under protest, seeming to weaken it by self-disparagement (136-48). As we have seen in II.iii, such withholding of information is likely to tantalize and infuriate Othello and lead him to a precipitous settling of accounts. "To be once in doubt/Is [once] to be resolved" (179-80). Iago creates a doubt so agonizing that the Moor will be induced to resolve his suspicions not by substantial evidence, but by "Trifles light as air" (319). Note the consummate hypocrisy and malice of Iago's arousing the suspicion by warning against it: "O, beware, my lord, of jealousy!" (165ff.). There is a parallel between Iago's attack on Othello here and on Brabantio in I.i.

Iago also works upon another set of vulnerabilities. Like everyone else, Othello believes Iago to be exceedingly honest, and Iago, playing the role of a native expert witness, comments on the cunning promiscuity of the average Venetian wife. On the heels of this, he strikes at Othello's marriage itself by representing as something sinister the deception without which the marriage could not have taken place (206-11; cf. 61.287-88). Notice that this dashes Othello's spirits more than a little (214-15). By attacking the precious new attach-

---

* One should note that in Elizabethan English, "jealousy" sometimes meant "suspicion, doubt, mistrust." This is the primary meaning of the word in lines 147, 165, 176, 192, 198 of the present scene. Iago eventually leads Othello into a degrading sexual jealousy, but he begins by suggesting to him that jealousy in the sense of vigilant suspicion would not be amiss.

ment to Desdemona, Iago is undermining what has become the very foundation of Othello's being. And then Iago stabs swiftly, staggeringly, directly at the Moor's sense of self, his sense of identity and worth (228-38): insultingly, he suggests to Othello's face that only foul and unnatural lust, "a will most rank," could make Desdemona choose someone so unlike herself in "clime, complexion, and degree" (compare Brabantio at 49.63-70 and especially 54.96-103), and that "better judgment" may well cause her to repent her choice. If normal instinct and good judgment will cause a wife to recoil in disgust from her husband, that husband is something less than a man; he is a thing (again, compare Brabantio's "such a thing as thou," 49.70), a kind of monster. When Othello accepts Iago's suggestion ("Haply for I am black," 262ff.), he accepts an insult that leads to profound injury of the self. By allowing it to be taken for granted that his black identity, his age, and his nationality are something naturally loathsome to Desdemona, he is in effect denying the validity and special worth of his particular manhood. For to consent to one's being taken for a monster is to consent to one's destruction as a man. Othello cannot lose faith in Desdemona's reasons for her choice without at the same time losing faith in himself.

From this point on, Othello's descent into the abyss of jealous passion is rapid and horrifying. He begins to sound more and more like the jealous Iago, subsisting on hatred ("my relief/Must be to loathe her," 266-67), taking on Iago's cynicism (all men are fated from birth to be cuckolds, 274-76) and his unpleasant language of animal sexuality ("I had rather be a toad," 269ff). Othello's language starts in fact to be contaminated by the Iago-strain from the beginning of his temptation: cf. "some monster in thy thought" (107), "Exchange me for a goat" (180). This process must be followed closely through III.iii and subsequent scenes, for it is the means by which Shakespeare shows us the mind of the victim cooperating in its own pollution and approximating in its vileness the mind of the victimizer. For the rest of Act III and all of Act IV, Othello's imagination, despite some patches of the old brightness, is "as foul/As Vulcan's stithy" (*Hamlet*, 100.85-86). When he returns to the stage after an absence of less than forty lines (288-326), we see with horror how deeply his mind has been poisoned by Iago's "Dangerous conceits" (322-26). Without a shred of concrete evidence, he has grossly exaggerated Iago's hints and warnings into near-conviction that Desdemona has in fact betrayed him (cf. 330, 335, 338, 342-43). Under the further proddings of his tormentor, Othello will settle for far less than ul-

rect "ocular proof" (356-57). Instead, Iago offers circumstantial evidence (391-405). And what does this amount to? When Othello hears a lurid tale of Cassio's talking in his sleep (410-23), he is ready to "tear [Desdemona] all to pieces" (428). When Iago merely reports that he saw Cassio wipe his beard with Desdemona's handkerchief, Othello exclaims, "Now do I see 'tis true" (441), and in fierce hatred pronounces vengeance against the supposedly guilty pair. This is, of course, a perversion of the process of judgment analogous to Iago's at the end of I.iii and II.i.

Perverted too are Othello's virtues of decisiveness, religion, and honor. "Like to the Pontic sea," he will rush "with violent pace" to a "wide revenge" (450-57); kneeling, he and Iago seal this bloody vow in a parody of a religious ceremony (457-66). Othello will now be swift to kill not merely out of justice and honor, as he later claims ("For naught I did in hate, but all in honor," 161.291; cf. also 126.210, 145.31-33, and 150-52.1-65), but in large measure out of the hatred and injured pride ("my name . . . is now begrimed and black," 383-84) expressed in this scene; he will not confront the supposed filcher of his good name (cf. 99.159) with the charges against him, but will be content to have him murdered in any way within three days (469-70); and he will himself murder his wife by "some swift means" (473-74). Finally, in the closing lines, we have a perversion of the military comradeship that has heretofore meant so much to Othello: "Now art *thou* my lieutenant" (475). Whereupon the man who in I.i boasted that he acted only for himself (41.38-62) replies, "I am your own forever." It is Desdemona, of course, who is Othello's own, even unto death and beyond. By the end of the scene, the union of Othello and Desdemona, based on love and forgiveness, has been replaced by the union of Othello and Iago, based on hatred and revenge.

III.iv

Throughout Desdemona's banter with the clown (1-22), which provides a brief but necessary plateau between peaks of emotion, we know that she is in danger. Our distress increases as the dialogue turns to the handkerchief, Othello's jealousy, and his approach (23-31). Everything Othello says is now full of hidden menace. Repelled by what he regards as Desdemona's duplicity—"O, hardness to dissemble!" (34)— he alludes riddlingly to Desdemona's moist palm as a sign of unrestrained sexuality (36-47) and believes he finds confirmation of her guilt in her untimely championing of Cassio (which, as Iago predicted at 89.359, undoes "her credit with the Moor") and her inability to produce the handkerchief upon request (51-98). Apart from regarding the handkerchief as something close to "ocular proof" (note Othello's emphasis on *seeing* the handerchief in Cassio's hand— 152.62,66; 158.212), the Moor values it as a symbol of sacred matrimonial love, first between his parents and now between him and his wife. (Nothing should be made of the trivial differences between his accounts at 55-56 and 158.213-14 of how his mother got the handkerchief. Shakespeare is occasionally inconsistent about such details.) In quasi-legal language, he describes it as a binding pledge and token, analogous almost to an engagement or wedding ring*—"that recognizance and pledge of love,/Which I first gave her" (158.211-12; cf. Emilia at 103.290). As such it stands at the center of his emotional life, and the magnificent poetry he lavishes upon it (55-75) is a sign of the preciousness of the love he believes Desdemona to have betrayed.

Stunned by Othello's unseemly rage, Desdemona informs Cassio that she has been unable to help him. When Iago hears of Othello's anger, he leaves, ostensibly to quench but actually to stoke the Moor's fire. As Desdemona and Emilia exit, the harlot Bianca enters and Cassio gives her the handkerchief he has found in his chamber. Iago's plot is working as well as evil heart could wish.

IV.i

Although Iago's hated rival Cassio is elevated at line 236 to command over Cyprus, IV.i is nevertheless the scene of Iago's greatest triumph over Othello. He controls Othello's emotions at will, conjuring up visions of Cassio and Desdemona in bed and allowing Othello to complete the fulsome picture for himself. As Othello does so, he suffers a simultaneous breakdown of language and of self-command, running on incoherently about "Noses, ears, and lips" and falling into a trance (36-45). When he awakens, Iago mocks and rebukes him with impunity and places him on the stage where he can spy on Cassio while Iago pretends to be talking about Desdemona (94-171). Now Othello is in the same position as Iago was at 72.165-75—standing off to a side, casting hate-filled glances and phrases at Cassio. (Thus Shakespeare uses stage movements and groupings to reinforce dramatic meanings;

---

* Elizabethan legal records show that handkerchiefs, in fact, sometimes served as tokens of betrothal or marriage in a private exchange of vows.

ask the class to find other examples of such use of the stage.) While Iago questions Cassio about Bianca, Othello's "unbookish jealousy" construes Cassio's "gestures, and light behaviors" (103-04) as evidence against Desdemona, and when Bianca gives Cassio the handkerchief, Othello takes that as proof that Desdemona is "such another fitchew [strumpet]" (146) as Bianca. Hence, when Desdemona speaks of "the love I bear to Cassio" and expresses pleasure in his promotion (233-37), her apparent brazenness infuriates her husband. As her kinsman Lodovico and the other Venetian officers look on in shocked disbelief, Othello strikes her, insults her, sends her home weeping, and dashes off muttering, "Goats and monkeys!" (263). He is echoing Iago's "Were they as prime as goats, as hot as monkeys" (107.400).

Yet the ensign's conquest over the soul of the general is not really complete. Iago has perverted Othello's "loving, noble nature" (76.289), but he has not destroyed it. He has prevailed upon Othello to murder Desdemona not in Iago's way, by poison, but rather in Othello's way, in an inversion of the Moor's characteristic sense of justice: "Strangle her in her bed, even the bed she hath contaminated" (209-10). But Iago cannot make the Moor forget Desdemona's beauty, sweetness, gentleness, "high and plenteous wit and invention" (191-92), nor can Iago eradicate the Moor's belief that such qualities can and should cohere with moral goodness. It is the disjunction between Desdemona's virtues and her seeming vileness that leads to the Moor's heartrending lament, "But yet the pity of it, Iago. O Iago, the pity of it, Iago" (197-98). Utterly isolated in his evil and emptiness, Iago is insensible to pity, incapable of that fellow-feeling which Wilfred Owen, in his poem "Insensibility," calls "the eternal reciprocity of tears." It is in fact the nobility which can be discerned even in Othello's perversion, the love he cannot forget even in his murderous hate, that make his fall so full of tragic pity and terror.

IV.ii

From the beginning of IV.ii to the point where Othello kills Desdemona, a few frail hopes are nourished by Othello's inquiry (1-23), Emilia's suspicions (129-43), Roderigo's brief revolt (171-202), Iago's misgivings (149.128-29), Othello's tears and kisses (150.1-22), and Emilia's knocking on the door when her mistress is "Not yet quite dead" (153.85). But in each instance, the hopes are abortive, and Othello's blinding jealousy, his "compulsive course" (109.451), his habitual decisiveness and follow-through ("Being done, there is no pause," 153.82) forestall delay or interruption of the tragic murder.

Othello sees Desdemona as sickeningly false, a "fair devil" (110.475), whose heavenly exterior conceals a rotten, hellish core. Here in IV.ii, where Othello treats Desdemona as a prostitute and Emilia as her bawd, this heavenly-hellish contrast occurs again and again. It tears Othello apart, and in his speech at lines 46-63 we see the deepest sources of his anguish. Sexual union with Desdemona has been for him the most intimate engagement of his entire being: "to be discarded thence" (59) is to be thrust out from "there where [he has] garnered up [his] heart,/Where either [he] must live or bear no life" (56-57). That is why the thought that Desdemona has casually sought sexual pleasure elsewhere and has lightheartedly given Cassio the sacred handkerchief merely to "gratify [reward] his amorous works" (158.210), is so appalling to him. How impudent can the strumpet be? * Why, even when she tries to deny her guilt—"Alas, what ignorant sin have I committed?" (69)—she has the effrontery to use the language of the seventh commandment: "Thou shalt not commit adultery" (*Exodus* 20.14). Furious, he repeats the word "committed" four times in nine lines (71-79). When he exits, he sees himself more than ever as the representative of divine justice, following the Lord's injunction to punish adultery by death.†

Othello's behavior leaves Desdemona stunned, "half asleep" (96). She is living through a nightmare; despite Iago's hypocritical assurances that all shall be well (169), she will not live to see the end of it.

IV.iii

Night has already come (3). As Othello accompanies Lodovico partway to his chambers, he orders Desdemona "to bed on th' instant" and asks her to dismiss Emilia (7-15). What follows is perhaps the single most poignant scene in Shakespeare. Desdemona's premonitions of death (23-25), her interpolated small talk with Emilia about unpinning and Lodovico's good looks (35-40), her struggle to keep poor Barbary out of her mind and her surrender to her preoccupa-

---

* In the Quarto, Othello's speech at lines 70-79 concludes with the outburst, "Impudent strumpet!"

† "If a man be found lying with a woman married to an husband, then they shall both of them die . . . so shalt thou put away evil from Israel." (*Deuteronomy* 22.22.)

tion as she breaks out into Barbary's willow song (26-58)—
all this is beyond praise. By magnifying our pity for Desdemona, the scene also magnifies the horror of her impending murder. That horror is further intensified by the absoluteness of Desdemona's purity. In contrast with the easygoing Emilia, who regards the world as "a great price for a small vice" of adultery (70-71), Desdemona would not "do such a deed for all the world" (65, 69, 80-81; cf. 136.162-63). And, again in contrast with Emilia, she wishes to requite evil not with evil but with good (89-108).

V.i

Outside, on a dark street, Roderigo tries to kill Cassio, but both are seriously wounded (Cassio very possibly by Iago's attack from the rear). Hearing Cassio cry out, Othello is inspired by Iago's example ("Thou teachest me," 33) to complete the double vengeance by killing Desdemona in her "lust-stained" bed (31-36). Nothing so much shows the perversion of the Moor's free and open nature as his calling the author of a treacherous nighttime ambush an honest, just, and noble friend. Iago thereupon puts his seal to the worthy title by killing his accomplice Roderigo, who gasps out "O damned Iago! O inhuman dog!" (62). Iago pretends concern for Cassio, tries to drag a red herring across the trail by accusing Bianca, and sends Emilia to the citadel to "tell my lord and lady what hath happed" (127).

V.ii

In this great last scene, all the strands of plot, character, language, and motif are woven into a triumphant design. As Othello enters with a light, the struggle between his love and his determination to deal out God's vengeance for sin resolves itself in tears: "This sorrow's heavenly;/It strikes where it doth love" (21-22). There are beauty and terror in this blasphemous comparison of himself to a stern but compassionate God, as there are in the words he repeats to convince himself that the murder is justified: "It is the cause, it is the cause, my soul./Let me not name it to you, you chaste stars./It is the cause" (1-3). Not since his arrival in Cyprus ("If it were now to die,/'Twere now to be most happy," 72.187-88) has he spoken with such simple power and beauty. Unlike the shallow Roderigo, who decides with a shrug, " 'Tis but a man gone" (144.10), Othello feels profoundly that something most precious will be lost forever should he once "put out the light" of Desdemona's life (7-15). Only a man of great soul could feel and speak in this way. But the Moor's soul is still distorted by hatred, pride, and jealousy, and when Desdemona awakens, his tone immediately becomes cold and curt. As she maintains her innocence, he is infuriated by her deathbed "perjury" (51,63), all the more brazen because of the ocular evidence, the handkerchief he *saw* in Cassio's hand (48-49, 62, 66). And when she weeps to hear that Cassio is dead, the judge who claimed he "would not kill [her] unprepared spirit" (31), seeing her once again as the "strumpet" impudently flaunting her sin to her husband's face (76-79; cf. 133.71-89), in a "bloody passion" (44) of jealous rage, puts her "to sudden death,/Not shriving time allowed" (*Hamlet*, 161.46-47). The irony is dreadful.

By another kind of irony, Iago is brought to inexorable justice through Emilia's instinctive adherence to the virtues he despises—love and duty. When Emilia defends her wronged mistress, Othello is as inexorably confronted with the full horror of his crime and self-deception. What shall be said of one who committed such a deed under the auspices of such a "demi-devil" (297) as Iago? To this question raised by Lodovico (287-89), and indeed by the whole play (see the preceding Introduction), Emilia, before she dies, offers a series of indignant answers (130-32, 154, 160-61, 230, 246) and Lodovico and Othello several more pertinent responses (279, 290-91). The fullest and most accurate answer is given by Othello himself, but his recognition is rightly delayed (334-52): only a tortuous ascent to light can balance so prolonged an immersion in darkness. Knowledge must precede judgment, "and the narrative in the end," as Doctor Johnson observed, "though it tells but what is known already, yet is necessary to produce the death of Othello." After he "Smothers" Desdemona (83 s.d.), Othello is in a state of distraction and shock (90-103), attempts to justify (128-214) an act that "shows horrible and grim" (200), and, when he learns that Desdemona is innocent, mounts two physical attacks on Iago (232-33, 282-83). Between these two sallies, Othello is obviously disoriented by his harrowing grief: when he finds the second sword (251), he seems at first to be threatening to escape, but instead stands, sword in hand, lamenting his fate and expressing unbearable remorse (256-78). The end of this speech is the nadir of an hysterical and almost animal suffering. A partial change seems to come over Othello with the wounding of Iago (283 s.d.). Shortly afterward, in response to Cassio's "Dear general, I never gave you cause" (295), we hear the spare and manly speech of the old Othello: "I do believe it, and I ask your pardon" (296).

But the great change comes when the remaining loose threads are tucked in (303-25). Othello now knows the whole truth of "what hath befall'n" (303)—knows simultaneously his own guilt and gullibility and Desdemona's transcendent faith and love—and his knowledge sets him free to speak and act like the Othello of old. His summation of the tragedy (334-52) throws out links to almost every important feature of the play. His first complete speech in I.ii referred to his service to the state; his last both begins and ends with such references. He recovers the full diapason of the language habitual to him before his fall. His opening lines are clear, soldierly, pointed (334-36); his later references to "the base Indian" * of the New World, to Arabian trees, and to the Syrian town of Aleppo (343-48) remind us of his romantic eventful history. Most remarkable of all, however, is the stern objectivity of his summation, a crucial part of which is closely modeled on the summary of "How these things came about" by the reliable choral character Horatio (*Hamlet*, 173-74.380-87). Both summaries are introduced by a four-word half-line ("So shall you hear," *Hamlet*, 173.381; "Then must you speak," 339), followed by four parallel object-clauses, each of which (except for *Hamlet*, 174.385) is introduced by the function-word *of*. (There are other minute similarities which cannot be discussed here.) In both speeches, the four object-clauses give an outline in chronological order, of the crucial events of the play. Othello might well say with Horatio, "All this can I/Truly deliver" (*Hamlet*, 174.386-87). His speech is far greater than Horatio's, however—morally by the degree to which objectivity about one's grave errors is more difficult for the offender than for an outsider, dramatically by the degree to which the tragic hero's own account of his tragedy is more powerful than a bystander's. With the last word of his account, Othello suddenly produces from his garments a dagger with which "He stabs himself" (352 s.d.). The surprise is great, for in this scene Othello has already been twice disarmed (232 s.d., 284 s.d.). Yet what else should we have expected? An officer carries small arms on his person: knowing Othello as we do, can we believe that he would wait a moment longer than necessary to execute just sentence on an offender?

Othello kissed his wife at the beginning of the scene; he

---

* This Quarto reading at line 343 is adopted by most editors. Elizabethan writers refer frequently to the ignorance of the Indians, who exchanged gems of great value for worthless trinkets.

kisses her now at the end. There is "No way but this" (354)—the way of honesty, courage, and expiation demonstrated in his final speech and act—to earn that profoundly moving dying kiss. The heroic lovers, each at his best fully worthy of the other, are united once again.

EPHIM FOGEL

SHORT-ANSWER QUESTIONS

1. What are Iago and Roderigo arguing about before they awaken Brabantio? (39-41.1-64) From their exchange, what reliable information can we gather about their characters and those of Cassio and Othello?

2. What sort of language do Iago and Roderigo use to characterize the union of Othello and Desdemona? (42-44.76-134)

3. What effect does such language have on Brabantio? (44-45.137-71)

4. What is Brabantio's attitude toward Roderigo's wooing of Desdemona before and after he learns of her marriage to Othello? (43.92-95 and 45.172) What does this reversal tell us about Othello's status in Venetian society?

5. Point out all the discrepancies you can find in this scene between Iago's outward behavior and his hidden intents? What effect does our knowledge of such discrepancies have on our response to later scenes in which Iago appears?

6. In what ways is Othello's behavior in I.ii different from what the first scene might have led you to expect?

7. According to Brabantio, by what means has Othello induced Desdemona to marry him? (49.61-78) Has he mentioned such an explanation earlier? (45.168-71)

8. What are the Duke and the Senators discussing at the beginning of I.iii? (50-52.1-43) Why does Shakespeare run the risk of boring his audience while the Senators take 43 lines to decide that the Turkish fleet is headed for Cyprus rather than Rhodes?

9. Do the Duke's and the First Senator's responses to Brabantio's charges against Othello in any way resemble their responses to the problem of Turkish intentions? (54.106-14)

10. In what senses does Othello admit that he is guilty of stealing Desdemona and using witchcraft on her? (53.78-81, 54.90-94, 56.168)

11. At 56.158, the Folio reads, "She gave me for my pains a world of kisses," the Quarto "a world of sighs." Which action—kisses or sighs—strikes you as more in keeping with the situation and with Desdemona's character?

12. What reasons do Desdemona and Othello give for her going with him to Cyprus? (59-60.243-69) Which spouse shows greater insight into himself?

13. What piece of advice to Roderigo does Iago repeat most insistently? (62-63.335-67) Why?

14. In what order do the characters land at Cyprus? (Pp. 65-72) What dramatic purposes are served by this rather than some other order?

15. Both Cassio and Iago agree that Othello's heart is now subject to Desdemona, "our great captain's captain" (68.74; cf. 87.314-18). What evidence in support of this view can you find in Othello's behavior when he lands at Cyprus? (72-73.179-210)

16. Iago says that he suspects both Othello and Cassio of adultery with Emilia (76.291-307). To what extent are such suspicions a probable consequence of the view of womankind expressed in the couplets he recites to Desdemona? (70-71.127-58)

17. What is ironical about Iago's statement, "I do love Cas-

THE TRAGEDY OF OTHELLO 209

sio well and would do much/To cure him of this evil"? (82.140-41)

18. As Othello inquires about the brawl during the night watch, his passion almost takes over from his "best judgment" (84.203-6). What is the reason for his near-loss of control?

19. "So will I turn her virtue into pitch,/And out of her own goodness make the net/That shall enmesh them all" (89.360-62). To what plan is Iago referring? Why does it give him such special pleasure?

20. "For thy solicitor shall rather die/Than give thy cause away" (94.27-28). Comment on the irony of this statement.

21. What exactly does the following passage mean? "For such things in a false disloyal knave/Are tricks of custom; but in a man that's just/They're close dilations, working from the heart/That passion cannot rule" (97.121-24).

22. What is Iago's explanation of Desdemona's choosing a husband so unlike her in "clime, complexion, and degree," and what is the effect of his explanation on Othello? (101.228-38)

23. How is the most important stage property in the play introduced, in the middle of III.iii? (103-05.285-321)

24. Under what circumstances does Othello demand "the ocular proof" of Desdemona's adultery, and what is Iago's response to this demand? (106-08.356-405)

25. "The Moor already changes with my poison," Iago boasts (105.322). By analyzing Othello's diction and metaphors, show how those changes are reflected in his invocation: "Arise, black vengeance, from the hollow hell!/Yield up, O Love, thy crown and hearted throne/To tyrannous hate! Swell, bosom, with thy fraught,/For 'tis of aspics' tongues" (109.444-47).

26. What vows do Othello and Iago make on their knees? (109-10.457-66)

210   TEACHING SHAKESPEARE

27. According to Othello, what is the history of the handkerchief he gave to Desdemona, and what are some of its unusual properties? (113.55-75) (If the student follows the account at 158.213-14—a minor inconsistency on Shakespeare's part, of no dramatic significance—he should receive credit for that part of the answer.)

28. What meanings does the handkerchief have to Othello? (103.290, 108-09.433-38, 113.55-68, 158.210-14)

29. How is the handkerchief transmitted from Iago to Bianca? (105.318-19, 117.187-90)

30. What makes Othello fall in a trance? (120-21.31-45)

31. In IV.i, Othello stands off to a side and casts hate-filled glances and phrases at Cassio (122-25.94-171). Has something similar occurred earlier in the play? (72.165-75)

32. What makes Othello cry out, "But yet the pity of it, Iago. O Iago, the pity of it, Iago"? (126.197-98)

33. Othello suggests one means of killing Desdemona and Iago another: which method does Othello accept, and why? (126.206-13)

34. Under what circumstances, and why, does Othello strike Desdemona? (127-29.219-60)

35. When Othello questions Emilia about Desdemona's chastity, does Emilia base her defense of her mistress mainly on evidence or on faith? (130-31.1-19)

36. Later in the same scene, Othello treats Desdemona as if she were a ──── and Emilia a ────. (131-33.27-92) (Ask the class to fill in the blanks.)

37. How do you account for Othello's reaction to Desdemona's question, "Alas, what ignorant sin have I committed?" (133.69-79)

38. Describe Roderigo's brief revolt against Iago and Iago's manipulation of Roderigo to bring his plot against Cassio to fruition. (137-39.171-245)

THE TRAGEDY OF OTHELLO   211

39. From whom did Desdemona first hear the "song of 'Willow'" and why can she not keep it out of her mind? (140-41.26-58)

40. How do Desdemona and Emilia differ in their views of adultery? (141-43.61-108)

41. How does the scene with Desdemona and Emilia affect our responses to the next two scenes, especially the final one? (Cf. the commentary on IV.iii.)

42. Why does Iago feel that he can only stand to gain from the encounter between Roderigo and Cassio? (144-45.11-22)

43. How do you account for Iago's badgering of Bianca? (144-49.78-125)

44. "It is the cause, it is the cause, my soul./Let me not name it to you, you chaste stars./It is the cause" (150.1-3). What does Othello mean by "the cause" and why does he repeat the phrase three times?

45. "Put out the light, and then put out the light" (150.7). How does Othello go on to distinguish between the two kinds of "light"?

46. Why does Othello smother Desdemona without allowing her time to "say one prayer"? (153.76-83)

47. Explain what Emilia means when she says, "I thought so then.—I'll kill myself for grief.—/O villainy, villainy!" (157.189-90; cf. 135-36.129-47)

48. How many times and under what circumstances is Othello disarmed in the final scene? (159-61.233-84)

49. What is the point of Iago's sardonic statement to Othello, "I bleed, sir, but not killed"? (161.284)

50. In his final speech, what is Othello's point in mentioning the incident in Aleppo? (163.347-52) You should give more than one explanation.

QUESTIONS FOR DISCUSSION

1. "Othello deals soberly and confidently with Brabantio's direct attack on his person and his marriage to Desdemona, but goes to pieces when Iago mounts a similar, but indirect, attack." Write an essay accounting as fully as you can for the difference in Othello's responses to each challenge.

2. When Lodovico asks Othello, "What shall be said to thee?", the Moor replies: "Why, anything:/An honorable murderer, if you will;/For naught I did in hate, but all in honor" (161.289-91). To what extent is this an accurate account of the feelings and motives which led him to kill Desdemona?

3. "Despite all the psychological realism of the portrayal of the chief characters, we should also think of the tragedy as a kind of morality play in which Othello is, as it were, Everyman, whose soul is a prize for which a devil called Iago and an angel called Desdemona compete." Discuss.

4. Write an essay showing how the language of Othello reflects the different states of his mind and feelings in the course of the play.

5. Discuss the different forms that jealousy takes in Iago, Roderigo, Bianca, and Othello. Should Brabantio be included in this list?

6. "Men should be what they seem;/Or those that be not, would they might seem none!" (98.126-27). How does the opposition between being and seeming apply to Iago, Cassio, and Desdemona?

7. "Othello's blackness, his thick lips, his identity as a Negro are highly interesting particulars, but they are not central to the Moor's tragedy." Discuss.

8. Trace the motif of judgment in *Othello,* taking "judgment" to mean both (1) the rational faculty in opposition to the five senses and the passions, and (2) a judicial or quasi-judicial process, a trial or kind of trial, in which a person is accused and defended and a sentence passed and executed.

9. "In something like the way Fortinbras and Laertes are foils to Hamlet, Iago and Roderigo are foils to Othello, and Emilia and Bianca to Desdemona." Discuss. By "foil" is meant a character who by contrast sets off or enhances the qualities of another character.

10. (The following question may be used in conjunction with a number of the longer speeches of Othello, including those at 102-03.257-78, 106.342-54, 109.439-47, 109.450-59, 113.55-75, 132.46-63, 150.1-22, 160-61.256-78, and 163.334-52.)

Write an *integrated* interpretation of the passage reproduced below, stressing the following points: the relationship of the passage to the incidents which lead up to it and to those which follow it; the ways in which the state of mind revealed by the speaker is or is not characteristic of him as he appears in the rest of the work; important elements of the whole tragedy which are contained in the passage.

(Give the passage selected in full.)

SAMPLE TEST

I. (30 minutes)

Write a well-organized essay on ONE of the following subjects.

1. "Othello deals soberly and confidently with Brabantio's direct attack on his person and his marriage to Desdemona, but goes to pieces when Iago mounts a similar, but indirect, attack." Write an essay accounting as fully as

you can for the difference in Othello's response to each challenge.

2. Othello's blackness, his thick lips, his identity as a Negro are highly interesting particulars, but they are not central to the Moor's tragedy." Discuss.

II. (30 minutes)
Write briefly on FIVE of the following.

1. In what ways is Othello's behavior in I.ii different from what the first scene might have led you to expect?

2. According to Brabantio, by what means has Othello induced Desdemona to marry him? Has he mentioned such an explanation earlier?

3. Both Cassio and Iago agree that Othello's heart is now subject to Desdemona, "our great captain's captain" (68.74; cf. 87.314-18). What evidence in support of this view can you find in Othello's behavior when he lands at Cyprus?

4. What meanings does the handkerchief have to Othello?

5. From whom did Desdemona first hear the "song of 'Willow'" and why can she not keep it out of her mnd?

6. "Put out the light, and then put out the light" (150.7). How does Othello go on to distinguish between the two kinds of "light"?

7. How many times and under what circumstances is Othello disarmed in the final scene?

AS YOU LIKE IT

INTRODUCTION

As You Like It is clearly one of the best of Shakespeare's comedies and has always been one of the most popular, but it presents so few problems and in general is so instantly appealing that teachers may have difficulty in deciding which aspects of it need the kind of careful study they are accustomed to give Shakespeare's plays. If, however, the dialogue needs little explication beyond that furnished by the notes, and if the ideas of the play are familiar to most amateur readers, students may still find themselves interestingly and profitably occupied by a study aimed at discovering why the play is so good—even if such an undertaking may be as difficult and dangerous as explaining a joke. Such a study might begin with Professor Albert Gilman's Introduction to the Signet Classic edition (pp. xxi-xxxiii) and Professor Helen Gardner's essay (pp. 212-30), two excellent examples of criticism that furnishes readers with new and illuminating ways to look at something they already understand and admire.

In Professor Gilman's Introduction the following observations will be especially useful: (1) "The play is chiefly concerned with two enduring human illusions—the pastoral ideal, or the dream of a simple life, and the ideal of romantic love." The history of pastoralism in literature and the origin of the word *romantic* should be explained, but it will be even more fruitful to consider how *enduring* these ideas are—particularly the pastoral convention that in the country people live a natural, therefore virtuous, life that is unavailable to people in the highly organized, complicated, and therefore evil, society of cities, and that the love of people who live on farms and ranches is more pure and intense than the love of men and women in the artificial society of great cities. (2) "The motives of the chief characters . . . are as simple and abrupt as the action of the play. . . ." Comparison of *As You Like It* with other Shakespearean plays will be instructive, for in general Shakespeare was less interested than modern authors in *why* characters feel, think, and act as they do. His genius was his ability to show *how* they do so, and to make his representations of human beings convincing. (3) "Englishmen in the Renaissance liked to construe life as an interaction of Fortune and Nature . . ." Though there is not much explicit discussion of this idea in the play, the topics of Fortune and Nature are useful in any judgment of the outcome. What happens to Rosalind and Orlando is not simply the consequence of their own virtue and will, but neither is it simply a matter of luck or other forces beyond their control. They enjoy gifts of nature in the characters they are blessed with, and they enjoy good fortune in the breaks of the game; but we see them, as we see other heroes, as deserving the "happy ending." (4) "The play is intended to suggest that human life can be harmoniously lived; that good sense, love, humor, and a generous disposition will produce happiness." Professor Gilman's development of this idea should be discussed in a way that will show how the contradictions within the pastoral ideal and the ideal of romantic love are reconciled by an understanding of the relativism implied in the title of the play.

From Professor Gardner's essay the following theses will be useful topics for class study and discussion. (1) This comedy, like some other Shakespearean comedies, is essentially different from a tragedy because it emphasizes the continuation of human life rather than the limits of one human life. Comedies that end with marriages remind us that life goes on; tragedies often remind us that our own life must have an end. In a consideration of *As You Like It* with reference to this point, it should be pointed out that the reason the audience does not feel cheated by the happy ending is that Shakespeare's Rosalind and Touchstone have clearly implied that the happiness or the continuing life promised by the conclusion will be just as imperfect as the happiness or the lives of most human beings. (2) In fantasies, improbability is not necessarily a flaw. Dreams are full of improbabilities and yet they sometimes express great and useful truths. A class might here become interested in the general question of literary art as imitation. Probability in plots is a relative matter, as Aristotle recognized when he said that a probable impossibility is better than an improbable possibility. Most of the coincidences in *As You Like It* are of the latter sort, but they are not offensive because the audience does not expect the same kind of probability in fantastic comedy as it does in tragedy. (3) As in other comedies of Shakespeare, the sense of place is more important in *As You Like It* than the sense of time. A comparison with *A Midsummer Night's Dream* and *The Tempest* will make the point and help illustrate Professor Gardner's definition of the Forest of Arden as the place where men find themselves. (4) The "discovery of truth in comedy is made through errors and mistakings" (p. 225). Comparison with *Twelfth Night, A Midsummer Night's Dream,* and *The Tempest* will help students understand the heuristic and aesthetic values of games that depend on disguise. "Hide and seek" has many intellectual and artistic forms.

Useful as these eight topics are as a guide to the study of the play, they will not lead students to its central value, to what most accounts for its excellence or to what they will remember long after they have forgotten the debate on the pastoral fallacy, the themes of gentility, Nature, and Fortune, and Shakespeare's use of an imaginary place as a setting for disguises and discoveries. Professor Gilman and Professor Gardner conclude their essays with discussions of Touchstone, Jaques, and Rosalind because they are, after all, what make the play memorable. Critical discussions of this marvelous trio often compare them with one another and point out interesting contrasts, but it is even more important to see how they are alike, because the quality they have in common is in fact the essential quality of the play itself. The style of Touchstone, Jaques, and Rosalind, like the style of the play, is the style of the fool. *As You Like It* is not to be taken seriously. Its style, its attitude, is that of the lighthearted mockery in which the art of the discourse is more important than the content. No study of the play is complete without a study of its style, simply because in a sense the chief value of the play is its stylistic achievement. And a study of the style of the play must be largely a study of the style of its three major characters, which is to say, a study of the way they speak. We know them by listening to them; Shakespeare created them by putting speeches in their mouths.

Touchstone, Jaques, and Rosalind are all jesters. They prefer jokes to sermons; they would rather play than be serious. They are by nature suspicious of earnest wisdom, and they scorn the pretentious. They would rather act a part than "be themselves," and they would rather play the fool than the sage. All three enjoy talking; all three look on conversation as an opportunity to exercise their wits, to call upon their powers of invention, to exploit their mastery of language. When they talk, they are concerned with how they talk, just as a poet or other writer might be. They talk like professional talkers, like people hired to entertain an audience. Of course all three are at times much interested in the force of their argument and in the persons they are addressing; but by and large they are most interested in maintaining a certain style, and that style is essentially the style of fooling.

In *Twelfth Night* (85.63-69) Viola explains what is required of a good fool: "He must observe their mood on whom he jests./The quality of persons, and the time;/And, like the haggard, check at every feather/That comes before his eye. This is a practice/As full of labor as a wise man's art;/For folly that he wisely shows, is fit;/But wise men, folly-fall'n, quite taint their wit." It is not hard to show how Jaques and Rosalind, as well as Touchstone, show their professional skill in the style of a fool.

There are other words for the characteristic style of a fool, a jester. One is *mocking*. Within a few moments after Rosalind first appears, she proposes that she and Celia "devise sports" (44.23); Celia suggests that they "sit and mock the good housewife Fortune" (44.30), and a few lines later she says that Nature has given them "wit to flout at Fortune" (44.44). Now what is meant by *mocking* or *flouting* is made clear by other references to the same activity. When Jaques describes his first meeting with Touchstone, he says he "met a fool/Who laid him down and basked him in the sun/And railed on Lady Fortune in good terms,/In good set terms, and yet a motley fool" (73.14-17). Whatever it was Touchstone did when he railed (a synonym for *mocked* and *flouted*), it is clear that its excellence was a matter of style—"in good set terms." Then later when he meets Orlando, Jaques at once challenges Orlando to a game of wits by mocking him, and when Orlando defends himself wittily, Jaques pays him the compliment of inviting him to sit down with him and "rail against our mistress the world and all our misery" (90.275-76). Apparently such railing would be amusing; it would be a sport engaged in not to persuade an audience but simply to please the contestants, like the singing matches of shepherds in classical and Renaissance eclogues.

Touchstone is, of course, a professional player, like such other court clowns as Feste in *Twelfth Night* and the Fool in *King Lear*. In the last act Shakespeare apparently wrote the scene with William simply to give Touchstone an additional opportunity to display his skill in railing. At the beginning of the scene Touchstone explains the motive of all who love to "fool" (or mock, chide, jest, or rail). He says, "we that have good wits have much to answer for. We shall be flouting; we cannot hold" (122.11-12), which is a jesting way to say that the jester mocks because he cannot help it—it is his nature, his attitude, his style. Touchstone has nothing against William; nor can he impress Audrey by his skill. His only motive is to enjoy the creative act involved in making the speeches he makes. Like a poet he is grateful for any occasion that may prompt him to create an artful piece of discourse.

All three, Touchstone, Jaques, and Rosalind, have a poet's passion for style. Their lives, as much as we see of them, consist of inventing speeches. They aim at a kind of impertinent, iconoclastic, aggressive brilliance. Railing is not the only style in which such brilliance of invention is possible, but in this play and in these three characters it prevails mainly because it is the style of verbal contest. It was a style Shakespeare was fond of. It appears in many of the comedies; even *Hamlet*, written about the same time as *As You Like It*, contains a fair amount of it.

Students should consider all of Touchstone's dialogue to discover the many kinds of "fooling" or flouting he is capable of. Then they should turn to Jaques and Rosalind. The audience is introduced to Jaques against the foil of Duke Senior, whose opening speech in Act II is an introduction to the Forest of Arden, a kind of utopia where good men occupy themselves with hunting and conversation. The Duke obviously enjoys the art of talk, but his own talk is in the style of sermons. His own "philosophical" style is serious, and Jaques' whole performance on the occasion of the stricken deer is a parody of the style of the serious moralizer. Jaques is railing at the whole world, animals as well as men, and his concern is not so much with the truth of what he is saying as with the way he says it. The act is so good he ends by weeping himself, amused, no doubt, by his joining the sobbing deer, who was only an excuse for an exercise in railing. Like the fool described by Viola, he "checks at every feather." He is no satirist bent on improving the world; he is a self-indulgent "poet" pleased by his power to discover those "thousand similes" the First Lord referred to (60.45). When he says he can suck melancholy out of an egg, he refers not so much to his melancholic disposition as to his ability to make almost anything the occasion for an exercise in mocking. His most famous speech, on the seven ages of man, illustrates the point. It is occasioned by a remark of Duke Senior, a short, serious, moralizing sermon that serves as a text for Jaques. It is not a necessary part of the plot; it is not part of an argument. His own personal convictions about the fate of man are just as irrelevant here as are Touchstone's ideas about books on the etiquette of quarreling when he gives his delightful performance on the "seven causes" (133-34.69-103). It is not Jaques' cynicism we should notice but the excellence of the "poem" he produces on the spur of the moment. It is, in fact, not cynical but deeply comic—and its style is the style of the fool. Jaques and Touchstone are friendly rivals in the art; and his admiration for Touchstone is one of our reasons for liking Jaques as we could not like a cynic (cf., Jaques' remark to Duke Senior at the end of the "seven causes" speech: "Is not this a rare fellow, my lord? He's as good as anything, and yet a fool," 134.104-05, where "He's as good at anything" means in effect that Touchstone can also suck mockery out of an egg).

Like Jaques, Rosalind is more than a jester. A fool is a human being manqué, and Rosalind is a gloriously complete human being. But her essential attitude and style are those of a mocker, a tease, free from the poison of hate or resentment and full of the wisdom that lets her mock herself and prevents her from taking herself any more seriously than she takes anything else in the world. The similarity of her style to that of Touchstone is best illustrated by the form of her first dialogue with Orlando in the Forest of Arden. In this exciting confrontation she first tells Celia her plan, the style she will assume in her address: she will "speak to him like a saucy lackey, and under that habit play the knave with him" (91.292-93). What she does is precisely in the manner of Elizabethan fools. She asks Orlando what time it is; he says there is no clock in the forest; and she then makes a wildly witty reply. Orlando replies as best he can in the same style; then Rosalind prepares to make her set-speech on the relativity of time. This preparation is in a form used by fools, by Feste and by Lear's Fool. She says, "I'll tell you who Time ambles withal, who Time trots withal" (91.305-06)—a statement that invites Orlando to say in effect, "Please do!" (Cf. Feste in *Twelfth Night,* 49.56-57: "Good madonna, give me leave to prove you a fool"; Olivia: "Make your proof"; and the Fool in *King Lear,* 65.141-42: "Dost thou know the difference . . . between a bitter fool and a sweet fool?"; Lear: "No, lad; teach me.")

Students will be able to illustrate at length Rosalind's love of fooling; only one example need be given here. When she privately confesses to Celia the extent of her love for Orlando, she begins with the plainness of direct expression: "O coz, coz, coz, my pretty little coz, that thou didst know how many fathom deep I am in love! But it cannot be sounded"

(114.196-98). "Many fathom deep" we can assume to be a figure, a metaphor, that was born of her passion—she did not search for it. But her sense of humor, her power to see and hear herself, are too strong to be overcome by her self-concern, and her attention is drawn, like that of a poet, to the words she has uttered; she adds, with a smile, "But it cannot be sounded." That extension of the figure in turn completely releases the impulse to mockery, and she must add ("We shall be flouting; we cannot hold," 122.12) the elaboration of a ridiculous simile: "My affection hath an unknown bottom, like the Bay of Portugal" (114.198-99). In the next speech she concludes the scene with a magnificent example of railing, not at Fortune but at Cupid, "That same wicked bastard of Venus" (114.202).

Touchstone is a fool, which is to say, not quite sane, as the world judges sanity. Jaques and Rosalind are, as we say, responsible people; but both recognize the humanity and even wisdom that are reflected in the impulse to fool, as well as the intellectual pleasure in the exercise of the human powers of wit and in the art of making things with words. Of course, Rosalind is more fortunate than Jaques—not because she is a better "poet," but rather because, whereas Jaques' exercises are mainly a means of pleasing himself, Rosalind's unself-centered fooling is the rhetoric of her love—for Celia, for Orlando, and for life itself.

THE ACTION

I.i

The playing time of the first scene is probably not more than ten or twelve minutes, but notice that during this time we learn almost all the necessary background of the story and we see the plot get well under way. In fairy tales, in romances, we expect a certain simplicity: characters, motives, even plots are conventional. In a sense we already know this story: it is the one about an ugly, mean, selfish older brother who tries to kill the handsome, honest, generous younger brother. The motives are simple: the greedy older brother wants even the little property the younger brother has a right to; and besides, bad people hate good people for being good, and look upon their popularity as a threat (160-63). Hate does not need explaining in fairy tales, and our play opens with prose expositions that remind us of such stories. We do not wonder why Oliver asks about Rosalind, nor do we object to the coincidence of Charles's appearance just as Oliver is seeking a way to injure Orlando. Even the fact that Oliver has already planned to challenge Charles does not seem objectionable, even though when we look carefully we see that by the use of this coincidence Shakespeare has wisely made it easier to get the plot moving. This is a romance, a comedy, and we expect bold strokes and conventional simplification.

I.ii

There is much disorder in the dukedom: Oliver plots unnaturally against his brother; Duke Frederick has driven his brother, the rightful duke, out of the country; and loyal followers of Duke Senior have gone into voluntary exile, abandoning their responsibilities and forfeiting their lands. In a small way this disorder is reflected in the relationship of Celia and Rosalind. Celia uses the familiar "thee" to Rosalind, the rightful "princess," whereas Rosalind, Celia's guest, feels obliged to use the formal "you" when she speaks to Celia. But that is minor; more important is the sense of love their dialogue expresses, especially in the contest of wits that they fall so naturally into. It develops from a proposal for "sports" (23), a game, a pastime, a way to pass time; and the game is an intellectual contest, not unlike the kind of teasing and witty sparring Shakespeare's lovers engage in in other comedies. Their exercises on the subject of Fortune (a nice subject for two girls about to intensify their struggle with bad fortune) are interrupted by the appearance of Touchstone, who is in a way a professional player of the game our amateurs are at. We learn a good deal about Celia and Rosalind during their dialogues with Touchstone (55-102): they are intelligent, quick, aggressive—they play the game well.

Against the background of this contest of wits we hear of the brutal physical contest of Charles and his victims; and suddenly we are witnessing a romantic tableau—a "sport," a contest, before the Duke, the "Princess," and "Lords" of the court. True to form (and to our expectations), Orlando impressively defeats the champion; and the "princess" falls in love with the brave young challenger. The stage action from line 229 to the entrance of Le Beau (248) should be clearly imagined, for the actors must here convey much of the miracle of love at first sight. Now Orlando has foiled his brother's scheme, won honor, fallen in love, and been forced to leave the court of the evil duke and return to the house of the evil brother Oliver. And we are confident that before long our hero will find the equally persecuted—the "heavenly Rosalind!" (279).

I.iii

Again, in the opening lines of this scene, we should help students see that what may read like artificial, insincere dialogue—unnatural, unladylike, unappealing—is Shakespeare's way of showing us the affectionate relationship between Rosalind and Celia, and of communicating the attractive vigor of the girls and the quality of the wits by which they must soon live. In the second episode of this scene (line 88 to the end of the scene), two things should be noticed. First, that Rosalind's decision to disguise herself as a man is more romantic than reasonable—surely there will be as much risk in her pretending to be a man as there would be if the two girls followed Celia's plan of simply making themselves as unnoticeable as possible (109-12). The disguise will in fact make more "sport" possible; it will be more fun. And second, notice how, in the same fairy-tale way, the girls equip themselves for this expedition by taking along Touchstone (as a plaything, so to speak) and all their "jewels and . . . wealth" (132). They look forward to the lark, as Celia in effect says in the last line of the act.

II.i

We, too, have looked forward to the Forest of Arden. All we know is that it is something like Sherwood Forest and that the life of the exiles there is as idyllic as life in the mythical "golden age"—no work, no war; they "fleet the time carelessly" (41.114-15), which must mean that in fact it is a world of play, of sport, of games. Now, with the beginning of Act II, we the audience have arrived in that world as spectators; and except for three short scenes, the rest of the play will be set here. In the first scene two things are worth emphasizing. Duke Senior's prologue-like description of life in the forest is not a perfectly clearly reasoned speech. He argues, in effect, as follows: life in the forest is more pleasant than court life because it is more natural, and it is safer because it is free of the envy that moves men to hurt one another; the rigors of winter are not so painful as the flattery of courtiers; the hardships can be made to produce something valuable; and, finally, nature is instructive and good. This paraphrase takes the charm from the passage, but it correctly suggests that Duke Senior is more like Gonzalo in *The Tempest* than like Prospero. He is a good old man but he is more idealistic and romantic than clearheaded. The other point to notice in this scene is that a careful study of the First Lord's description of Jaques suggests that Shakespeare has presented a kind of picture entitled "Melancholy," something like the pictures of various virtues and vices to be found in emblem books. The oak, the antique root, the brawling brook are perhaps more gothic or "melancholic" than pastoral. Jaques is lying down like the inactive melancholy man. Like the stag, Jaques is sequestered; he languishes, he moans, and in effect he also weeps tears into the brook, for he augments the misery of the world by citing examples of the world's evil.

Though his fellow "foresters" condescend a little to Jaques, he is nevertheless a man whose humor (melancholy) gives him the kind of clear head that Duke Senior lacks. Melancholy men, Elizabethans believed, were not necessarily pessimistic or cynical; they were rather men whose bittersweet pleasure was in seeing the world and man's condition, nature, and behavior with almost painful clarity. They did not always see the whole truth, but they saw some truths clearly. Nothing in the play suggests that Jaques' fellows disliked him, though Rosalind did not take to him.

II.ii

This scene is necessary to explain how Oliver gets into the forest; see 118.76.

II.iii

Shakespeare made this scene richer than the mechanical demands of plot required, and what he added should be noticed. In the First Lord's account of Jaques we heard how Jaques found sermons not in stones or running brooks, exactly, but in an event in the forest, the sight of a stricken deer. In the present scene, instead of a picture called "Virtue," we have something more like a parable; and *parable* seems an especially appropriate word for the episode because Adam's speeches have something religious about them. In this parable the good man, Sir Rowland, and his good son are rewarded for their goodness by the loyalty of their servant. And Adam is rewarded for his prudence and temperance by being prepared for this crisis in his old age. There seems little reason, to us, for Orlando's considering the option of becoming a highwayman. Shakespeare is only emphasizing, in the broad strokes characteristic of this kind of romance and this kind of parable, the sterling virtues of our hero. Finally, in lines 43 and 44 it should be noticed that by reference to God's providence expressed in the Old Testament and the New, Adam has unconsciously added a religious element to our conception of life in the Forest of Arden: the "golden age" is a classical, mythological idea of a life in which good men prevail; the story of Robin Hood is a secular, popular, folk version of a similar idea; and the Judeo-Christian idea that God will provide comes close to the ideal of man living like the lilies of the field, that neither toil nor spin.

II.iv

We are now one-fifth of the way through the play; except for one brief scene the rest of the play takes place in the Forest. What can happen in the rest of the play? Orlando must find Rosalind; Oliver must be killed or forced to change his ways; Duke Senior must be restored; and Duke Frederick must have his comeuppance. But we the audience are not children, and the simple resolution of this old fairy-tale plot will not make our evening in the theater worth our while. What students need most from here on is help in discovering the fun (and wisdom about life and human nature) that the remaining scenes are filled with. The heart of this scene, for example, is a discussion of the symptoms of love, with just a glance at another old topic: the assumption of youth that their experiences are unique.

But first in this scene we should point out that Touchstone's feeling about Arden sounds like Jaques', and as if to prove his point there enter two real shepherds not at all like the idyllic creatures of the pastoral ideal. Second, we should examine the cause for our pleasure in Touchstone's account of his love for Jane Smile. A shift in point of view and a shift in language produce a comment on the conventional ideas about the behavior of lovers. The speech, like others of Touchstone, is a touchstone, a means of testing the worth of the speech or idea that is placed beside it. Like all professional fools, Touchstone lives by probing received commonplaces and the pretensions of rhetorical discourse. Third, the arrangements for buying out Corin's master have the same simplicity and coincidental quality we have seen in other parts of the plot. Partly we enjoy in a childish way this dreamlike good fortune; partly we are glad to have the story taken care of in as simple a way as possible.

II.v

Here is another discussion. The subject once again is the folly of thinking that perfection in this life is possible, or more specifically of deceiving oneself into believing that nature is better than civilization. Students need to be shown the pleasure Jaques feels in his satirical comment, as well as the degree of humorous self-knowledge he shows in the simile in line 11. In his last two speeches in the scene Jaques implies that those who believe life in the country to be preferable to life in the city are "gross fools" (50), self-deceived by their "stubborn will" (48). The last speech is purposely obscure, and Jaques is using a common device of the Elizabethan fools, who enjoyed tossing out enigmatic statements containing just enough sense to tease their hearers. Notice that if Jaques's *ducdame* is a gyspy word, it may, by the free association characteristic of "foolish" talk, suggest the "first-born of Egypt" (55), since gypsies were so-called because they were thought to have come from Egypt. Fools sometimes let language take them where it will—which is part of the fun we find in their talk.

II.vi

This scene prepares us for the belligerent entrance of Orlando in the next scene by showing us that he and old Adam have arrived in the Forest of Arden and that old Adam is in desperate case.

II.vii

By now students should be prepared for Jaques' discovery of, sympathy with, delight in Touchstone. The tropes in the first three lines of Jaques' speech (12-14) communicate his pleasure: "*f*ool i' th' *f*orest" becomes "*m*otley fool" in a "*m*iserable world," and *fool* and *world* are almost a rhyme, like *food* and *foul* in the next line. Jaques is delighted to have found someone with a congenial sense of "humor." Like the melancholy Jaques in II.i, Touchstone is lying down; melancholy men are not doers. He rails at Fortune, as Jaques railed at man and Nature. And "In good set terms" (17), that is, with pleasure in the way he expresses himself, with pleasure in discourse. He preaches, that is, a mock sermon, taking as his text not a deer but a watch; and his sermon is inconclusive; it is no help to those who hear it except as seeing a truth is helpful. It ends with an enigma (31): he is "so deep contemplative." When Jaques says Touchstone's brain is dry, he is alluding to the Elizabethan assumption that the humor of melancholy is dry and cold, characteristics supposed to account for the clarity of understanding in the melancholy man; and when he says Touchstone "hath strange places crammed/With observation" (40-41), he refers to a theory about the way memory supplies the imagination with stored-up experience, stuff to be used in making his witty analogies.

Jaques turns now to a debate with benevolent old Duke Senior. Jaques' defense rests not so much on the good accomplished by his freedom to criticize, to say what he thinks and to describe the world as he sees it, as on the fact that his satire can do no harm. It is the "liberty" (47) of the fool that he envies (that, indeed, he practices); in this lack of restraint, this lack of fear of what people will think of the fool, or do to him, in this lack of responsibility for what he says, Jaques sees a way to happiness for the melancholic man.

Is Duke Senior serious in his charge that Jaques' private

life has been sinful? The strong terms in which he makes the charge have persuaded some critics to believe that the Duke speaks the truth and that Jaques is, therefore, a less attractive person than he would have been had we not known this about his character. But we know that the Duke has said he loves to argue with Jaques (61.67), and he may here be only egging him on.

Orlando's aggressive entrance provides an opportunity for brief comment on the subject of true gentility ("gentleness," 102), a favorite with Elizabethans and with Shakespeare. Orlando seems to have erred in assuming that the good breeding implied in the term *gentleman* (see the derivation of the word) can be found only in the courts, or at least not in this "desert inaccessible" (110). Jaques and Duke Senior bring him up short.

When Orlando describes the Forest of Arden as a place where "Under the shade of melancholy boughs" men may "Lose and neglect the creeping hours of time" (111-12), he reminds us of Jaques under the oak and Touchstone's discourse on time. But one of the most interesting variations on the subject of time is Jaques's speech on the seven ages of man (139-66). It does not, of course, reflect Shakespeare's view of life any more than does Macbeth's "Life's . . . a poor player/That struts and frets his hour upon the stage/And then is heard no more" (*Macbeth*, 124.24-26). We are not even sure how accurately it expresses Jaques' view. It is simply a handsome performance. Those who like it and assent to its partial truth are not all pessimists. We smile with Jaques; we are not depressed by his details. Our fondness for babies is not diminished by our being reminded of their noise and their smell, or our pleasure in little boys by our memory of their whining and their resistance to education, or our love for lovers by their ridiculous behavior. The soldier, the justice, the old man, and the senile man are all as Jaques describes them. We do not think them worthless because each has its own set of ridiculous characteristics. What Jaques shows us is a fool's-eye view of man—clear, practical, and bittersweet. The appearance of young and noble Orlando and old and loyal Adam complements, or comments on, the vivid, seven-figured moralized painting Jaques has just finished.

Ingratitude is an appropriate theme for a song sung by Duke Senior and the other exiles; but its meaning is enriched by the context, by the fact that it follows a demonstration of true gratitude and friendship. Though we recognize it as a lyrical celebration of the goodness of "This life" (183) in the Forest of Arden, a song echoing the idea Duke Senior uttered

AS YOU LIKE IT   229

in his opening speech (59.1-17), the "gentleness" of Orlando is not the consequence of his life in the Forest. Is the emphasis in the song on man's ingratitude or on the last line of the refrain? The ambiguity is not out of place in a scene that has shown both the satirist's view and the idealist's view of life; and not out of place in a play called *As You Like It*.

III.ii

This long scene consists, after Orlando's opening soliloquy, of a sequence of five dialogues:

1. (Lines 11-87). Here is more "sport"—a playful discussion, a game with language played to entertain the players. Touchstone's "Hast any philosophy in thee, shepherd?" (21-22) is his way of pointing up what he has just been doing: parodying the pretensions of learned discourse. Even so he manages to speak good sense about the mixed blessings of pastoral life. Corin is no man for paradox, and he cannot be accused of parody; he simply knows the facts.

2. (Lines 88-122). The two "poems" represent two points of view, of course; but Orlando's passion is expressed very badly, whereas the fool's detachment, his "liberty," produces a certain witty elegance. All Touchstone's conceits (hart, cat, garments, sheaf and bind, cart, nut, rose, prick) are part of his "touchstone" technique, by means of which fuzzy abstractions are tested against the "facts" of life. Rosalind knows the truth of both views.

3. (Lines 123-250). Rosalind may suspect (she must certainly have a wild hope) that Orlando is the author of these poems, but she finds them funny; she sees them with her wit. She does not lose her critical detachment. And during the following dialogue with Celia, her excitement over the impending discovery does not subdue her wit till Orlando is named (210); after that only Celia is able to play their witty game.

4. (Lines 251-91). As audience we identify with Rosalind in this exciting view of her lover; but as critics we are also able to admire Shakespeare's inspired decision to show Orlando against the foil of Jaques. Jaques is right; Orlando's "worst fault . . . is to be in love" (279). He is not without a kind of stolid wit and manly self-possession that make him a proper object of Rosalind's love. When we see Jaques through Rosalind's eyes, we see *his* worst fault—that he is not, cannot be, in love.

5. (Lines 292-425). What makes this confrontation of Orlando and Rosalind a classic of dramatic writing is Shakespeare's skill in imitating the tensions of the conventions of

courtship. We feel first, of course, the tension of the disguise: Rosalind is hiding; will Orlando find her? Rosalind feels both the tension of her disguise and the tension of her necessarily concealed love. Most social conversation consists of a series of improvisations, but the conversation of two people strongly attracted to one another but not yet permitted the frankness of lovers is in a sense all artifice. Neither can say what he means; neither, in fact, can talk directly about what is on his mind (or in his heart). Shakespeare thought of a lovers' dialogue as like a fencing match or dance.

Rosalind's strategy is to "play the knave with him" (293), but what follows is all free-style, all improvisation. Like Touchstone and Jaques, Rosalind can produce a little concert, or one-man show, of invention; here her purpose is to hold Orlando's attention—to hold, in fact, Orlando's presence. He must not get away. Like Touchstone, she takes "time" for her topic; but her "sermon" is full of life (not a little like the life in Jaques' Seven Ages speech). The speech works; Orlando asks where she lives and gives her a chance to find a way into a second subject: "courtship" leads to "love" (341) and love, to the sickness of love. And with a little help from Orlando, Rosalind gets to her overwhelming subject: Orlando (353). Now she is off the ground, in full flight—free and in complete control. Her invention can fly in the heady air of love. And she has moved closer to Orlando, has begun the aggressive teasing that Shakespeare saw as a large part of the joy of courtship. Then, when she hits on the madness of love, she thinks of the strategem of proposing a cure for Orlando's sickness. A game within a game! And what makes it exciting for us is what makes it attractive to Rosalind—it is a game for high stakes.

It is worth remarking that when she describes her previous success with the therapy she proposes (408-11), she says she drove her "suitor . . . to forswear the full stream of the world and to live in a nook merely monastic"; that reminds us of Jaques' decision at the end of the play.

III.iii

What Touchstone says about the poet's dependence upon an intelligent, sensitive, responsive audience, as well as his reference to the truth of fiction and the true fiction of love is a brilliant comic variation on part of the subject of our play.

The speech on marriage and the necessary dangers thereof anticipates Rosalind's similarly affirmative attitude toward the mixed blessing of marriage (see 112.139-49).

III.iv

Rosalind is subdued and in no mood for repartee. We see in her "the pale complexion of true love" (50); still, since the sport proposed by Corin involves lovers, Rosalind is game.

III.v

The Silvius-Phebe affair probably amused Shakespeare's audience in a way not available to students today, for it seems to be in part a satire on the literary convention of the faithful lover and his cruel mistress. Still, among the varieties of love contained in our play, we have no trouble in recognizing the type that is parodied here. Phebe is a full, living character—not a two-dimensional caricature—and her two long speeches in this scene establish our interest in this subplot with its variations on our theme. Her first speech reveals a really cynical, self-regarding wit—a contrast to the humane and genuine wit, not only of Rosalind but of Jaques and Touchstone. Her second speech is a picture both of infatuation and of self-deception. Her falling in love with Rosalind is comic, and our pleasure in the play is compounded by the complexity she adds to the plot.

Rosalind is naturally on the side of the lover, but the motive for her long speech (103.35-63) is perhaps most of all her love of "sport." The performance only makes us love Rosalind more—for her vitality, her intelligence, her understanding of her fellow human beings.

IV.i

A confrontation between Rosalind and Jaques might under other circumstances be very fruitful, but at the moment their interests are too far apart to produce real communication. Jaques' speech on melancholy may usefully be compared with Mercutio's speech on dreams (*Romeo and Juliet,* I.iv). Jaques' reference to his travels seems to be related to a contemporary notion about the characteristic melancholy of men whose travels abroad made them malcontents.

The rest of the scene, after Jaques' exit, may be considered as a climax or high point: it contains the mock marriage of Orlando and Rosalind, and Rosalind's declaration of her love. The scene is all Rosalind's, of course; it is, perhaps, the point at which we begin to be convinced that the play is Rosalind's, that for all the fun and wisdom of Jaques and Touchstone's melancholy sport, we still know that there is something imperfect in it. We may begin to see that Rosalind is a kind of goddess, embodying not simply a feminine life force but the great human health that sometimes is an equal match for Fortune. She is a heroine—a heroic woman—which is to say that she is a superior human being, a winner, as are a number of the other women in Shakespeare's romantic comedies.

But first our attention should be directed to the easy self-confidence, the steady light touch with which she directs all the action here. Thanks to her disguise and her situation, she can be frank and open in all she says; and we can enjoy a courtship and marriage in which there are no lies. The tone of Rosalind's eight or ten speeches must convey both her strength and her love, both her self-sufficiency and her need for Orlando. Notice how much of what she talks about, that is, how much of the "matter" (76) of her speeches, consists of things and actions from the nonromantic world, which she prefers to the world of the romances of Troilus and Leander (92-102). Cock-pigeons, parrots, apes, and monkeys (143-46) are from Elizabethan London life; and doors, casements, beds, women's tongues, and nursing children (154-55; 161; 165-67) are from all domestic life.

IV.ii

The song's reminder of women's inconstancy makes us consider that all women are not Rosalinds, but the primary function of the scene seems to be to fill in the lapse of time between IV.i and IV.iii.

IV.iii

This scene, consisting of two episodes, is a good example of Shakespeare's dramatic skill, his ability to abridge the narrative of a romance in order to maintain the speed of exposition necessary in a play. We learn all we need to know about Phebe's infatuation, her egocentricity, and the limits of her imagination simply by hearing Rosalind read the eighteen lines of her wretched "verse" epistle. (Students should notice why it is a bad, or a ridiculous poem.) And in the remaining hundred lines of the scene Oliver gives us a vivid account of Orlando's noble kindness and courage, and Rosalind, by swooning, gives dramatic evidence of her love. Oliver's forty-odd lines of narrative (99-121, 128-33, and 139-57) have a pictorial quality that is like both the description of melancholy

Jaques under another oak (60.31) and the ornamental style of prose romances. Finally, we should notice that, after Rosalind recovers, she is still her witty self, unable to resist the temptations of playful irony even in this moment of strong feeling.

Here Rosalind's love for games, for sport, is combined with other motives to drive her and our plot to its romantic resolution. Here she prepares for the discoveries of Act V scene iv. Rosalind claims to be able to "do strange things" (126.59) and to be a "magician" (127.71). In what does Rosalind's magic consist? She has power to "do strange things" because like all wizards (from Middle English *wis*, meaning wise) she knows more than her subjects or her audience. But we may begin here to speculate about what other powers she possesses. Rosalind seems to be almost like a goddess, for all her very human traits; and she presides over the resolution of all the conflicts of the play in a way that reminds us of Prospero. Rosalind's powers are very feminine, however; and we must not forget that though she wants every woman to find the right man, her overwhelming aim is to marry Orlando—to love him and keep him for the father of her children.

V.i

Both scenes i and ii prepare us for the play's ending, in which Rosalind, by the aid of the magician with whom she has, "since I was three year old, conversed" (126.60), will bring all the paralleled and contrasted love affairs of the play to a simultaneous conclusion. In this scene, Touchstone, in a brilliant display of his superior courtly manners ("It is meat and drink to me to see a clown; by my troth, we that have good wits have much to answer for." 10-12), disposes of William, the dangerous rival for Audrey's hand.

V.ii

In this scene, making a virtue of necessity ("Is't possible that on so little acquaintance you should like her?" 1-2), Shakespeare belatedly brings Celia and Oliver together as lovers; then the disguised Rosalind promises Orlando to produce Rosalind and arrange for him to marry her when Oliver marries Celia, once more confronts Silvius and his recalcitrant Phebe, and—in a closing speech—promises to solve the problems of all of them by marriage the next day. We notice that Touchstone and Audrey are not included in this promise, so that, when the time comes, Touchstone is forced, as he puts it to the Duke, to "press in here, sir, amongst the rest of the country copulatives" (133.56-57) in order to be married to Audrey.

V.iii

This scene serves to indicate the necessary passing of time between scene ii and scene iv, but it is also an overture to the last "act"—a "pastoral" overture, in which the civilized conventions of *rings* are joined with the universal natural generative forces of *springs* (16). It reminds us that though "life was but a flower" (27), the flower is an almost irresistible blessing.

V.iv

The last scene is almost a little play in itself; as it opens, Rosalind reminds all the others of what they have promised to do if she performs her magic, and we share their suspense about the outcome, even though our experience with such stories and our knowledge of the facts make us confident of the outcome. What we anticipate is a scene of recognitions, in which everyone in the play who is in the dark will discover the truth and in that discovery find a fulfilling resolution. One common type of game or play consists of fooling (or frustrating) someone only to give him the pleasure of release that comes from being undeceived.

The suspense is made pleasant not only by our anticipation but by the interlude of fooling provided by one last performance by Touchstone (35-105). These seventy lines of dialogue allow Rosalind time to disappear and transform herself into a beautiful woman; but they also give Touchstone time for his fine comic commentaries on marriage and on the artificiality of court life. Students should be given the chance to consider why Touchstone's explanation of his decision to marry Audrey is so funny and so memorable. But students will need some help with the seven causes. In the broadest sense Touchstone is ridiculing the pretentions of learning. His whole analysis of the types of retorts sounds like a parody of useless and pedantic treatises that classify and subclassify all manner of things. But in fact, the satire here is more specific; in the Elizabethan age there were many books on how to do things—dance, fence, ride, behave in polite society, etc. Touchstone's speech sounds as if he had in mind either a handbook on "honor" or one on how to defend himself (cf.

Mercutio's scorn for Tybalt, who fought "by the book," in *Romeo and Juliet*, 102.103).

When Rosalind and Celia reappear, there is soft music in the background, and they are conducted by Hymen. We do not think of this supernatural addition to our romantic but nevertheless "natural" plot as the work of Rosalind's magic. We do not really worry about how or why the god gets into the act; but if we do, there are two ways to explain the phenomenon. One is that, like other Shakespearean comedies, this one very easily slipped into the conventions of the masque, and if the form of the masque is explained to students, they will see how easily an Elizabethan audience would have accepted this shift in dramatic form. Notice that in addition to the song (141) and the dance (198), which in themselves delight us (and may remind us of the masque in *The Tempest* or the ending of *A Midsummer Night's Dream*), we have a kind of ballet-like figure in the symmetry of the four couples. But more to the point is that in the final scene Rosalind has given up her role of presiding genius in order to become a participant in the consequences of her "magic." The god Hymen has taken the place of "divine" Rosalind, and must preside at the nuptial rites.

In the Epilogue, students should be reminded, the audience enjoys meeting the *actor*, not the character of the play. The effect is something like an intermediate step between the illusion inside the theater and the real world we meet when we walk out; or like the effect at the end of a puppet show when the puppeteer suddenly stands up and shocks our sense of proportion by the incongruity between his size and the size of the puppets we have been watching. Rosalind's Epilogue can profitably be compared with those of Puck (in *A Midsummer Night's Dream*) and Prospero (in *The Tempest*): all are announcements that the sport, the game, the fooling—the play —is over.

Scott Elledge

SHORT-ANSWER QUESTIONS

1. Does Orlando's opening speech sound like the beginning of a story you have heard before? What kind of story? In what respects?

2. In 38.39, what is offensive about Oliver's question?

3. What is the effect of Oliver's insult to Adam in 40.81?

4. Does the news Charles brings (40-14.96-115) sound like a story you have heard before? What kind? How?

5. What have Robin Hood (41.113) and the golden world in common?

6. Does it seem plausible that at this particular moment (so apropos for Oliver) Orlando should plan to wrestle Charles? If not, why don't we feel that Shakespeare is being unfair—or unrealistic?

7. Is it necessary for Oliver to be as villainous as Shakespeare makes him in 42.132-51? Shouldn't such evil characters be reserved for tragedies?

8. Oliver's soliloquy at the end of scene i tells the audience two important things. What are they?

9. Is Celia serious about mocking Fortune? (44.30) As a "sport" (44.25), what could this proposal mean?

10. If Rosalind is not really replying to Celia in 44.39-41, what is the point of her speech? Why introduce "Nature"?

11. Why does Touchstone swear by his "knavery"? (45.72)

12. What does Celia's reply mean in 46.85-88?

13. What is the effect of Le Beau's account (47.117-23) heard against the background of the witty chatter of Celia, Rosalind, and Touchstone?

14. Does what Orlando says in 49.175-82 impress Rosalind? Isn't Orlando's self-pity obnoxious?

15. Why does Celia also seem to be on Orlando's side? (50.200 and 203)

16. What happens on the stage between the time Rosalind

AS YOU LIKE IT

gives the chain and the time she and Celia leave the stage? (51.235-46)

17. What does Rosalind's speech to Duke Frederick (55.57-63) add to our concept of her character?

18. In 59.5, explain why the substitution of *but* for *not* would not essentially change the meaning? One consequence of Adam's fall was the introduction of "seasons."

19. What does the Duke mean by "custom" (59.2)? By "persuade me what I am" (59.11)? By "tongues in trees," etc. (59.16-17)?

20. How seriously is Duke Senior upset by the thought of killing deer? (60.21-24) On what do you base your judgment?

21. Why does the First Lord give so many details in his account of Jaques in 60.25-43? What does the *way* he tells it suggest about his feeling for the deer?

22. What happens to our interest in the deer during the First Lord's second speech (60-61.45-63)?

23. In Adam's speech in 63.2-14, what suggests his age?

24. Why do we accept Orlando's judgment of the good old days (65.56-63) when we disapprove of the kind of "slavery" that is implied?

25. How does the language of Silvius (66.23ff) differ from that of, say, the noblemen, or of Celia and Rosalind?

26. Somehow Touchstone's comment on Silvius' speech (67.44-54) seems more than just funny. Why does it suggest some kind of wisdom?

27. We do not know why II.vi is in prose, but the kind of prose it is contributes to the atmosphere, or tone, of the play. How?

28. How do you know Duke Senior is jesting in 72.1-2?

29. Make a list of Jaques' reasons for envying the fool (74-75.44-87).

238   TEACHING SHAKESPEARE

30. In 76.101 what does Duke Senior mean by "gentleness"? It is defined in the next twenty-five lines.

31. In Amiens' song (78-79.174-90) what does "the green holly" seem to stand for? What is it in contrast to? Is the song merry or melancholy?

32. Is there any sense in Touchstone's fooling reply to Corin's question in 81.13-22? In the dialogue that follows, does Corin seem to be a dolt? Which comes off better in the discussion, the court or the country?

33. Why isn't Orlando's poem (84.88-95) a good poem? What is good about Touchstone's parody of it (100-12)? The poem Celia reads proposes a series of topics for future poems; what are they? (125-34)

34. When Orlando and Jaques meet (89.249ff.), Orlando proves equal to Jaques' game of wit. What contrasts in the two men are revealed in the dialogue?

35. Why does Rosalind decide to "play the knave" (91.293) with Orlando? And what does she mean by the phrase? In 92.332, why does Rosalind add "like fringe upon a petticoat"? Why does she go into such detail about her old uncle (92.339ff)? In what follows (to the end of the scene) what is it that makes Rosalind's aggressiveness so attractive?

36. In what respect is Touchstone like a poet? (96.11-15) When Jaques calls him a "material fool," does he mean that Touchstone is wise? What kind of appealing truth is in Touchstone's speech on marriage? (97.46-61) What is there about Touchstone's speeches (and attitudes) in this scene that reminds us of Rosalind and Jaques?

37. Why does Celia tease Rosalind in scene iv?

38. How do you know that Phebe (102.8ff.) is not just teasing Silvius? Is Rosalind's long and spirited criticism (103.35-63) consistent with her character? Is Rosalind just teasing Phebe? How does the presence of Phebe add to the meaning of the play as a whole? That is, is the Phebe-Silvius plot simply one more funny element in the play?

AS YOU LIKE IT

39. Jaques and Rosalind have some traits in common, but when they meet in Act IV, scene i, they are not congenial. Why?

40. In Rosalind's speeches on love (110.89-102), and married women (112.139-49), and women's constancy (112-13.160-68), do you think she is only playing a game with Orlando—or is she saying what she believes? Why do you think so?

41. What does "like the Bay of Portugal" (114.199) do to the effect of Rosalind's confession of love? Does it make Rosalind seem less sincere? And why does she abuse Cupid in the next speech?

42. What is the purpose of Act IV, scene ii? Which themes established in the play are brought together in the song? (115.10-19)

43. Phebe's verse (117.41-64) is worse than Orlando's; why?

44. What accounts for the vividness of the story of Orlando's discovery of Oliver? (119-20.105-57) Why does Rosalind insist that she only pretended to faint? (121.168 and 182)

45. By the time we get to Act V one would think Shakespeare had introduced enough characters without bringing in Audrey's rejected suitor, William. Why did Shakespeare write Act V, scene i?

46. In Act V, scene ii, Rosalind, clearly in command, prepares for her last "sport," her last "game"; how does the effect of lines 82-104 contribute to our sense of play?

47. What sort of person does Touchstone pretend to be in his scene beginning at 132.39? How does the way he speaks make what he says so comic? What is it about his choice of words that indicates his tone? Do you think "an ill-favored thing, sir, but mine own" (133.59) is cynical? What do we call statements as "Rich honesty dwells like a miser, sir, in a poor house" (60-61)? What happens to the meaning of the statement when Touchstone adds "as your pearl in your foul oye

ter"? Why not "as the pearl in the foul oyster"? In 134.102 what is the effect of "your"? How does Touchstone say, "Much virtue in If"?

48. What is the verse form of Hymen's speeches (134.108-15, 135.125-30)? Why didn't Shakespeare write them in prose—or in iambic pentameter?

49. At the end of the play how many people have been "converted" (136.161)? Who are they? How many, and who, have experienced a change in fortune? Which characters at the end of the play seem to have been essentially unchanged? Why were they immune to the power that affected everyone else?

50. If you were producing the play, presumably with a woman playing the part of Rosalind, would you omit the Epilogue? Why?

QUESTIONS FOR DISCUSSION

1. What are some of the ideas about life and human affairs that Rosalind and Touchstone would agree on?

2. Why will Orlando be a better husband for Rosalind than Jaques?

3. Jaques, Rosalind, and Touchstone all talk about time; compare and contrast their ideas. What happens to our sense of time in the play?

4. What is gained by setting most of the action in the Forest of Arden? Shakespeare could have written essentially the same story with only courts or cities as background.

5. How are the forces of hate and disloyalty and ingratitude overcome in the play?

6. To what extent is the play satirical?

7. Judging from your observation of Jaques, how would you define melancholy?

AS YOU LIKE IT

8. Judging from your observation of Touchstone, how would you describe an Elizabethan court clown?

9. Why might actors or people who enjoy acting be especially fond of this comedy?

10. The plot is highly complicated and full of surprising coincidence; why isn't it a melodrama?

SAMPLE TEST

I. (15 minutes)

Is the emphasis in this play on love or marriage? Explain.

II. (10 minutes)

Does the play suggest that men generally behave better in a pastoral setting than in a courtly or urban setting? Explain.

III. (20 minutes)

Answer eight of the following questions briefly:

1. Why does Jaques envy the Fool?

2. Why, according to Duke Senior, does Jaques wish to be satirical?

3. Why was Rosalind exiled?

4. How was Duke Frederick converted?

5. How does Touchstone treat William?

6. What is the moral of the song, "It was a lover and his lass"? (129-30.13-32)

7. How was Oliver's character changed?

8. What does *moralize* or *sermonize* mean? Give a few examples from the play.

9. When Rosalind decides to "play the knave" with Orlando, what does she mean and what is her aim?

10. What does Orlando discover when he meets Duke Senior and his followers in the Forest of Arden?

TWELFTH NIGHT, or, WHAT YOU WILL

INTRODUCTION

With *Twelfth Night* Shakespeare brought romantic comedy to perfection. He had already achieved some brilliant successes in this form, notably with *A Midsummer Night's Dream* (1594-96) and *As You Like It* (1599-1600), but *Twelfth Night* reveals a sureness of technique and a maturity of outlook which distinguish it from even the best of its predecessors. A glance at the chronological table in the Prefatory Remarks of the Signet Classic Shakespeare (pp. xii-xiii) suggests that Shakespeare at the time he wrote this play (probably in 1599 or 1600, shortly after *As You Like It*) was nearing an important turning point in his career. The next eight or nine years were to be devoted to the writing of tragedy (including the four "great" tragedies, *Hamlet*, *Othello*, *King Lear*, and *Macbeth*) and to some experiments in a new, more realistic kind of comedy (*All's Well That Ends Well* and *Measure for Measure*). Only at the end of his career did he return to something like romantic comedy in plays like *The Winter's Tale* and *The Tempest*. But Shakespeare had developed in the interim, and the products of his last three or four years as an active playwright are in no sense mere repetitions of his earlier successes. They represent, in fact, a third kind of comedy—one allied more closely to the relatively early romantic comedies than to the realistic comedies of his tragic period, but in essence different from both. For Shakespeare's most characteristic work in the comic vein, however, we look not to these late plays but to the plays of the 1590's, and particularly to *Twelfth Night*, which crowns the rest.

While the action of *Twelfth Night*, like that of most of Shakespeare's romantic comedies, is extremely complex, it is handled with such skill that we are never in doubt about what is going on. On analysis it is possible to distinguish four strands which make up this action: (1) Orsino's wooing of Olivia, (2) Olivia's wooing of Viola, (3) the separation and reunion of Sebastian and Viola, (4) the gulling of Malvolio. The first three, which are so closely bound together as to be inseparable, constitute the main plot of the play. The fourth stands apart from the others as the subplot. It is not, however, absolutely independent: in Act III, scene iv, and again in Act IV, scene i, characters of the subplot collide with those of the main plot, with interesting results. There are also, as we shall see, some important thematic connections between the two plots.

All three strands of the main plot are dependent in one way or another on Viola's disguise as the page Cesario. The device of the disguised heroine (a favorite with Shakespeare) is more than a theatrical trick. As Herschel Baker points out in his Introduction (pp. xxix-xxx), it is thoroughly in keeping with the twin themes of dissimulation and deception which are so important in this play. Nevertheless, the device sometimes strikes modern readers and audiences as offensively artificial and improbable. It is helpful if we remind ourselves that in Shakespeare's theater female parts were played by boy actors (see the interesting discussion by Harley Granville-Barker on p. 178); but a situation in which a boy actor impersonates a woman who pretends to be a boy creates its own problems of credibility, even though these are not the same problems a modern audience feels. A more important consideration is the attitude toward Viola's disguise implied in the following words which Duke Orsino addresses to Cesario (46.30-34):

> . . . they shall yet belie thy happy years
> That say thou art a man. Diana's lip
> Is not more smooth and rubious; thy small pipe
> Is as the maiden's organ, shrill and sound,
> And all is semblative a woman's part.

The Duke says, in effect, that Cesario looks and sounds more like a woman than a man. To Shakespeare's original audience this was a reminder that the boy actor playing Viola-Cesario was supposed to be a woman; and, what is more important, it suggests that Viola's disguise as Cesario was meant to be less than fully convincing. The point is that Shakespeare is not particularly interested in fooling his audience. On the contrary, he continually helps them see through the disguise lest they fail to appreciate the ironies of Viola's delicate position (see, e.g., 54.182; 62.25-28; 71.22-35; 89.143, 159-62). Although the other characters are deceived, the audience is never allowed to forget that Cesario is really a woman.

There are any number of additional details equally bothersome to someone expecting a more convincingly "realistic" play. Why, for example, does Viola decide to take service with Duke Orsino (39.52-61)? Shakespeare provides no convincing answer, although he surely expected an audience to see Viola's embarking on an uncertain course of action as an indication of her character. "What else may hap," she says, "to time I will commit" (60)—a statement which reveals an attractive mixture of impulsive optimism and courage. In this case the speaker's general attitude is more important than the particulars of her plan. Or what of the marriage of Olivia and Sebastian? Olivia thinks that she is marrying Cesario, and Sebastian, although puzzled by the lady's proposal (119.1-21), is willing enough to go through with the ceremony. Such things do not happen in life—or at least not very often. But they do happen as a matter of course in fantasy, in fairy tales, and in romantic comedy; and when they do, we do not demand a perfectly logical or rational explanation.

Twelfth Night, of course, is neither a fantasy nor a fairy tale. Shakespeare does not in this play forsake the world of experience for a world of pure imagination, as he does to an extent in *A Midsummer Night's Dream.* He does, however, view the world of experience in such a way that some of the hard facts of everyday reality are blurred, distorted, or even ignored, so that other, less immediately obvious truths may be brought into sharper focus. This, in brief, is the method of romantic comedy. In the marriage of Olivia and Sebastian, the very disregard for surface realism or plausibility emphasizes an important truth, one which Sebastian himself makes explicit at a later moment in the play (131.259-60):

> So comes it, lady, you have been mistook.
> But nature to her bias drew in that.

Sebastian is telling his newly married wife that her natural inclinations ("nature") prevented her from marrying a woman ("to draw to the bias" means to follow one's inclinations or inborn tendencies). In wooing Cesario, who is really a woman, Olivia was unwittingly going against her nature as a woman. But Olivia has been acting contrary to her nature in another way as well. Her unreasonable vow to mourn the death of her brother by cutting herself off from all human society was itself unnatural (see the commentary on Act I, scene i). Nature, however, cannot be opposed for long, and Olivia soon finds herself married to Sebastian, in spite of her own intentions and in defiance of the logic of probability which governs the affairs of everyday life. The very implausibility of the marriage thus becomes a proof of the power of natural instinct.

It is evident that the "nature" which Olivia has unsuccessfully opposed is closely related to love. In fact, the behavior of almost every character in the play sheds some light on this all-important question. Viola's love for Orsino is outgoing and self-effacing; its characteristic expression is devoted and self-sacrificing service to her lord, even to the point of death (see 126.132-38). Antonio's love for Sebastian is of the same kind: he gives freely of his possessions (94-95.38-46) and is prepared to risk personal danger for the sake of his friend (60.45-48). Orsino's love for Olivia and Olivia's love for her dead brother, by contrast, are basically self-centered. Both in fact are practicing a kind of solipsistic self-love which is hardly love at all. The most notorious practitioner of self-love, however, is Malvolio. In this respect he functions within the play as a grossly exaggerated reflection of Orsino and Olivia. His ridiculous pride is fully exposed in Act II, scene v (see the commentary), and suitably punished in Act IV, scene ii, when he is imprisoned in a dark room as a madman. The implications of Malvolio's punishment are clear: self-love is a foolish madness which inevitably robs one of freedom. We should recall in this connection that both Orsino and Olivia lead extremely confined and restricted existences throughout most of the play. Orsino remains effectively imprisoned within his own palace until the last act; his wooing of Olivia is conducted by emissaries like Valentine and Cesario. Olivia's confinement is, if anything, more extreme. In her excessive grief for her brother's death, she has converted her palace into a cloister and herself into a recluse (see 36.27-31). Although they are unaware of it, both are suffering the punishments of self-love; indeed, confinement or imprisonment, whether literal or figurative, is no more than a logical extension of that perverted form of love which is unable to reach beyond itself to others.

Aside from Malvolio, the character who does most to alert us to the follies of self-love is Feste the Clown. (See the commentary on Act I, scene v, for the significance of his role as "fool.") Throughout most of the play he preserves a distance between himself and the action going on about him, and as a result he is able to observe and comment more acutely. He points up the absurdity of Olivia's excessive grief (49.56-71) as well as the skittishness of Orsino's sentimentality (73.73-79), and in doing so helps an audience maintain a properly critical attitude toward such folly. His more general comments on human affairs (e.g., 84.39-40; 114.4-6) are also perceptive, and they frequently contain indirect references to the goings-on in Illyria as well.

But Feste is not simply a perceptive critic of foolishness; he is also one of Shakespeare's merriest jesters. There is no bitterness in his criticism, and much of his banter is simply high-spirited good fun. He is a skillfully balanced character, in much the same way that *Twelfth Night* is a skillfully balanced play. The play's title and subtitle seem to promise inconsequential fun and gaiety, mere merriment without meaning (see the Introduction to the Signet edition, pp. xxiii-xxiv). And yet, as we have seen, Shakespeare is obviously very much interested in questions which are anything but trivial. Although they are treated comically, the questions are serious ones, and without them the play would be much less than it is. The most difficult task facing a teacher of the play is to convey a sense of this subtle and complex balance of the serious and the comic, the significant and the frivolous. This relationship is not simply a matter of peaceful coexistence, as if one half of the play could be labeled "serious" and the other half "comic." The two aspects are often so intimately related that a single event like the imprisonment of Malvolio can be at once uproariously funny and profoundly meaningful. To treat one to the exclusion of the other is to do an injustice to the whole.

In practice, it is usually preferable to concentrate on the more important characters and the action. Much of the humor and simple good fun of *Twelfth Night* are not immediately apparent to an untrained reader, and a teacher would do well to devote a large measure of his time and energy to pointing out these features of the play. Ideally, a student's awareness of the more serious thematic implications of the characters and action will develop indirectly as he is led to examine more closely Shakespeare's skill as a comic dramatist, particularly his skill in controlling our responses by means of comparison and contrast. Above all, a student should be made to realize that *Twelfth Night* is not a play to be appreciated only by a trained critic with specialized knowledge of Shakespeare and his times. Training and practice will help one understand and appreciate more fully, but the fundamental enjoyment to be derived from the play is available to any sympathetic and interested reader.

THE ACTION

I.i

Shakespeare did not write his plays to be read but to be acted on a stage. Students should be reminded of this frequently and encouraged to imagine scenes or incidents as they would appear in performance. Sometimes it is necessary to know certain facts about the kind of theater for which Shakespeare wrote (see Prefatory Remarks, pp. xiii-xvii), but more often common sense and an attentive reading of the dialogue and stage directions will suffice. In this scene, for example, students should not overlook the simple fact that Orsino, the central figure, is a duke—that is, a nobleman of great rank and power. (He is occasionally called a count, but the discrepancy is not important. Although Shakespeare is vague about the political and social structure of Illyria, evidently Orsino, whatever his proper title, is a person of some significance, perhaps the head of state.) He is richly dressed and accompanied by a sizable retinue of lords, attendants, and musicians, all of whom are doing their best to humor their lord. The musicians are playing sweet and soulful music which Orsino at first finds pleasing. One phrase, in fact, is so lovely that he has it repeated: "That strain again!" (4). A moment later Orsino suddenly commands the musicians to stop (7), and the mood changes slightly as he reflects on the impossibility of sustaining his delicate and highly refined emotional state (9-15). The solicitous Curio tries to distract his lord by proposing a more active, vigorous diversion: "Will you go hunt, my lord?" (16). But Orsino turns even this helpful suggestion to thoughts of his unrequited love for Olivia (17-24). He can think of nothing else.

There is something incongruous about this opening scene. We expect to hear some talk of state, for the dominant figure is obviously a politically and socially prominent person, and the appearance of lords and attendants suggests an official or semiofficial occasion. Instead we hear only of Orsino's personal feelings. To suggest the quality of these feelings to your students it will help to read the first fifteen lines of the scene aloud—but only if you can play the "ham." For Shakespeare intends Orsino to be more than a trifle foolish in his languishing lovesickness. To be done right the speech must be overdone: an actor must sigh frequently, roll his eyes heavenward, perhaps even press the back of his hand to his forehead. We soon realize that although Olivia's refusal to return his love has made Orsino miserable, there is a large measure of enjoyment in his misery (notice his reference to the "sweet pangs" of love, 71.16). Orsino sees himself in the role of a fashionably melancholic lover disdained by a fair but cruel lady, and his emotional life is centered not on the lady but on his own feelings as spurned lover. An audience made aware of Orsino's condition cannot help finding him laughable.

If your students can be persuaded to look at Orsino's sentimentalizing with a critical eye, they will probably have no trouble reacting properly to Valentine's message from the Countess Olivia (25-33). The message introduces information essential for understanding what is to follow, but it also gives us a glimpse of a foolishness comparable to Orsino's. Olivia has spurned Orsino's love because of her vow to mourn the death of her brother ("A brother's dead love," 32 = "love for a dead brother"). The terms of her vow are, of course, extravagant: she will veil herself like a nun ("cloistress," 29) for seven years and make a practice of weeping daily for her brother. Mourning is proper enough under the circumstances, but this is clearly unreasonable. Feste the Clown will cleverly demonstrate the foolishness of Olivia's behavior in a later scene (see 49.56-71), but your students should be aware of it even in Valentine's message here in scene i. Olivia, indeed, seems to enjoy her sorrow as much as Orsino enjoys his lovesickness.

Once students have been encouraged to adopt a critical attitude toward Orsino and Olivia, however, they should not be allowed to become too critical. Both characters are decidedly sympathetic. Whatever satire Shakespeare directs at them is of the most gentle and harmless sort, for their follies are after all not very serious or long-lived. Hazlitt's distinction between the "ludicrous" and the "ridiculous" may help to make this point (see his essay on pp. 169-71): we laugh at Orsino and Olivia but we do not despise them; we recognize their shortcomings but take an indulgent attitude toward them.

I.ii

The mood of this scene contrasts sharply with that of scene i, just as Viola contrasts with both Orsino and Olivia. There is none of the languor and overripeness associated with Orsino's sentimentality. Viola is alert and inquisitive (notice how many questions she asks in this brief scene), eager to be doing something about her unfortunate situation. Although she has good reason to think that she (like Olivia) has lost a brother, she gives no thought to mourning. She is unreservedly hopeful and optimistic despite the harrowing experience (the shipwreck, described by the Captain, 8-17) which she has just been through. Her vitality provides a welcome relief from the oppressive atmosphere of Orsino's court.

It is futile to argue over the reasonableness or unreasonableness of Viola's plan (52-61) or the inconsistency pointed out in the note to line 62. (See the preceding Introduction.) Some scholars have tried to account for such difficulties by supposing that Shakespeare revised his play, but this is by no means certain.

I.iii

This scene introduces us to the world dominated by Sir Toby Belch, the irresponsible and disreputable uncle of Olivia. "I am sure care's an enemy to life," he proclaims (2-3), and Sir Toby is all in favor of "life." He has little use for such conventional virtues as industry and sobriety, and as we learn later (see especially 92.55-56), he has been cheating his drinking companion, Sir Andrew Aguecheek, with impossible hopes of winning Olivia as his wife. He is also one of the chief conspirators in the gulling of Malvolio which forms the subplot of the play. By all rights, then, he should be a complete scoundrel; but like Falstaff, whom he resembles in many ways, he is not. More than likely your students will instinctively find him an altogether likable (if not admirable) character, and rightly so. There is no need to analyze this reaction at great length, but you might call attention to his wit and cleverness as reasons for our generally favorable response to him. Note also the refreshing candor with which he characterizes himself (e.g., 10-13): he knows what he is and makes no pretense of being anything else.

A comparison with Sir Andrew Aguecheek will prove instructive. Sir Andrew's misunderstanding of "accost" (51) and *"pourquoi"* (90) is an index to his intellectual obtuseness. (Sir Toby's description of Sir Andrew in lines 25-28 is mockingly ironic and not meant to deceive Maria.) The put-down he receives from Maria (65-78) and Sir Toby's comments on his hair (94, 96-97, 99) suggest a condition of sexual impotence (see note to 72) and general physical debility. The name Aguecheek is itself revealing: the ague is a disease which leaves its victim pale and weak. ("Agueface," 43, is Sir Toby's comic perversion of Sir Andrew's family name. Sir Toby later calls Sir Andrew "a thin-faced knave," 129.207. See also 105.274-76.) Sir Andrew, of course, is unaware of his own stupidity, and apparently he thinks of himself as healthy and good-looking (e.g., 97.131-32). Unlike Sir Toby, he entertains false notions of himself. We can only guess at his accomplishments as a dancer, but part of the fun of this scene surely derives from the sight of this lean, sickly, and weak-witted individual prancing about the stage like a puppet at Sir Toby's direction (see 137-38).

I.iv

When this scene opens Viola has already disguised herself as a man, Cesario, and taken service with Duke Orsino. She has, in fact, become the Duke's trusted confidante (see 12-14; "you" is addressed to the attendants) and undertakes to woo the Lady Olivia for her master. This situation provides the basis for much of the action to follow; Viola is the link between the two great houses, and her disguise as the page Cesario is the pivot on which the main plot turns.

In Viola's aside which ends the scene, we learn that she has fallen in love with Orsino. This is the first of several amusing complications which grow out of the disguise situation. It is a mistake to worry about the improbability of this turn of events; what matters is the way the healthy directness and engaging frankness of Viola's statement emphasize the contrast between her and Orsino.

I.v

Three important characters make their first appearance in this scene: Feste the Clown, Malvolio, and Olivia. Feste and Malvolio are servants in Olivia's household, the first her professional jester or entertainer and the second her steward or chief administrative officer in charge of buying provisions and managing the other servants.

Notice that Feste's speeches are labeled "Clown," while in the dialogue he is always called "fool." In the context of this

TWELFTH NIGHT, OR, WHAT YOU WILL   253

play "Clown" is to be understood as the theatrical term applied to an actor who specialized in comic roles; "fool," on the other hand, is equivalent to jester—in Shakespeare's day a person usually attached to the household of a prince or nobleman to provide entertainment for the master and his guests. Sometimes these jesters were so-called natural fools (or simply "naturals")—that is, simple-minded or mentally defective people (see 40.29 and note). Feste is obviously not of this type. He is consistently witty and shrewd, a perceptive observer of the people and situations about him. In this respect he is very much like the Fool in *King Lear*. Although he sometimes speaks what appears to be sheer nonsense, usually his comments have a satiric point (see the preceding Introduction).

Fools in Shakspeare's time customarily wore a parti-colored uniform known as "motley" (see 55-56: the point of Feste's retort is that although he is dressed like a fool he is not stupid) and enjoyed an extraordinary freedom of speech, even when addressing their patrons (see 94-95: "There is no slander in an allowed fool, though he do nothing but rail [criticize]"). Shakespeare turns the professional jester's license to good dramatic purpose by having his fools serve as acute commentators on his other characters. Feste's catechizing of Olivia (56-71) is a good example. A fool's license was not unlimited, however, and a successful fool would have to know when and how much to exercise his critical wit (see 85.61-69).

Malvolio appears only briefly in this scene. His "self-love" and "distempered appetite" (90-91), fully developed in later scenes, are only suggested here. He is an important official in Olivia's household, a sober and serious man with a strong sense of responsibility. The frivolity and disrespect for authority of people like Feste and Sir Toby are, naturally enough, offensive to him. His hostile attitude toward Feste in particular is evident in this scene (72-89), and subsequently Feste has occasion to remind Malvolio of his unkind words (see 135.375-79). It will be convenient to postpone a fuller treatment of this character until his return in Act II, scene iii.

When Viola enters to Olivia at line 165 we have the beginnings of the second major complication arising from Viola's disguise as Cesario. Despite her vow, Olivia admits the page to her presence and unveils her face (233-35); and before the scene is finished, she has fallen in love with "him." Your students should note signs of this development as early as line 278: "You might do much." A few lines later the signs are even clearer: "Let him [i.e., Orsino] send no more,/ Unless, perchance, you come to me again" (281-82). In reading these lines there should be a brief pause after "no more" and a slight emphasis on "you." After Viola-Cesario leaves, Olivia tells us explicitly that she feels herself falling in love (294-99; the "plague" in this context is love). The ring which she sends by Malvolio (300-07) is of course her own and not Viola's or Orsino's; Olivia is simply making an excuse to see Cesario again (see Act II, scene ii). Your students should not be disturbed by this violation of Olivia's vow. Having seen as early as scene i that the vow was a ludicrously unnatural one, they should be prepared to see it give way to more normal and healthy instincts.

II.i

Sebastian and Antonio, first introduced in this scene, round out the cast of significant characters. (Fabian and the Priest have not yet appeared, but neither is essential to the play.) We learn that Sebastian, Viola's brother, has not been drowned. And since he looks very much like his sister (25-26; see also 109.391-95), we can anticipate a further complication arising from Viola's disguise as a man. We are also aware that all the complications of the intricate Orsino-Viola-Olivia triangle must be resolved when Sebastian and Viola meet face to face.

Antonio's casual reference to the "many enemies" he has in Illyria (45) should not be overlooked. It takes on some importance later on (see 107.331-44). In the context of the present scene it serves to emphasize the selflessness of Antonio's friendship for Sebastian (see the preceding Introduction).

II.ii

This brief scene is a continuation of the line of action begun in Act I, scene v. Malvolio "returns" the ring to Viola (see note to line 12), who is immediately aware that Olivia has fallen in love with Cesario (22). This realization leads to her reflection on the evils of disguise and the frailty of women (27-32; see Introduction, pp. xxix-xxx). Viola then summarizes the confusions that have developed thus far (33-35), only to conclude "O Time, thou must untangle this, not I;/It is too hard a knot for me t' untie" (40-41). Note that Viola has said much the same thing before (39.60) and that it reveals her character. Neither Olivia nor Orsino would be likely to say it.

II.iii

The first seventy-one lines of this scene prepare for what is to follow. Students may be questioned about the circumstantial setting implied in the dialogue and directed to look closely at Sir Andrew's lines for additional evidence of his foolishness.

When the scene opens it is very late at night (or early in the morning), and Sir Toby and Sir Andrew have been carousing for some time. They are joined by Feste the Clown, who contributes his share to the noisy celebration ("caterwauling," 72, as Maria calls it—literally, the wailing of cats) which is being carried on in complete disregard for the comfort of other members of Olivia's household. Malvolio tries to restore peace and quiet, but he is no match for Sir Toby and Feste. They accuse him of being a kill-joy—one who tries to impose his own narrow and self-righteous code of behavior on others: "Dost thou think, because thou art virtuous, there shall be no more cakes and ale?" (114-15; "cakes and ale" is a proverbial symbol of merriment). The accusation does not fit the situation at hand, for Malvolio is simply doing his duty; but it does characterize his general outlook on life—an outlook which Sir Toby and Feste find intolerable.

After Malvolio has been laughed off the stage, Maria proposes her scheme for tricking the steward. This scheme exploits Malvolio's least likable and most indefensible trait—what Olivia has earlier referred to as his "self-love" (50.90). Maria hopes to embarrass him, not so much because he is sober, responsible, and virtuous, but because he is "an affectioned ass," one who is "so crammed, as he thinks, with excellencies that it is his grounds of faith that all that look on him love him . . ." (147-52). This consideration will help to create the proper perspective for those later scenes in which we actually see Malvolio victimized.

II.iv

This scene advances the action very little; it is an interlude between the formation of Maria's plot in the previous scene and its execution in the following scene. Its principal purpose is to bring to our attention once more Orsino's lovesickness and Viola's difficulties in loving the lovesick Duke. Both Feste's song in this scene (51-66) and the one he sang for Sir Toby and Sir Andrew in the previous scene (64.40-45, 48-

53) are love songs, but they differ greatly in diction, rhythm, tone, and theme. Each is appropriate to its context.

The conversation between Orsino and Viola which rounds off this scene (80-125) intensifies the irony of Viola's position. Notice particularly the effect of Orsino's comments on the shallowness of women's emotions (94-104). The audience is aware that these words are spoken to a woman whose love is deeper and more lasting than the speaker's.

II.v

After the interlude of scene iv we reach one of the high points of the subplot. Malvolio is the principal object of mockery in this scene, but notice that Sir Toby is also ridiculous in his inability to control himself as he overhears Malvolio putting on airs. He is especially upset by Malvolio's negligent use of the name "Toby" without the honorific "Sir" which belongs to a knight. When Malvolio speaks of "my kinsman Toby," for example, Sir Toby is reduced to inarticulate indignation: "Bolts and shackles!" (55-56). The word "Toby" in line 68 is spoken with a special mocking emphasis.

Malvolio's pride or self-love is fully revealed even before he reads the letter which Maria has planted in his path. He pictures himself as Olivia's husband, "Count Malvolio" (35), exercising his authority over people who are presently his social betters. His daydreaming reveals not so much his political or social ambition as his overactive imagination feeding on an exalted sense of his own merit and importance. Fabian's analysis is essentially correct: "Look how imagination blows him," he says (42-43). After Malvolio finds the letter with its cryptic riddle, his imagination again goes to work. Confronted with the mysterious inscription "M, O, A, I," he resolves to "crush this a little" in order to make it mean what he wants it to mean (138-40). In this way he is able to convince himself that Olivia is in love with him—a conclusion which suits perfectly his sense of his own importance. (At this point you might question your students about the possible significance of the play's subtitle, "What You Will.")

Sir Andrew's particular brand of foolishness is also apparent in this scene (see especially 78-82). Be sure that your students do not overlook his habit of echoing Sir Toby. He has done this on occasion earlier in the play (e.g., 42.62; 64.34; 65.56; 69.163), but in the excitement of having successfully duped Malvolio he is unable to contribute a single thought of his own. Each of his five comments on page 82 is a mindless, parrot-like repetition of Sir Toby.

III.i

In this scene the disguised Viola is once again acting as Orsino's ambassador to Olivia. Her encounters with Feste and Sir Toby are marked by clever word play, most of which is explained in the notes on pp. 83-87. (The point of Sir Andrew's "I'll get 'em all three all ready," 92-93, is that he is impressed by the elegant, courtly diction of Viola and plans to make use of such words as "odors," "pregnant," and "vouchsafed" in his own conversation. Probably he jots these words down in his notebook.)

In her interview with Cesario, Olivia makes a frank confession of her love (151-54). She admits that the sending of the ring by Malvolio (Act II, scene ii) was a trick, and she realizes that Cesario must understand the reason for it. Her love, she feels, is by now perfectly obvious ("a cypress, not a bosom,/Hides my heart," 123-24). Although disappointed by Cesario's response, she has not given up hope of eventually winning "his" affections ("Yet come again," 165).

III.ii

The purpose of this scene is to lay the groundwork for two incidents to be presented in Act III, scene iv—the duel between Sir Andrew and Cesario and the appearance of the gulled Malvolio. The latter is a continuation of the action of Act II, scene v; it is "the fruits of the sport" (82.198). Maria's detailed description of Malvolio's behavior (68-83) is calculated to whet our appetite for what is to follow. Similarly, Sir Toby's accurate estimate of Sir Andrew's valor (61-64) and Fabian's comment on Cesario (65-66) give us a good idea of what to expect from the forthcoming duel.

III.iii

Before satisfying our expectations, however, Shakespeare reminds us that Viola's brother, Sebastian, is near at hand. He and Antonio were first introduced in Act II, scene i; at that time Sebastian had expressed his intention to go to Orsino's court, and Antonio had decided to follow him despite the personal danger involved. The present scene gives more details about Antonio's background and explains the reason for the danger he faces in Illyria (25-37). This information is helpful in understanding the following scene.

III.iv

Shakespeare in this scene draws together several lines of action which have hitherto been developed more or less independently. Matters are advanced considerably, yet by the end of the scene nothing has been settled conclusively. Shakespeare cleverly satisfies many of our expectations even as he creates new ones. The tricking of Malvolio, for example, reaches a hilarious climax in the first part of the scene (1-132), but Sir Toby promises more to come: "we'll have him in a dark room and bound" (141-42). The plot to force Sir Andrew and Cesario into a duel, proposed in the first scene of this act, is then developed slightly (148-208), interrupted briefly by another conversation between Olivia and Viola (209-25), and finally brought to a head in lines 322-23. Just as it is about to be concluded, however, Antonio enters, followed closely by the Officers (330) who arrest him. In the confusion which results, the duel is temporarily forgotten, but at the end of the scene (397-408) we have reason to expect more to come of this situation.

Most of the fun of this long and complex scene is dependent upon visual rather than verbal effects. Consider the sight of the sober and serious Malvolio strutting about the stage in yellow stockings and with a forced smile on his lips. There is nothing particularly subtle or sophisticated about this kind of humor. The same can be said of the abortive duel between Sir Andrew and Cesario. Neither one wants to fight the other, and probably both try to run away. (When Sir Toby tells Sir Andrew that "Fabian can scarce hold him yonder," 292-93, we should picture Cesario trying to escape and Fabian holding him back. Sir Toby deliberately misinterprets this action in order to frighten Sir Andrew.) The sudden appearance of Antonio (carefully prepared for in the previous scene) with his quite understandable confusion at Cesario's failure to recognize him, produces the same kind of laughter with an added undertone of seriousness. Viola's disguise has created a further complication, and one which may have dangerous consequences.

Sir Toby's behavior when the Officers enter is striking in performance but easy to overlook when we are reading the play. Except for his brief comment to Antonio (332), he remains silent until the Officers have left the stage (384). His silence is not like him and forces us to consider why he has nothing to say. On the stage, a good actor will make Sir Toby's silence eloquent.

When Antonio has left the stage in the company of the Officers, Viola muses on the possible significance of what has just happened. She has good reason to think that her brother was not drowned after all ("He named Sebastian," 391), and we would expect a more realistically conceived heroine to fit all the pieces of the puzzle together and immediately resolve the difficulties stemming from her disguise. But Shakespeare is not writing a detective story. We must grant him the privilege of postponing his final resolution even as he prepares us for it.

IV.i

With the appearance of Sebastian in this scene we know that this resolution is not far off. He is the one person required to dispel the confusions involving Orsino, Olivia, and Viola. But Shakespeare chooses to intensify the confusions before resolving them. In this brief scene, Feste, Sir Andrew, Sir Toby, and Olivia all mistake Sebastian for Cesario. Sir Andrew suffers a beating as a result (26), and we learn later that Sir Toby receives the same treatment (see 128-29.192-211). Olivia's mistake produces an altogether different result; the last two lines of this scene (64-65) suggest what it will be, and this suggestion is confirmed in Act IV, scene iii.

IV.ii

The action of this scene has been prepared for by Sir Toby in Act III, scene iv (see 100.141-42). Malvolio has been judged a madman and confined to a dark room (the usual treatment for the insane in Shakespeare's time). The indignity of the situation is here intensified by Feste, who pretends for a time to be Sir Topas, the curate, and in this guise taunts Malvolio. For the implications of Malvolio's imprisonment, see the preceding Introduction.

By now Sir Toby is ready to bring the entire Malvolio affair to a close. He knows that Olivia will be offended at his treatment of her steward (who is, after all, a trusted and valuable servant—see especially 97.64-66) and that it will not be safe to continue the "sport" any longer (69-73).

IV.iii

Sebastian is thoroughly confused by the treatment he receives from Olivia, but decides to take advantage of his good fortune. Olivia has arranged for a secret marriage (28-29), which takes place between the end of Act IV and the beginning of Act V. Such a turn of events is highly improbable in life, but it is consistent with the tone of the play and a suitable outcome of the confusions and mistaken identities which have been developed throughout this and the preceding act. Furthermore, the very improbability of this situation embodies an important theme of the play (see the preceding Introduction).

V.i

The final resolution of all difficulties and misunderstandings is achieved economically in a single scene. With the entrance of Orsino, Viola (still disguised), and Orsino's lords (7), the stage begins to fill rapidly: first Antonio and the Officers (49), then Olivia with her attendants (97), the Priest who has married her to Sebastian (150), followed shortly by Sir Andrew (171) and Sir Toby and Feste (189). All of the many confusions resulting from Viola's disguise are brought forward once more and passed quickly in review. Antonio, Olivia, Orsino, the Priest, Sir Andrew, and Sir Toby all accuse Cesario of deception or disloyalty, and only the audience knows that "he" is innocent. At this climactic moment, with the attention of all concerned (including the audience) focused on Viola, Sebastian finally makes his entrance (208). This is the moment for which the audience has been waiting since Sebastian's first appearance in Act II, scene i. When it finally comes here in the last scene of the play, an audience feels more than a sense of inevitability, for the climactic organization of the scene produces excitement and even surprise. We know that Sebastian will come, but we do not know exactly when he will come. With the appearance of each new character we half expect the suspense to be broken, but instead it is intensified.

When Sebastian finally does arrive on the scene, all the other characters are naturally dumbfounded. Orsino speaks for the others as he points in amazement to each of the twins in turn: "One face, one voice, one habit, and two persons—/A natural perspective that is and is not" (216-17). What to Orsino and the others is a "Most wonderful" mystery (see 225) is then explained in the dialogue between Sebastian and Viola (226-58).

The dialogue itself may provoke questions from your students. First of all, why is it so long? It takes Sebastian and Viola the space of some fifty lines of conversation to recognize one another, whereas we might expect the truth to dawn on both of them the moment Sebastian came onstage. Furthermore, why do they insist on bringing forth such detailed evidence in support of their instinctive belief that they are in fact brother and sister? Viola says that her father had "a mole upon his brow," and Sebastian exclaims that *his* father also had a mole upon his brow (242-43). But even this remarkable coincidence is not enough. Viola notes that her father died when she was thirteen years old, and Sebastian responds that *his* father died when his sister was thirteen years old (244-48). Surely all of this is quite unnecessary to establish their identities. Some of your students may notice a related peculiarity: Viola never does say explicitly that she is Viola; she only offers to "bring you to a captain in this town,/Where lie my maiden weeds" (254-55) and thus confirm the circumstantial evidence which all but proves that she is Sebastian's sister.

All of these peculiarities are the result of Shakespeare's attempt to avoid a melodramatic or sentimental mood for the conclusion of his play. (We have seen how Shakespeare invites a critical attitude toward Orsino's melodramatic sentimentality.) A similar reunion of brother and sister in real life would be an occasion for joyful weeping and wordless embracings, but Shakespeare knew that such as emotional display would be inappropriate for a play like *Twelfth Night*. (Note how the references to tears and embracings in lines 240 and 251 recognize and at the same neutralize these conventional responses.)

The emotionally subdued recognition scene leads naturally to the final entrance of Malvolio. (The arrangement of events here is further evidence that Shakespeare did not wish to have the reunion of Sebastian and Viola dominate this last scene.) The straitlaced steward, last seen in his darkened prison, is released at Olivia's command (317) and given a chance to present his grievances. When it is clear that he has in fact been duped, Olivia generously agrees to let him be "both the plaintiff and the judge/Of [his] own cause" (356-57). Fabian then reveals the details of Maria's plot, insisting that the entire affair is an occasion for laughter, not revenge (357-70). Malvolio, however, is unable to accept this conclusion, and he leaves the stage with an angry threat—"I'll be revenged on the whole pack of you!" (380)—which seems to endanger the joyous tone of this concluding scene. Some actors and critics, in fact, have tried to make Malvolio a semitragic figure, a righteous man who has been punished unfairly and who deserves to be revenged on his enemies. (See the essay by Charles Lamb on pp. 172-74.) This was certainly not Shakespeare's intention, and you should take care that your students are not misled by such an interpretation. As we have seen in the analysis of Act II, scene iii, the plot against Malvolio was aimed not at his virtue but at his vice—notably his pride or self-love. Fabian makes the same point in confessing his part in the trick (363-64) and adds that the tricksters have only evened the score against Malvolio (369-70). Olivia's final comment, when properly understood, agrees with this view. When she says that Malvolio "hath been most notoriously abused" (381), she seems at first to be completely sympathetic to Malvolio. The tone of voice in which she delivers this judgment, however, is important. The key word is "notorious"—one of Malvolio's favorite words, in fact one which he has used twice in this scene alone (331, 345; cf. 117.90-91 and 115.48). Olivia is actually mocking her servant, if only in the most lighthearted manner.

When Malvolio has left the stage, it is possible to return to the major business at hand, the forthcoming marriage ceremonies. Shakespeare's romantic comedies almost invariably end on this note. The obstacles to love—mistakes, misunderstandings, or even occasionally malice—are overcome, and the resulting harmony takes the form of a marriage celebration which usually involves several couples. In *Twelfth Night*, the two principal marriages are supplemented by a third, the marriage of Sir Toby and Maria (see 364-66). Of the characters who have engaged our interests, only three remain unmarried. Malvolio, and to a lesser extent Sir Andrew, have been unable to escape from the confinement of their foolish pride, and for this reason are fittingly excluded from that celebration symbolizing a love which is directed outside oneself to another. The case of Feste is something else again. His final song, which brings the play to a close, injects a note of melancholy into the festive proceedings and reminds us of the existence of a world more familiar to us than the world of romantic comedy. As the shrewd and detached observer of human folly, Feste cannot be expected to share wholeheartedly in the joyous celebration to come. The refrain of his song—"For the rain it raineth every day" (394)—is itself an exaggeration, and it is not intended to undercut the play's happy conclusion, but it does remind us that romantic comedy provides only a partial view of existence. The delicate balance of mood and tone so characteristic of *Twelfth Night* is thus maintained right to the end.

BARRY ADAMS

SHORT-ANSWER QUESTIONS

1. Why does Olivia respond unfavorably to Orsino's wooing? (36.25-33)

2. What does Viola suppose has happened to her brother? (37.3-5)

3. How does Viola plan to enter the service of Duke Orsino? (39.52-61)

4. What is Sir Toby's attitude toward Olivia's grief? (39.1-3)

5. What does Maria think of Sir Andrew Aguecheek? (40.23-24, 29-33)

6. Why is Sir Andrew staying with Sir Toby? (43.102-05)

7. How does Feste the Clown prove Olivia a fool? (49.56-71)

8. What does Malvolio think of Feste? How does his attitude differ from Olivia's? (50.72-96)

9. Who is said to be "sick of self-love"? (50.90)

10. What is the immediate result of the first meeting of Olivia and Viola? (57-58.280-99)

11. Why does Olivia ask Cesario if he is a comedian? (53.168-72)

12. Why does Olivia send her ring after Cesario? (58.301-07; see also 87.113-19)

13. Who is Antonio, and what danger does he face in Illyria? (60.45-46; see also 94.25-37)

14. When does Viola perceive the danger of her disguise as Cesario? (62.27-32)

264   TEACHING SHAKESPEARE

15. To whom and under what circumstances does Sir Toby say the following: "Dost thou think, because thou art virtuous, there shall be no more cakes and ale?" (67.114-15)

16. Why does Maria wish to fool Malvolio? (68.146-53)

17. What do we know about Maria's handwriting? (69.159-61)

18. What kind of song does Feste sing for Orsino? (72-73.51-66)

19. How does Malvolio try to interpret "M. O. A. I."? (80.125, 138-41)

20. Who is "The Fortunate Unhappy"? (81.159)

21. What is Viola's opinion of Feste as a fool? (85.61-69)

22. How does Viola react to Olivia's frank confession of love? (89.159-64)

23. How does Fabian provoke Sir Andrew to challenge Cesario to a duel? (90.18-30)

24. What does Sir Toby think of Sir Andrew's valor? (92.61-64)

25. Why does Antonio give his purse to Sebastian? (95.44-46)

26. Why does Olivia suspect that Malvolio is mad? (96-97.16-58)

27. How is Malvolio treated for his madness? (100.141-42; see also Act IV, scene ii)

28. How would you describe the letter which Sir Andrew composes as a challenge to Cesario? (101.153-78)

29. Why does Sir Toby decide not to deliver the letter? (102.192-204)

30. What is Cesario's reaction to Sir Andrew's challenge? (104.250-54)

TWELFTH NIGHT, OR, WHAT YOU WILL   265

31. How and why does Sir Andrew propose to avoid the duel with Cesario? (105-06.294-98)

32. How is the duel actually prevented? (107.324-26)

33. What is the result of the first meeting of Sir Andrew and Sebastian? (112.24-36)

34. Who is Sir Topas the curate? (114.1-3)

35. How does Sir Topas test Malvolio's sanity? (116.51-62)

36. When and why does Sir Toby begin to have misgivings about the trick he has played on Malvolio? (116.69-73)

37. How does Sebastian react to Olivia's treatment of him? (119.1-21)

38. Why does Orsino threaten to kill Cesario? (125-26.117-31)

39. How does Cesario respond to this threat? (126.132-36)

40. Why does Sir Toby need a surgeon? (128.175-76)

41. How do Sebastian and Viola recognize each other? (130.242-48)

42. What happens to the Captain who rescued Viola from the sea? (131.275-77)

43. Why does Olivia ask Fabian (rather than Feste) to read Malvolio's letter to her? (132.291-301)

44. How does Olivia plan to make amends to Malvolio for the trick played upon him? (134.355-57)

45. Who reveals the details of the trick to Olivia, and how does he excuse the trick? (134.357-70)

46. Why does Sir Toby marry Maria? (134-35.364-66)

47. What is Feste referring to when he says, "thus the whirligig of time brings in his revenges"? (135.378-79; cf. 50.74-89)

48. What is the substance of Malvolio's last words? How does he leave the stage? (135.380)

49. Which of the important characters are not planning to marry at the end?

50. Describe the tone of Feste's concluding song.

QUESTIONS FOR DISCUSSION

1. *Twelfth Night* is one of Shakespeare's most musical plays. Discuss the various kinds of music in the play and the uses to which Shakespeare puts them. Consider also the different attitudes toward music expressed in the dialogue.

2. Olivia accuses Malvolio of being "sick of self-love" (50.90). Which of the other characters are suffering from the same disease? How seriously are they infected?

3. Viola's disguise as the page Cesario is one of the most conspicuous features of *Twelfth Night*. Show in what ways it is absolutely essential to the action of the play. Consider what would happen without it.

4. After Malvolio has been tricked into wearing yellow stockings and going cross-gartered in Olivia's presence, Fabian says, "If this were played upon a stage now, I could condemn it as an improbable fiction" (100.133-134). Discuss the implications of this statement with reference to its immediate context and the entire play.

5. "Some of Shakespeare's most important characters are the least interesting, and conversely some of his least important characters are the most interesting." Discuss this paradox with reference to Sebastian and Sir Andrew, or Antonio and Maria.

6. Sir Toby claims that the gulling of Malvolio is done "for our pleasure and his penance" (100.143-144). How

TWELFTH NIGHT, OR, WHAT YOU WILL

accurate is this statement? Are the elements of pleasure and penance balanced, or does one of them predominate?

7. Both Orsino and Malvolio have very distinctive speech habits. Analyze or describe these habits by comparing and contrasting the style of a passage like 35.1-15 with that of a passage like 81.160-80 or 98.67-88.

8. In her first interview with Olivia, the disguised Viola says, "what is yours to bestow is not yours to reserve" (54.186-87). What does she mean? How relevant is this idea to the play as a whole?

9. Discuss the different kinds of humor in *Twelfth Night* (for example, visual and verbal, satiric and nonsatiric). Try to characterize the type of laughter provoked by each.

10. Many of the characters in *Twelfth Night* besides Malvolio are called "mad" on occasion (see, e.g., 52.136-37; 66.87; 95.13-14; 112.27; 113.61; 119.1-21). Discuss the different uses of the term in two or three passages. To what extent is it possible to say that the play is *about* madness?

SAMPLE TEST

I. (30 minutes)

Provide *brief* answers for all of the following.

1. Why does Olivia respond unfavorably to Orsino's wooing?

2. What is Sir Toby's attitude toward Olivia's grief?

3. How does Feste the Clown prove Olivia a fool?

4. Why does Olivia send her ring after Cesario?

5. What kind of song does Feste sing for Orsino?

6. How does Viola react to Olivia's frank confession of love?

7. Why does Orsino threaten to kill Cesario?

8. How does Cesario respond to this threat?

9. How do Sebastian and Viola recognize each other?

10. How does Olivia plan to make amends to Malvolio for the trick played upon him?

II. (20 minutes)

Compose a clear, unified, and coherent essay in answer to the following question. Cite specific examples and illustrations whenever possible.

> In her first interview with Olivia the disguised Viola says, "what is yours to bestow is not yours to reserve." What does she mean? How relevant is this idea to the play as a whole?

THE TRAGEDY OF KING RICHARD THE SECOND

INTRODUCTION

In *Richard II* Shakespeare fashions the warp and woof of tragedy from the historical account of a man who was king and who played his role intensely, if not convincingly. Richard II, ill-fated like the star-crossed lovers in *Romeo and Juliet*, was destined for destruction partly because of his inadequacy to life, partly because of his poetic illusions about kings and men, and partly because of history's decree. Shakespeare, the man with the "largest and most comprehensive soul," often culled his dramas from the life records of men. He distilled from human nature, wherever he found it, the sensitivities and fears, the good and evil, the lights and darknesses of human souls. In a sense, *Richard II* is something like a masquerade where persons, history, and the stuff of life seem at times to be postures and impostures. Richard freely played his moments, sometimes toyed with them, until his moments were all counted and he saw himself as nothing (142.38-41).

Richard II was completed probably about 1595 during Shakespeare's early period. Chronologically placed between *Romeo and Juliet* and *A Midsummer Night's Dream* (see Prefatory Remarks, p. xii), it shares with both dramas a lyric mood, exuberant imagery, and a poetic expression that is at one moment dramatically imperative and at the next rhetorically self-conscious. The earlier histories, *Richard II* and the three parts of *Henry VIII*, as well as *King John*, which may have been written before *Richard II* although published later, are generally speaking less sensitively conceived character studies. In *Richard II* Shakespeare apparently passed his apprenticeship in tragedy, preparing for the more fully tragic characters of Hamlet, Lear, Brutus, and others in his mature tragedies. In addition he initiated the tetralogy of chronicles covering the stormy reigns of Richard II, Henry IV, and Henry V.

Presumably the student who undertakes the study of *Richard II* will be equipped with some knowledge of Shakespeare's drama. Ideally he will have had sufficient experience with Shakespeare's plays to ensure him a basic understanding of tragedy as Shakespeare wrote it. But history or chronicle as dramatic matter may be unfamiliar to him. The Elizabethans saw history as a comment not only on the past but also on their own situation. The Elizabethan historian searched out and presented accounts of former times with at least a partial purpose of pointing a finger at his own time. Shakespeare, who undoubtedly was acquainted with contemporary history (see The Sources of *Richard II*, pp. 151ff.), probably saw, as his fellow Elizabethans did, parallels to current events. Recent studies stress political interpretations and influences on Shakespeare, particularly in his histories. He takes historical events to prove that "All the world's a stage" (*As You Like It*, 77.139). Despite its historical orientation, however, the basic order of *Richard II* is poetic, lyric, and tragic.

Elizabethan England was politically unsettled, and the English people, we are told, remembered Richard II as a sovereign who was deposed, as a self-centered believer in the divine right of kings and as a martyr to history. Elizabeth was aware that her subjects were comparing her to Richard II. On one occasion she is reported to have said, "I am Richard II!" It is not surprising that the abdication scene was omitted from early quartos and not included until the Fourth Quarto was published in 1608 after the death of Elizabeth (see Textual Note, p. 148). On the eve of the abortive Essex rebellion *Richard II* was performed. The abdication scene was included as a prelude to the anticipated overthrow of Elizabeth. The political situation governs the movement of the play, therefore, and the predicament of Richard provides for the assessment of character and action.

The divine right of kings, a commonly accepted doctrine in Elizabethan England, depends on a belief in loyalty, order, and authority, based on a universal law of justice and retribution under a provident God and a divinely appointed ruler. The order is disturbed by crimes; if the wrong is the king's, the world supposedly suffers from the violation of order. In *Richard II* the Gardener exclaims, "O, what pity is it/That he had not so trimmed and dressed his land" (109.55-56). In Richard's eyes his anointing implies a sacredness and a kind of insulation from reality (93.54-57; 102.76-80). Gaunt rep-

THE TRAGEDY OF KING RICHARD THE SECOND 271

resents an affirmation of this view, but he balances it against the judgment of personal responsibility (49.37-38; 69.104-14). Carlisle's endorsement gives a religious sanction (93.27-28; 116.125-27). Religious metaphor is a logical expression of such an attitude; for Richard, especially, scriptural and Christian imagery is an expression of policy as much as belief.

Students will approach *Richard II* more comfortably if the play's historical background is clarified. The selections from Holinshed in the text (pp. 157-90) make that background clear and provide an opportunity for discussion of Shakespeare's use of sources. Some comment on the events will prove helpful. The action of the play occurs during the last two years of Richard's reign, and it involves a struggle for power among the descendants of Edward III. Richard was the son of the famed Black Prince, the dashing hero of English chivalry. The Black Prince died one year before his father, Edward III. By immediate consent of Parliament, Richard, just ten years old, succeeded his grandfather and received the crown, which he later lost to his cousin, Henry Bolingbroke, Henry IV.

Other sons of Edward III and their offspring are important to Richard's story: John of Gaunt, Duke of Lancaster, was father of Henry Bolingbroke, who also has the title of Duke of Hereford; Edmund of Langley, Duke of York, was father of Aumerle; and Thomas of Woodstock was the Duke of Gloucester. The other children of Edward III are unimportant to the play. The affairs of the kingdom were discharged under a regent until Richard reached the age of twenty-three, when he dramatically took the power into his own hands, dismissing and appointing ministers and officials according to his own pleasure. When Act I begins, Richard has two uncles surviving, Gaunt and York, Gloucester having died in questionable circumstances.

The action of the play is circular. In the first acts Richard is surrounded by flatterers, suspicions, and intrigue; at the end the new king, Henry IV, has acquired the crown, the throne, and also the flatterers, the suspicions, and the intrigue. At the center of the circular structure is the kingship. Concentric, as it were, are the imperatives of obedience and loyalty to the king, and of concomitant respect of the king for the rights of his subjects. In linear development there is a neat balance of contrasts and oppositions in characters and events. Situations are repeated in the play with characters exchanged. This balance is particularly notable with Richard and Bolingbroke. The skill of both is tested by the disloyalty of their followers; Richard acts impulsively and foolishly; Bolingbroke is efficient and practical. Richard banishes traitors; Bolingbroke forgives when it is advantageous (cf. I. iii and V.iii). Both men use their followers; both are concerned with family loyalties, etc.

Shakespeare often places characters against a larger philosophical pattern of moral responsibility for human actions, especially in kingly persons. In *Richard II* he adapts to this purpose the Boccaccian *de casibus* theory of the rise and fall of noble persons. The historical context becomes a kind of fate not only recording but molding, even evoking, the hero and the villain. The fall of a king, the punishment of a villain, etc., all occur under a tragic impulse that universalizes the characters until the action becomes an image of the fate of man in general. Shakespeare seems to be saying in *Richard II* that something is "rotten" in the state of man, and paradoxically, something glorious, too. The glory sometimes needs the rotten to make its appearance on the stage of man.

It is advisable for high school students to read *Richard II* as tragedy constructed out of historical characters and actual events. The play was written before Shakespeare's tragic sense was fully developed and during a period when his style still echoed something of the detachment of the comic mode which marked his early plays. Such distance prevents a personal insight into Richard as he is caught in the grinding wheels of history. We meet Richard at his height and see him cast down and destroyed. He is the type of character destined to be diminished. His struggle against his fate may be ineffective and unreal, but he is eloquent and charming as he falls. Just as Richard is propelled downward by an inevitable destiny, so Bolingbroke follows an ascendant destiny. Shakespeare uses the struggle between the two to construct a plot, but he uses drama, poetry, and humanity to construct Richard.

Richard II, called an "unripened Hamlet" by William Butler Yeats, has been compared with Brutus as ill-suited to his situation. He is a lesser Lear who must be deprived of his kingship before he can come to grips with his own reality; like Romeo, he too easily lets loose his hold on life. Winston Churchill described the historical Richard as an enigma, having in his nature "fantastic error and true instinct." Richard seems to see himself as the center of a ritualistic, ceremonial existence into which he has been almost literally born a king. He is essentially not committed to belief, to his sovereignty, nor even to life. Even the retrovertive ceremonial of the abdication precludes the reality of suffering that purges and restores. Ironically, then, Richard is seen as inferior despite his sovereign position. Suffering evokes a shadow and a nullity (142.31-41). Communication is difficult to Richard's sensitive soul; rhetoric and poetry are as close as he can come to a working dialogue with the world and its people. His inability really to suffer, his aloneness amidst people—he seems only to act suffering—these are his true sufferings. Richard rejected his portion in life; his death is a final shunning of life.

There are no soul-searching soliloquies in *Richard II*. Indeed, there scarcely could be. Richard cannot face himself, actually or in the mirror, and others seem only on the periphery of his introverted consciousness. There is no one to reveal the inner truth. Even the solitary thoughts of Richard in prison are not truly interiorized (141.1-41). Motives in the play are often not clearly defined. Characters emerge from traits typical of their position in life rather than from their own individuality; even Richard comes alive only when he begins to act. Other characters could have been cut from the same cloth, though in different patterns. Had the situation been different, Bolingbroke easily could have been the play's hero. York is the wise old man, phrasing maxims of experience like another Polonius, shortsighted, expedient. Aumerle, while loyal to Richard, is thoughtful enough of himself when his part in the conspiracy is disclosed. Notably lacking in the play is the real common man, and missing with him is the humor which he can express for Shakespeare. Even the Gardener and his companion, the "Man," are only mouthpieces expressing the conventional view of Richard and his England. They never have the delightful reality of a Gobbo, a gravedigger, a drunken porter or a philosopher-fool.

In summary, then, the students should recognize that the basic historical facts which form the plot of *Richard II* have been given a dual focus in the tragic conflict of Richard and Bolingbroke. This conflict itself develops the many-faceted character of Richard as he copes with his illusions and submits to his destiny; at the same time it builds a tragedy on the imbalance of strength and weakness in his character. All characters in the play can be evaluated by their relation to this duality. Finally, poetic qualities, rhetoric, and verbalization, profuse but precise imagery, emphasize the neat symmetry of the play's construction and enforce its tragic implications.

THE ACTION

I.i

The play opens in Windsor Castle where the king is officially king and where he exerts his sovereignty. The next time the action is placed in this setting, the court is a "kingless" one, presided over by the Duke of York while Richard is in Ireland (II.ii). In scenes iii and iv of Act V, Richard has been dethroned and a new king wields power, ironically surrounded by the same kinds of problems which Richard faced in the early scenes of the play. Throughout the play the setting is in this way appropriate to the action, even if not highly significant.

The first nineteen lines are briefly introductory, establishing a formal tone and initiating the duel and the conflict which ultimately cost Richard his throne. Richard employs the royal plural, emphasizing his sovereignty (for example, 5,15). His address to his uncle is formal and publicly respectful. His interest in Hereford's motives (8-10) prepares us for his later leniency toward his cousin. We may guess even so soon that Richard has reason to be wary of Bolingbroke. Richard's speech just before the entrance of the disputants (15-19) shows his typical consciousness of position and his consistent use of eloquent rhetoric. The couplet (18-19) closes the section with a neat parallelism. Shakespeare often used the couplet in his early plays to close off one sequence from the succeeding action or to terminate an important speech (cf. Introduction, p. xxiv).

The speeches of Bolingbroke and Mowbray constitute a verbal match that parallels the duel. At first it seems to be only a formal interchange of charge and countercharge of treason. Something more serious is suggested by Richard's rather realistic acknowledgment that only one of these men can be telling the truth. The challenge sets a pattern for the total action of the play, which also involves the life and death of the participants and leads to the rise and fall of kings. Already a converging of themes is apparent in the fusing of the conflict of sovereignty and treason with the problem of "honor or death" introduced by Mowbray (166-69).

Bolingbroke is quite proper in his words, protesting loyalty and devotion (30-34), and putting the requirements of the chivalric code before those of family loyalty (70-71; cf. Mowbray's charge, 58-60). His denunciation of Mowbray is strong, with parallel structures repeated for rhetorical emphasis (91, 92, 96). Bolingbroke introduces the biblical imagery to make appropriate but ironic reference to Gloucester's death. Since Richard knew best his own responsibility for his uncle's death, the reference to sacrificial Abel (104) cuts two ways. Bolingbroke assumes the role of avenger of Gloucester's death (105-08). Since Richard, the King, is better placed to seek revenge, it is possible to see in this claim by Bolingbroke an incipient aspiration to the throne. At the end of the scene a proud Bolingbroke refuses to apologize to Mowbray, lest by doing so he discredit his position. Bolingbroke appears determined, assured, and righteous. His confident manner suggests success in the duel and prepares us for his ultimate triumph in his conflict with Richard.

Mowbray creates an impression of sincerity and loyalty. As defendant he stands to win sympathy. His response to Bolingbroke's accusations begins with "cold words" (47), in a mood of restraint that conceals deep personal feeling, but he quickly becomes intense and passionate, breaking the previously established formal tone. He insists on his loyalty to the King, his liege-lord (78-79). The code of chivalry will be the test of his loyalty. He admits to some wrongs and thus disarms the audience. His admission is unsettling to Richard, who can ill afford the risk of having his own political sins revealed. Mowbray vehemently rejects a peaceful solution; he refuses to retract the challenge since he values his honor equally with his life (182-85).

At the end of this scene Richard sets forth his conception of sovereignty (196). At fleeting moments during the play Richard shows a deceptive candor. Both appeals having been rejected, Richard cannot settle the quarrel by command; however, he can command the time and place for the testing of justice. Richard vows, almost lightly, by his sovereignty itself that justice will be impartial (117-21). In his first appearance Richard seems more the representation of authority than a person of authority. He is in the potentially tragic situation of a man not in relation to his society; his tragic isolation thus begins to emerge, even while he is in a favorable situation.

The allusions to chivalry and honor in this scene provide the context for the conflict. They define Richard's position as King and clarify his relation to "Old" and "time-honored" Gaunt (1), as well as to Bolingbroke and Mowbray. Note the number and range of images used by Richard: raging sea and fire (19); figures from falconry (109); disease and medicine (152-59); heraldic lions and leopards (173-74). Repeated references to blood and bleeding establish the tone of tragedy (cf. Symphonic Imagery, p. 207ff.). Blood also emphasizes the theme of family loyalty. In Elizabethan understanding killing in "hot blood" was a lesser crime than killing in "cold blood." The latter indicated a lengthy, deliberate quarrel like the feud in *Romeo and Juliet* (51, 58, 71, 103-04, 113, 119, 149, 153, 172, 194). Mowbray opens a new theme when he comments on man as "gilded loam, or painted clay" (179) when honor is lost. This figure speaks to the condition of Richard as the drama moves on.

I.ii

Exposition continues into the second short scene with Gaunt's stark confession of complicity in the death of his brother, Gloucester (1). Ironic candor marks this scene also, since the conversation is between Gaunt and Gloucester's widow. The further forthright statement that Richard is responsible for the murder (4-5) clarifies Richard's actions in the preceding scene and reveals the real significance of the Bolingbroke-Mowbray conflict.

Gaunt also introduces the idea of the divine appointment of kings. Recognizing Richard's responsibility for much of the evil, he categorically assigns the office of revenge to God or to God's minister, the King (37-41). Unlike Bolingbroke he accepts no personal responsibility for avenging his brother's death or for his own part in it.

The Duchess, a choric character, presents a rather unconvincing plea for vengeance. Little personality shows through her oratorical manner. At this point the student may need clarification of the Tree of Jesse passage (cf. Symphonic Imagery, p. 223). The persons of the play and their complex relationships can profitably be discussed at this point. Note again the references to blood as fusion of life and death (10-22). Formal acceptance of God's will marks the ineffectiveness of the Duchess' complaint. Her position is as uncertain as her speech. Few true interrogatives occur in the play; most

THE TRAGEDY OF KING RICHARD THE SECOND   277

are purely rhetorical. However, the Duchess questions acutely
the whole play and its essentially "love-less" tale (9-10).
"Brotherhood" is almost as meaningless as her words prove,
and love has no true place in the play.

I.iii

In the lists at Coventry, medieval pageantry is achieved
through the action and the dialogue because Shakespeare's
plays were performed with a minimum of scenery. The flexi-
bility of action that was made possible by the indeterminate,
sceneryless stage also allows Shakespeare to telescope time.
The entire action of this play covers less than two years. Ignoring the time intervals of actual history, Shakespeare
makes the development of character and the dramatic action
continuous.

The suggested splendor of the tourney makes Richard's
show of kingship seem pathetic. Note the stage directions
calling for the flourish of trumpets when the royal procession
enters, the show of officers charged with the proper conduct
of the tourney, and the "champions" in battle array. The formality of the dialogue, the identification of causes and persons, even the King surrounded by his favorites, make a romantic and courtly spectacle. The mediation of the Marshal
emphasizes the detachment of the King from the duel and
the opponents. Evidently Richard is seated on a platform of
some kind (perhaps the upper area of the stage). When he
comes down to Bolingbroke, he leaves behind, to some degree, his regal posture and greets him as cousin (55).
Note the significance of Richard's descent at Bolingbroke's
request (54), a foreshadowing of later descents. Note, too,
the kissing of the hand and, especially, the formal bowing of
the knee. These actions are repeated with increased significance in later encounters.

Students may contrast the actions of Bolingbroke and
Mowbray, both before and after the halting of the duel. Bolingbroke is bold and presumptuous. Mowbray sincere and
deeply grieved. Bolingbroke capitalizes on family ties. His
claim that his cause is that of God and the King (40) only
echoes similar phrases of Mowbray (17-25). Bolingbroke's
position is strengthened when Richard, descending to em-
brace him, calls him "Cousin" (55). He in turn calls Aumerle "cousin" (64), and identifies his father among Richard's
courtiers (76).

Richard's conduct as he commands the trial to commence
(99) and then throwing down the warder as soon as the

charge is sounded (117-18) is of critical importance. Within twenty-nine lines Richard has made clear the ambiguity of his position. His actions—impulsive, unmotivated, perhaps unrealistic—reveal the character who dominates the drama. They antagonize Bolingbroke, his formidable opponent.

The decision to halt the combat is Richard's. He has, of course, consulted with his council (124), as a king should, but the plan he follows is clearly his own. For the first time Richard has resorted to subterfuge. Having no way of solving his problem, he banishes its cause. His assertion that his whole object is to preserve peace is only empty rhetoric (123-38). It is not easy to assess the disproportionate sentences Richard pronounces on the disputants. Richard must have good reason to trust Mowbray's silence about the death of Gloucester. Mowbray himself underscores the situation with his ironic description of his sentence as a "speechless death" (172). Richard's leniency toward Bolingbroke seems both foolish and unfair. The four-year reduction in Bolingbroke's sentence is typical of the mistaken actions of Richard. It is difficult to find a moment when Richard makes a deliberate, or even a definite, wrong decision in this tragic descent; rather he goes through a series of experiences in each of which he fails to act prudently. In his final words to Bolingbroke, Mowbray predicts the outcome of Richard's decision on this occasion (200-204).

The conflict between Bolingbroke and Mowbray is apparently settled with words. "How long a time lies in one little word. . . . such is the breath of kings" (212-14), Bolingbroke exclaims when his banishment is reduced. This remark emphasizes one of the most important ideas in the play. Richard has met his problem with an eloquently expressed but practically dangerous solution. He appears, in his delight in the verbal excitement of his own eloquence, not to see that he has dramatically changed the lives of several persons. Life and death for very real people depend on what he says; with a word he can shorten the misery of Bolingbroke's exile. But these things do not seem so real to him as the fine words he uses. (Cf. discussion of *"tongue, . . . mouth, speech* and *word,"* pp. 213ff.)

Bolingbroke's brief acceptance of his sentence, unmarked with feeling, is strangely acquiescent. In the reference to the sun (145-47) kingly power is obliquely suggested. Elizabethan imagery equated England with the universe, the king with the sun, etc. His exile from his native land does not remove Bolingbroke from his "country's light" into "shades of endless night" destined for Mowbray (176-77). Gaunt reinforces this point by suggesting that a wise man can learn to live wherever the "eye of heaven" shines (274). In a philosophical discourse of paternal advice he sententiously comforts his son. One is reminded of Polonius' farewell advice to Laertes in *Hamlet*. Gaunt's aphorisms are more serious, and perhaps more insidious. ("Think not the King did banish thee,/But thou the King," 278-79.)

I.iv

In this scene, too, Richard shows a tendency to overvalue merely verbal achievements. "Cousin" bumps against "cousin" (20) and "craftsmen" are wooed with "the craft of smiles" (28). The "lining" of coffers punningly makes "coats" (61). Finally Richard profanes the solemn moment of Gaunt's dying with a frivolous joke: "Pray God we may make haste and come too late!" (64). The general "Amen!" of his sycophants closes the first act with a resounding hollow sound (65).

This scene is a footnote on the character of Richard, and, in a lesser degree, of Aumerle and the Dukes. Aumerle is loyal to Richard; for Bolingbroke he has little regard. Bushy and Green are typical sycophants.

In the first act Richard has committed himself uncompromisingly to the position that he will not abdicate. He is confident of his position and power; he is King by divine right, by circumstance, and by his own assurance. He foresees that Bolingbroke, already a favorite of the commoners, will return as an enemy (20-36). This awareness is couched in legalistic terms: "reversion" (35), the right of succession or future possession; "coffers" (43); "revenue" (46); "blank charters" (48). Richard's haste to acquire Gaunt's property and consequently to deprive Bolingbroke of it aggravates the initial injury of banishment. The student should realize that Richard's heartless humor indicates a selfishness and a lack of true feeling for his uncle. He presents an unpleasant facet of his personality in this scene, displaying an inner crudeness that is in jarring contrast with the nobility and royalty that supposedly characterize a king.

II.i

Gaunt, named "Old" and "time-honored" by Richard in the opening lines of the play (41.1), lies ill, awaiting the King's visit. York, with choric wisdom and simple truth, tersely asserts the vanity of hoping that Richard will take Gaunt's advice (4). Gaunt, the voice of age and experience and suffering, demonstrates for us the proper balance of "voice," "breath," and "life" (5-16). His dying speech brings to the surface the reality of suffering. Just as it has been difficult to reach the reality of characters like Richard behind the rhetoric of their dialogue, so it has been impossible to come close enough to their humanity to comprehend their suffering. York proposes that Richard be told the truth; he implies a tone of ill-feeling, possibly distrust. He evokes the prophetic voice of Gaunt (31-68). The famous patriotic words of the dying man are endowed with a greater sincerity because he is dying; they express a deep respect for England and loyalty to the King. Again there is a convergence of themes: loyalty to the King; love of the land; a respect for breeding, rulers, family bonds, and the warrants of living and dying. The stage is set for a king, even though he be a weak one. Such a noble land as Gaunt describes deserves a noble ruler.

As Gaunt puns on his own name, he suggests something of Cassius' "lean and hungry look," the look of a watcher (73-83; cf. *Julius Caesar*, 43.194). He predicts (125ff.) a new royalty, new loyalties born of present dying, illness, and disease. The dying Gaunt fathers from the tomb a new king; Gaunt's sickness is health compared with the illness imputed to a healthy Richard. The "thousand flatterers" who "sit" (100) in Richard's crown are a disease which will bring death and suffering. Gaunt reminds us that Richard is mortal and a man like any other despite his singularity as King (104-14).

As may be expected, Richard, consistently rejecting truth, becomes enraged. He rejects Gaunt, and indirectly Gaunt's son (146). The announcement of Gaunt's death gives this unfeeling Richard no pause. "So much for that," he says as if washing his hands (155). And he moves immediately to deprive the banished Bolingbroke.

Choosing to ignore immediate dangers, Richard concerns himself with his problems abroad. Trusting to York's sense of duty and loyalty, he appoints his uncle Regent. This move is foolish in the light of York's frankly expressed remarks. Equally foolishly, Richard then sails to battle on foreign soil, leaving the disgruntled lords to discuss his weaknesses and failings. They are beginning to feel that the wrongs Richard has done (241ff.) justify Bolingbroke's claims. Already the descent of Richard has begun; and the complementary rise of Bolingbroke, assisted by Northumberland and his sons, has also begun. Loyalty recedes as the King departs.

II.ii

Again the scene is Windsor Castle, the setting for critical actions. The Queen, only a shadow of the sovereign, holds brief converse with Richard's favorites. Even to please the King she cannot feign happiness. In 1396 Richard II married the daughter of Charles V of France. Actually she was a child-bride, but the Isabel of the play speaks as an adult. She shows an honesty not found in many persons in this play, and her loyalty to Richard creates sympathy for him. An audience should feel that a man so loved has some good qualities.

The Queen speaks not of words, but of thoughts, the shadows of words (30-32). Her thoughts, like the words so lightly tossed out in earlier scenes, are empty too, because, the Queen agrees, her nameless grief is "nothing" (34-40). She has been reduced to the nothing that Richard will face in prison (142.38-41). Here once more is the theme of reality and appearance; the Queen constructs a fragile hope (43-45) which, shadow-like, is destroyed by the startling news of Bolingbroke's return and his increasing military strength (49-51, 58-61). Her hope destroyed, the Queen can feel only grief and the approach of death (62-66) and its shadow-dispersing reality. When York enters, she asks not for thoughts but for words, "comfortable words" (76).

York is again the voice of truth and prophecy. Since the King stood to England as the preserving power of God, York sees "a tide of woes/Comes rushing on this woeful land at once" (98-99; cf. 120-21). The woe seems to enter the kingdom through the Queen, who remains silent and inactive in this part of the scene, suffering in the shadow of Richard's wrongs. She can be paralleled with the Duchess of Gloucester, who has died in her own grief, unheard and unaided (50.44-74). York calls the Queen "sister," as if she almost were the Duchess; then he calls her "cousin" (104). York, one of the few who must make a definite choice, admits that choice is difficult because conscience and duty are on Richard's side.

Richard's favorites set the scene for disaster; Bushy says, seeming to foresee the tragic outcome, "We three here part that ne'er shall meet again" (142).

II.iii

The abrupt entrance of Bolingbroke and Northumberland is made in the "high wild hills and rough uneven ways" (4).

The return of Bolingbroke to England, the woes of the Queen and of York, the dilemma of the favorites, all these signal upheaval. The dialogue becomes less lyric and less rhetorical. It is the language of men who stand close to dangerous realities and who know how to accept a challenge. Manliness and courage are implied, and business-like attitudes. Action may be expected. (Northumberland and Percy continue as companions of Bolingbroke in the succeeding plays that deal with Bolingbroke's reign, the two parts of *Henry IV*.)

Loyalty to Bolingbroke is evident in all who have gathered around him. The youthful Percy is specially devoted to him, in marked contrast with the elderly York, who may well be the only man present who recalls the old regime. Note the change in language, the conscious play on words (86-88), and the rhetorical questions (89-95). York speaks of the "anointed King" and his heritage (95). York sounds like the voice of age addressing youth, fearful of the rebelliousness of youth. Note the formality of York's address; Bolingbroke, by contrast, speaks in familiar terms of kinship. These two graphically express the conflict of loyalties that confronts them all. York's vulnerability and his honesty force him to recognize that Bolingbroke has some right on his side, but he charges that the wrong way has been chosen to achieve these rights. He will "remain as neuter" (158), a clearly impossible position, but one that will ease him away from his loyalty to Richard when another is king. Bolingbroke has already pledged himself to "weed and pluck" the land (166), a task that belongs to the King. The images here, especially that of the "caterpillars of the commonwealth" (165), are taken up again in the garden scene later on.

II.iv

This brief scene is primarily exposition. The people are fearful that Richard will not return. The frightening natural phenomena (7-17) reflect the turmoil in the world when a king has sinned or is sinned against. Students may remember similar occurrences in *Julius Caesar*, *Macbeth*, and *Hamlet*. And so the act closes with a strong sense of foreboding. The rapid descent of the "shooting star" (19-20), debased as it falls to earth, and the setting sun, so like the decline of a king, are images reminiscent of *Romeo and Juliet*. The climactic third act is clearly rehearsed in these lines.

III.i

This scene depends for its effect on the audience's remembering the last part of the second scene in Act II (81.122ff). Bushy and Green have met the fate they feared. Bolingbroke acts with the power and presumption of a king. Like Richard earlier in the play, he commands and lives are changed, sometimes terminated. Still professing love and loyalty to Richard, he deprives him of the props of his kingship. Claiming that he seeks only the redress of his personal wrongs, he establishes his own code of justice. Note his respectful concern for the Queen, who remains the shadow of the King, the bond connecting Richard to England.

III.ii

A critical point in the tragedy begins here. With two acts completed and two more to follow, the action, at least quantitatively, is almost half completed; and yet interest in Richard as a person is only just beginning. Having seen Bolingbroke potentially victorious, the student may see Richard as foil to both Bolingbroke and fate. In his weakness Richard develops a sense of reality that he has not previously had. As human qualities come to the fore, sympathy is aroused. This Richard, who almost childishly exposes his ambiguities, is not violent, not military, but highly vulnerable.

Richard's rhetoric increases in intensity but not always in logic. He not only plays at being king, he plays his own idea of a king. His failing confidence is only thinly masked. His posturing is only vaguely convincing, and the depth of his feeling is perplexing, perhaps even to Richard. The melodramatic gesture of kneeling to touch the earth, *his* England, suggests a kind of sincerity, a welcome note of patriotism. Contact with the land reassures him. Security comes first from the land, and secondarily, after Carlisle's reminder, from his divine appointment (57). The relation of king to land is a "natural" one; like a mother, his land should warm and protect him (8-27).

Richard's uneasy bravado reveals uncertainty and reminds us of his incompetence. Lines 36-62 may be difficult for the student. Like many of Richard's speeches, this one toys with the logic of thought and of sentence structure, creating an admirable rhetoric in its fine words. Images seem heaped together, as if many things are piled onto Richard at this point. He asserts that a king is like the sun; that night and day indicate a nebulous evil and good, a time for guilt and a time for innocence; the "golden crown" (59) becomes a "hollow" (160) one (cf. p. 224). "Not all the water in the rough rude sea/Can wash the balm off from an anointed king" (54-55). Richard adopts religious metaphor to affirm his invulnerability as a king.

Brought back to the practical problem by Aumerle's reminder (82), Richard attempts to recall his "coward majesty" (84), but immediately begins to think again of his weakened position. He seems ready to capitulate. For the first time Richard entertains the realistic view that his kingship has possible limits, that it may be terminated by human forces (93-103, 177, 210-13, 215-18).

Richard's words, after he learns of the death of his favorites, beg for analysis (145-77). Richard has changed moods rapidly. He easily cries treachery when he believes that his friends have betrayed him; too readily he condemns. The news that they died for their loyalty to him evokes no real sorrow or even brief encomium. Instead, self-pity consumes Richard. Death of friends reminds him of the death of kings (156), and so Richard is moved to words not to action. He talks of the end of things, of dispensing of properties by will, of hollow crowns and antic Death, of final gestures and closing ceremonies (144-177). These lines detail his last stand on the stage. Defeat is imminent; Richard has seen through his fanciful image of a king and begins to explore the novelty of being human. Yet this new experience is short-lived. For the easily swayed, emotion-filled Richard again becomes "bright" as an "eagle" at the prodding of loyalty (102.68).

Recall again Richard's early actions; decisions were then reached with his counselors about him. Of these counselors none seemed so true as Carlisle. It is important to recognize this man as a true ecclesiastic, not a time-serving appointee. His admonitions (27-32.178-85) are in direct contrast to Richard's shallow thinking and nearsighted views. Carlisle respects the anointed king, but he is also aware of the folly of Richard's present course.

III.iii

The meeting between Bolingbroke and Richard contrasts strongly with the banishment scene. The pageantry of the tourney is replaced by a military setting with real armies offstage. Bolingbroke has the military power, but Richard still possesses the crown. Again Richard descends to his cousin, just as he had in the lists before the charge was sounded (53.54).

Again the speech of Bolingbroke and his followers is direct and pointed. The lines are brief until Richard's appearance is imminent. The principal linguistic device is the pun; no fanciful figures are used.

Bolingbroke's greeting is less courtly than formerly; his words are self-assured and threatening (41-47). He anticipates conflict with images of storm and conquest. He heralds Richard's appearance with attention to externals, "and mark King Richard how he looks" (60). He compares Richard with the red sun at dawn which foretells a storm (61-63). York's rejoinder is a sad comment, "Yet looks he like a king . . . Controlling majesty" (67-69).

The interchange between Northumberland and Richard is dramatic. Richard, unsure of his position and woefully aware of his folly, capitulates even before descending. In the banishment scene Richard had remained distant, almost detached. Here he throws himself into his defeat almost as if he relishes the role. He has no capacity for compromise; having given the first inch, there is for him no return—he relinquishes all in a magnificent gesture. His action constitutes a submission rather than an acceptance of his destiny. He invites his own catastrophe. The inevitability of his defeat makes his regal attitude almost absurd.

III.iv

The allegorical character of the garden scene accounts for the obvious coincidence which places the Queen conveniently in the shadows while the Gardener discusses England (the garden) and the deposition of the King. The Elizabethan theory that order and proportion in the kingdom derive from the King is clear. The Gardener and the Man are like the characters of a morality play. As allegorical characters, they define the chaotic state resulting from the misdeeds of the King. Their voices seem to be the voices of the English people who look to Bolingbroke now to prune and dress the land and to return it to "law and form" (41).

This scene is built on contrast and contradiction. The Gardener is productive; he plays a generative role. Richard has become degenerate; he is now a destructive force in England. The Man is curious to know why they should attempt to keep their walled-in garden orderly when the land at large is overrun with evil (40-47).

The Queen, like Richard, must go to London to encounter woe (97; cf. 107,206). Her ineffective curse on the Gardener's art (101) demonstrates her powerlessness as Queen.

All that she will claim as place in England is a spot where rue has been planted in testimony of her queenship (104-07).

IV.i

Westminster Hall, a scene of regal glory and of coronations, is ironically chosen for the un-crowning of Richard. It is a regal stage on which Richard may enact his deposition. Once again Richard is kingly, noble in mood at least; and yet there is little in his actions that is manly. He is pathetic; he is human. Once his humanity is revealed, he can evoke sympathy. As does Lear's, his test comes when he is stripped of the trappings of a king. The tension of something within Richard vibrates against all the characters, even against his own conduct: he finds it difficult to drop suddenly all his kingly habits. In this episode Shakespeare has gathered many of the characters of the play, as if to validate the "un-kinging" of Richard.

The death of Gloucester becomes throughout the play a more and more meaningful image of the tragic consequences of expediency. With each reference there is an increasing urgency; a kind of compulsion overspreads the characters (cf. 44.98-108; 45.132-34; 48.1ff.; 69.104-05; 69.124-38; 71.163ff.). Guilt-ridden, they are caught in the revolving action and tossed about as the wheel carries Bolingbroke higher and Richard lower (183-88).

At the beginning of the play Bolingbroke is in a situation parallel to Richard's at the end. Aumerle, holding on to a waning loyalty to Richard, now faces Bolingbroke's followers. The flatterers of Richard have been well replaced. The challenges and the gages are tossed freely as the decision is made for "swords and lances [to] arbitrate" (48.200).

Carlisle stands apart from the action. His attitude is certain to be disapproved of by Bolingbroke. First Carlisle gives the news of Mowbray's death, the consequence of the earlier trial and his banishment. Perfunctorily Bolingbroke consigns Mowbray and his quarrel to the bosom of Abraham (103-04) and turns his attention to Richard and the throne. Carlisle's moment is brief but eloquent. Carlisle is always marked with a solemnity not found in any other character in the play. Sincerely religious, he is prophetic and incisive. He views the political changes in England and Bolingbroke's conduct as unnatural and irreligious. Carlisle is devoted, not just to Richard, but to the idea of godlike majesty. In his famous speech on obedience to God's "deputy elect,/ Anointed, crownèd, planted many years" (126-27), he is so orthodox

THE TRAGEDY OF KING RICHARD THE SECOND 287

that he must be arrested (114-49). Having already assumed
the kingship, Bolingbroke has no other answer for him. Carlisle expresses a truth that cannot be evaded. At the end of the
long abdication scene he is heard again as an augur of doom
for England and Bolingbroke (321-22).

Richard's conduct during this scene is a summation of his
character: posturing, gesturing, a fusion of fact and illusion,
perplexing, and provocative. First he indulges in theatrics,
only thinly disguising the truth of the situation. He compares
himself to Christ, persecuted and delivered up to his enemies
(169-70; 238-41). Intensity as much as pathos marks Richard's command performance. With an almost playful gesture,
he calls on Bolingbroke to grasp the crown. For a tense moment they hold the crown between them. Typically, Richard
cannot commit himself to defeat. If Richard is not king, he is
nothing (200-21). "Oh, that I were a mockery king of
snow," he cries (259). Indirection is an imperative for Richard. When he confesses himself a traitor to the kingship, he
obliquely includes all around him in the same judgment. "For
I have given here my soul's consent/T' undeck the pompous
body of a king" (248-49). Moral evaluation, even of kings, is
measured by loyalty to the kingship.

The "mockery king of snow" frets meanwhile with the
shadow and substance of his own reality. Again Richard
would see his own self, would grasp the humanity that had
earlier insinuated itself into his words. However, the mirror
shows no more of the reality than others can see. It only images, reproduces a face, a semblance of a person. It is the
mirror, not the crown, that Richard tosses away. Richard's
mood is interrogative; he makes no affirmation. Unlike Lear,
he cannot come to grips with himself. Deposed and submissive, he remains irrepressible. Bolingbroke holds the crown,
but Richard has stolen the show—"A woeful pageant" (320).

A brief episode closes the scene with the promise that "A
plot shall show us all a merry day" (333). A plot devised by
"holy clergymen" (323-24) ratifies Richard's kingship and
condemns Bolingbroke's usurpation. Also, the cycle of downfall of the mighty begins again with Bolingbroke poised at the
top.

V.i

On a street in London, where Richard is only a man, no
longer a king, the Queen sees her "fair rose wither" (8). The
productive, life-giving images used by the Queen earlier
(II.9-13) are replaced by figures of destruction and death,
(11-15; 29-34). When Richard speaks to her he gives a sum-

mary of his own life and death, seeing his career as another instance of the prince fallen from high estate. "Tell thou the lamentable tale of me" (44; cf. 97.155-56). The pretty little scene of separation adds no depth to Richard's character; he remains self-centered and acquiescent. But the Queen's feelings about him increase our sympathy for the victimized Richard.

V.ii

The action of this scene reinforces the parallel between the position of Bolingbroke now and of Richard at the beginning of the play. York speaks sadly of the mistreatment of Richard and the acclaim of Bolingbroke. The juxtaposition is viewed through the eyes of York, who is always loyal to the king, whether Richard or Bolingbroke. His personal feelings must be muffled because his allegiance belongs to the throne (39-40). The pseudo-domestic drama involving York, his wife, and their son, produced by the plot to kill Bolingbroke, reemphasizes the theme of loyalty to the king as the measure of men's virtue.

V.iii

The opening lines of this scene are a bridge to events in the Henry IV plays that are the sequel to *Richard II*. Bolingbroke is surrounded by a mockery of his own obeisance to Richard when he was charged with treachery in the first act. Wiser than Richard was, he pardons Aumerle and paves for himself at least one easier road to follow.

V.iv

The obvious purpose of this brief scene is to motivate the murder of Richard.

V.v

Richard had almost achieved a moment of truth when he called for the mirror in the deposition scene. Then, however, there were spectators, and he turned the occasion into a performance; here, in prison, he is alone and achieves as much self-revelation as he is capable of. Even at this point he would populate his prison in order to recreate a world for himself. However, having rejected his own humanity and failing to gain an understanding of mortality, he passes over even words and entertains himself with thoughts. Thoughts, too, he rejects because they are concluded with a cipher. When removed from history and real life, un-kinged, unmade as it were, Richard can look for ease, for then he will have no shadows with which to flirt (1-41). And thus Richard turns to view his own time-wasted existence (49). As his time runs out, Richard briefly encounters humanity in the groom who remembers him as king.

When Exton and the murderers rush in, Richard is moved to physical action for the first time in the play. He has nothing left for defense. His eloquence and show of majesty are as empty now as his barren cell. In a rapid action in which Richard must be violent, brave, and authentic, he kills two of his attackers before he himself dies, slain by an impetuosity not unlike his own. "O, would the deed were good!" (114).

SISTER RITA CATHERINE HOMMRICH

V.vi

Windsor Castle witnesses a bloody initiation of Bolingbroke's reign. Carlisle, alone, merits a stay of execution; that stay is Bolingbroke's tribute to truth and honor (24-29). In the final encounter, Richard, even in death, exerts a power against Bolingbroke. His death reveals unwanted truths to Bolingbroke. He vows to make a pilgrimage to expiate his crime. Blood has marked the start of his sufferings.

SHORT-ANSWER QUESTIONS

1. What effect is created by Richard's initial address to his uncle, York?

2. Does Richard arouse any feeling when he greets Bolingbroke as cousin and asks for the charge? (41.8-11)

3. The speeches of Mowbray and Bolingbroke are similar in language. How are these men distinguished in personality?

290   TEACHING SHAKESPEARE

4. What charge does Bolingbroke make against Mowbray? (44.87-108)

5. To what wrongs does Mowbray admit? (45-46.132-41)

6. What does Mowbray mean when he remarks that deprived of honor "Men are but gilded loam, or painted clay"? (47.179)

7. What is the significance of throwing down the gage or raising the gage?

8. What admissions does Gaunt make at the beginning of Act I, scene ii? (48.1-3)

9. The Duchess of Gloucester is a choric character. What information does she add?

10. How does Richard communicate with the two men who have come to duel? Why does he not address them directly? (51.7)

11. Why does Richard descend from the royal seat? (53.54)

12. What reason is given for halting the combat? (55.125ff.)

13. What sentences are pronounced on the disputants? Why was a distinction made? (56.139-43, 148-53)

14. Why is Bolingbroke's term of banishment lessened? (58.207-11)

15. How does Richard react to the news that his uncle, John of Gaunt, is ill? What aspect of Richard's character is revealed? (64.59-64)

16. Gaunt, speaking from his deathbed, claims to be a prophet. What predictions does he make? Is his patriotism sincere? (66-67.31-60)

17. Gaunt creates a somber kind of humor in the speech that puns his name. Comment on the significance. (68.73-83)

18. Why does Richard become angry at Gaunt's words? (69.115)

THE TRAGEDY OF KING RICHARD THE SECOND 291

19. What is Richard's reaction to the announcement of Gaunt's death? (70.153ff.)

20. What action does Richard take? How does this action complicate previous events? (72.209-10)

21. How does Northumberland arouse sympathy for Bolingbroke? (74.238-45, 252-55, 258)

22. What is the Queen's attitude toward Richard? (75.5-13)

23. Explain Bushy's words to the Queen about shadow and grief. (77.14-27)

24. What tragic function is fulfilled by Bushy, Bagot, and Green? (II, ii)

25. Bolingbroke returns at a critical moment in the play. Is there any evidence that his ambitions are overweening? (84.59-62, 85.70-73, 86.112-35)

26. Percy's devotion to the Duke he has never seen is striking. Does he appear to be sincere? Is there any significance in his attitude?

27. Explain York's attitude toward Bolingbroke when they first meet after the return of the latter? (85-88.83-160)

28. Why does Bolingbroke have Bushy and Green executed? What does such an action indicate?

29. Explain Richard's action when he returns to England. (92.4-26)

30. How do Carlisle and Aumerle compare with Richard's earlier advisers?

31. What message does Salisbury bring to Richard? How does Richard react? (94.64-74)

32. Has Richard changed from the person we saw him to be at the beginning of the play? (104.142-74)

33. What predictions are contained in the couplet that ends Act III, scene ii?

292   TEACHING SHAKESPEARE

34. What message does Bolingbroke plan to send to Richard as he prepares to meet him at Flint Castle? (101.30-47)

35. What does Northumberland report to Bolingbroke about Richard? (106.182-83)

36. What place does the Gardener have in the narration of events?

37. Why do the lords challenge Aumerle at the beginning of Act IV?

38. What warning does Carlisle give to Bolingbroke? (116.114-49)

39. When he is called on to relinquish the crown, why does Richard become reluctant after he had already agreed to do so?

40. What interpretation do you give to these words of Richard's:

    O, that I were a mockery king of snow,
    Standing before the sun of Bolingbroke,
    To melt myself away in water drops! (121.259-61)

41. Why does Richard throw down the mirror? (122.275-90)

42. What is to become of the Queen after she separates from Richard? (126.22-25)

43. What document does York take from his son? (131.56ff.)

44. What consequent action does York take? Aumerle? The Duchess?

45. How does Bolingbroke receive their pleas? (139.128-35)

46. What prompts Exton's action against Richard? (140.7-11)

47. In the prison at Pomfret Richard comments to himself: "I wasted time, and now doth Time waste me" (142.49). What is the significance of these words?

48. Richard so often in critical moments backs away from

real struggle. Is this true in the death scene in the prison?

49. What final judgment does Bolingbroke pronounce on Carlisle? (146.24-26)

50. What is Bolingbroke's reaction to the news of Richard's death? (147.34-36, 38-52)

QUESTIONS FOR DISCUSSION

1. Does Richard have an authentic place in his world? Is he capable of malice? Of any real emotion? What evidence to support your answer can be found in the action of the play?

2. In view of his final mastery over Richard, does Bolingbroke assume the role of hero in the play?

3. Discuss the tragic function of the following images in *Richard II*:

    a. Crown
    b. Earth
    c. Garden
    d. Blood
    e. Illness and disease

4. a. How important to the action of the play are the facts of history?
   b. Explain Shakespeare's use of history to develop the tragic character of Richard II.

5. Can we see Richard independently as a character or do other characters reveal him to us? What relation is established between Richard and Gaunt? Richard and York? Richard and Bolingbroke? Richard and the Queen? Richard and his favorites?

6. Humor, which Shakespeare often uses as a foil for tragic action, is notably omitted in *Richard II*. Does this omis

sion constitute a flaw, or is it a necessary outcome of conditions in the play?

7. The abdication scene brings Bolingbroke and Richard into direct conflict over the crown. How does the interaction at this time reveal their characters?

8. The garden scene in Act III is both allegorical and symbolic. How does the conversation between the Gardener and the Man help to point the real meaning of the play?

9. Much of the action in *Richard II* involves intrigue and conflict between male characters. What dramatic necessity is answered by the Queen? The Duchess of Gloucester? The Duchess of York?

10. In the abdication scene Bolingbroke asks Richard if he is willing to surrender his crown. What is the significance of Richard's reply: "Ay, no; no, ay: for I must nothing be" (119.200)?

SAMPLE TEST

I. (45 minutes)

1. Does Richard have an authentic place in his world? Is he capable of malice? Of any real emotion? What evidence to support your answer can be found in the action of the play?

2. What does Mowbray mean when he says that deprived of honor "Men are but gilded loam, or painted clay"?

3. What tragic function is fulfilled by Bushy, Bagot, and Green?

4. What place does the Gardener have in the narration of events?

5. What is the significance of the warning Carlisle gives to Bolingbroke?

II. 45 minutes

1. The Garden scene is both allegorical and symbolic. How does the conversation between the Gardener and the Man help to point the real meaning of the play?

2. What interpretation do you give to these words of Richard:

    O, that I were a mockery king of snow,
    Standing before the sun of Bolingbroke,
    To melt myself away in water drops! (121.259-61)

3. What is Richard's reaction to the announcement of Gaunt's death?

4. What is the Queen's attitude toward Richard?

5. Richard so often in critical moments backs away from real struggle. Is this the case in the death scene in prison?

III. 45 minutes

1. Discuss the tragic function of the following images in *Richard II*.

    a. Crown
    b. Earth
    c. Garden
    d. Blood
    e. Illness and disease

2. Explain Richard's action when he returns to England from the expedition to Ireland.

3. What is Bolingbroke's reaction to the news of Richard's death?

4. When he is called on to relinquish the crown, why does Richard become reluctant after he had already agreed to do so?

5. How do Aumerle and Carlisle compare with Richard's other advisers?

IV. 45 minutes

1. The abdication scene brings Bolingbroke and Richard into direct conflict over the crown. How does the interaction at this time reveal their characters?

2. In the prison at Pomfret Richard comments to himself, "I wasted time, and now doth Time waste me" (142.49). What is the significance of these words?

3. Why does Richard throw down the mirror?

4. What final judgment does Bolingbroke pronounce on Carlisle?

5. Percy's devotion to Bolingbroke, whom he has never seen, is striking. Does he appear to be sincere? What significance do you find in his attitude?

THE HISTORY OF HENRY IV (PART ONE)

INTRODUCTION

The play usually known as *Henry IV, Part One* is in fact not a part of a play but one of four history plays, each complete in itself, in which Shakespeare has brought to a resolution a dramatic action selected from the successive reigns of Richard II, Henry IV, and Henry V. In *Richard II* he concentrates attention only on the last turbulent two years of the king's reign, which comes to an end when he is deposed (and presumably murdered) and his cousin, without clear title, comes to the throne as Henry IV. The so-called *Henry IV, Part One* concerns itself only with the rise and partial suppression of a rebellion against the King during a single year of his reign. *Henry IV, Part Two*, the least effective of the four plays, brings Henry IV to his death. He now has a firmer *de facto* claim to the throne to pass on to his son, who is crowned in this play as Henry V. The last of the plays—*Henry V*—is primarily a celebration of Henry V's exploits at Agincourt (1415) and his subsequent wooing of Kathcrine of France.

Characters appear and reappear in two or more of these plays as determined by history and by Shakespeare's dramatic intents. The King Henry IV whom we get to know in the play we are reading plays a prominent part in *Richard II*, where he is known as Bolingbroke, a name given to him because he was born in Bolingbroke castle in Lincolnshire. The rebels in *Henry IV, Part One*, seeking to justify their uprising against the King, find a way to deny his right to the throne by calling him Bolingbroke, as they do for example at 56.135 and 60.239. His son, Prince Hal, is referred to but does not appear in *Richard II*. He has a prominent role in the two Henry IV plays and is of course the hero of *Henry V*. Falstaff appears for the first time in *Henry IV, Part One*, is rejected by Hal when Hal becomes King, and is only mentioned in *Henry V*, when the circumstances of his death are reported. But so clearly are each of these plays autonomous, so distinct is the action of each one, and so completely are the characters revealed by each action, that we will be well advised not to think of the plays as sequels or of the characters as men who preserve their identities as they would in a modern tetralogy.

But history is a continuum even if these plays are not. If the characters are largely determined by the roles they play in the separate works, the role they play in history is largely predetermined. The plays are history as well as drama, and Shakespeare as we know made generous use of Holinshed's *Chronicles of England, Scotland, and Ireland* (see pp. 157-70). However often Shakespeare has chosen from the reigns of these kings only those episodes which suit his purpose, and however often he has taken conventionally acceptable liberties with the facts in order to sharpen his dramatic conflicts, he was inevitably conditioned by the broad outlines of England's history during the first decades of the fifteenth century. We should remember that from 1400, the approximate date of the action of *Henry IV, Part One,* to 1600, the approximate date of the writing of the play, England had emerged to take its place under Elizabeth as a European power. Henry IV had contributed his part to the developing idea of English kingship. Henry V, as the popular hero of Agincourt, had become as well-loved a figure in Shakespeare's England as King Alfred, who let the cakes burn. England's sense of the past stretched after a fashion from Shrewsbury through Agincourt to the victory over the Spanish Armada in 1597. How many Englishmen at the close of the sixteenth century knew anything of Henry IV's reign it is impossible to estimate. How much they learned from Shakespeare's play we can only guess. But since we must read the play as both history and drama and follow the characters as they encounter their historical as well as their dramatic destinies, we need to be able to find our way among the complex relationships that genealogy sets forth. A chart may prove especially helpful in a play where the rebellion against the King is so much of a family affair and where the King's title to the throne is legitimately in dispute.

Richard II closes with Bolingbroke vowing to "make a voyage to the Holy Land" (147.49) that he may rid himself of what guilt he is willing to assume in the death of Richard. *Henry IV* opens with Bolingbroke, now King, reaffirming his intention, a "twelvemonth old," to carry out this pilgrimage

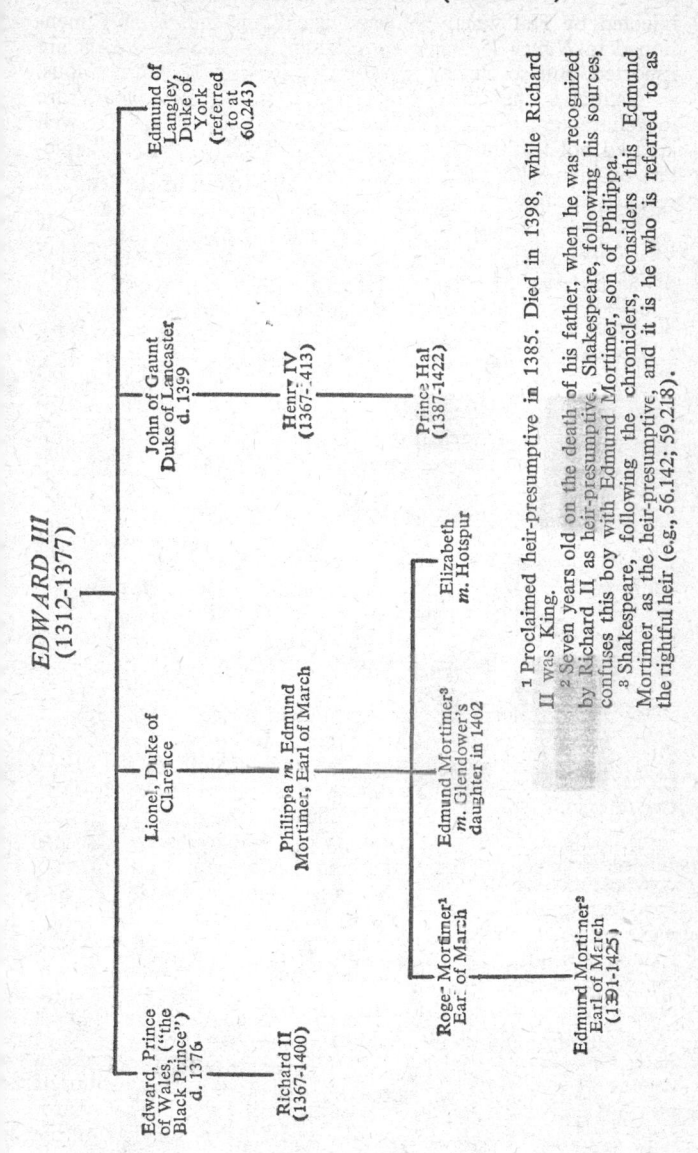

THE HISTORY OF HENRY IV (PART ONE)

EDWARD III (1312–1377)

- Edward, Prince of Wales, ("the Black Prince") d. 1376
  - Richard II (1367–1400)
- Lionel, Duke of Clarence
  - Philippa *m.* Edmund Mortimer, Earl of March
    - Roger Mortimer[1] Earl of March
      - Edmund Mortimer[2] Earl of March (1391–1425)
    - Edmund Mortimer[3] *m.* Glendower's daughter in 1402
    - Elizabeth *m.* Hotspur
- John of Gaunt Duke of Lancaster, d. 1399
  - Henry IV (1367–413)
    - Prince Hal (1387–1422)
- Edmund of Langley, Duke of York (referred to at 60.243)

[1] Proclaimed heir-presumptive in 1385. Died in 1398, while Richard II was King.

[2] Seven years old on the death of his father, when he was recognized by Richard II as heir-presumptive. Shakespeare, following his sources, confuses this boy with Edmund Mortimer, son of Philippa.

[3] Shakespeare, following the chroniclers, considers this Edmund Mortimer as the heir-presumptive, and it is he who is referred to as the rightful heir (e.g., 56.142; 59.218).

(40.18-29). But news of the battle of Holmedon (September 14, 1402) causes him to turn his attention to domestic affairs, and from this date Shakespeare traces the rise of a conspiracy against constituted monarchy to its partial defeat at the battle of Shrewsbury on July 21, 1403, when Hotspur is killed. From the point of view of history, the play portrays one incident in the slow and painfully achieved growth of the ideal of nationalism, one incident in English history occurring a quarter of a century before France rejected the nationalistic ideal in the defeat and death of Joan of Arc. When Shakespeare writes his play, the Tudor dynasty is firmly established. The Lancastrians, represented by Henry IV, are not nearly so firmly entrenched. Carefully, then, Shakespeare causes us to withdraw our sympathy from the rebel cause in order that, after the rebellion is met and scotched, centralized power may more firmly hold the throne. With intellectual honesty he develops the historical theme, and indeed he is not unsympathetic with the monarchial ideal. He respects Elizabeth even if his respect stops short of adulation. He disapproves of civil war as any Englishman as near as he to the War of the Roses might disapprove; and he, like his fellow countrymen, knows that England under Elizabeth is well off. And also like his countrymen he knows that the question of Elizabeth's successor is in doubt, and can with sympathy follow Henry IV as he attempts to stop a rebellion when a group of nobles rise against him on the partial pretext of supporting the "true heir."

But while interpreting this period historically, Shakespeare is busy making drama of his material and inevitably discloses something of his own feelings about the events, as the meaning he finds in the whole action begins to become apparent to him. Much of the historical significance, the drama in the action, and the developing meaning of the play emerges simultaneously in scene after scene, and it is of course only for the purpose of clarity that we turn our attention first to one and then to the other. We can see, however, that as drama the events become a conflict of opposing wills and desires with such generalized and abstract forces as the Welsh and Scotch opposition embodied in Glendower and Douglas, and the position of the powerfully individualistic and kingmaking barons represented by the Percys of Northumberland, father, son, and uncle. Against the plotting, coldly calculating Earl of Worcester is set the plotting, shrewdly calculating English King. Shakespeare senses real dramatic possibilities in the somewhat equivocal position of a king who with some justice may be called an usurper. All the better for his play if he can resolve the conflict in a single-handed struggle between two characters. To achieve this resolution he makes the King (actually thirty-seven years old) seem an old man, worn and tired by his efforts to unite England, and presents as protagonist and antagonist the forty-year-old Hotspur and the seventeen-year-old Hal as two young men of equal age, who might have been exchanged for each other in their cradles (42.85-88). Historically, the action takes place within a year, but Shakespeare compresses it within three or four months. Drama is making demands, if easily acceded ones, upon history.

Personalities clash in the drama. Henry enrages Hotspur. Worcester thereupon directs the uncontrolled anger of Hotspur to further a plan of his own making. Both know Hotspur and use that knowledge to bend him to their wills. Henry lies to drive Hotspur into open opposition; Worcester lies to keep him there. The weakness of the conspiracy, which must be shown if we are to see the historical implications of the play, are set forth dramatically by showing the antipathetic natures of the conspirators, and nowhere does drama serve so superbly the ends of history as in the scene at Bangor where Hotspur and Glendower clash (III.i) or in the scene at the rebel camp near Shrewsbury when Hotspur faces the defection of his allies (IV.i).

Even in a play that came as early in his canon as *Henry IV*, Shakespeare has begun to see the dramatic opportunities in the conflict between those who cling to the medieval ideal with its emphasis on the individual, the personal virtues, and the personal vices, and those who espouse the emergent ideal of nationalism with its emphasis on the citizen, the civic virtues, and the civic vices. Richard II, Henry's earlier opponent, had none of Henry's sense of responsibility to the state. With a stronger hand and a strong sense of the responsibility of kingship, Henry sets about to weld a nation out of the looser, wilder, unstable elements of a feudal society. Quieting the occasional twinges of conscience that come as he thinks of his throne resting on the foundation of betrayal and regicide, he sets about in this play to betray his supporters, the Percys among others, as he had betrayed his king, scheming for their deaths, as he had for Richard's, that England may one day become in fact a nation. The final struggle is between Hal, who by Act III turns out to have many of the qualities of his father, and Hotspur, who for all his admirable qualities is as irresponsible as Richard II, as irresponsible in his realm as Falstaff is in Eastcheap tavern. When we seek to discover where Shakespeare's deepest sympathies lie, perhaps we feel that he approves of the Prince of Wales and does all he can for him, but that Hotspur, to be condemned by the historical implications of the play, is closer to the direct line of his heroes that leads from this play to Brutus and to Hamlet and ultimately to Macbeth, Othello, and Antony. Edmund Wilson thinks that even "from Falstaff through Brutus to Hamlet is not such a great step." In the acting history of the play, it is the parts of Falstaff and of Hotspur that have always attracted the great Shakespearean actors.

Both history and drama demanded Falstaff. From the *Chronicles* Shakespeare learned that Hal was a dissolute youth who reformed in time to become a popular idol as Henry V. In *The Famous Victories of Henry the Fifth* (pp. 179-233) he finds among the companions of Hal's dissolute days a character called Sir John Oldcastle. Shakespeare's Falstaff, derived at a great remove from Oldcastle, will be a dramatic means to account for Hal's dual nature, if such it can be called. During the period covered by the first two acts of *Henry IV* the Prince shows himself impolitic but not dissolute. He shows himself irresponsible, and upon this ground his father bases his long charge in the middle of the play's progress (III.ii). Falstaff is in every sense the apotheosis of irresponsibility. But to reduce Falstaff to this dramatic function is to sadly underestimate his role. Shakespeare lent him so profusely his own wit and wisdom that Falstaff seems to have grown not only too large for his dramatic function but even too large for the play. Perhaps this aspect of Falstaff may not seem readily apparent. We can see, however, that as Falstaff began to seize Shakespeare's imagination, he saw that he could use him to set up parallels between the comic and the serious plot and thus make the comic plot a commentary on the serious action.

The kind of commentary provided will be pointed out in the discussions of individual scenes. For now it is enough to see that Falstaff dominates the scenes in which he appears, as does Henry. Falstaff is to be the victim of a plot, as was Henry, and Falstaff like Henry turns the plot upon its plotters. Falstaff lies as Henry lies. The reconciliation of Henry and his son—at the heart of the serious plot—is presented first in rehearsals of the reconciliation scene in which Hal and Falstaff play the roles of the King and his son. These parallels are in the first two acts. As the play moves to its conclusion, the contrasts between the same material used both seriously and comically become more significant. The line becomes thinner between courage and foolhardiness, between wisdom and craft, between loyalty and treachery, between valor and discretion. By the constant alternation of the two plots Shakespeare conveys something of the puzzle of life. Its irony, later to cause him such great concern, begins to become apparent in the closing acts. It is impossible to see how this could have come about without the presence of Shakespeare's Falstaff.

THE ACTION

I.i

The opening speech of the King establishes at once a link in the sequence of historical events between this play and *Richard II*. *Richard II* closes with Henry's vow to make a voyage to the Holy Land (see the preceding Introduction). A year has elapsed (28) and the King's council is concerned with "forwarding this dear expedience" (33), when news arrives of domestic troubles of quite different sorts. The student should carefully distinguish between the situation in Wales and that in Northumberland. He should see that both Mortimer and Hotspur are fighting on the King's side and perhaps be advised even this soon that it is this Mortimer whom Shakespeare mistakenly assumes was recognized by Richard as heir-presumptive and should have been reigning at Richard's death instead of Henry (see the genealogical chart in the preceding Introduction). He should be told that by the law of arms Hotspur was entirely within his rights in refusing to send the King any prisoners except those of royal blood, but that Shakespeare's Hotspur, unaware of the law of arms, never claims that he is within his rights in holding the prisoners for himself. At this point we can only speculate on what may have been Hotspur's motive and wait to decide whether Westmoreland is right in attributing his actions to the "teaching" of his uncle, the Earl of Worcester (94-97).

The fighting in both Wales and Northumberland has been almost incredibly bloody, with a thousand killed and their bodies mutilated in Wales (42-46), and "Ten thousand bold Scots, two and twenty knights, Balk'd in their own blood" (68-69), casualty figures not exaggerated by Shakespeare but taken from Holinshed (pp. 158-59). As we read of these encounters we recall Henry's opening speech (5-18) in which in phrase after telling phrase he describes the civil strife that

304

has occurred during his ascent to the throne. The same phrases, we discover, will prove equally appropriate to characterize the struggles that lie ahead, struggles that we are soon to learn are to be at least in large part precipitated by the King himself. In fact we might even suspect that he knew Englishmen were not to march one way in "mutual well-beseeming ranks" (14), that if he really thought he would ever go to Jerusalem, he is self-deceived. But too much must not be deduced from such speculations. His opening speech, like many passages in Shakespeare, must not be thought of as solely characterizing the speaker. Furthermore, whatever part Henry may have had in promoting civil strife, both earlier and later, there is no reason to think that he does not believe it to be as peculiarly inhumane as he describes it. We must be prepared to suspend judgment, to wait and see how much he may have the good of his country at heart and how much his mere personal advantage. If we find him an arch dissembler, we will usually be aware of his dissembling and wonder why his victims are not also aware. Later in this scene (77-89), when he wishes that Hotspur might have been his son instead of young Harry, he is speaking both as a father and as a king who hopes to be succeeded by a ruler not as essentially irresponsible as he had found Richard II. We need not doubt his sincerity in this speech, even though we already sense that trouble will arise between the King and Hotspur, and even though events will prove that Henry is as wrong about one of these young men as about the other. Hotspur is not "sweet fortune's minion" (82). "Riot and dishonor" do not stain Prince Hal's brow (84-85), as we are to see in the second scene of Act I. In bringing these two young men to our attention in this opening scene, Shakespeare has given us our first hint of the roles that they are to play as protagonist and antagonist in the action that lies ahead. We are not aware of these roles at this time, but we will have cause to remember the speech as the play moves on.

Two minor points should be noted. At a time of crisis for Henry, the Prince of Wales is noticeably absent from his councils. And in a scene which must provide us with solid blocks of exposition, Shakespeare almost makes us feel that there is action where there is none. Notice that in Westmoreland's speech (49-61) the news from Holmedon is reported as "uneven and unwelcome" (50), the issue "Uncertain" (61). Immediately Sir Walter Blunt, "new lighted from his horse" that has sped so fast he is "stained with the variation of each soil" between Holmedon and London (63-64), arrives to bring to the court "smooth and welcome news" (66) of Hotspur's victory.

I.ii

Frequently—indeed, too frequently—comic scenes in early drama are interludes that have little or nothing to do with the action in the serious plot, but in this play Shakespeare, sanctioned by the few references to the dissolute youth of the actual son of Henry IV, is provided with the mechanical means of integrating the comic scenes with the serious ones. If history advised him that Hal was to reform, then the ends of history can be served by showing us what he reformed from. But once provided with this easy justification for including comic scenes in a serious drama, he began slowly to see far richer possibilities in the alternating of scenes from the two plots than the mere possibility of showing us the dual nature of the young prince. By creating Falstaff as an attraction to draw Hal away from the court when we clearly see that Poins, Bardolph, Gadshill, and Peto would not serve, he created a character who would more and more force a consideration of the implications of the serious plot from another point of view.

Even in this scene (which we may assume takes place at the Prince's residence, for certainly not at the royal palace or in a tavern) we see how clearly Falstaff dominates the action, as Henry had dominated the first scene. We see that Falstaff entertains the idea of giving over his wicked life to escape damnation (100-02) as Henry had planned a pilgrimage to atone for his sins. When he eagerly agrees to be one in a highway robbery and the Prince finds this no "good amendment" (106) in his life, Falstaff points out that robbing is his vocation, and " 'Tis no sin for a man to labor in his vocation" (108-09), whether he be king or highwayman. We see that all is not well in Falstaff's kingdom, for there are those among his followers who are hatching a plot against him. And we see that the state of England is no more stable, no less lawless, no more under the control of responsible men in Falstaff's England than in the England that Henry must seek to rule. As Falstaff says, "the poor abuses of the time want countenance" (159-60).

The Prince moves easily among the members of this group, and, though they are familiar with him, they never really forget that he is the King's son. He is happiest when trying to match his wits in verbal combat with Falstaff, but is really not very good at it and comes off second best. But it is

THE HISTORY OF HENRY IV (PART ONE)   307

clearly fun for him, though unfortunately the reader is so
plagued with footnotes designed to translate into modern English the vocabulary of this particular "underworld," that
much of the apparent fun escapes him.

The soliloquy which closes the scene needs some attention.
If we read it as a speech solely designed to characterize the
Prince, he comes off pretty badly. Some of the qualities of
Hal implied in this speech may be true qualities, for there is
a sense in which Hal is the son of his father. But we have
watched him in action throughout this scene and will watch
him in others. In this action he is not the prig, the self-consciously politic planner that the speech suggests he is. He has
not been playing the part of an irresponsible young man in
order that his reformation may come as a surprise and win
him favor in the eyes of those whom he was deliberately deceiving. We will do well to take this soliloquy as Shakespeare's understandable, if somewhat ill-advised, notice to the
audience that they are not to be unduly alarmed by the early
image of himself that the Prince is creating.

I.iii

This is obviously an important scene, for Henry is to show
his hand and so is Worcester. The King begins the attack,
and we should ask with what justice he accuses the Percys of
"indignities" (2). If he has in mind only Hotspur's refusal of
prisoners, we shall soon see that no indignity was intended by
this refusal. Worcester takes up the challenge and intentionally (for we cannot believe that he is ever inadvertent) reminds the King of the debt of gratitude which he owes the
Percys. The King promptly dismisses him and the two men
are not to meet again until late in the play. Was the King
finding too onerous the debt of gratitude that Worcester reminded him of? Did he see that a king whose power was dependent upon kingmakers rather than upon Parliament could
never be the king of a truly united country? Was he moved
by fear, or merely seeking a cause for a break with those
whom he once needed to bring him to power?

While Henry was making the speech in which he summarily dismisses Worcester, Northumberland sought to interrupt
him but was ignored (21). When permitted to speak, Northumberland seeks to explain his son's denial of the prisoners,
and we see here that the Percys are not claiming his right to
them but merely urging that he spoke impetuously or was
misrepresented. Hotspur's speech in explanation is a fine one,
but in expressing his contempt for the pestering popinjay

acting as the King's emissary, he reveals his single-mindedness, his complete commitment to the profession of arms. In concluding with the request that the report of his action not come between him and the King, he demonstrates that generosity of spirit, that quickness to act on impulse and to retract as quickly, that is his strength and his weakness in the world of Bolingbroke and Worcester. Good honest Walter Blunt is as convinced by Hotspur as we are.

But Hotspur, it seems, has made one proviso, a proviso that the King, were he seeking conciliation, might be quick to grant unless his devious plans include driving the heir-presumptive Mortimer into the opposition. In rejecting Hotspur's proviso the King picks his words and phrases carefully, disclosing that his knowledge of how to drive Hotspur into opposition is the result of having taken Hotspur's measure. "Foolish Mortimer" has "willfully betrayed" the lives of those in his command (79-80), perhaps to secure the hand of Glendower's daughter in marriage. With little justice and with little truth, the King gives his reasons for not ransoming "revolted Mortimer" (91). Hotspur's reply is a splendid defense of a soldier behaving as a soldier should behave, and we do not question his sincerity because he is defending his wife's brother. But the King, having worked Hotspur up to this peak of protest, now risks a lie of such proportions that even he will not wait for Hotspur's reply. After accusing Hotspur of lying, he asserts flatly that Mortimer never encountered, never even dared encounter, Glendower, and promptly dismisses Northumberland and his son as he had earlier dismissed Worcester.

The King has had his way with Hotspur. It remains now for Worcester to have his way, and Worcester will move with as sure knowledge of his nephew as the King had had. Hotspur reports without any show of proof that the King trembled in fear "even at the name of Mortimer" (142), even though, strangely enough, he seems not to have known that Mortimer had been proclaimed heir until his father and uncle tell him of the proclamation (143-54). Hotspur recalls that it was his father and uncle "that set the crown/Upon the head of this forgetful man" (158-59), yet seems to ignore for a moment that Henry was joined first by Northumberland, then by Worcester, and finally at Berkeley Castle in Gloucestershire by Hotspur himself (243-47). When his anger against the King has reached an inordinate height, Worcester cannily drops hints of a plot he is hatching, carefully baiting the hook for Hotspur by emphasizing its extreme danger (188-91). Worcester knows that in support of an action where danger lies (193) and where honor is at stake (199-205), Hotspur can be counted on, though both Worcester and Northumberland lose patience with him as he continues to allow his indignation free play in speech after speech, including in his indictment "that . . . sword-and-buckler Prince of Wales" (228). As he speaks of the Prince, he shows the contempt of a Percy for the lower classes that infest the taverns of London, and sadly underestimates the young man who will bring an end to his career at Shrewsbury. When Hotspur cools down a bit, Worcester reveals a plan the details of which we should take care to have in mind. We should see how Worcester plans to draw Douglas, Glendower, and Mortimer into the rebel camp. After Worcester's final word of warning to Hotspur (289-90), the scene is rapidly brought to a close. That this warning was ignored, we shall discover in Act II, scene iii.

II.i, II.ii

Although the action in these two scenes shifts from an inn yard at Rochester to the highway near Gad's Hill, the scenes should be considered together. In the first scene Gadshill (a man as well as a place) is dispatched by the robbers to make sure that their intended victims with three hundred gold marks will be on their way to Gad's Hill. Beyond letting us know that the robbery is about to get under way, the scene gives us a glimpse of the unsavory condition of a typical inn of the period. Shakespeare permits Gadshill to have his one moment of importance in the play, as he boasts to the chamberlain of the presence in his gang of those who "for sport sake are content to do the profession some grace" (72-73). The chamberlain, we learn, will get his cut if all goes well (94-95).

In the second scene Falstaff is again to dominate the action. Poins has removed Falstaff's horse, and the loss assumes in Falstaff's opening speech the colossal importance of a betrayal as Falstaff shows how incongruously he can elevate the unimportant. If at the close of this speech he calls down "A plague upon it when thieves cannot be true one to another" (27-28), he will later have a greater reason to do so. The Prince and Poins, following their plan, withdraw from the scene, the travelers enter, and Falstaff falls upon them, crying "They hate us youth" (85), addressing them as "fat chuffs," shouting that "young men must live" (89-91). Having robbed the travelers, Falstaff is busy dividing the spoils and unprepared for the surprise attack that comes. We must assume that they think the officers of the law are upon them. Bardolph, Gadshill, and Peto immediately take to their heels and Falstaff, left alone, strikes a blow or two, and then follows the others. Much—far too much—has been made of Falstaff's cowardice in abandoning the booty. For why, left alone, should he risk arrest when the penalty is hanging? As we shall see in scene iv, the source of the amusement does not lie in Falstaff's running away, but in his accusing Poins and Prince Hal of cowardice, thus permitting them to turn the tables on him, since it was he that ran and not they. At the close of this scene Prince Hal and Poins are laughing at Falstaff's roars as they watch him larding the "lean earth," trudging away on foot (109).

II.iii

Hotspur is at Warkworth Castle in Northumberland, a stronghold of his father. Contrary to Worcester's caution, Hotspur has revealed the plot against the King to the unidentified writer of the letter he is reading. In branding the undertaking as dangerous, the author of the letter is as surely increasing Hotspur's zeal as had Worcester in Act I, scene iii. In describing his allies as "uncertain" and the time as "unsorted" (12), the author of the letter calls forth from Hotspur a prompt denial, and by increasing the odds against the venture, he increases Hotspur's determination to proceed. We sense, however, that all will not be well and that through just such a move as Hotspur has made in enlisting an additional ally, the King will get wind of the plot. We soon learn that Hotspur, manifesting his singleness of purpose, has for two weeks been leading his forces into battle in his dreams. Inactivity weighs heavily upon him, for he needs to translate intent into action without delay. In the closing portion of this scene we watch Lady Percy, all unbeknownst to her husband, learn all that she wished to know about what is going on in his mind and troubling his sleep.

II.iv

Before the entrance of Falstaff we watch Hal exhibiting his pride in having acquired the lingo, the argot of the taverns, the vocabulary of tapsters and tinkers. It is a richly colored speech, as full of figures as is Hotspur's, though both are drawn from markedly different arenas of experience. Hal is as much devoted to the talk of the tavern as Hotspur to the talk of the battlefield, and each, of course, thinks the other as single-minded as he is.

Before Prince Hal meets sterner competition, he and Poins are to get poor Francis thoroughly upset and confused, and we watch Hal as he seeks to find a question to which Francis' inevitable "anon" will be so accidentally inappropriate that the Prince can come down hard on him. Concluding that Francis has "fewer words than a parrot," that "His industry is upstairs and downstairs, his eloquence the parcel of a reckoning" (99-102), Prince Hal's thoughts leap at once to Hotspur, whose industry is the killing of "six or seven dozens of Scots," whose eloquence is reporting the trifling number of those he has slain (103-09). We ask ourselves whether Hal's judgment of Hotspur is more, or less, accurate than Hotspur's earlier judgment of Hal (I,iii).

Falstaff enters to test whether an attack is the best defense. His sack is filled with lime, his friends have proved themselves cowards, and "There is nothing but roguery to be found in villainous man" (124-25). There is to be much talk of courage, much of honor, as there had been in the serious plot. Falstaff amasses a mountain of outrageous lies to preserve his equanimity, his dominance, and Henry, as we may be reminded, had told just as outrageous lies to secure his throne. Hotspur's courage, undaunted and magnificent, if foolhardy, is mocked by the reduction of courage to the hacking of a sword, the pricking of a nose with straws. Genuine courage will make for brave deeds; pretended courage makes for uproarious laughter; one kind of courage will leave death and destruction in its wake, the other will be drowned in the roars of an evening's entertainment in a tavern.

With the arrival of Sir John Bracy from the court a serious note is struck. The rebellion is under way, but as Falstaff characterizes the rebels, the comic atmosphere of the scene is not dissipated. Nor is it to be dissipated when it is clear that Hal must return to court. The serious reconciliation of father and son is to be parodied in two forms in the tavern, with Falstaff first playing the role of Henry and then of Hal. Ostensibly the rehearsal is for the purpose of giving the Prince an opportunity to prepare himself to confront his father, but what happens is something quite different. Falstaff, either as King or as Prince, dominates the episodes and turns both opportunities into apologies for his own life. Despite what Falstaff is up to on both occasions, he plays the King by parodying the speeches of all grieving fathers to all repentant sons in a rhetoric as stately and pompous as that of Henry's. When the roles are reversed and Hal plays the King to Falstaff's Hal, the Prince so forgets the intention of these rehearsals as to pour forth a string of abuse upon Falstaff in the lingo of the tavern, with no regard to the character of the King. Falstaff, picking up the challenge, speaks quietly but eloquently in his own defense.

The scene closes with the arrival of the sheriff and his men on the track of Falstaff, who has been easily identified as one of the Gad's Hill robbers. The Prince urges Falstaff to hide while he disposes of the sheriff, and a few moments later, when he has assured the officer of the law that justice will be effected, he looks behind the arras to find Falstaff "Fast asleep . . . and snorting like a horse" (529-30), exhibiting his magnificent composure.

III.i

As we see the essentially antipathetic character of each of the rebels assembled in Wales, we see where the real weakness of the rebellion lies and anticipate its failure. We can scarcely imagine natures more radically different than those of Glendower and Hotspur, and as their personal differences are disclosed, we see Shakespeare seeking to suggest the inevitable differences between Celt and Saxon. That Glendower could have cuckolded the devil and then enlisted him under his banner does not seem entirely impossible. His is a simple, trusting nature, given to dreams, to sentiment, to the expression of unabashed emotion, often sentimental, but touching the commonplace at times with the radiance of romance. For all our understanding of Hotspur's impatience with him, Hotspur does not show himself in the best of lights, and Mortimer, the heir-presumptive but generally the forgotten man, is hard put to keep the peace between them. For all the softness of Glendower's speech, we question which man is more self-assertive than the other, and may wonder if one is any more the victim of his illusions than the other.

When the map is produced, showing the tripartite division of England and Wales among the three rebels with the strongest claims (71-80), we must assume that Shakespeare knew how his own audiences would feel, that sympathy at this point can scarcely be with the rebellion. But the disclosure of the division of the country serves another purpose. True to his nature, Hotspur protests that the course of the river Trent deprives him of a "huge half-moon" (99) of his territory, and even when Mortimer points out that when the river bends north into Hotspur's territory, it soon bends south into his, Hotspur characteristically declares that he will change

THE HISTORY OF HENRY IV (PART ONE)   313

the course of the Trent (113). A moment later, equally characteristically, Hotspur decides to drop the whole question (136).

Hotspur's volatile temper erupts three times during this scene and over matters of decreasing importance: his differences with Glendower, his quarrel over the course of the river Trent, and his discomfort with the failure of his wife to swear a "good mouth-filling oath" (256). In each incident, though with decreasing intensity and consequence, he seems to break forth into violent action, in the same fashion as he has graphically described the behavior of those forces beneath the earth that bring about earthquakes, toppling down steeples and towers in a brilliant though wasteful display of pent-up forces (26-33). Worcester in his single speech in the scene (176-88) sums up Hotspur's failings in the calm, measured tones of which he is master, and though Hotspur professes to have been "schooled" by his uncle, neither Worcester nor we really believe him.

III.ii

This scene at the very center of the play marks the actual reconciliation of father and son, of Prince and King, and gives assurance that the defeat of the rebels, which we had anticipated in the preceding scene, will bring the play to its conclusion. We need to follow carefully the twists and turns of Henry's speech, and also to see the responses that Hal makes to each portion of it. We should see to what extent, if any, Hal is moved to his decision by what his father says, to what extent, if any, we are witnessing a change in Hal or merely a change in his condition.

The King has opened the play by describing himself as "shaken" and "wan with care" (39.1), and so he opens his speech to his son. His conscience had led him to his plans for a pilgrimage to the Holy Land because of his share in the deposition and death of Richard; he now would persuade himself that Hal is the scourge of Heaven sent to punish him for his "mistreadings" (11). How else to explain the search for "barren pleasures, rude society" (14) in a son of the Lancastrian line? We should note that the King does not believe that Hal is morally corrupt any more than we do. He has shown a strange (and impolitic) taste for low company. In reply Hal tells his father that many reports that have reached his ear have been invented or exaggerated to win the favor of the King. He shows little, if any, of the mood of the penitent. The King again professes wonder as to how a Lancastrian could have acquired such tastes—"affections" (30)—and then moves easily and naturally to speculate about what would have happened to him had he been like Hal. As he describes the manner and intent of his mode of life (46-59), we are reminded of the professed policy that Hal set forth at the close of Act I, scene ii, but are more convinced of the truth of what Henry says than we were by Hal.

Inevitably the King moves to a description of his predecessor Richard and in doing so reveals his concern for his country, for as Richard was, so now is Hal. Where will England be if Hal's fate is to be "but as the cuckoo is in June,/Heard, not regarded" (75-76)? We should see that the King's concern is in part for his son, but in part—and perhaps in larger part—for his successor. Hal is now as Richard was. Hotspur is now as the King was when he made his move to seize the throne (93-96). As we follow the King through all of these comparisons, we must recognize that these are steps in a carefully conceived argument, and that Henry's descriptions of both Richard and Hotspur are carefully tailored to produce the effect he hopes for. His characterization of Richard is indirectly a characterization of himself, and we are pretty sure that Henry was never like Hotspur. But throughout his whole speech, and especially at the end when he turns to celebrate the military accomplishments of Hotspur, the King has prepared the way for Hal's ringing declaration: "Percy is but my factor, good my lord,/To engross up glorious deeds on my behalf" (147-48). On reflection, we may find it a little difficult to believe that honors can be acquired in this fashion as they are in prizefights, but, other times, other customs. Were we listening to this scene rather than reflecting upon it, we might be persuaded, as Henry was, that "A hundred thousand rebels die in this!" (160). As the scene closes we see that Henry, well-informed as to the moves of the rebels, is ready to proceed with confidence to suppress the rebellion, a confidence that we did not feel the rebels had when preparing to move into the fight at the close of the preceding scene. At the close of the scene that immediately follows Hal's reconciliation, we will find Falstaff ready to meet the rebel's challenge in his particular way.

III.iii

We move from the reconciliation of Henry and Hal immediately to Eastcheap, where Falstaff professes to be in the mood of the penitent, ready to conclude, as Henry had been in addressing Hal, that "Company, villainous company, hath been the spoil" of him (10-11). Having proposed a pact with Bardolph in which Falstaff will amend his life if Bardolph will amend his face, Falstaff moves into a magnificent extempore performance in celebration of Bardolph's nose, a performance which in its incongruity and exaggeration reminds us of his description of the attack of those men in Kendall-green who assaulted him on the highway, (II.iv) and of his elaborate apologies for himself when he and Hal were rehearsing in anticipation of Hal's summons to court (II.iv).

With the entrance of the Prince, the hostess of the tavern enlists Hal's aid in calling Falstaff to account for debts long overdue, and we are to witness the last of the scenes in which the Prince matches his wits with Falstaff as Falstaff parries all verbal thrusts aimed at him, and finally manages to his satisfaction to get the hostess in a position where he can triumphantly announce: "Hostess, I forgive thee" (176). As the scene closes, the Prince is in a more serious mood. He has procured for Falstaff "a charge of foot" rather than of horse (192-93), and though Falstaff dislikes the idea of walking rather than riding into battle, he thanks God for the rebels, for "they offend none but the virtuous" (197). Hal leaves, proclaiming that "The land is burning, Percy stands on high,/ And either we or they must lower lie" (209-10), and Falstaff meets the challenge: "Rare words! Brave world! Hostess, my breakfast" (211). Consider again the closing lines of each of the three scenes in this act.

IV.i

In this scene conspicuous weaknesses in the rebel cause are to be disclosed, weaknesses that in a sense we have anticipated in watching Worcester's attempt to keep Hotspur in check, in hearing Hotspur read a letter from a friend who is cautiously withdrawing from what he believes to be an ill-timed venture, and in witnessing the clash of personalities among the rebels assembled at Bangor. Now we are to learn from Northumberland's letter that he is sick and that some of his friends are not yet prepared to join the rebellion (23-24; 32-33), and that Glendower's forces will not be ready to march for fourteen days (125). Worcester speaks in his customary voice of cautious wisdom, pointing out what may be inferred from Northumberland's absence. But just as Hotspur has asked, impatiently and irrationally, how his father has "the leisure to be sick/ In such a justling time" (17-18), he tells Worcester, just as irrationally, that it will lend luster to their enterprise if they dare move into battle without the aid of Northumberland (75-81). Douglas alone abets him in the illogical position that he has adopted (53-55), but take it he has and maintain it he will, despite the final blow that comes when Vernon arrives to tell him of the strength of the King's forces and to report that "the madcap Prince of Wales" (94) seems like "an angel dropped down from the clouds/To turn and wind a fiery Pegasus/And witch the world with noble horsemanship" (107-09). In a speech magnificent in its foolhardiness, Hotspur cries, "Let them come" (111), and looks forward to meeting Hal in single combat. The scene closes with Hotspur, unmindful of the fact that he may well be sacrificing the lives of thousands of men in a waning cause, shouting, "Doomsday is near. Die all, die merrily" (133).

IV.ii

Scarcely have the echoes of Hotspur's speech died on the unlocalized stage of the Elizabethan theater when Falstaff and his company march on. With the same maddening incapacity to take seriously the world and its institutions, its schemes and its projects, he has at first impressed those men who he knows have both reasons for remaining at home and the resources to buy their release from service. He is left with "a hundred and fifty tattered prodigals" (34-35), the ragtag and bobtail of London's population, with but "a shirt and a half" (42-43) in all his company, and the need to find what linen they can come by "on every hedge" (48-49). When accosted by the Prince for assembling such a group of scarecrows, Falstaff replies: "Tut, tut, good enough to toss; food for powder, food for powder, they'll fill a pit as well as better. Tush, man, mortal men, mortal men" (66-68). As we are trying to make out what to think of this speech, we remember Hotspur saying, "Doomsday is near. Die all, die merrily" (125.133).

IV.iii

The rebels are camped at Shrewsbury, and Hotspur is for joining battle at once, again seconded by Douglas. Worcester is now joined by Vernon in an attempt to dissuade him. Douglas, with little cause, accuses Vernon of being afraid, and Vernon is stung to reply, firmly repudiating the charge. Vernon in Hotspur's camp is the counterpart of Sir Walter Blunt among the King's men. They are both loyal followers, both clear-sighted, both honest and forthright, one in the service of an irrational leader, the other in the service of a devious

THE HISTORY OF HENRY IV (PART ONE) 317

king. Vernon urges Hotspur to put off the fight until the next day, for he is in possession of information that makes the battle an even more dubious one than it had seemed when we learned that Northumberland and Glendower were delayed. The forces under Vernon's cousin have not arrived, Worcester's horses have just arrived but are tired, the rebels are outnumbered by the King's forces.

What Hotspur's decision would have been we never learn, for at this point Sir Walter Blunt arrives with an offer from Henry to listen to all grievances and to pardon all offenses. Since he is reported to have thirty thousand men (124.129) and the rebels only ten thousand (132.9), the King may be said to be leading from strength, but to what extent he is now willing to go in meeting the rebels' demands, we may have reason to question. In Act V, scene i, Worcester will show that he has his doubts. In any event, we can see that Shakespeare's material is running a little thin, for Hotspur, in replying to Blunt, leads us through all the stages in Henry's progress to the throne, pointing out again how the Percys joined him in this progress, though he had told them that all he sought was the restoration of the lands and title of Duke of Lancaster, of which Richard had deprived him (60-62). Blunt interrupts to say, "Tut! I came not to hear this" (88), and we sympathize with him. Hotspur then turns to recount more recent grievances: his refusal to ransom Mortimer, his dismissal of Worcester from his council board, and his driving of Northumberland from the court. By these acts Hotspur contends that the King drove them to "seek out/This head of safety" and "to pry/Into his title" (102-04). When Blunt asks if he shall return this answer to Henry, Hotspur, in one of those reversals of position which we have learned to expect, tells him not to do so and that Worcester will come on the next day to talk with the King. He even goes so far as to assure Sir Walter that the rebels may accept the King's grace and love.

IV.iv

This is a scene of little importance. In it we are told again what we already know, and learn only that Glendower's delay was occasioned by his being "overruled by prophecies" (18) and that the Archbishop of York is about to muster his forces in anticipation of being visited by the King should Hotspur be defeated. Actually Shakespeare is looking forward in this scene to *Henry IV, Part Two*, when the Arch bishop of York will be considered under the "unfinished business" of *Part One*.

V.i

At the King's camp the day dawns forebodingly, as Shakespeare's days frequently do when the moment of decision is at hand. In the King's company are the Prince of Wales, Lord John of Lancaster, Sir Walter Blunt, and—surprisingly —Sir John Falstaff. As Hotspur had assured Sir Walter Blunt, Worcester arrives for his second and last encounter with the King. He has essentially little more to say than to repeat what Hotspur has said to Blunt in Act IV, scene iii, but he takes slightly longer to say it. In fact the tenor of his speech is what he had compressed into four lines at their first meeting (I.iii). Henry dismisses his charges as mere excuses "To face the garment of rebellion" (74). Hal, in a dramatically effective speech, offers to let the whole issue rest on single combat between him and Hotspur, and Henry agrees, repeating the same offer he had made earlier through Sir Walter Blunt. When Worcester leaves, we note that the Prince does not believe that Hotspur will accept his challenge (115).

When the others leave and Falstaff is left alone on the stage, he has his say on the subject of honor, hitting upon the form of questions and answers to be found in the catechism of the Church. We may feel that this speech is appropriately placed at the close of the first scene of this act and preceding the second scene. Both the King and Hal would readily see Hotspur slain, the man who the King had said was "the theme of honor's tongue" (42.80), the man whom Prince Hal had called a "child of honor and renown" (110.139), the man who himself had said that he thought it "an easy leap/To pluck bright honor from the pale-faced moon" (58.199-200). The King had just made Worcester an offer which we suspect he does not mean and which we feel sure Worcester does not believe, but, as we shall see in the following scene, he will not risk telling Hotspur what the King had offered. Armies are to clash for Hotspur's honor, for Bolingbroke's throne, for Worcester's skin. "What is in that word honor?" Falstaff asks (134-35).

V.ii

Worcester and Vernon return to the rebel camp with Worcester convinced that Hotspur must not be told of what he first calls "The liberal and kind offer of the King" (2).

THE HISTORY OF HENRY IV (PART ONE)   319

We soon discover, however, that Worcester is willing to believe that the King may well forget Hotspur's part in the rebellion, but not that of Northumberland or of Worcester himself; that the King's offer may be a kind one to Hotspur, but that "We, as the spring of all, shall pay for all" (23). To Hotspur, then, he reports that "There is no seeming mercy in the King" (34). Henry has lied to Hotspur to drive him into rebellion; Worcester lies to keep him there.

Hotspur is told, however, that the Prince has challenged him to single combat, but nothing seems to come of this challenge save as it provides Vernon with another opportunity to speak in glowing praise of the reformed Prince of Wales. Hotspur's response to this praise is more restrained than his earlier response, and though he plans to seek out Hal on the battlefield, he has no thought of settling the whole issue on the outcome of this meeting, nor has he been advised that the Prince had proposed so doing. He rallies his men for battle, maintaining, as we would expect him to, that "the arms are fair,/When the intent of bearing them is just" (87-88). With his cry of "Esperance! Percy!" (96) we surely cannot withhold our sympathy from this young man whose weakness is so much a consequence of his strength, and who is going to his death as the victim of such cold-blooded manipulation.

V.iii

Sir Walter Blunt, one of many men "Semblably furnished like the King himself" (21), is killed by Douglas, and Hotspur appears to tell Douglas that had he fought in this fashion at Holmedon, he would not have been defeated. Falstaff, for all his reputation for self-preservation bordering on cowardice, is in the thick of the fight, though all but three of his hundred and fifty soldiers have lost their lives. When the Prince enters, he cannot resist boasting that he has killed Hotspur; when the Prince leaves he is standing over the body of Sir Walter Blunt, saying, "I like not such grinning honor as Sir Walter hath" (58-59).

V.iv

Here again this scene on the battlefield consists chiefly of vignettes, and we can do little more than move with the action from one incident to another. We watch the Prince urging his father not to retire from the fight lest his retirement alarm his friends. We hear the Prince refuse to be led to his tent because of a "shallow scratch" (10) and hear him pause for a moment in generous praise of his younger brother (16-19). Douglas appears to challenge what may prove to be yet another "counterfeit" (27) of the King, but on this occasion has found Henry himself. Henry is hard pressed by Douglas when the Prince comes to his aid. Douglas, we are advised, *"flieth"* (42 s.d.), but without acquiring the reputation for cowardice that Falstaff acquired when he had fled at Gad's Hill.

With the entrance of Hotspur, the long-awaited encounter is at hand. As we had expected, Hal kills Hotspur, and Hotspur, dying, professes he could better face the loss of life than the loss of "those proud titles" Hal has won from him (78). Percy, as Hal had predicted, has proved to be his "factor," and Hal is ready to speak generously over Hotspur's body.

Meanwhile Douglas has returned to attack Falstaff, who falls to the ground feigning death. The stage is now set for Falstaff's last jest. Giving the body of Hotspur a fresh wound in the thigh, he lifts him over his shoulder, intent on claiming the prize. The Prince arrives, surprised to find Falstaff on his feet since he had left him earlier for dead. He is to be even more astounded when Falstaff claims that both he and Hotspur were only momentarily out of the action, that both arose to fight "a long hour by Shrewsbury clock" (146), until Hotspur fell. In the face of this preposterous tale, Hal concedes that "if a lie may do" Falstaff grace, that he will "gild it with the happiest terms" he knows (155-56). A retreat sounds. The King's forces have won.

Perhaps we may feel as Napoleon was said to have felt when he read this scene, that the cut and thrust of swordplay should not have been allowed to prove Hal the better man.

V.v

The play is to come to a close with the forces of the rebels shattered but more work left for the King's forces, work to be concluded in *Henry IV, Part Two*. Worcester and Vernon have been taken prisoner and are to be killed by the King's orders. Vernon and Blunt, the two loyal followers, are both to die, but at least Sir Walter was allowed to die in battle at the hands of Douglas rather than at the hands of the executioner. Douglas, fleeing again, fell over a cliff and was so bruised that he could be taken prisoner. The Prince asks for the privilege of setting Douglas free without ransom, ostensibly because he had fought bravely but perhaps also for reasons as politic as those so dear to his father's heart. The King

THE HISTORY OF HENRY IV (PART ONE) 321

dispatches Lord John and Westmoreland to take care of Northumberland and the Archbishop of York. He and Hal will move against Glendower and Mortimer. We had almost forgotten Mortimer, but ostensibly it was because the King had refused to ransom him that forty thousand Englishmen met at Shrewsbury.

WILLIAM SALE

SHORT-ANSWER QUESTIONS

1. Does a speaker in the first scene give us an approximate date for the action of the play? (40.26)

2. What "heavy news" comes from Wales, and why is it described as "heavy"? (40.37-46)

3. Is the news from Northumberland also "heavy"? (41.50,66)

4. How has Hotspur displeased the King? (42.91-94) and whose fault is it said to be? (42.94-95)

5. What plan does Poins propose to Falstaff? (48.128-37)

6. What plan does Poins propose to the Prince? (49.164-70)

7. How does the Prince explain the company he keeps? (51.201-07)

8. What does Worcester say that causes the King to dismiss him? (52.9-12)

9. Whom does Hotspur blame for his having refused the King the prisoners he has captured? (53.32)

10. After Hotspur has apologized to the King for withholding prisoners, how does the King anger him again? (54.84-85; 55.112-13)

11. What reason is offered for the King's feeling about Mortimer? (56.143; 57.144)

12. What opinion does Hotspur express of the Prince of Wales? (59.228)

13. Who is the "fawning greyhound" that Hotspur met at Berkeley Castle? (60.245-249)

14. What reasons does the unknown author of a letter give Hotspur for not joining him in the rebellion against the King? (71.10-11; 72.12-14)

15. How does Lady Percy learn that something is troubling her husband? (73.48)

16. At what point in the game that Poins and the Prince are playing with Francis does the Prince achieve what he had really set out to do? (78.62-68)

17. When Francis leaves the scene, the Prince is reminded of Hotspur. Why? (79.99-102)

18. Can Falstaff be said to believe that an attack is the best defense? (80.114)

19. What excuse does Falstaff have to offer when the Prince and Poins tell him that it was they alone who went off with the booty? (85.268-71)

20. What is Hotspur's reply to Glendower's contention that the whole earth shook at his birth? (97.17-19)

21. How did the rebels propose to divide the country after the successful completion of the rebellion? (98.73-74; 99.75-78)

22. Why and how did Hotspur propose changing the course of the river Trent? (99.94-104)

23. Who speaks as peacemaker in III.i and with what effect? (102.176-89)

24. What objection does Hotspur have to the oaths his wife swears? (105.249-59)

THE HISTORY OF HENRY IV (PART ONE) 323

25. In his opening speech in III.ii, how does the King seek to account for the behavior of his son? (106.4-11)

26. How does the Prince account for the reputation he has in his father's eyes? (107.23-28)

27. Why does the King dwell at such length upon the character of Richard II? (108.85-88)

28. Why does the Prince hope that Hotspur's honors were even greater than they are? (110.144-48)

29. Falstaff asks the hostess if she has inquired as to who picked his pocket (113.54-55). Who did pick his pocket and what did he take from it? (95.534-41)

30. When Falstaff cries "Rare words! Brave world," what occasions this outburst? (119.209-211)

31. For what two reasons have Northumberland's forces failed to arrive at the rebel camp? (121.31-33)

32. How does Hotspur think that his father's absence can be turned to the advantage of the rebels? (122.43-52) Does Worcester agree? (122.59-67)

33. Is the opinion that Hotspur expresses of the Prince of Wales essentially the same as he had expressed earlier in the play? (123.94-96; 59.228)

34. Hotspur says, "This praise doth nourish agues," (124-111). What praise? By whom? Of whom? (123.97-101;124.102-09)

35. How long will Glendower be delayed in joining the rebel forces? (124.125)

36. What sort of men did Falstaff first impress into the army and why? (125.12-15; 126.16-23)

37. Compare Falstaff's "Tut, tut, good enough to toss," with Hotspur's last line in the preceding act. (127.66; 125.133)

324 TEACHING SHAKESPEARE

38. What bad news does Vernon bring to the rebel camp? (129.19-24)

39. After Sir Walter Blunt tells the rebels that the King bids them name their grievances, what grievances of Mortimer and of Worcester does Hotspur specify? (131.93-96,99)

40. What reply does Hotspur tell Sir Walter Blunt to take to the King? (132.108-11)

41. When Worcester tells the King that he has not sought rebellion, what does Falstaff say? (135.28)

42. Why does Worcester compare the King to young cuckoos? (136.59-64 and note)

43. How does the Prince propose to settle the whole issue between the King and the rebels? (137.99-100) Does he think his proposal will be accepted? (138.115)

44. Why does Falstaff call his speech on honor a catechism? (138.141)

45. To what extent does Worcester think the King's forgiveness will go? (139.16-23)

46. How does Worcester describe the King's offer to Hotspur? (140.34)

47. When Vernon speaks in praise of Prince Hal, is there any difference in Hotspur's response than in his response to Vernon's earlier praise of Hal? (141.69-74; 124.110-11)

48. When Douglas kills Blunt, who does he think he has killed? (143.5-6) Why?

49. When the Prince asks Falstaff for his pistol, what is it that Falstaff gives him? (145.53-54)

50. Why did Falstaff wound the corpse of Hotspur? (150.127-28, 149-51)

QUESTIONS FOR DISCUSSION

1. Describe in detail Worcester's plot against the King and show the means he uses to insure that Hotspur will join with him in this plot.

2. How has the rivalry and the eventual meeting of Hal and Hotspur been prepared for from the first scene of the first act until Hotspur dies at Shrewsbury?

3. In what variety of ways throughout the play are we advised of the weaknesses of the rebel cause?

4. What aspects of Hotspur are revealed in the scenes at Warkworth Castle (II.iii), at Bangor (III.i), and at the rebel camp near Shrewsbury (IV.i)?

5. Comment on the acting of Hal and Falstaff in the two scenes at the Boar's Head Tavern when Hal is preparing for his reconciliation with his father (II.iv).

6. Discuss the variety of lies that are told in this play.

7. Discuss the ways in which Falstaff suggests our consideration of the material of the serious plot from another point of view.

8. After reading the selections from Holinshed's *Chronicles* (pp. 157-70), discuss some of the ways in which Shakespeare has departed from history in the interest of drama.

9. After reading this play, Napoleon was said to have felt that the cut and thrust of swordplay should not have been allowed to prove Hal a better man than Hotspur. Considering the way in which Shakespeare presents these characters, what do you think led Napoleon to this conclusion?

10. George Lyman Kittredge described Henry IV as one of

the most baffling of all Shakespeare's complex characters. What do you think Kittredge had in mind?

SAMPLE TEST

I. (30 minutes)

Write a well-organized essay on ONE of the following subjects.

1. Describe in detail Worcester's plot against the King and show the means he uses to insure that Hotspur will join with him in this plot.

2. Discuss the ways in which Falstaff suggests our consideration of the material of the serious plot from another point of view.

II. (30 minutes)

Write briefly on FIVE of the following.

1. How has Hotspur displeased the King? And whose fault is it said to be?

2. How does the Prince explain the company he keeps?

3. What reason is offered for the King's feeling about Mortimer?

4. What objection does Hotspur have to the oaths his wife swears?

5. Why does the King dwell at such length upon the character of Richard II?

6. Falstaff asks the hostess if she has inquired as to who picked his pocket (113.54-55). Who did pick his pocket and what did he take from it?

7. Why does Falstaff call his speech on honor a catechism?

THE TEMPEST

INTRODUCTION

The Tempest is usually conceded to be Shakespeare's most philosophical play, that play in which his uses of poetic and dramatic imagery seem most self-consciously intended to order a comprehensive vision of human life. Certainly it is the most extreme example of the kind of play which he was writing toward the end of his career, the romances or tragicomedies which include *Pericles*, *The Winter's Tale*, and *Cymbeline*. In these works he sacrificed the penetrating character studies of his so-called tragic period for relatively flat characters, abandoned the strategy of boring inward in favor of encompassing great breadth, and relinquished the values of episodic tightness of structure ("tightness" here relative to Renaissance standards of structure) for the loosely orchestrated, free-breathing kind of action characteristic of romance, rich in associative, metaphorical, and symbolic possibilities. In these plays, and in *The Tempest* quite conspicuously, he can be accused of a certain carelessness about dramatic technique, almost an unwillingness to trouble with technical problems which he had long before solved for himself as a playwright; thus we find him indulging such obvious technical crutches as the long expository speech of Prospero to Miranda in I.ii and the outsized, extra-dramatic masque in IV.i. But it is crucial to see that even these so-called weaknesses are used to positive advantage: the loose, romance-like actions—in *The Tempest* a largely invented action (see The Source of *The Tempest*, Signet Classic edition, pp. 125-39) —enabled him to work most easily and expansively with the patterns of pardon and reconciliation and of resurrection and continuance so important in his late work; the machinery of spirits and mythological figures, of masques, music, and "miracles," gave him a rich array of devices for bringing associative and symbolic dimension to his actions; indeed, the very looseness, untidiness, and misty uncertainty of these plays became integral to their strange, mellow, philosophical temper. Like the romantic comedies, the romances end with an emphatic sense of affirmation, yet they are much graver in tone in that they chiefly celebrate, not love and youth, but the total fabric of life as a sad and very beautiful thing.

Of the collection of elements which Shakespeare has combined in *The Tempest* to produce what Prospero at one point, glancing at the play itself, calls "this insubstantial pageant" (104.155), probably none is more important than the cause of most of the play's key events, Prospero's magic. In some sense the play is about the changes which Prospero effects through his magic, the promise of human life which he clarifies through his magical project. To understand Shakespeare's intention on this score, it is necessary to see that the kind of magic involved would have been recognized by the Elizabethans as natural magic, a kind of magic clearly distinguished from black or diabolical magic and associated with medieval science and the activities of great learned men. More precisely, this was the magic that was worked, not through the devil's power and after some unholy alliance with the demonic world had been made, but through a knowledge of nature, and more specifically a knowledge of the occult power that was believed to inhere in natural things. It was the magic of savants like Albertus Magnus and Roger Bacon; it was associated with books and an advanced understanding of mathematics and of the properties of stones, herbs, and magnets. In the popular mind, understandably, it took on the character of a kind of superhuman wisdom, while the natural magician became a figure remote and mysterious, capable of almost anything because capable of bending nature to his will.

On these associations Shakespeare has built the fable of a master-magician who undertakes the master-project of briefly controlling and directing all the life within the arena of the play. Prospero's aims, we learn, are neither to avenge his wrongs nor to perfect the materials on which he is working, but to renew the figures that have come under his sway and to support the promise of that renewal with the fresh beginning implied in the marriage of Ferdinand and Miranda. Prospero's clarification of the possibility of a "brave new world" (115.183), indeed, associates the play in important respects with other Renaissance utopian works, which also play off the dream of what might be against the reality of what is. In *The Tempest,* Prospero's magic is the quantity normally missing in experience by which to see, if only briefly, what might be.

Prospero's project, in any event, provides the matrix for both the events of the play and the highly special atmosphere in which they transpire. With Prospero standing by as a kind of providential father, it is entirely probable that characters will drift from moment to moment, as in a dream; that spirits, mysterious music, and nature herself will participate in the human action in such a way as to suggest that somehow all being is involved in the effort at hand; that human life itself on the island will seem universalized, as if seen from a great distance. It is these features of the play that give it its abstract, philosophical character; that prompt us to view the action so as to emphasize not the individual careers represented but patterns of lost and found, death and rebirth, and appearance and reality—that prompt us, in short, to a sense of life of extraordinary breadth and depth. In embracing its materials hopefully, yet without sentimentality, *The Tempest* communicates a mood of wise acquiescence of rare authority. Because it was Shakespeare's last play, at least the last written entirely by him, it is sometimes thought to contain his summary reflections on art and life.

THE ACTION

I.i

The play opens with a short, explosive scene aboard the foundering ship transporting King Alonzo of Naples and his party from Tunis, where they have just celebrated his daughter's marriage to the King of Tunis, to Naples. All is confusion, noise, and frantic activity—all underscored dramatically by hurried entrances and exits, shouted orders, curses, and screams. As the Shipmaster and Boatswain make their final efforts to save the situation, Alonzo, Sebastian, Antonio, Ferdinand, and Gonzalo appear on deck to be met by the Boatswain's annoyance and abrupt command that they leave the seamen to their work and return to their cabins. His curt insistence (16-18) that conventional class distinctions disappear in the face of a threat so elemental as the storm is a first preparation for the detached, rather abstract view of humanity fostered later. The responses to his insolence, moreover, provide some preliminary distinctions among the characters: Gonzalo, at first conciliatory, is then mildly amused at his boldness and inclined to see it as a favorable sign in that it suggests a hanging rather than a drowning destiny for the Boatswain; Sebastian and Antonio are so bitter and quarrelsome that Antonio, suggesting his narrowness and vindictiveness of spirit, accuses the crew of drunkenness and incompetence (56). Then, with confused cries within of " 'Mercy on us!' 'We split, we split!' 'Farewell, my wife and children!' " etc., Gonzalo is left alone to conclude the scene with the wry observation—another touch which skillfully qualifies the seriousness of the scene—that he would give up a great deal of sea for a very small piece of safe dry ground (64-67).

In addition to this scene's obvious function of preparing for the coming of Alonzo and his associates to Prospero's island, it introduces a few of the elements that will give the later action dimension and depth, and not the least of these is the storm itself. Reminders of the storm occur frequently in the play—at the beginning of II.ii, for example, during the mock-banquet in III.iii, and at the departure of the dancers in the masque in IV.i—and in the very next scene (I.ii) we hear of the storm in which Prospero and Miranda had started out on what he calls their "sea sorrow" (47.170). In some real sense, storm is the condition with which the world as represented by the play begins, the condition from which it is coming and in which everything of consequence is born. This whole first scene—short and rapid though it is—provides a fleeting image of a society of men in chaos, men struggling, quarreling, praying, terrified, helpless. It is upon this image of humanity that Prospero works.

I.ii

Had any serious expectations been aroused by the first scene, however, they are immediately suppressed by what we learn at the beginning of this scene, a scene so full of expository and preparatory matter that it could be called mechanical and clumsy if it did not accomplish so many things so skillfully. In Prospero's first lines, and throughout the scene, we are forced to attend to, among other things, the extent of his power and control. "Be collected./No more amazement Tell your piteous heart/There's no harm done . . ./No harm" (13-15), he says, in assuring Miranda that all is well with the castaways, and he then proceeds to a recital of acts and, toward the end of the scene, to the performance of others which confirm his mastery. This assurance that little or nothing will happen that Prospero does not intend draws attention away from the action as adventure and focuses interest early on why it is being made to work out as it is.

Having reassured Miranda and put aside his magician's robe, Prospero first undertakes to complete Miranda's education by telling her the story of their exile. A long narrative, effectively broken up by interruptions and comments by both Prospero and Miranda, Prospero begins it by asking Miranda what she herself remembers of her earliest childhood. But she remembers little; all she recalls from "the dark backward and abysm of time" (50) is like a dream, a sense, that is, of a life both real and unreal. This is the first occurrence in the play of the dream sense that will gradually clarify one of the play's chief themes. Prospero then tells her that twelve years before he had been the Duke of Milan and had made a grave error in leaving the practical business of government to his brother Antonio because he preferred to pursue his "secret studies" (77). By thus neglecting his worldly responsibilities, Prospero admits, he awakened an evil ambition in his brother, who, taking advantage of his trusting nature, gradually replaced his ministers with his own and, when the time was ripe, allied himself with Prospero's enemy, Alonzo of Naples. The alliance of Antonio and Alonzo then removed Prospero, though they dared not kill him because of his popularity with the people. Instead, they put him to sea with Miranda in a rotten, unseaworthy boat that "the very rats/Instinctively [had] quit" (148-49); and there Prospero and his child would almost certainly have perished if Antonio and Alonzo's agent in this design, the kindly Gonzalo, had not provided them with food, water, clothes, and other "necessaries" (164), including certain "volumes" from Prospero's library (167). Aghast at this remarkable account, Miranda had earlier touched on one of its key ambiguities when she asked, "What foul play had we that we came from thence?/Or blessèd was't we did?" (60-61), to which Prospero had replied "Both, both, my girl!" (61). Toward the end of his tale he elaborates on the contradictions inherent in this seeming catastrophe by discerning a "providence divine" (159) in their rescue: in the raging winds that, despite their violence, saved them; in the presence of the child Miranda, "a cherubin" (152) whose smile filled Prospero "with a fortitude from heaven" (154); in the unexpected and in many ways irrational kindness of Gonzalo. Prospero concludes the story of their "sea sorrow" (170), a story which already offers clear parallels to the disaster presumably suffered by the characters in the first scene, by admitting again that he with the help of "bountiful Fortune" (178) has brought his enemies to the island; furthermore, he implies that he must take full advantage of their presence because his favorable star is now at its height and "Will ever after droop" (184). But he declines at this point to elaborate further on his design and, instead, casts Miranda into a sleep.

With Miranda asleep, Prospero calls in his aide, the spirit Ariel, and together they review the events of the shipwreck as Prospero had predetermined them. Ariel reports that he had boarded Alonzo's ship during the storm and so terrified everyone aboard with fire, lightning, and explosions that Alonzo and Antonio and their followers had quit the ship and made for shore. Now the ship is safe in a cove; the sailors are asleep in her hold; Alonzo, Antonio, and the others are safely on the island, and the rest of Alonzo's convoy, convinced that the vessel was lost, has departed from Naples. From Ariel's account, at least two important aspects of Prospero's control emerge: that it extends to inward as well as to outward matters, for they speak of "this coil" that infects his victims' reason with "a fever of the mad" (207-09); and that it entails in this instance the careful division of the castaways into "troops" (220). Both details suggest what becomes clearer in Prospero's later treatment of Ferdinand, that his aims do not reach merely to revenge, or even to a simple justice, but beyond, to some constructive end that is still not clear.

But this portion of the scene also has important functions beyond exposition. With Ariel's appearance, and immediately thereafter Caliban's, Shakespeare introduces and deliberately forces a comparison between two symbolic figures who tell us a good deal both about Prospero's power—they are his servants—and about the material upon which he is working. Their appearance at this point, moreover, as the situation is being unfolded and the action being readied to go forward, serves to adjust our perspective on the action as a whole, to prompt us to view Prospero's grand design with some of the detachment with which we are forced to see his management of these creatures who so clearly epitomize the broad components of the human nature which he is manipulating.

Ariel is a creature of air and spirit who is associated in his activities in the play with flight, music, poetry, and loveliness. But, as the commentary on his nature which Prospero's review of his situation reveals, he is scarcely idealized. Like the spirit, he is intent upon his liberty (245), even at the expense of all other considerations. Prospero calls him "Moody" (244) and a "malignant thing" (257) and reminds him, as he must frequently (261-63), apparently, of the time when he was the slave of Sycorax, Caliban's sorceress-mother, enforced to "earthy and abhorred" (273) labors, and finally imprisoned in physical nature in "a cloven pine" (277). From this condition Prospero, through his superior art, has freed him, and now he serves Prospero on the understanding that with the completion of Prospero's project he will be liberated. Having thus reproved him, Prospero orders him to take the shape of a water nymph and to become invisible to all others; chastened, Ariel obeys and leaves.

Prospero then awakens Miranda and tells her they must visit Caliban. It should be noticed here how Shakespeare all but ignores the pretext for this portion of the scene in the interests of forcing the juxtaposition of Caliban and Ariel; though Prospero speaks of "other business" (315) for Caliban, in addition to fetching wood, he never speaks further of it in the scene. Shakespeare's justification for this loose end is the contrast that Caliban forces with Ariel: Caliban is called "Dull thing" (285) and is quickly associated with earth and lower nature—with all, more generally, that is most intractable in human nature. Early in their relationship Prospero had loved him and had tried to educate him; he had taught him language and the natural wonders of the island. But Caliban had repaid him by trying to ravish Miranda: he is a creature "Whom stripes may move, not kindness!" (344), "Which any print of goodness wilt not take,/Being capable of all ill!" (352-53). Of such unmanageable, rebellious natures, however mitigated by sympathetic traits, the Elizabethans took the pessimistic, hardheaded view revealed in Prospero's solution to the problem of Caliban: since he needs Caliban and cannot conceive of a life without him, he constrains him to obedience with threats of physical pain (369-71).

Upon Caliban's dismissal, Ariel brings in Ferdinand to the accompaniment of the song "Come unto these yellow sands" (375), and Prospero actively takes up his great project. It should be pointed out how subtly the play has moved from the noisy confusion of the opening scene through the quiet scene between Prospero and Miranda to the distinctly less realistic scenes involving Ariel and Caliban to bring us to the special, strangely poetic atmosphere of Ferdinand's scene. Ferdinand insists on these special values in his first lines, as he tries to identify the source of the mysterious music, "I' th' air or th' earth?" (388), and comments on the rich sense of otherness that he feels and felt as

> Weeping again the King my father's wrack,
> This music crept by me upon the waters,
> Allaying both their fury and my passion
> With its sweet air. (391-94)

He rightly associates the experience with a kind of spell. Then Ariel begins to sing again, "Full fathom five thy father lies" (397), to intensify the sense so prominent in the play from this point forward of meanings and beauty close but just out of reach, as in a dream. Actually, the song misrepresents the facts, since Alonzo has not been drowned, to point in choral fashion to the deeper action in which this lost group from civilization has been cast up by the sea to undergo "a sea change/Into something rich and strange" (401-02), and it accomplishes this commentary even as it insists once again, as Ferdinand has already done and as Prospero will frequently do, on the wondrous interpenetration of physical nature (sea, earth, air), the spirit world (Ariel and the mysterious music), and humanity in the total effort in process to produce a "change."

The song finished, Ferdinand confronts Prospero and Miranda, and with his stunned response to the girl, and hers to him, Prospero executes an important step in his plan ("It goes on, I see," 420). Miranda's simple, entirely ingenuous character, it should be noticed, is highly appropriate to Shakespeare's purposes here. Like virtually all the characters in the play, she is given a notably flat characterization, in her case one of such inexperience that she seems almost a personification of innocence. Shakespeare uses this innocence not only to give Prospero a reason to act as her educator, and us a reason to feel that in her he is preparing a wonder (consider her name), but to give her with some probability the superlatively flattering comments about the human beings she meets, remarks that in some sense Shakespeare means but that he uses largely to hint at potential dimensions in the human material on which Prospero is working. Of Ferdinand she says, "What is't? A spirit? . . . /It carries a brave form./ . . . I might call him/A thing divine" (410-19). In his turn Ferdinand, not so unspoiled but also capable of wonder, thinks her "the goddess/On whom these airs attend!" (422-23). Finally, the most elaborate and important of the purposes accomplished here is Prospero's preparation for the impressively symbolic marriage to take place later between Ferdinand and Miranda—Miranda not simply as a personification of innocence but also as an agent of faith and trust (cf. "There's nothing ill can dwell in such a temple," 458; "Sir, have pity./I'll be his surety," 475-76).

Once Prospero is assured, in any case, that love is working its charm in the young people, he confides to us in an aside that he must make it more difficult than it seems to be to them. Accordingly, he accuses Ferdinand of being a usurper and a spy, and, when Ferdinand tries to resist an undignified imprisonment, he subdues him with a charm. Again Prospero's power to work on the minds and spirits of his subjects is clear: he speaks of infusing Ferdinand's "conscience" with "guilt" (471-72), of depriving his "nerves" of "vigor" (485-86); for his part, Ferdinand admits that his "spirits, as in a dream, are all bound up" (487), but also grants that the enchantment of having found Miranda is such that he will happily endure his "prison." Pleased at his progress ("It works," 493), Prospero leads Ferdinand away, confiding to Ariel as he goes that soon he will be free, while Miranda assures Ferdinand that all will be well.

II.i

The action turns to Alonzo and his party and takes up the treatment of the castaways by groups, that is, by turning in successive scenes to the respective groups into which Prospero has divided humanity on the island—the nobles, the lovers, and the servants. This scene deepens the picture of one level of the humanity on which Prospero is working by providing a highly detailed picture of the nobles at cross-purposes—bickering, scheming, mocking each other, and finally plotting murder. Much of the dialogue has relatively little function in the subsequent chain of events beyond clarifying the characters on this one level; in fact, a good bit of it consists of Gonzalo and Adrian's attempts to distract Alonzo from his sorrow at the supposed loss of Ferdinand, attempts which center chiefly in their comments on the natural wonders of the island, and Antonio and Sebastian's mocking of their wonderment. Adrian speaks of the "subtle, tender, and delicate temperance" (45) of the climate and of the island's sweet air, lushness, and fertility, while Gonzalo marvels at the newness and freshness of their clothes. But Antonio and Sebastian bring to the same facts a meanness and pedestrian quality of mind and spirit that prompts them to ridicule; showing themselves men incapable of listening to others, particularly when the talk implies sensibilities finer than their own, they then pass from ridicule to cruel recriminations by reminding Alonzo that it was he who, against opposition, consented to his daughter's marriage to the King of Tunis and he, accordingly, who was responsible for the voyage that has ended in shipwreck and Ferdinand's death ("The fault's your own," 140). Gonzalo reproves them for the unkindness: "The truth you speak doth lack some gentleness,/ And time to speak it in. You rub the sore/ When you should bring the plaster" (142-44); but they mock even this gentle and entirely justified criticism. In this way the scene proceeds, rather aimlessly from the point of view of the structure of events in the play, but lending depth to distinctions and perceptions of great importance to Prospero's aim to refashion briefly the human material that has come under his sway. Likewise, Gonzalo's description of his ideal commonwealth, which predictably Antonio and Sebastian also ridicule, has no practical function except, that coming as it does in a place of emphasis in the scene and calling attention as it does to a utopian example, it underscores the play's long-range aim to examine human possibilities.

The scene does not take up the forward movement of Prospero's project until Ariel, invisible to the nobles, comes in to the accompaniment of "solemn music" and charms Alonzo and his company, with the exception of Antonio and Sebastian, into a sleep. Given this opportunity, Antonio is quick to point out to Sebastian that, since Ferdinand is drowned, and Alonzo's daughter is in distant Tunis, he has only to eliminate Alonzo to rise to the throne of Naples. Sebastian raises a question about "conscience" (279), but Antonio derides that "deity" (282) and offers his own example in Milan to persuade him that he must seize the occasion. Sebastian agrees and offers to reward Antonio with relief from a tribute which Milan pays to Naples, and together they plan to murder Alonzo and Gonzalo. Before they can strike, however, Ariel returns, again to the accompaniment of music and a song, and, since he has by this time let Antonio and Sebastian's natures go as far as Prospero intended them to, he awakens Gonzalo by singing in his ear. Gonzalo starts up, sees Antonio and Sebastian with their swords drawn, and awakens Alonzo and the others. After a confused account of the noise which had wakened them, the group goes off to hunt further for Ferdinand, and Ariel goes to report to Prospero.

II.ii

In another part of the island, meantime, Caliban complains bitterly, as he gathers wood, of Prospero's practice of punishing him by sending spirits in various forms to pinch him; vengeful, yet incapable of calculated cunning, he admits that, though he knows the spirits hear him, he "needs must curse" (4). When Trinculo, Alonzo's jester, appears, accordingly, Caliban takes him to be a spirit and falls flat on the ground. Trinculo marvels at "this monster" (31) for a moment, but, himself terrified by the thunderclaps that punctuate the scene as a whole to keep the condition of tempest before us, he quickly joins Caliban under his cloak. In this position Alonzo's butler Stephano, reeling drunk and singing a ribald song, finds them.

With this scene, then, the action moves to the third "troop," the servant group, in whom are represented minds and sensibilities even less satisfactory in most respects than those found among the nobles. The scene is largely in prose, except for those of Caliban's speeches which deal with the island and in which he is yoked to its magic, and in it a grotesque alliance is struck by these temporarily masterless servants. Most of the dialogue concerns their discovery of each other: first Stephano's discovery of Trinculo as a separable part of the four-legged monster under Caliban's coat, then their discovery of Caliban, and his of them. In the drinking and high-spirited talk by which Stephano and Trinculo explain how they came to be here, a natural zest and even a certain fellow-feeling are evident among them. But if Shakespeare concedes these qualities to them, he also clearly represents their loutishness and their proneness to serious error. Caliban, having mistaken Trinculo for a spirit earlier, now mistakes Stephano for a god and his wine for "celestial liquor" (122); Stephano, moreover, accepts him as his subject. When they have drunk deep of Stephano's wine, they all stagger out as Caliban sings of freedom and, paradoxically, leads the way.

In brief, the scene introduces the third of the groups which constitute the rough cross-section of humanity on whom Prospero works, and sets up a parallel in the alliance of Stephano, Trinculo, and Caliban to the alliance struck in the previous scene by Antonio and Sebastian. If the servants are in some respects more attractive at this point than the noble conspirators, it should also be pointed out that, as with Caliban, they should probably not be viewed sentimentally. In Shakespeare's view these are clearly the least tractable and manageable of human beings; in them we can expect Prospero's magic to have least effect.

III.i

The scene shifts again to the lovers to discover Ferdinand executing the task set him by Prospero, carrying and piling some thousands of logs. Normally, he admits, the work would be "heavy" and "odious" (5), but under these circumstances, with the chance to be near Miranda, he does not mind it. Miranda then comes in, followed by Prospero, who remains unseen by the lovers, and laments Ferdinand's labors and offers to help him. He gallantly refuses and they fall into conversation, while Prospero comments so as to underscore clearly that he has planned not merely their falling in love but their marriage, which here he asks heaven to "rain grace" on (75-76). But Ferdinand and Miranda carry out Prospero's purposes without prompting. He asks her name, and she, breaking her father's command, tells him; then he praises her as the most perfect woman he has even known, admitting as he does that he has known other women and loved them. In the mutual confessions that follow, Miranda takes the lead, asking him first if he loves her; then, calling on the aid of "plain and holy innocence" (82), proposing marriage to him. They agree and go out, while Prospero lingers to comment that, though he cannot feel their happiness at this turn of events, nothing could make him happier. He then returns to his book and project.

Again it should be pointed out that, though the scene advances the action, it does little to deepen or particularize the characters of Ferdinand and Miranda. They remain relatively flat, and we care about them and, like Prospero, rejoice in their proposed union largely because of its meaning. Here, as elsewhere in this play and in Shakespeare's later plays, characters elicit sympathy and interest as they crystallize and are enriched by meanings. In this scene Miranda's association with innocence is again clear in her touching, almost poignant, naiveté. Ferdinand, by contrast, knows the world and has known love before, but he has not been spoiled by this knowledge. It is possible, in discussing the lovers and in attempting to understand that part of Prospero's plan which they represent, to argue that Ferdinand represents the best that the world of men can offer while Miranda represents the best to be found in a world apart from people: he is in a sense the best of experience, she the best of innocence. Prospero desires a union of these creatures and in that union intends to lay some part of the foundation for the world to which he will return at the end of the play.

III.ii

The action next shifts to the low-life characters, Caliban, Stephano, and Trinculo. Stephano continues to ply Caliban with wine and asks him to speak to them, while Trinculo ridicules the "Servant monster" (3). When Caliban complains about Trinculo's ridicule, Stephano cautions Trinculo, asserting that his subjects "shall not suffer indignity" (39-40), and then Caliban kneels, like a vassal to his lord, and presents his "suit" (42). At this point Ariel enters, still "invisible" (44 s.d.), and listens as Caliban tells Stephano about Prospero and Miranda, and then interrupts the account with cries of "thou liest" (47), delivered in such a way as to make it appear that Trinculo has uttered them. Trinculo denies several times that he has spoken, but when one of the cries seems leveled at Stephano, he strikes Trinculo for his impudence. Caliban, again speaking in verse to the others' prose, then urges Stephano to murder Prospero and make Miranda his woman, and, persuaded by Caliban's praise of Miranda's beauty, Stephano assents and proposes that he will be king of the island, with Miranda his queen and Trinculo and Caliban his viceroys. By this time in high spirits, Stephano starts to sing a song, which Caliban interrupts by saying that he has the wrong tune. Before Caliban can give him the right tune, however, Ariel plays it "on a tabor and pipe" (129 s.d.) to plunge the three conspirators into confusion. Trinculo is terrified at the mysterious music; Stephano feigns a courage but is equally frightened; only Caliban is relatively unmoved, largely, as he explains, because "the isle is full of noises,/Sounds and sweet airs that give delight and hurt not" (140-41). In his description of the island's strange music, "strange" because it moves Caliban to a sense of beauty that he can never be entirely sure of, as if he were somehow between waking and sleeping, Caliban identifies a fitful consciousness of experience better than his own, a potential in himself that is painful because it is so rudimentary. Reassured, the plotters go off in the direction of the music, again led by Caliban.

The principal functions of the scene, then, are to tighten the analogy with the noble group, especially with Antonio and Sebastian, by duplicating their plot with a second murder plot, and to give further exposure to the mentalities and sensibilities to be focused on this level of humanity. As Caliban, Trinculo, and Stephano plan the murder of Prospero, we see that it is not problem-solving intelligence that they lack, or even a rudimentary capacity for appreciating beauty, so much as a disposition to place a high value on humanity. They talk about dignity, but Caliban and Trinculo, at least, are continuously subject to indignities. Moreover, by repeating the murder scheme in this line of action Shakespeare generalizes our sense of the depravity of the human material on which Prospero is working. Although neither the noble conspirators nor these servants seem distinctly worse than ordinary human beings, in both lines of action Shakespeare carefully sounds a base note of pessimism by tying the characters to a decision to murder.

III.iii

In yet another part of the island the nobles have exhausted themselves with hunting Ferdinand; they stop to rest, and Antonio and Sebastian, apart, agree to execute the murders that night. At this moment they are interrupted by "Solemn and strange music" (17 s.d.) as Prospero appears, unseen, above them (see Prefactory Remarks, Shakespeare's Theater, pp.xiv-xv), and then by "strange Shapes" (17 s.d.) which bring in a banquet, dance and greet them kindly, invite them to eat, and then depart. The nobles' responses to these "Shapes" are largely consistent with what we have already seen of their natures: though all are stunned by the otherworldly music and what Sebastian calls a "living drollery" (21), only Gonzalo has complete faith that the spirits are friendly creatures who intend them good; Sebastian and Antonio wish to take advantage of the food that in their view the "Shapes" have stupidly left behind; Alonzo suspects a trick. After Gonzalo has persuaded them, but before they can actually start eating, however, Ariel, in the form of a harpy, reappears to an accompaniment of thunder and lightning and causes the banquet to disappear. Having transfixed them with this fear, Ariel then indicts the "three men of sin" (53)—Alonzo, Antonio, and Sebastian—and explains that destiny, the sea, and his "fellow ministers" (65) working through the natural elements have brought them to the island to make them suffer for their wrongs. When he has finished, he "vanishes in thunder" and then "to soft music" the "Shapes" return, dance and mock the nobles, and carry off the table (82 s.d.). Prospero, who has been watching from above, comments that his project is progressing as he had planned: his enemies are now "knit up/In their distractions" (89-90). After he has gone off to rejoin Ferdinand and Miranda, Alonzo marvels at the way the sea and the winds, together producing a mysterious music, have provoked him to a sense of guilt and of his sins' relation to his present sorrow. After the others have gone, Gonzalo remains briefly to comment to Adrian on their "ecstasy" (108), this strange working of conscience that has begun to "bite the[ir] spirits" (106).

In this scene, then, the patterned treatment of the separate groups continues, tracing the execution of Prospero's project step by step; but as the project nears its climax, outward events become more fantastic and less important than inward events. The mock-supper and magic feats in this scene are merely occasions for representing—by means of Ariel's indictment, the nobles' responses, and Prospero and Gonzalo's comments—the nobles' progress in the direction Prospero has chosen for them. Prospero's statement "My high charms work. . . . They now are in my pow'r" (88-90) confirm for us that they are afflicted as he intends them to be; his use of sounds from the sea and the wind and of helpers that seem peculiar to the island, moreover, reinforces our sense that somehow all nature is involved in the temporary chastening that is under way.

IV.i

In this scene the action returns to the lovers and consists largely of the masque with which Prospero entertains them. Again it should be clear that the pretext for the masque is rather feeble—Prospero says that he has promised to show the young folk some "vanity of [his] art" (41)—and in the episodic structure, the masque is an extra-dramatic element, one inessential to the unfolding of the action. Shakespeare uses it for its associative and symbolic value, to bless, as Prospero wishes to, the symbolic union of Ferdinand and Miranda, and in doing so to provide an occasion for developing a perspective of unusual comprehensiveness on both the masque and the play itself.

The action is really quite simple. Prospero, having explained to Ferdinand why he has been difficult and having warned him to remain chaste in his relation with Miranda until their marriage is concluded, then calls upon Ariel to bring on the "rabble" (37) to perform the entertainment. The masque consists, first, of an invocation by Iris, the goddess of the rainbow and Juno's messenger, of Ceres, the goddess of agriculture; Ceres, associated throughout the speech (60-72) with fertility and abundance, is asked to entertain Juno and to assist in celebrating this "contract of true love" (84). In answer to Ceres' question about Venus and Cupid, Iris replies that they will not be present to trouble this perfect union with lawless passion. When Juno, the queen of the gods, has appeared, she and Ceres sing a two-part song blessing the nuptial couple with fertility and long life. Ferdinand is delighted with the proceedings, and in answer to his question about the spirit-performers, Prospero explains that they are the figures of his thought, "called to enact/[his] present fancies" (121-22). Then the masque continues as Juno and Ceres send Iris to call in a group of nymphs and reapers, who dance a "graceful dance" (138 s.d.) combining visually the mythological and realistic orders of existence elusively present and mixed throughout the play. But, suddenly recalling at this point the plot of Stephano, Trinculo, and Caliban, Prospero abruptly stops the dance and dismisses the dancers. Seeing Ferdinand "dismayed" (147) at this sudden turn, he explains that the entertainment is only an illusion, associating it, as he does, with the deeper illusions of art and life.

Prospero's commentary on his entertainment (148-58) contains the most explicit references in the play—perhaps in all Shakespeare's plays—to Shakespeare's conscious concern with the multiple levels of meaning embodied in his action. At the most obvious level Prospero is speaking of his spirits —"These our actors" (148)—which he has conjured up for the masque; they have vanished, he points out, just as, he implies, the larger "pageant" (155), the life he has brought to the island and ordered there, will vanish. Secondly, however, the spirits are the actors in the play *The Tempest:* like the spirits in the masque, they have created a vision of life which will also, like "the great globe itself" (153; in this first sense, the Globe Theater), vanish and "Leave not a rack behind" (156). Finally, the "vision" referred to (151) is to be seen as a metaphor for all life, an image of life crystallized, an image, that is, presented in terms of life's basic, essential elements and relationships, and, like life, also an illusion. The lines "We are such stuff/As dreams are made on, and our little life/Is rounded with a sleep" (156-58) insist on this broadest of applications. It should be pointed out, moreover, that Prospero is not in the least depressed by this statement: he begins this speech by telling Ferdinand to "be cheerful, sir" (147), and what he says is entirely consistent with his activities in the play. Seeing life as an illusion or dream does not prevent him from seeing it, as Ferdinand and Miranda see the brief and fleeting image of the masque, in terms of what life promises, in terms of a condition in which humanity seems worthy of itself, nor does it prevent him from committing himself to it and trying to do something about it. On the contrary, seeing life as a dream, insubstantial and evanescent, enhances and mellows his love for it. It is in part this understanding that liberates his humanity for the pardon and reconciliation of the final scenes.

The remainder of the act, then, deals with Prospero's preparation to meet the threat of Stephano, Trinculo, and Caliban. Ariel reports to him that the conspirators, still reeling drunk, have been led by his tabor music into a filthy pool. Then, after Prospero and Ariel have hung an array of fine garments on a line, they come in, Stephano and Trinculo fuming at Caliban because they have lost their bottles and smell so foully, Caliban urging them to be quiet and assuring them that all will be well. When they see the finery displayed on the line, Stephano and Trinculo rejoice at their good fortune, and set about putting it on, while Caliban, suspecting a trick, heatedly tells them to leave it alone. But they refuse to listen to him and dress themselves as the new aristocracy. As they are giving orders to steal the rest, however, spirits in the shape of dogs suddenly come in and, to "A noise of hunters" drive them out (254 s.d.). Prospero, who with Ariel has looked on throughout, orders the "goblins" (258) to punish them with pinches and cramps and then turns to conclude his labors with the speech "At this hour/Lies at my mercy all mine enemies./Shortly shall all my labors end . . ." (262-64).

V.i

This last long scene of the play begins with Prospero's brief review of his project, now "gather[ed] to a head" (1). All is as he ordained, Ariel assures him, and his charms work so potently in Alonzo, Antonio, and Sebastian that were he (Ariel) human, he would be compassionate. Taking up this cue, Prospero then explains to him that he has intended compassion all along, that his purpose was to move the sinners to a sense of guilt and penitence, but no more. Accordingly, he instructs Ariel to release them from the bonds that hold them, while he prepares to break the charm that has held their "senses" (31), to which end he draws a magic circle with his staff and elaborately invokes the "elves of hills, brooks, standing lakes, and groves," the spirits of the sea, and the "demi-puppets" of the night—all the creatures that have aided him in his art (33-50). Having invoked them, however, Prospero does not call upon their aid once more but suddenly and dramatically abjures his magic, breaking his staff and "drown[ing] his book" (57) to the accompaniment of solemn music. Despite all that he has accomplished through his magic, as well as all that conceivably he could accomplish, he seems by his description of it as "this rough magic" (50) to judge it unworthy of the human material on which he has used it. Although it is clear that he could have done much more than he has, he feels that the "rare action" (27) consists in renouncing his art, renouncing, that is, the inadequate perfection which it might have produced, for the flawed but human condition that he accepts. Having made a fresh beginning possible and having nourished a profound promise in the marriage of Ferdinand and Miranda, Prospero chooses to go no further and implies by his choice that the greater good lies in forgiveness and reconciliation.

Even as Prospero casts off the trappings of his art, Ariel leads in Alonzo, Antonio, Sebastian, and the others, the first three still dazed by the charm that is dissipated during the next speech. Prospero receives them, greets "Holy Gonzalo" (162), and describes the process of their recovery from the "inward pinches" (77) that still afflict them; as they recover, Ariel dresses Prospero in his robes of state, singing, as he does, "Where the bee sucks, there suck I" (88), a song which once again calls attention to the mysterious and marvelous blend of natural, spirit, and human elements in the action before us. When Ariel has been dispatched to fetch the Shipmaster and the Boatswain, Prospero declares himself the "wrongèd Duke of Milan" (107) and welcomes his guests more elaborately. He parries their questions about the wonders they have seen by assuring them that he will explain everything presently; he confides to Antonio and Sebastian in an aside that he knows of their vicious plan but "will tell no tales" (129); he forgives the wrongdoers everything, demanding, as he does, that his dukedom be restored; he counters Alonzo's lament that he has lost a son with the misleading claim that he has lost a daughter. But even this single note of anguish he then resolves happily by leading the party to his cell, where they discover Ferdinand and Miranda playing chess. With this discovery there are fresh reunions and fresh amazement; from Ferdinand, Alonzo, and the others there is amazement that they have found each other alive, from Miranda, in her innocence, amazement at the beauty of such creatures: "How beauteous mankind is! O brave new world/That has such people in 't" (183-84). With these rediscoveries the scene is charged with a sense of mellow, melancholy rejoicing as the lost are found and the supposed dead returned to life, as the possibility of a fresh beginning becomes increasingly real. Gonzalo discerns the hand of beneficent providence in the proceedings, when he says,

> Look down, you gods,
> And on this couple drop a blessed crown!
> For it is you that have chalked forth the way
> Which brought us hither. (201-04)

At this point Ariel returns with the Shipmaster and Boatswain, and from the latter the group learns that the ship is safe and that the crew has been sleeping in the ship's hold, as "in a dream" (239). Again Prospero parries questions about this wondrous matter with the promise that he will presently explain everything; then, driven in by Ariel, Caliban, Stephano, and Trinculo appear in their "stolen apparel" (255 s.d.) to complete the group. As Antonio and Sebastian laugh at these grotesque figures, echoing their earlier mocking tone in such a way as to imply that they, at least, have not entirely changed, Prospero identifies the errant servants and "this thing of darkness" (275) as his own. Stephano and Trinculo, still dazed by drink and their recent torments, are sulkily submissive; Caliban, suggesting more clearly that he has learned something, is angry at his own stupidity in having mistaken "this drunkard for a god" (297) and quick to obey Prospero in the hope that he will be forgiven. With all souls accounted for, Prospero invites the party to spend the night in his cell, where he will pass the time by telling them his story, and promises that the next day they will all sail for Naples, where Ferdinand and Miranda will be married. Assuring them of "calm seas, auspicious gales" (315), the fitting ending to a project he had begun in tempest, he dispatches Ariel to this final task, repeating his promise that when it is completed, Ariel will be free, will, more precisely, be released "to the elements" (318). As he draws the human family around him—"Please you, draw near" (319)—the play concludes.

ANTHONY CAPUTI

SHORT-ANSWER QUESTIONS

1. How does Gonzalo's response to the Boatswain's insolence in I.i (38.29-34; 40.57-59) serve to undercut the seriousness of the threat facing the ship?

2. What is Antonio's explanation of the disaster (39.56-58) in I.i? Is there any evidence for it?

3. How does the shortness of Prospero's first lines in I.ii (41.14-16) support his authority?

4. What is the purpose of the interruptions in Prospero's narrative to Miranda (pp. 43-47) in I.ii?

5. How, precisely, had Antonio contrived Prospero's exile? (45. 120-32; 46.138-51)

6. For what purpose does Shakespeare risk the improbability of Gonzalo's including among the things with which Prospero was exiled the "volumes that/[He] prize[d] above [his] dukedom"? (47.167-68)

THE TEMPEST

7. What preserved Prospero from despair at the time of his exile? (46.152-58)

8. How many evidences of "providence divine" (47.159) can you find in Prospero's safe passage to the island?

9. Why was Ariel imprisoned in "a cloven pine" (51.277) when Prospero found him? (51.272-74)

10. By what details is Caliban associated with animal nature? (pp. 53-55)

11. Who are the three men Miranda has seen (58.446) by the end of I.ii?

12. What natural wonders on the island have impressed Gonzalo and Adrian? (pp. 62-65)

13. What does Sebastian's argument in II.i that the entire disaster is Alonzo's fault turn on? (66.128-39)

14. What is the immediate purpose of Gonzalo's description of his ideal commonwealth in II.i?

15. What is to be Antonio's profit for helping Sebastian to the throne of Naples? (73.296-98)

16. How are the different accounts of the noises which awoke Alonzo and his party in II.i consistent with their earlier responses to the island?

17. If Antonio's plot had succeeded in II.i, in what respects would Sebastian's situation have been analogous to his?

18. Caliban twice thinks Trinculo and Stephano to be creatures other than they are in II.ii. What sorts of creatures does he think them? (77.65; 79.121-23)

19. Who speaks verse in II.ii, and who prose? Why?

20. Explain the makeup of the "most delicate monster" (78.93-94) which Stephano discovers in II.ii. (78.93-112)

21. What sound from nature recurs through II.ii? (75.s.d.; 76.38)

22. In III.i, what command of Prospero's does Miranda break? (83.37)

23. What does Miranda's name mean literally?

24. Who proposes marriage to whom in III.i? (85.81-83)

25. In III.ii, why does Caliban decide not to serve Trinculo? (86.25)

26. What medieval convention do Caliban and Stephano imitate when Caliban proposes his plot to him? (89.91-99)

27. What prompts Stephano to strike Trinculo in III.ii? (88.75-81)

28. What does Caliban insist that Stephano do first in his plot against Prospero? (89.95-97)

29. What occurs in III.ii to indicate to Caliban, Stephano, and Trinculo that "others" are present? (90.129-39)

30. On what evidence does Gonzalo believe in III.iii that the "strange shapes" are friendly? (93.30-34)

31. Who are the "three men of sin" referred to by Ariel? (94.53)

32. Explain Ariel's meaning when he says that the sea has "requit" Prospero's exile. (95.71)

33. Name several precise ways in III.iii in which the human action is tied closely to physical nature.

34. What is the evidence in III.iii that Prospero's project is going as he intends it to? How would you describe his progress to this point? (95.83-92)

35. In Greek story who are Iris, Ceres, and Juno?

36. What threat had Venus and Cupid posed to the "contract of true love" being celebrated in IV.i? (101.94-98)

THE TEMPEST

37. In what sense are the spirits in IV.i expressions of Prospero's mind, according to him? (103-04.148-58)

38. In addition to goddesses and nymphs, what nonmythological figures take part in Prospero's masque in IV.i? (103.s.d.)

39. For what two reasons are Stephano and Trinculo angry with Caliban in IV.i? (105.199-200, 106.208)

40. Which of the three, Caliban, Stephano, and Trinculo, argues against stealing the fine garments which Prospero and Ariel leave displayed for them in IV.i? (106.224)

41. In V.i Prospero states his aim regarding the nobles clearly. What is it? (109.20-32)

42. In renouncing his magic what signs of his art does Prospero renounce dramatically? (110.50-57, 111.s.d.)

43. How much time has the action on the island, from shipwreck to reconciliation, covered? (115.186; 117.223)

44. Which discoveries seem like rebirths in Act V?

45. What other service does Ariel perform while he is fetching the Shipmaster and the Boatswain? (117.221-26)

46. What in Antonio and Sebastian's responses to Caliban, Stephano, and Trinculo (118-19.263-66) suggests that these nobles have not been greatly changed by their experience?

47. What evidence is there that Caliban has learned something from his experience? (120.295-98)

48. What have Caliban and his companions been doing since they were set upon by spirits in the form of hunting dogs? (118.253)

49. With what does Prospero intend to entertain his guests during the night before their departure? (120.303-07)

50. What is the Prospero of the Epilogue calling for when he asks to be released from his "bands"? (121.9)

QUESTIONS FOR DISCUSSION

1. Discuss the evidence in the play that suggests injustice in Caliban's situation. Why has Shakespeare qualified his portrait of this "beast" in this way?

2. Discuss the different reactions of Adrian and Gonzalo, on the one hand, and Antonio and Sebastian, on the other, to the wonders of the island. What do these differences indicate of differences of mind and sensibility?

3. Discuss the promised marriage between Ferdinand and Miranda, what Prospero in III.i calls a "Fair encounter/Of two most rare affections!" (84.74-75). To what extent can it be understood as a union of the best of innocence and experience?

4. Discuss Alonzo's speech in III.iii (96.95-102) with reference to the function of physical nature in the play, both as a context and as a force.

5. Discuss Prospero's speech in IV.i (103.148-58), beginning "Our revels now are ended," giving particular attention to the multiple references of words and phrases. Comment on the importance of the tendency here to merge orders of reality in the play as a whole.

6. In V.i Prospero says, "They being penitent,/The sole drift of my purpose doth extend/Not a frown further" (109.28-30). Discuss the evidence in this act which illuminates what Prospero has accomplished with the nobles, and what not.

7. Discuss a selection of the songs in the play. What are their dramatic functions? What are their atmospheric functions? How do the words deepen or render more precise our perception of the action?

8. Discuss Ariel as a commentary on spirit and/or Caliban as a commentary on the flesh.

9. Discuss the evidence in the play, besides Prospero's renunciation of his magic, that Prospero prefers the flawed human world to any which his magic might create.

10. A famous historian once argued that many of the lives of great men—men who have changed the course of history—reveal a pattern of withdrawal and return, that is, a pattern by which the man withdraws from society for a time and comes to a new vision of it, and then returns to impose his vision on it. How satisfactorily does this theory describe the experience of Prospero? With what great men might he be usefully compared?

SAMPLE TEST

I. (30 minutes)

Write a well-organized essay on ONE of the following subjects.

1. Discuss Prospero's speech in IV.i (103.148-58), beginning "Our revels now are ended," giving particular attention to the multiple references of words and phrases. Comment on the importance of the tendency here to merge orders of reality in the play as a whole.

2. In V.i Prospero says, "They being penitent,/The sole drift of my purpose doth extend/Not a frown further" (109.28-30). Discuss the evidence in this act which illuminates what Prospero has accomplished with the nobles, and what not.

II (30 minutes)

Write briefly on FIVE of the following.

1. What preserved Prospero from despair at the time of his exile?

2. What is the immediate purpose of Gonzalo's description of his ideal commonwealth in II.i?

3. Explain the makeup of the "most delicate monster" (78.93-94) which Stephano discovers in II.ii.

4. What does Caliban insist that Stephano do first in his plot against Prospero?

5. Explain Ariel's meaning when he says that the sea has "requit" Prospero's exile.

6. How much time has the action on the island, from shipwreck to reconciliation, covered?

7. Which discoveries seem like rebirths in Act V?